RSF: The Russell Sage Foundation Journal of the Social Sciences

Immigrants Inside Politics/Outside Citizenship

VOLUME 2 · NUMBER 3 · JUNE 2016

RSF: The Russell Sage Foundation Journal of the Social Sciences ISSN 2377-8261

The Russell Sage Foundation
The Russell Sage Foundation, one of the oldest of America's general purpose foundations, was established in 1907 by Mrs. Margaret Olivia Sage for "the improvement of social and living conditions in the United States." The foundation seeks to fulfill this mandate by fostering the development and dissemination of knowledge about the country's political, social, and economic problems. While the foundation endeavors to assure the accuracy and objectivity of each book it publishes, the conclusions and interpretations in Russell Sage Foundation publications are those of the authors and not of the foundation, its trustees, or its staff. Publication by Russell Sage, therefore, does not imply foundation endorsement.

Board of Trustees
Sara S. McLanahan, *Chair*
Larry M. Bartels
Karen S. Cook
W. Bowman Cutter III
Sheldon H. Danziger
Kathryn Edin
Lawrence F. Katz
David Laibson
Nicholas Lemann
Martha Minow
Peter R. Orszag
Claude M. Steele
Shelley E. Taylor
Richard H. Thaler
Hirokazu Yoshikawa

Mission Statement
RSF: The Russell Sage Foundation Journal of the Social Sciences is a peer-reviewed, open-access journal of original empirical research articles by both established and emerging scholars. It is designed to promote cross-disciplinary collaborations on timely issues of interest to academics, policymakers, and the public at large. Each issue is thematic in nature and focuses on a specific research question or area of interest. The introduction to each issue will include an accessible, broad, and synthetic overview of the research question under consideration and the current thinking from the various social sciences.

RSF Journal Editorial Board
Elizabeth O. Ananat, Duke University
Annette Bernhardt, University of California, Berkeley
Karen S. Cook, Stanford University
Sheldon H. Danziger, RSF President
Janet C. Gornick, The CUNY Graduate Center
Jennifer Hochschild, Harvard University
Douglas S. Massey, Princeton University
Mary E. Pattillo, Northwestern University
James Sidanius, Harvard University
Mary C. Waters, Harvard University
Bruce Western, Harvard University

Copyright © 2016 by Russell Sage Foundation. All rights reserved. Printed in the United States of America. No part of this publication may be reproduced, stored in a retrieval system, or transmitted in any form or by any means, electronic, mechanical, photocopying, recording, or otherwise, without the prior written permission of the publisher. Reproduction by the United States Government in whole or in part is permitted for any purpose.

Opinions expressed in this journal are not necessarily those of the editors, editorial board, trustees, or the Russell Sage Foundation.

We invite scholars to submit proposals for potential issues through the *RSF* application portal: https://rsfjournal.onlineapplicationportal.com/. Submissions should be addressed to Suzanne Nichols, Director of Publications.

To view the complete text and additional features online please go to **www.rsfjournal.org**.

Russell Sage Foundation
112 East 64th Street
New York, NY 10065

ISSN (print):   2377-8253
ISSN (electronic): 2377-8261
ISBN: 978-0-87154-990-7

Immigrants Inside Politics/Outside Citizenship

ISSUE EDITORS
James A. McCann, Purdue University
Michael Jones-Correa, Cornell University

CONTENTS

In the Public but Not the Electorate: The "Civic Status Gap" in the United States **1**
James A. McCann and Michael Jones-Correa

Part I. The Migrant Experience, Civic Integration, and Social Capital

Migration Status and Political Knowledge Among Latino Immigrants **22**
Susan K. Brown and Frank D. Bean

Emigrant Politics, Immigrant Engagement: Homeland Ties and Immigrant Political Identity in the United States **42**
Roger Waldinger and Lauren Duquette-Rury

Healthy Skepticism or Corrosive Cynicism? New Insights into the Roots and Results of Latino Political Cynicism **60**
Melissa R. Michelson

Politicized Immigrant Identity, Spanish-Language Media, and Political Mobilization in 2012 **78**
Sergio I. Garcia-Rios and Matt A. Barreto

Part II. The Social Dimensions of Political Engagement

A Different Hue of the Gender Gap: Latino Immigrants and Political Conservatism in the United States **98**
Katharine M. Donato and Samantha L. Perez

Religion and the Political Engagement of Latino Immigrants: Bridging Capital or Segmented Religious Assimilation? **125**
David L. Leal, Jerod Patterson, and Joe R. Tafoya

Part III. Political Participation and Partisanship

Latino Electoral Participation: Variations on Demographics and Ethnicity **148**
Jan Leighley and Jonathan Nagler

The Hispanic Immigrant Voter and the Classic American Voter: Presidential Support in the 2012 Election **165**
Michael S. Lewis-Beck and Mary Stegmaier

Incorporation of Latino Immigrants into the American Party System **182**
David O. Sears, Felix Danbold, and Vanessa M. Zavala

Political Identity Convergence: On Being Latino, Becoming a Democrat, and Getting Active **205**
Leonie Huddy, Lilliana Mason, and S. Nechama Horwitz

Part IV. Study Appendix

Key Design Features of the 2012 Latino Immigrant National Election Study **230**
James A. McCann and Michael Jones-Correa

In the Public but Not the Electorate: The "Civic Status Gap" in the United States

JAMES A. McCANN AND MICHAEL JONES-CORREA

"You're going to have a deportation force, and you're going to do it humanely."

—Donald Trump, candidate for the 2016 Republican presidential nomination, discussing the deportation of the eleven million undocumented immigrants currently residing in the United States (BBC 2015).

The 2016 presidential campaign is well under way, and debates concerning immigration have taken on ominous tones. Candidates from both major parties have talked about enforcement along the border, but the view of immigrants among Republicans vying for their party's nomination is darker. Candidates promise to end "illegal" immigration, to track immigrants like FedEx packages (Spodak and Scott 2015), to dramatically increase the deportations of those in the United States without papers, and to reverse the executive order signed by President Obama deferring enforcement for those who arrived in the United States as children with their undocumented parents (Peoples and Caldwell 2015). The candidate leading the polls through the fall of 2016 called deporting the eleven million undocumented immi-grants living in the United States "cheap, 'doable' and humane" (BBC 2015).

This vitriol is both a reflection of and a reaction to a remarkable feature of life in the United States today: the growing ethnic diversity across the nation, a phenomenon driven largely by the settlement of migrants from Latin America and Asia (see figure 1). According to the most current census figures, nearly 16 percent of the adult population in the United States is foreign born. Among these immigrants, more than half, or approximately one of every twelve adults living in the country at this moment, are not American citizens.[1]

These noncitizens are in fact a heterogeneous mix—legal permanent residents, refugees, asylum seekers, people who entered the country without administrative authorization, and people who entered with a visa but overstayed (see figure 2).

The image of immigrants portrayed in the 2016 presidential primary debates is of people who are not part of the United States, even though they reside in the United States. They are freeloaders or lawbreakers, sitting on the sidelines of civic life, making few contributions. But this is far from the case. The major-

James A. McCann is professor of political science at Purdue University. **Michael Jones-Correa** is professor of government and Robert J. Katz Chair of the Department of Government at Cornell University.

We thank Sheldon Danziger, Aixa Cintrón-Vélez, Geri Mannion, Elizabeth Cohen, Suzanne Nichols, Ann Marie Clark, and the anonymous reviewers for much helpful assistance and feedback. Direct correspondence to: James A. McCann at mccannj@purdue.edu, Department of Political Science, Beering Hall, Purdue University, 100 N. University Street, West Lafayette, IN 47907; and Michael Jones-Correa at mj64@cornell.edu, Cornell University, White Hall, Ithaca, NY 14583.

1. By recent historic standards, this percentage is rather high. In 1970, the number of foreign-born noncitizens over eighteen stood at only 2 percent of the total adult population (that is, one out of every fifty people).

Figure 1. Number of Immigrants and Their Share of the Total U.S. Population

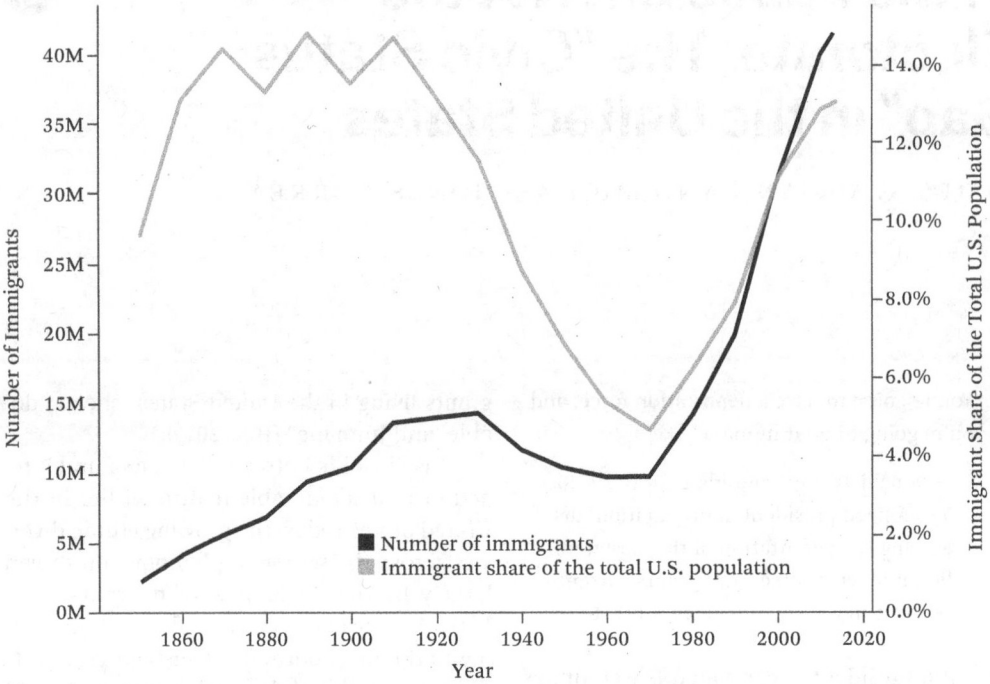

Source: Authors' compilation based on Gibson and Lennon 1999; Migration Policy Institute 2015.

Figure 2. U.S. Foreign-Born Population 2012

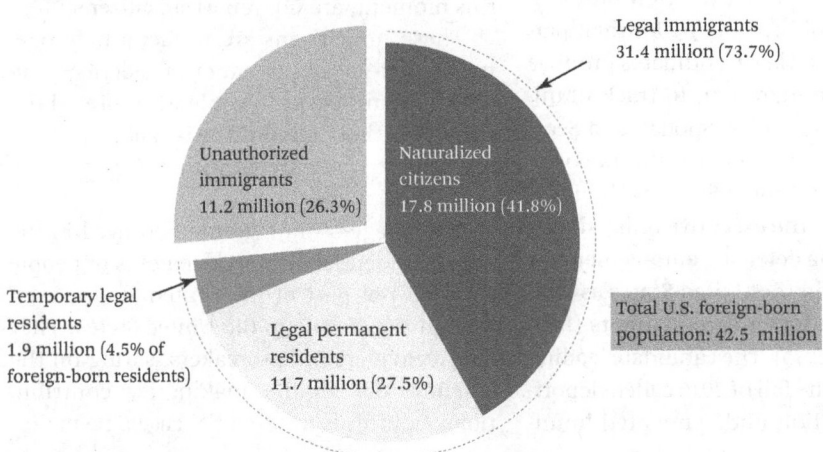

Source: Brown and Stepler 2015.
Note: Pew Research Center estimates for 2012 based on augmented American Community Survey data from Integrated Public Use Microdata Sample (IPUMS).

ity of immigrants, even those here without papers, have lived in the United States more than a decade (see figure 3). They are residents, not tourists or people just passing through the country. They are customers and neighbors and coworkers. In short, they are part of how we think of the public, even if not necessarily part of the electorate.

In the nineteenth century, immigrants, even without being citizens, could be part of

Figure 3. Immigrants Who Have Lived in the United States More than Ten Years

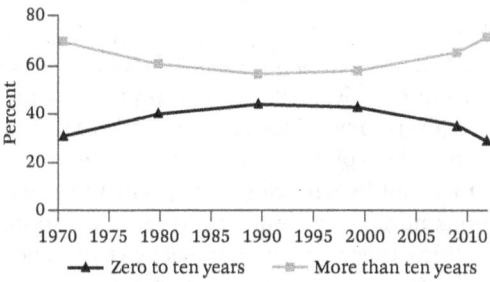

Source: Brown and Stepler 2015.
Note: Pew Research Center tabulations of 1970–2000 decennial censuses and 2010 and 2013 American Community Surveys (IPUMS).

the public and the electorate: at least twenty-two states allowed noncitizen residents to register and vote. However, since the 1920s, only American citizens have had the right to vote in federal and state elections. In a few scattered municipalities around the country, noncitizens can still vote in local contests for school board and other offices.[2] These exceptions, however, prove a general rule: to be a citizen is to be a voter, or at least a potential voter within the electorate. On occasion, lawmakers or news commentators charge that large numbers of noncitizens are finding ways to vote illegally. Little to no evidence, however, supports such a claim.[3] Noncitizens in the United States may be long-term residents but not voters.

In the United States and other democracies, the tendency to equate political representation with voting by citizens is widespread. In an election, voters are charged with holding leaders and parties accountable for past actions in government and steering the future course of policymaking. Representation in this mold consists of a time-delimited delegation of authority from the mass public to lawmakers. This is an inherently noisy process. Some citizens may choose not to vote, and those who turn out may choose candidates based on considerations that have little to do with the past performance of government officials or the future course of public policies. Nonetheless, evidence is ample that government officials study the preferences of voters closely, perhaps to a fault. Even in an era of safe congressional seats and diminishing electoral competition in many parts of the country, officeholders take campaigning and elections quite seriously.[4]

This fact of political life raises a larger the-

---

2. In Chicago, noncitizens are eligible to vote in school board elections, and in Maryland six cities grant voting rights to noncitizens under certain conditions. The political scientist Ronald Hayduk notes that several municipalities are currently considering extending the franchise to allow noncitizens to vote in local races (2015). But most recently, on March 3, 2015, a ballot measure to this effect failed in Burlington, Vermont, by a margin of 58 to 42 percent.

3. Audits of voting registration records in a number of states and local jurisdictions show the incidence of noncitizen registration and subsequent turnout to be low—vanishingly low. In a probe of alleged illegal voting during the 2004 gubernatorial election in the state of Washington, for example, two instances of noncitizen voters, both university students, were discovered; nearly three million voters in total took part in this election. More recently, Ohio Secretary of State John Husted reported in March of 2015 that after an extensive investigation of voting records, forty-four noncitizens may have voted illegally in that state since the 2000 elections. Husted, who had earlier anticipated that the number of confirmed noncitizen voters would run into the thousands, concluded after this audit that noncitizen voting is not a "systemic or widespread problem." In Colorado, an analysis of voting fraud spanning many years resulted in early 2015 in the conviction of one noncitizen voter, a Polish national. As part of a plea agreement, the defendant was ordered to complete forty-eight hours of community service and was put on supervised probation for two years (for more detail on these audits and outcomes, see Henderson 2012; Lerner 2015; Johansson 2015; and Thompson 2015; see also Marouf 2012, 66–73).

4. After spending significant amounts of time with congressional representatives and following them in their travels back to the home constituencies, Richard Fenno notes that "members of Congress do have an idea of who votes for them and who does not. . . . They have a pretty good idea. . . . They worry a lot. They exhibit great caution in making perceptual judgments. . . .They rarely allow themselves the luxury of feeling 'safe' electorally. They do not take their reelection constituency for granted" (see Fenno 1978, 19–20). This is the central mes-

oretical question: in a democratic system, should the preferences and needs of the substantial noncitizen resident population be taken into account in some fashion within policymaking processes? In short, should noncitizens count? As a matter of public administration in the United States, noncitizens certainly "count." As residents, they are far from invisible in the eyes of many state and federal entities, and states and localities take their needs into account—even as the benefits immigrants receive have been curtailed.[5] They count, too, toward the apportionment for legislative districts, which historically has been based on the total population within a locality, irrespective of voting eligibility—though this norm came under review by the Supreme Court in 2015.[6] Noncitizens are also recognized as taxpaying members of society. Immigrants without a social security number are required to file tax returns annually—even if they will never see any benefits. Furthermore, under federal Selective Service rules, nearly all foreign-born male noncitizens under twenty-six must register for the draft.[7] Supporting the country financially and protecting it—these are the fundamental responsibilities of the members of a democracy. In the United States, citizens and noncitizens alike share in these duties.

We consider whether noncitizen residents have a right to political representation, given that they have some degree of recognition as part of American society. Is it proper and just for government officials to respond exclusively to members of the electorate? Or are members of the public who cannot participate in elections nevertheless entitled to representation? Political theorists have approached these questions from a variety of perspectives.

Discussion of the empirical research literature in this area examines how foreign-born noncitizens in reality behave in politics. If by some accounts noncitizens deserve political representation, how much potential is there for immigrants without voting rights to send signals to government officials through the participatory activities available to them? Voting is one way for many to have a voice in politics, the most common way, to be sure, but hardly the only way. If the ballot box is closed to foreign-born noncitizens, are other avenues of engagement pursued, so that government leaders might conceivably take their views into account?[8]

---

sage of another classic work on congressional representation, *Congress: The Electoral Connection* (Mayhew 1974).

5. Congress passed the Personal Responsibility and Work Opportunity Reconciliation Act (PRWORA) in 1996, significantly limiting the eligibility of both undocumented immigrants and legal permanent residents for welfare and other public benefit programs such as Aid to Families with Dependent Children (AFDC), now Temporary Aid to Needy Families (TANF).

6. On April 4, 2016, the Supreme Court ruled that states are justified, in light of well-established administrative practices and arguments endorsed by the framers at the time of the constitutional founding, to apportion legislative seats based on total population rather than an estimate of the number of registered or eligible voters (*Evenwel v. Abbott*, case no. 14-940). Under current law, each U.S. congressional district must include approximately seven hundred thousand residents. Sanford Levinson (2013) estimates that the number of undocumented foreign-born residents of California equates to three such seats using the rule of "one representative equals seven hundred thousand constituents"; in Texas, the number of undocumented immigrants is the equivalent of two seats. If the Court had ruled to restrict the apportionment count to the voting-eligible population or to the actual number of registered voters when district lines are drawn, major political consequences would surely have followed. The more rural areas of the United States, which tend to lean Republican, would likely benefit in this instance. The justices chose not to rule on whether a state could legally draw districts to equalize the voter-eligible population rather than the total population; they indicated only that creating districts based on the full count of residents irrespective of voting eligibility was constitutionally sound.

7. The only exceptions to this are seasonal agricultural workers on H-2A visas, diplomatic personnel and their families, international students, and tourists.

8. If exclusion from the ballot box impedes other kinds of political engagement—for example, group activities

Much more work is needed to discern how noncitizens find their way into political activity, and what impediments to democratic engagement are most severe. With this motivation, we conducted a special survey of the Latin American–born population during the 2012 campaign season. The evidence from this survey is the basis for the papers included in this issue of *RSF*.

SHOULD A LACK OF VOTING RIGHTS MEAN A LACK OF VOICE IN REPRESENTATION?

From the standpoint of democratic theory, the existence of a sizable population that is formally outside the boundaries of the electorate raises questions. First and foremost, is this civic status gap troubling? That is, does the gap make American politics less representative? A number of approaches to answering these questions are possible.

For a political system to be fully democratic, every adult living within its domain and subject to its laws should have a say in how those laws are created, assuming that they are not temporary residents or intellectually impaired in some way. This is the ethical principle of inclusion and representation held by political theorists such as Robert A. Dahl and Iris Marion Young (see in particular Dahl 1989, chapter 9). The expansiveness of this premise, which Dahl labeled a categorical principle, is striking. On these grounds, few could be rightfully excluded from democratic politics. Dahl couples his categorical principle of inclusion with an emphasis on equality of voice. In short, in a democracy, the signals directed toward government officials should reflect the rich diversity of groups and interests within the public, and all members should have comparable opportunities to influence policymakers. This is echoed in Young's work, which argues that "the normative legitimacy of a democratic decision depends on the degree to which those affected by it have been included in the decision making processes and have had the opportunity to influence the outcomes" (2000, 5–6).

The roots of this perspective extend to the classical liberal writings of John Locke and the constitutional framers of the United States. As Dahl notes, "the argument is grounded on the moral axiom that no person ought to be governed without his consent" or "required to obey laws that are not of his own making" (1989, 122). In James Madison's seminal defense of the U.S. Constitution in the *Federalist Papers* and other writings, the founder spoke of a venerable "Republican Principle" under which just governments are obligated to take the full expanse of public opinion into account when devising policies (Sheehan 2004, 1992). "Public opinion sets bounds to every government, and is the real sovereign in every free one," argued Madison in a 1791 piece for the *National Gazette* (1962, 170).

Although this categorical principle of inclusion is straightforward in theory, its application in practice can be ambiguous. At what point does a person transition from a child, for instance, who lacks the standing to participate in the electorate, to an adult with full political rights? At the age of eighteen? At twenty-one? Citizens should clearly be included within the boundaries of the political system. But what about the varied group of residents in the United States—refugees, student-visa holders, legal permanent residents, guest workers, undocumented residents and their children, and others—who may not be citizens but are often

---

that are essentially expressive, such as attending protest rallies, or more conventional participation in election campaigns—it may still be possible for noncitizens to be represented in government. This would come about if officials or advocacy organizations step into the role of a "trustee" for this population (for an extensive discussion, see Pitkin 1967). In this latter vein, the duty of the representative to his or her constituents is said to consist of a devotion to their larger "interests" rather than simply their momentary opinions as expressed—or not expressed—through voting and other channels. The philosopher Edmund Burke is most closely associated with this perspective. Some have suggested that the surest way to represent noncitizens who lack voting rights is for leaders to adopt this "trustee" role (see, for example, Cohen 2014). If the available evidence indicates that foreign-born noncitizens express little to no voice in day-to-day politics, then some form of trusteeship would indeed be the most appropriate mode for representation.

also clearly not temporary either? These residents may live out their lives in the United States without full access to this country's system of political representation. And what exactly is the line between a temporary visitor and a permanent resident, anyway? When does a transient stop being a transient within a political system and become instead a resident?

Some theorists have argued that not even residence itself is a necessary prerequisite for political standing. Current practice in the United States affords citizens who may opt to reside abroad a right to political engagement equal to that of their co-nationals living within the country, even though they will inevitably experience the laws and politics of the United States in quite different ways. The political philosopher Robert Goodin goes further, arguing that neither citizenship nor physical residence is a necessary requirement, in an era of increasing globalization, for political standing. Invoking a principle of democratic inclusion in sympathy with Dahl's, Goodin posits that all individuals whose interests are affected by the policies of a government are rightfully entitled to have a say in how those decisions are made. This implies that even people living on the other side of the world who are not formally connected to the political system of that country should be included somehow in its democratic deliberations. However, although Goodin sees such an unorthodox stance as ethically defensible, he concedes that it is logistically unworkable (2007; see also Dahl 1970 and Rehfeld 2005). In any case, political community is not necessarily contiguous with geographic space.

Dahl recognized that fitting his one-size-fits-all categorical principle of democratic inclusion to the real world of politics would require compromises and judgment calls. To a certain extent, the criteria for incorporation would be worked out in practice, and boundaries for exclusion would be established. "Egalitarian inclusiveness," however, was his priority. If applied, his principle would surely encompass the vast majority of foreign-born noncitizens living in the United States today. As estimated in the 2013 American Community Survey, noncitizens over eighteen have lived in the country for an average of fifteen years. Nearly 80 percent have spent five or more years in the United States. These are certainly not transients; these are individuals subject to government policies for a sustained period. As such, Dahl, Young, and Goodin would argue they should rightfully be considered participants in democratic society.

These theorists take the principle of inclusiveness as their starting point, whereas others start with the premise that questions of democratic inclusion have to be considered in particular historic contexts, where traditions and deep-seated cultural values shape beliefs about who belongs in the political community and who does not. This is a more particularistic, situational perspective, one that Dahl refers to as a contingent standard. This is a not-uncommon position. Michael Walzer, for instance, argues for the legitimate exclusion of nonmembers to enable the redistribution of public goods to members (1983). The boundaries of membership are drawn by geography. This, in fact, is how most liberal democracies function, offering full membership rights—citizenship—for those who are legal residents, and no rights at all for those not residing. Those who reside temporarily or illegally are entitled, at best, to partial membership.[9]

In a democracy, the conditions whereby some individuals or groups are invited to join and others are kept outside the fold could be said to stem from the collective judgments of the already-incorporated members of society. "By its very nature, a *demos*," writes Elizabeth Cohen, referring to a set of people comprising a given political unit, "must discriminate. It must develop a rule stating who is and is not included in the *demos* and then turn over enforcement of that rule to the state" (2014, 1051; this theme is also explored in Dovi 2009). In the United States, the offices of the U.S. Citi-

---

9. Elizabeth Cohen expands on this notion that citizenship rights are a gradient, not a binary. People are granted differentiated bundles of citizenship, with some holding "semi-citizenships" or partial rights. These semi-citizenships, she argues, are inevitable in any democracy. "People may possess some but not all" of the fundamental political/democratic rights, or may have a "weak version" of those rights (2014, 1048–49; see also 2009).

zenship and Immigration Services are charged with enforcing these rules. Under current law, approximately half of the noncitizen population, even individuals who have resided in the country for many years, have no standing to be represented as coequal participants in the political community by virtue of the fact that they do not have the legal authority to reside legally in the United States. The law has drawn the boundary in such a way to exclude them from inclusion in the political community. In fact, some have argued that by their voluntary presence in the United States noncitizen residents might be said to "consent" to their restricted political status. After all, immigration restrictionists have argued, noncitizens always have the option to leave and return to their countries of origin. However, if federal administrative laws are viewed as manifestations of collective democratic judgments, even permanent legal immigrants cannot be considered coequal participants in American politics. Immigrants who are not naturalized American citizens but are legally recognized as permanent residents possess certain statutorily and even constitutionally recognized rights—but not the right to vote.

There is thus a clash between two reasonable ethical perspectives on democratic inclusion. One way to resolve this clash, at least partly, might be to recognize that the collective preferences of the *demos* are difficult to ascertain in practice. Just as the application of Dahl's principle of egalitarian inclusiveness to the everyday world of politics requires compromises, which entail some potential members being excluded, an interpretation of the will of the *demos* should be approached with an appreciation of uncertainties and inexactness. Federal administrative policies concerning immigration and naturalization are traceable to the *demos* in certain senses. Legislative representatives are elected, and the current policy infrastructure in this area is a legacy of past congressional actions. Administrative agencies are overseen by the president, who of course is also elected. However, the connections between national immigration policies and the *demos* are not as tidy as Cohen's quote implies. The members of the political community do not simply formulate rules for inclusion or exclusion, and then order administrative entities to act. Nominally democratic connections are insufficient in and of themselves to provide moral legitimacy to administrative policies without some recognition of the contingencies and uncertainties surrounding the will of the *demos*.

Furthermore, it is not hard to find other ways to gauge the general attitude of the *demos* toward noncitizens, methods that lead to a different interpretation. Research on how ordinary Americans view American identity—that is, the traits that make someone distinctly American—indicates that citizenship is closely linked with being a "true" member of the country (Theiss-Morse 2009, 88). This would seem to justify excluding the large noncitizen population from civic and political life based on democratic principles. But common notions of citizenship in the American context are not strongly linked to ethnicity, religious practice, or national origin. Some see whites, Christians, and the native born as particularly American, but the majority of Americans do not. This leaves open the possibility of genuine acceptance in many quarters of the diverse foreign-born population. Moreover, that citizenship is so closely tied to conceptions of American identity need not imply a widespread principled commitment on the part of the *demos* to impose a hard separation in public affairs between noncitizens and citizens. When asked in interviews whether immigrants without residency papers should be deported, remain in the United States only temporarily as guests, or have the opportunity to become a citizen, the modal attitude by a wide margin in survey reports since the mid-2000s has been to extend to undocumented residents some kind of avenue to citizenship.[10] Americans are deeply committed to the status of citizenship

---

10. In June 2011, for example, 64 percent of the respondents in a survey sample stated a preference for permitting undocumented immigrants to become citizens. Only 21 percent favored deportation, and even fewer (13 percent) preferred allowing the undocumented to remain but only temporarily as guest workers. These breakdowns are rather stable across many years (see Muste 2013, 409; Segovia and Defever 2010, 387).

as a key marker of national identity but show relatively little desire to restrict the boundaries of this designation.

These observations suggest that the ethical judgments derived from either the categorical or contingent perspectives on democratic inclusion are not poles apart. Both frameworks could justify recognizing noncitizens as participants or potential participants in American democracy, participants whose voices should not be ignored. What are the contours of this voice? Does a lack of citizenship rights have a bearing on democratic involvement? We consider these questions next, for they touch directly on the potential quality of representation.

DOES A LACK OF VOTING RIGHTS MEAN A LACK OF VOICE IN REPRESENTATION?

"The tools of social research have made it possible, for the first time, to determine with reasonable precision and objectivity the extent to which the practice of politics ... conforms to the assumptions of the theory of democratic politics," declared Bernard Berelson in his 1952 presidential address to the then-fledgling American Association of Public Opinion Research. "The closer collaboration of political theorists and opinion researchers should contribute new problems, new categories, and greater refinement and elaboration to both sides" (314). Decades later in a retrospective essay to commemorate the fiftieth anniversary of that same organization, Philip Converse echoed Berelson's point. "From the very outset in the 1930s, public opinion polling has been closely wedded to the study of popular democratic politics" (1987, S12). These remarks frame our discussion in this section. If individuals without citizenship rights have the standing to be heard in politics, as some theorists have maintained, then it is incumbent on social scientists to examine the volume and clarity of their voice. What is the relationship between citizenship status and actual democratic practice? Does a lack of citizenship rights lessen the potential for effective representation? Diminish or distort political expressions above and beyond exclusion from the ballot box?

Over the last eighty years, much has been learned through systematic survey research about how political engagement and "voice" vary across many different social and demographic categories—gender, sexual orientation, race and ethnicity, religious denomination, generational cohort, marital and family status, occupation, income bracket, educational attainment, and region, among other groupings. Indeed, the scholarly literature on the contours of participation and public opinion in the United States and other democracies is voluminous. Studies of mass-level political behavior make up perhaps the largest body of work in the entire discipline of political science. Against this backdrop, however, relatively little is known about the political participation and aspirations of foreign-born noncitizens, and how their levels of involvement and aspirations compare with those of the U.S.-born population. Given that individuals without voting rights are able to take part in politics in any number of ways, and many democratic theorists would evaluate the quality of representation in the United States based in part on how well the system responds to the voices of noncitizens, reasons to include noncitizens in the sampling frames of major national opinion polls are compelling. If this were standard practice, social scientists could put a finer point on the political preferences and activities of individuals who are part of the public but not yet in the electorate, thereby enriching theoretical debates about their potential for effective democratic incorporation.

Yet, regrettably, the major academic survey archives that researchers, teachers, journalists, and policymakers routinely turn to when seeking information on the ebb and flow of political attitudes and involvement throughout the United States are essentially silent on the political behavior of noncitizens. Take, for example, the long-running American National Election Studies (ANES) series. Since the 1940s and continuing during each major national election campaign, the ANES has conducted extensive interviews nationwide with approximately 1,500 to 2,000 individuals per election year. This is a high-investment undertaking, in that surveys typically take place in the households of respondents. ANES questionnaires contain literally hundreds of items. Perceptions of the principal candidates running for office, partisan attachments, ideological stances and public policy preferences, evaluations of incumbent officeholders, attitudes toward the political system on the whole, levels of involvement in a multitude of civic and political groups—all of these topics among others are regularly covered in ANES interviews. The ANES polling archive is rightly viewed as a crown jewel within the political science community. Countless scholarly articles, books, classroom lectures, and newspaper stories have drawn findings from the datasets in this archive. But throughout the long history of the ANES, only U.S. citizens have been eligible to take part in interviews.[11] Until recently, this feature of the design did not greatly affect sampling coverage. In the 1960s, 1970s, and 1980s, a survey of the electorate could for all practical purposes be considered a poll of the entire American public. Today, however, a representative survey of persons with voting rights leaving out the 8 percent of U.S. residents over eighteen who are not citizens will not necessarily cover the full range of political attitudes and behaviors within the total adult population, and the ANES series can shed no light on how noncitizens compare to citizens.

Another widely accessible academic survey of political attitudes and behavior is the Cooperative Congressional Election Study (CCES) series, launched in 2006 and fielded in each election cycle since. Unlike the ANES, CCES interviews are conducted through the Internet, which allows sample sizes to be far larger. This opens new analytical possibilities for survey researchers. Comparisons across social and demographic groupings can be much more granular if one is working with, say, thirty thousand cases rather than two thousand. The sampling frame for these studies, however, is similar to that of the ANES: the CCES is designed to capture political attitudes and involvement within the electorate—not the public at large.[12]

In contrast to the ANES and CCES survey archives, the Gallup organization since the 1930s has fielded thousands of surveys with the aim of covering the public in its entirety. Many of these polls are archived for general use and have been well plumbed over the years by social science researchers, teachers, and news commentators. These opinion studies undoubtedly include a good many noncitizens, because Gallup generally selects study participants at random without regard for civic status and sample sizes are often quite large. Given that the firm usually conducts interviews in

---

11. In advance of the fielding of the 2012 ANES, the demographers and statisticians designing the sampling framework anticipated that as many as 270 noncitizens might be approached for participation in the study through random selection. When this happened, interviewers had no choice but to terminate the survey.

12. Respondents in the CCES are selected using matched random sampling techniques. The firm carrying out the polling begins with two lists—one listing of all consumers over eighteen in the United States and another with adults who have agreed to take part in an opt-in Internet-based survey. In the first stage of sampling, a random set of consumers is drawn. For the consumers in this set, key demographic variables such as age, income, education, race, and gender are noted. In the second stage, a matching algorithm is used to identify individuals in the opt-in Internet list who most closely fit the demographic profiles in the consumer file. The goal in this two-stage process is to obtain a representative sample of voters, including Americans who are eligible to vote but have not registered to vote in the current election. These procedures are described at the CCES website, http://projects.iq.harvard.edu/cces/book/sample-design (accessed May 20, 2015). Even though the intended sampling population is the voting-eligible public, it is theoretically possible given the matching procedures that some noncitizens might fill out a CCES survey. For this reason, respondents are asked to indicate whether they are foreign born and, if so, whether they are citizens; this allows CCES users to screen out noncitizens when estimating models of voting choices. In each installment of the CCES, very few respondents have marked that they are noncitizens. In the 2006 round, for example, 0.83 percent of the CCES participants fell in this category. The organizers of the CCES strongly caution against analyzing this tiny subsample of self-identified noncitizens who were unintentionally included in the study (see Ansolabehere, Luks, and Schaffner 2014). One recent attempt to analyze CCES data on noncitizens sparked a great deal of controversy among political methodologists (Richman, Chattha, and Earnest 2014).

English, the noncitizens taking part would not be fully representative of the entire foreign-born noncitizen population. Yet even a biased sample could contribute to our sense of how civic status shapes democratic engagement. As a matter of long-standing internal policy at Gallup, however, foreign-born respondents are not asked whether they are naturalized citizens.[13] Consequently, it is not possible with Gallup data to compare foreign-born noncitizens with immigrants who have naturalized or to the U.S. born in general.

The random sampling techniques that Gallup pioneered to select respondents have been widely emulated throughout the polling industry for many years. It is thus conceivable that noncitizens have taken part in surveys conducted by the *New York Times*, the *Washington Post*, and other major media outlets. As with Gallup polls, many of these studies are publicly archived for general use. The Interuniversity Consortium for Political and Social Research at the University of Michigan and the Roper Center for Public Opinion Research index hundreds of such surveys. We are not aware, however, of any instances in which the citizenship status of foreign-born respondents was recorded in these polls. It appears that the policy at Gallup to avoid this topic is widely shared across the polling departments of leading news organizations. This was the case even in a 1995 *Washington Post* Poll on Race Relations, an ambitious national survey with oversamples of ethnic minority groups. Many participants in this study would not have been American citizens, but the *Washington Post* did not include an item to ask about this (Lien 2001, 232). As with the ANES and CCES, these surveys cannot help sharpen our understanding of the noncitizen population.

This brief overview of polling archives is far from comprehensive. Our intention is simply to demonstrate that the most prominent and sophisticated surveys of public opinion and political activities in the United States are better suited for examining the voting public than the public as a whole, and particularly that growing portion of the public that falls outside the formal boundaries of the electorate. To map and model political engagement among foreign-born noncitizens and assess how these patterns compare with American citizens (who have voting rights), one would ideally wish to administer an exceedingly large survey so that enough immigrants are included to make generalizations. One would also have to be sensitive to language barriers and devise strategies for overcoming the natural reticence on the part of many immigrants to participate in these kinds of studies. These challenges in principle could be met, but a survey of this magnitude would certainly be costly—perhaps prohibitively. It is not surprising, then, that such systematic polls of the 8 percent of the adult population in the United States that is excluded from the electorate have not yet been conducted. Immigrants who have not acquired voting rights arguably have a right to be represented in a democratic system. But capturing their many diverse voices in a representative public opinion poll may not be feasible.

More feasible is to conduct surveys within particular ethnic populations, where both U.S.-born respondents and immigrants—noncitizens as well as naturalized citizens—are included in the sampling frame. In the last several decades, many studies along these lines have been administered within the Latino and Asian American communities.[14] Among the most extensive and influential are the fol-

---

13. In a personal nonconfidential correspondence dated April 13, 2015, a data specialist on the staff of the Gallup Poll reported that "we contact people with a variety of citizenship statuses—including people who might be living in the U.S. illegally. For this reason a question about citizenship was deemed too sensitive to ask on our survey." Gallup's concern about sensitivities notwithstanding, no evidence suggests that foreign-born survey respondents are reluctant to report their actual citizenship status (see McCann and Nishikawa 2012, 101; Jones-Correa and McCann 2013). As discussed, foreign-born respondents in more specialized ethnic surveys are routinely asked about their citizenship.

14. Since the 1990s, more than half of all immigrants in the United States have come from Latin America, and nearly 30 percent are Asian born (see Migration Policy Institute 2015).

lowing, all of which are publicly available for independent analysis.[15]

Surveys of Latinos

The Citizen Participation Study (CPS), conducted by Sidney Verba, Kay Lehman Schlozman, Henry Brady, and Norman Nie, was fielded in the spring of 1990. In spite of its name, the sample included seventy-three foreign-born Latinos who were not naturalized citizens. Although the number of noncitizens was not large, the fact that Verba and his colleagues extended the sampling frame in this way at all was noteworthy given that the central focus of the study was on citizen involvement.[16] Data were gathered through in-person interviews.

The Latino National Political Survey (LNPS), conducted by Rodolfo de la Garza, Angelo Falcon, F. Chris Garcia, and John A. Garcia, was fielded between July of 1989 and March of 1990. In total, 2,817 Latino respondents of Mexican, Puerto Rican, or Cuban heritage took part, 38 percent of whom were non-naturalized immigrants. The organizers of this study sought to cover up to 85 percent of the Latino population in the United States at that time, with interviews conducted in person.[17]

The Latino National Survey (LNS), conducted by Luis Fraga, John Garcia, Rodney Hero, Michael Jones-Correa, Valerie Martinez-Ebers, and Gary Segura, was fielded by telephone between November 2005 and August 2006. This telephone survey is by far the largest of its kind, both in terms of the span of time in which data were gathered, the number of states covered (fourteen states plus the District of Columbia), and the sample size ($N = 8,634$, including 3,778 noncitizens) (for overviews of findings, see Affigne, Hu-Dehart, and Orr 2014; Fraga et al. 2011).

Surveys of Asian Americans

The Pilot National Asian American Political Survey (PNAAPS), conducted by Pei-te Lien, was fielded by telephone between November 2000 and January 2001. Many ethnic groups were covered in this study (Chinese, Korean, Vietnamese, Japanese, Filipino, and South Asian), the total sample size of which was 1,218, of whom 388 were foreign-born noncitizens. Sampling took place in five major metro areas with substantial Asian American populations: Chicago, Los Angeles, New York, Honolulu, and San Francisco (for more information, see Lien, Conway, and Wong 2004; Wong 2006).

The 2008 National Asian American Survey (NAAS), conducted by Karthick Ramakrishnan, Jane Junn, Taeku Lee, and Janelle Wong, was fielded by telephone between August and October 2008. This study included the same ethnic groups as the 2000–2001 PNAAPS, but was much larger. In total, 5,159 respondents were polled, including 903 immigrants who were not U.S. citizens (for the study design and core results, see Wong et al. 2011).

In the fall of 2012, we extended the research

---

15. As with our canvassing of the major public opinion archives in the United States, this overview of survey resources for studying noncitizen populations in particular is hardly comprehensive. We identify here those polls that are broadly national in scope and have attracted the most scholarly attention.

16. The major work that is based on the Citizenship Participation Study is Sidney Verba, Kay Lehman Schlozman, and Henry E. Brady's *Voice and Equality* (1995; see also Verba et al. 1993). Verba, Scholzman, and Brady recognize the theoretical ambiguities surrounding conceptualizations of the "public" in an era when it is possible to reside in the United States for a prolonged period but not have citizenship rights (1995, 231 note 6). The authors do not attempt to resolve these ambiguities. Rather, they make the case, as we do here, that survey research on democratic engagement will make the greatest theoretical contributions if a more expansive understanding of the "public" is taken to heart. As they put it, "There are a number of philosophical questions as to whether noncitizens are appropriately part of the universe for a participation study. Although it could be argued that, from the perspective of democratic theory, this should be a study of citizens only, we did make a deliberate choice to interview noncitizens. Noncitizens are affected by American laws, and many are permanent residents (legally or illegally).... Thus, we decided to include noncitizens since they can always be separated in analysis."

17. The central findings from the National Latino Political Survey are presented in tabular form in Rodolfo de la Garza and his colleagues' *Latino Voices* (1992).

program on civic status and political engagement by fielding the Latino Immigrant National Election Study (LINES), a large-scale nationally representative survey of foreign-born Latinos from Spanish-speaking countries. This survey was designed both to coincide and to mesh with the ANES that year. Further details about the LINES survey and the papers in this issue of *RSF* follow in the next section. Before turning to LINES, we review some of the broader lessons to date about noncitizen involvement in politics. These lessons form a baseline on which LINES researchers can build.

The first lesson is that immigrants without citizenship rights are not politically quiescent. Exclusion from the ballot box is not tantamount to civic silence. This was very much evident in the outpouring of social movement activity between February and May 2006 in response to a harsh anti-immigrant measure that at the time was under consideration in the U.S. Congress. Sizable rallies took place not only in major urban centers like Los Angeles and Chicago but also in smaller cities and towns such as Fort Myers (Florida), St. Paul (Minnesota), and Goshen (Indiana). Not all of the participants in these events were themselves foreign born. Yet immigrants, particularly Latino immigrants, were the primary driving force behind this mobilization, including a good many noncitizens (see Bada, Fox, and Selee 2006; Barreto et al. 2009; Zepeda-Millán 2014; Voss and Bloemraad 2011).

If we consider more prosaic forms of involvement, findings from the 2006 LNS indicate that among foreign-born Latinos who were not citizens, 10 percent reported participating in political groups, nearly 80 percent stated that they had participated formally or informally in collective initiatives to solve community problems, and nearly one in five had contacted a government official about a particular concern. Rates of participation among Latino noncitizens were found to be somewhat lower in the 1990 CPS and the 1989–1990 LNPS but are nonetheless noteworthy. In the CPS, 13 percent of the Latino noncitizens reported an affiliation with a political organization, 5 percent had participated in informal community groups, and 7 percent indicated that they had made contributions to election campaigns, among other activities. The NLPS gauged involvement in somewhat different ways. In this study, 6 percent reported signing a petition, 5 percent expressed political views symbolically by wearing a button, and 4 percent had written a politician. Fewer respondents reported attending rallies, volunteering for a campaign, or making political donations (see Levin 2013, 547; Verba, Schlozman, and Brady 1995; Leal 2002, 361).

For Asian immigrants without voting rights, the 2008 NAAS reports that nearly 20 percent worked to solve a community problem, 5 percent contacted government officials, and another 5 percent contributed to political causes. These percentages are fairly comparable to what was recorded several years earlier for this population in the 2000–2001 PNAAPS. In this study, 14 percent of noncitizens had worked with others on community problems, 6 percent had written or telephoned a public official about a concern, and 6 percent had donated to a campaign (Wong et al. 2011, 60; Lien, Conway, and Wong 2004, 150).

Generalizing from these results, we are confident in asserting that a fairly large number of noncitizens are enthusiastic about taking part in politics even if they are unable to vote. Advocacy groups and government officials seeking to represent the interests of noncitizens could, if they listen closely, pick up these signals. There is, in short, the potential for some forms of delegate representation.

A second lesson, however, is that civic status casts a shadow over political practice: for both Latinos and Asian Americans, citizens participate more frequently than noncitizens. This appears to be true for a wide array of activities—signing petitions, expressing viewpoints by wearing a button or displaying a bumper sticker, communicating directly with officeholders, volunteering for campaigns, and attending community meetings. The gap between citizens and noncitizens is somewhat narrower for unconventional oppositional forms of participation, such as engaging in protest demonstrations, but it is still apparent. These patterns are in keeping with a statement Rodolfo de la Garza and Louis DeSipio made more than twenty years ago: "Lack of citizenship serves to exclude participation in electoral activities and can make involvement in nonelectoral activities even less likely" (1994, 18).[18] Although it is possible for lawmakers and advocates to hear the voices of noncitizens, the raised voices of members of the electorate are often louder, more persistent, and more noticeable.

By way of illustration, consider these selected findings. In the 1990 CPS, nearly three times as many Latino citizens as noncitizens reported informal activity in local community groups to deal with a problem than noncitizens (14 versus 5 percent); approximately twice as many Latino citizens were affiliated with a political organization (27 versus 13 percent); and Latino citizens were more than twice as likely as noncitizens to take part in campaigns (8 versus 3 percent). Similar distinctions emerge in other major studies of the Latino population, and this gap between citizens and noncitizens is evident even when focusing solely on foreign-born Latinos. In the more recent 2005–2006 LNS, the rate of participation in political groups for Latino immigrants who had become naturalized American citizens was over twice that of Latino noncitizens (23 versus 10 percent); naturalized citizens were also twice as likely to have contacted government officials about an issue (Levin 2013, 547). Among the respondents in the 2000–2001 PNAAPS, foreign-born citizens were twice as likely as noncitizens to write or telephone an official or donate to a political campaign. These differences are echoed in the 2008 NAAS. By a 2:1 ratio, the citizens in this study were more inclined than noncitizens to make political contributions and get in touch with someone in government (Lien, Conway, and Wong 2004, 150; Wong et al. 2011, 60).

Anyone taking the democratic principle of equality of voice to heart and wishing to see the full public represented in politics would find these distinctions troubling. No formal legal barriers restrtict volunteering on a campaign, working for a political party, attending meetings of a local city council, or getting in touch directly with a government official. But surveys of the foreign-born population imply that barring noncitizens from registering to vote implicitly sets up obstacles to other avenues of political expression.

How this barrier, which is a product of federal administrative law, compares with other barriers to involvement remains an open question—a third lesson from the existing academic literature. Students of participation have long recognized a wide array of economic, social, and attitudinal factors that impede political activity. It is an unfortunate fact of political life that participation is costly. It takes time, material resources, and a certain level of expertise. Many people in the United States—individuals without a great deal of formal education, those on the lower rungs of the economic ladder, or people without as much life experience—may find themselves ill equipped to take part in politics. This may be especially true for much of the foreign-born population. The great majority of immigrants settle in the United States after their formative childhood years. Without an early familiarity with governing institutions and processes, American politics may appear mysterious for quite some time after arrival. Immigrants for whom English is not the first language face further challenges in acquiring information about the issues that most affect them.

Political parties, interest groups, and informal social networks help orient individuals toward politics and prompt involvement.[19] However, it may take time for immigrants to develop deep and meaningful connections to political and social organizations. Noncitizens in particular could be especially reluctant to establish ties to the larger community, given their more precarious standing in American civic life. When assessing the contours of political voice for the foreign born, we should therefore be mindful of not only the civic status gap but also variations in economic status and well-being, exposure to American politics, and par-

---

18. Along similar lines, Gary Segura, Harry Pachon, and Nathan Woods write that "being a noncitizen is likely to be a substantial impediment to civic engagement, and noncitizen status does indeed reduce the likelihood of engagement in government" (2001, 89).

19. The canonical statement on this is Robert Putnam's *Bowling Alone* (2001).

tisan and group ties and identities. The ways that different forces shape political participation are most fruitfully explored through multivariate analyses. To what extent does a formal designation of citizen or noncitizen affect actual engagement in politics once other potentially debilitating factors are taken into account?

Turning to previous research, we encounter a mixed bag of results and conjectures. Working with the Citizen Participation Study, Sidney Verba and his colleagues examine who takes part in time-intensive political activities, such as working with others informally in the community to accomplish a certain political goal or attending meetings to deal with a particular issue. After statistically controlling for the education level of the survey respondent, the strength of attachment one feels to a political party, the information one has about political processes in the United States, family income, and various other factors having to do with organizational ties and personal resources, whether an individual was eligible to vote did not matter in the least in shaping involvement. Nor did civic status have a noticeable effect on the tendency to engage in informal political discussions (Verba, Schlozman, and Brady 1995, 358). The implication of these findings for our discussion of the civic status gap is plain to see: exclusion from the electorate is not necessarily the obstacle that de la Garza and DeSipio made it out to be. Immigrants appear to have higher barriers to cross—barriers having to do with socioeconomic status, group belonging, and civic skills.

Subsequent research on Latino involvement in politics has not questioned the importance of socioeconomic status as a critical dividing line separating participants from nonparticipants, and that partisan and group attachments, as well as familiarity with American politics, are among the strongest predictors of involvement is scarcely debated. However, in a 2002 piece that drew from the 1989-1990 LNPS, David Leal argues that civic status matters far more than Verba and his colleagues give it credit for. Its effect on a wide range of activities cannot be washed away statistically by taking into account an individual's level of education, family income, age, views of the major political parties, and a host of other factors. Leal speculates that the seeming insignificance of civic status in the earlier analysis could stem from differences in sampling between the CPS and the LNPS.[20] Drawing from the 2005-2006 Latino National Study, Ines Levin (2013) suggests that, after controlling for social and economic background characteristics, whether a Latino immigrant has become a naturalized citizen is only moderately relevant when predicting political involvement. This conclusion is somewhat at odds with both the Leal and the Verba and colleague pieces. Levin shows that citizens are more likely to contact government officials, particularly non-Latino government officials, but there is no measurable difference between citizens and noncitizens in other forms of involvement (participation in political groups and attendance at community meetings to address particular problems).[21] Several more specialized studies of the Mexican immigrant population in particular have found that citizenship status does not have a large impact on political involvement once these same kinds of control variables are taken into account (see Lien 1994; Barreto and Muñoz 2003; McCann and Nishikawa 2012).

Much less systematic multivariate research has been conducted on the Asian American immigrant population. One study based on a sample of California residents in the 1980s found that citizens—both U.S.-born and foreign-born naturalized Asian Americans—

---

20. Other statistical analyses of participation based on the LNPS similarly conclude that civic status has a significant impact even when controlling for socioeconomic status, age, the time a respondent has lived in the United States, language abilities, partisanship, interest in American politics, and contacts with various political organizations (see Martinez 2005; Wong 2006, 222).

21. Levin's findings are in keeping with those presented by Karthick Ramakrishnan (2006, 252). Using data from the September 2002 Volunteer Supplement of the Current Population Survey, Ramakrishnan shows that among immigrants, civic status is unrelated to the incidence of volunteering in local community groups once length of stay in the United States is controlled.

were much more likely to take part in activities other than voting than noncitizen immigrants were. This relationship held up even when controls were put in place for socioeconomic status, group identifications and ethnic ties, age, partisanship, gender, and country of origin. In contrast to this, another piece that drew from a different survey, the 2000–2001 PNAAPS, concluded that for Asian Americans, citizenship status did not have a notable impact on political activities other than voting when a comparable set of control variables was factored in (Lien 1994, 251; Wong 2006, 224).

Taking a step back from the many works mentioned, it appears that little can be said with confidence about the impact of citizenship status on democratic practice relative to other economic, social, and cultural forces. Conventional wisdom in many circles claims that acquisition of citizenship rights is a key milestone in the course of immigrant incorporation. If it is the case, however, that the division of the foreign-born population into incorporated citizens and unincorporated noncitizens has no noteworthy bearing on everyday political involvement, that would be an intriguing finding—a welcome result for some, because it would speak to the potential for substantive democratic inclusion even in the face of administrative barriers, or an unwelcome result for those who wish to make membership and standing within the political system unambiguous. Whatever the normative viewpoint, it is important for empirically minded social scientists to arrive at a clear picture. So far, we do not have such a picture.

To advance our understanding of political engagement within the noncitizen population, it would be most beneficial to gather survey data during major political campaigns. American politics, after all, by virtue of its constitutional design follows a recurring cycle. During campaign periods, participatory opportunities abound, and in most parts of the country the airwaves are full of mobilization messages. For this reason, a long-standing tradition within political science is to survey the public most keenly during election campaigns, when elite-mass communication is most intense. These are moments when any similarities or differences between citizens with voting rights and noncitizens should stand out in greatest relief. Only one of the studies discussed, the 2008 survey of Asian Americans, was fielded at such at time. More surveys along these lines are needed.

It would also move scholarship in this area forward if the noncitizen category were disaggregated. Included in this grouping are legal permanent residents (green card holders) who are similar to U.S. citizens in various respects, immigrants who entered the United States without papers, and individuals who have some form of government-issued identification but are not permanent residents. These statuses might well be linked in very different ways to political engagement in practice. Pooling them all under the label of noncitizen creates a classification that is rough at best.[22]

In addition to comparing immigrants within the noncitizen population based on their particular administrative statuses, it would be helpful to gather survey data that permit wider comparisons across the public. As noted, some researchers compare noncitizens within a particular ethnic group to foreign-born coethnics who have become naturalized citizens. Other studies have compared noncitizens with all coethnics, including the U.S. born. Still others compare noncitizens with the U.S. public at large. Theoretically, any of these lines of comparison could be informative. The most useful survey designs would permit multiple levels of comparisons so that, say, foreign-born Latinos who are not American citizens could be compared with naturalized Latino immigrants, Latinos in general, the African American community, the Asian community (immigrant and native born), the Anglo community, and the country in general.

The nationwide LINES survey we fielded in 2012 had these three qualities—the scheduling of interviews to coincide with the peak of the campaign season, extensive instrumentation that allows for a richer recognition of noncitizen statuses, and a design that easily links with the ANES, so that the political attitudes and involvement of foreign-born noncitizens can

---

22. In his piece on noncitizen participation, Leal refers to the bluntness of this dichotomy (2002, 370).

be compared with naturalized immigrants and members of other ethnic and racial groups within the mass public. The features of this design are discussed in the following section.

THE 2012 LATINO IMMIGRANT NATIONAL ELECTION STUDY

Some weeks after the formal kickoff of the 2012 presidential campaigns, we conducted the LINES, a nationally representative survey of 1,304 foreign-born Latino adults. Interviews were administered over the telephone, with respondents selected at random using listings provided by marketing research firms. Approximately 60 percent of the LINES participants were not U.S. citizens, a proportion that comports with estimates from the U.S. Census.[23]

Unlike previous polls of Latinos, such as the LNS and the LNPS, only immigrants from Spanish-speaking Latin American countries were targeted for interviewing. Although this sampling strategy was more narrowly focused than earlier studies of ethnic populations, the findings can be placed in a much broader context. This is because LINES was fielded in parallel with the ANES: the first wave of data gathering for both studies took place before the election, and then a follow-up round was conducted shortly afterward. Most of the questionnaire items for LINES—the measures of political participation, views of the parties, attachments to particular social groups, and levels of trust in American policymakers, among others—were adapted directly from the ANES.[24] These two studies thus readily allow joint analysis.

This was our way of making the study of public opinion and political behavior during a major campaign cycle more representative of the public at large. It was not possible to cover the entire noncitizen population. The challenges of surveying immigrants from regions other than Latin America would have been insurmountable. Given constraints, interviews were conducted only in English or Spanish, which meant that Brazilian immigrants could not be included in the sampling frame either, though of course they are considered Latin American born. Nevertheless, the coverage of LINES encompasses most of the current noncitizen population, especially noncitizens who lack residency documentation.[25] Participants who have been largely invisible to election-year public opinion researchers now stand out.

The many contributors in this issue of *RSF* offer the first fruits of this initiative. We do not list the claims of each piece one by one. Readers are encouraged to see for themselves how the authors have exploited the novel features of the LINES surveys. By way of heralding these works, we emphasize here that when put alongside other subgroups within the American public, Latino immigrants—including noncitizens—appear relatively engaged in politics. Federal administrative policies that deny particular rights to immigrants who have not gone through the process of naturalization should not be seen as affixing a kind of Scarlet Letter that pushes foreign-born noncitizens to the periphery of civic life. Several of the articles in this issue chart the ways that noncitizens become involved in politics. One piece finds that undocumented Latino immigrants are less likely to become informed about American politics relative to legal permanent residents and U.S. citizens. This could have an effect on the quality of participatory signals. Others suggest, however, that attachments to political parties and political outreach, a sense of ethnic consciousness feeling that one is Hispanic or

---

23. The LINES codebook provides more details about the survey firms that carried out the interviews, sampling weights, and other technical information. Support for this study came from the Russell Sage Foundation, the Carnegie Corporation of New York, Cornell University, the Purdue University Global Policy Research Institute, and the Office of the Vice President for Research at Purdue University.

24. In 2012, the ANES produced questionnaires in both English and Spanish, and an oversample of Latino citizens was conducted. The LINES questionnaire drew directly from the wordings in the ANES survey so that the two studies could be seamlessly integrated for analysis.

25. An estimated 60 percent of the unauthorized immigrant population in the United States today is Mexican origin. Approximately 80 percent of unauthorized immigrants emigrated from a Latin American country.

Latino, exposure to Spanish-language media, and transnational connections can help pull immigrants, both citizens and noncitizens, toward the political process. In the tradition of the ANES, the 2012 LINES dataset is available to all for fresh analyses on the publication of this issue. Given the novelty of incorporating noncitizen respondents into the framework of an election-year survey, much fresh ground is to be tilled. An appendix provides additional technical details about the study and information about downloading it for further analysis.

In closing, we should recognize that any assessment of how federal migration policies and administrative categories influence political participation and public opinion among the foreign born is inherently dynamic. Government regulations and enforcement norms change. It is possible that the day-to-day implications of being a citizen or noncitizen could vary over time. Political scientists investigating the interface between public policies and political behavior must be mindful of these dynamics.

As of this writing, government statutes concerning immigration and naturalization are in a state of flux. In November 2014, President Obama announced an executive order that would permit approximately half of all undocumented immigrants to remain in the country at least through the end of his term without fear of deportation. The legality of this action is currently being contested, and the U.S. Supreme Court is expected to rule on it in 2016. It is not clear whether this Obama administration order will stand, and perhaps be a harbinger of more wide-ranging immigration policy reform, or whether the Court will strike it down. The LINES survey provides a key snapshot of administrative status and democratic engagement in 2012. As new policies in this area are enacted and evolve, the study can serve as a springboard for future surveys to explore the changing contours of immigrant political engagement—and, most importantly, the potential for effective representation. Throughout the 2016 campaign season and beyond, issues concerning immigration and multiculturalism will undoubtedly continue to receive a great deal of attention, remaining very contentious. Simplistic and disparaging caricatures of the foreign born are now commonly aired in many circles. At this pivotal juncture, social scientists have a professional and moral obligation to shed much needed light on the political orientations and aspirations of immigrants, citizens and noncitizens alike.

REFERENCES

Affigne, Tony, Evelyn Hu-Dehart, and Marion Orr, ed. 2014. *Latino Politics en Ciencia Política*. New York: New York University Press.

Ansolabehere, Stephen, Samantha Luks, and Brian Schaffner. 2014. "The Perils of Cherry Picking Low Frequency Events in Large Sample Surveys." *CCES News*, November 5, 2014. Accessed May 20, 2015. http://projects.iq.harvard.edu/cces/news/perils-cherry-picking-low-frequency-events-large-sample-surveys.

Bada, Xóchitl, Jonathan Fox, and Andrew Selee, eds. 2006. *Invisible No More: Mexican Migrant Civic Participation in the United States*. Washington, D.C.: Woodrow Wilson International Center for Scholars Mexico Institute.

Barreto, Matt A., Sylvia Manzano, Ricardo Ramírez, and Kathy Rim. 2009. "Mobilization, Participation, and *Solidaridad*." *Urban Affairs Review* 44(5): 736–64.

Barreto, Matt A., and José Muñoz. 2003. "Reexamining the 'Politics of In-Between': Political Participation Among Mexican Immigrants in the United States." *Hispanic Journal of Behavioral Sciences* 23(4): 427–47.

BBC. "Donald Trump Defends His 'Humane' Deportation Plan." *BBC News*, November 11, 2015. Accessed January 14, 2016. http://www.bbc.com/news/world-us-canada-34790293.

Berelson, Bernard. 1952. "Democratic Theory and Public Opinion." *Public Opinion Quarterly* 16(3): 313–80.

Brown, Anna, and Renee Stepler. 2015. "Statistical Portrait of the Foreign-Born Population in the United States, 1960–2013." *Pew Research Center Hispanic Trends*. Accessed February 2, 2016. http://www.pewhispanic.org/2015/09/28/statistical-portrait-of-the-foreign-born-population-in-the-united-states-1960-2013-key-charts/#2013-fb-authorized-pie.

Cohen, Elizabeth. 2009. *Semi-Citizenship in Democratic Politics*. New York: Cambridge University Press.

———. 2014. "Dilemmas of Representation, Citizenship, and Semi-Citizenship." *St. Louis University Law Journal* 58 (Summer): 1048–49.

Converse, Philip E. 1987. "Changing Conceptions of Public Opinion in the Political Process." *Public Opinion Quarterly* 51: S12.

Dahl, Robert A. 1970. *After the Revolution?: Authority in a Good Society*. New Haven, Conn.: Yale University Press.

———. 1989. *Democracy and Its Critics*. New Haven, Conn.: Yale University Press.

Dovi, Suzanne. 2009. "In Praise of Exclusion." *Journal of Politics* 71(3): 1172–86.

Fenno, Richard F. Jr. 1978. *Home Style: House Members in Their Districts*. Boston, Mass.: Little, Brown.

Fraga, Luis, John Garcia, Rodney Hero, Michael Jones-Correa, Valerie Martinez-Ebers, and Gary Segura. 2011. *Latinos in the New Millennium*. New York: Cambridge University Press.

de la Garza, Rodolfo, and Louis DeSipio. 1994. "The Link Between Individuals and Electoral Institutions in Five Latino Neighborhoods." In *Barrio Ballots*, edited by Rodolfo de la Garza, Martha Menchaca, and Louis DeSipio. Boulder, Colo.: Westview Press.

de la Garza, Rodolfo O., Louis DeSipio, F. Chris Garcia, John Garcia, and Angelo Falcon. 1992. *Latino Voices: Mexican, Puerto Rican, and Cuban Perspectives on American Politics*. Boulder, Colo.: Westview Press.

Gibson, Campbell J., and Emily Lennon. 1999. "Historical Census Statistics on the Foreign-Born Population of the United States: 1850 to 1990." Working Paper no. 29. Washington: U.S. Census Bureau.

Goodin, Robert E. 2007. "Enfranchising All Affected Interests, and Its Alternatives." *Philosophy and Public Affairs* 35(1): 40–68.

Hayduk, Ronald. 2015. "Immigrant Voting." Accessed May 20, 2015. http://ronhayduk.com/immigrant-voting/.

Henderson, Ana. 2012. "Citizenship Verification, Obstacle to Voter Registration and Participation." *Race, Poverty, and the Environment* 19(1). Accessed January 16, 2016. http://reimaginerpe.org/19-1/henderson.

Johansson, Brandon. 2015. "Gessler Voter Sting Nets One Conviction Despite Accusation of Widespread Fraud." *Aurora Sentinel*, March 13, 2015. Accessed January 16, 2016. http://www.aurorasentinel.com/news/gessler-voter-sting-nets-1-conviction-despite-accusation-widespread-fraud/.

Jones-Correa, Michael, and James A. McCann. 2013. "The Effects of Naturalization and Documentation Status on the Participation of Latino Immigrants." Paper presented at the annual meeting of the American Political Science Association. Chicago (August 28–September 1, 2013).

Leal, David. 2002. "Political Participation by Latino Noncitizens in the United States." *British Journal of Political Science* 32(2): 350–70.

Lerner, Kira. 2015. "Ohio's Huge Voter Fraud Investigation Turns Up Nearly Nothing," *ThinkProgress*, March 13, 2015. Accessed January 16, 2016. http://thinkprogress.org/election/2015/03/13/3633472/husted-noncitizen-voters/.

Levin, Ines. 2013. "Political Inclusion of Latino Immigrants: Becoming a Citizen and Political Participation." *American Politics Research* 41(4): 535–68.

Levinson, Sanford. 2013. "Who Counts? Sez Who?" Childress Lecture at Saint Louis University School of Law, November 1, 2013. *Saint Louis University Law Journal* 937 (2014): 937–89.

Lien, Pei-te. 1994. "Ethnicity and Political Participation: A Comparison between Asian and Mexican Americans." *Political Behavior* 16(2): 237–64.

———. 2001. *The Making of Asian America Through Political Participation*. Philadelphia, Pa.: Temple University Press.

Lien, Pei-te, M. Margaret Conway, and Janelle Wong. 2004. *The Politics of Asian Americans: Diversity and Community*. New York: Routledge.

Madison, James. 1962. "Public Opinion." In *The Papers of James Madison*, vol. 15, edited by James M. Banner, Thomas A. Mason, Robert A. Rutland, Jeanne K. Sisson, Robert J. Brugger, Robert Rhodes Crout, Dru Dowdy, Susannah H. Jones, and Fredrika J. Teute. Charlottesville: University Press of Virginia.

Marouf, Fatma. 2012. "The Hunt for Noncitizen Voters." *Stanford Law Review Online* 65(66–72). Accessed January 16, 2016. http://www.stanfordlawreview.org/online/hunt-noncitizen-voters.

Martinez, Lisa M. 2005. "Yes We Can: Political Participation in Unconventional Politics." *Social Forces* 84(1): 135–55.

Mayhew, David R. 1974. *Congress: The Electoral Connection*. New Haven, Conn.: Yale University Press.

McCann, James A., and Katsuo Nishikawa. 2012. "Engaging Immigrants in American Democracy." In *De la Cultura Cívica*, edited by Julia I. Flores Dávila. Mexico City: Universidad Nacional Autóma de México.

Migration Policy Institute. 2015. "Immigrants Countries and Regions of Birth." *U.S. Immigration Trends*. Accessed May 20, 2015. http://www.migrationpolicy.org/programs/data-hub/us-immigration-trends#source.

Muste, Christopher P. 2013. "The Dynamics of Immigration Opinion in the United States, 1992–2012." *Public Opinion Quarterly* 77 (Spring): 409.

Peoples, Steve, and Alicia A. Caldwell. 2015. "Cruz Immigration Plan Would Suspend Work Visa Program," *The Big Story*, November 14, 2015. Accessed January 16, 2016. http://bigstory.ap.org/article/2f572d185cd847f4a21ec1f8764d7ea7/cruz-immigration-plan-would-suspend-work-visa-program.

Pitkin, Hanna Fenichel. 1967. *The Concept of Representation*. Berkeley: University of California Press.

Putnam, Robert. 2001. *Bowling Alone: The Collapse and Revival of American Community*. New York: Simon & Schuster.

Ramakrishnan, S. Karthick. 2006. "But Do They Bowl? Race, Immigrant Incorporation, and Civic Voluntarism in the United States." In *Transforming Politics, Transforming America*, edited by Taeku Lee, S. Karthick Ramakrishnan, and Ricardo Ramírez. Charlottesville: University of Virginia Press.

Rehfeld, Andrew. 2005. *The Concept of Constituency: Political Representation, Democratic Legitimacy and Institutional Design*. New York: Cambridge University Press.

Richman, Jesse, Gulshan Chattha, and David Earnest. 2014. "Do Noncitizens Vote in U.S. Elections?" *Electoral Studies* 36: 149–57.

Segovia, Francine, and Renatta Defever. 2010. "The Polls—Trends: American Public Opinion on Immigrants and Immigration Policy." *Public Opinion Quarterly* 74 (Summer): 387.

Segura, Gary, Harry Pachon, and Nathan Woods. 2001. "Hispanics, Social Capital, and Civic Engagement." *National Civic Review* 90(1): 85–96.

Sheehan, Colleen A. 1992. "The Politics of Public Opinion: James Madison's 'Notes on Government.'" *William and Mary Quarterly* 49 (October): 609–27.

———. 2004. "Madison v. Hamilton: The Battle over Republicanism and the Role of Public Opinion." *American Political Science Review* 98 (August): 405–24.

Spodak, Cassie, and Eugene Scott. 2015. "Christie: Track immigrants like FedEx packages." *CNN Politics*, August 29, 2015. Accessed January 14, 2016. http://www.cnn.com/2015/08/29/politics/chris-christie-fedex-packages/.

Theiss-Morse, Elizabeth. 2009. *Who Counts as an American? The Boundaries of National Identity*. New York: Cambridge University Press.

Thompson, Chrissie. 2015. "Noncitizens Voted in Greater Cincinnati." *Cincinnati Enquirer*, March 12, 2015. Accessed January 27, 2016. http://www.cincinnati.com/story/news/politics/2015/03/12/non-citizens-registered-vote-cincinnati-jon-husted/70224542/.

Verba, Sidney, Kay Lehman Schlozman, and Henry E. Brady. 1995. *Voice and Equality: Civic Voluntarism in American Politics*. Cambridge, Mass.: Harvard University Press.

Verba, Sidney, Kay Lehman Schlozman, Henry Brady, and Norman Nie. 1993. "Race, Ethnicity and Political Resources: Participation in the United States." *British Journal of Political Science* 23 (1993): 453–97.

Voss, Kim, and Irene Bloemraad, ed. 2011. *Rallying for Immigrant Rights*. Berkeley: University of California Press.

Walzer, Michael. 1983. *Spheres of Justice: A Defense of Pluralism and Equality*. New York: Basic Books.

Wong, Janelle. 2006. *Democracy's Promise: Immigrants and American Civic Institutions*. Ann Arbor: University of Michigan Press.

Wong, Janelle, S. Karthick Ramakrishnan, Taeku Lee, and Jane Junn. 2011. *Asian American Political Participation*. New York: Russell Sage Foundation.

Young, Iris Marion. 2000. *Inclusion and Democracy*. Oxford: Oxford University Press.

Zepeda-Millán, Chris. 2014. "Weapons of the (Not So) Weak: Immigrant Mass Mobilization in the U.S. South." *Critical Sociology*. doi: 10.1177/0896920514527846.

PART I
The Migrant Experience, Civic Integration, and Social Capital

Migration Status and Political Knowledge Among Latino Immigrants

SUSAN K. BROWN AND FRANK D. BEAN

This paper invokes a membership-exclusion theoretical model of immigrant integration to investigate political incorporation. Specifically, we examine the extent to which unauthorized migration status is associated with general and particular political knowledge and with other kinds of structural incorporation. In the analyses, we use data from the initial wave of the 2012 Latino Immigrant National Election Study (LINES) targeting adult immigrants from Spanish-speaking countries in Latin America. Consistent with theoretical expectations, we find that unauthorized Latino immigrants have significantly lower levels of general political knowledge than green card holders, those with other government IDs, or naturalized citizens, and that the difference between the unauthorized and the legal groups holds up when controls are introduced for exposure (quantity and quality of time in the country) and various kinds of structural incorporation, although differences among the legal groups do not. Thus, forms of structural integration mediate the effects of exposure on acquisition of general political knowledge by legal immigrants, but they do not for unauthorized immigrants, providing evidence that membership exclusion severely restricts political incorporation. At the same time, unauthorized immigrants show more awareness about changes in the unemployment rate than legal immigrants do, a result consistent both with their main reason for migration (to work) and with their having recourse only to collective action as a form of political expression.

Keywords: political incorporation, unauthorized migration, membership exclusion, political knowledge

Many discussions of immigrant political incorporation begin by focusing on race and ethnicity (Hochschild et al. 2013). In the U.S. case, this seems appropriate, given that most of the migration to the United States in the last half-century has been non-European (Bean, Lee, and Bachmeier 2013). Such discussions tend to veer toward either the optimistic or pessimistic, depending on whether they take as their model the successful integration of the descendants of European immigrants of the early twentieth century or the lingering socioeconomic disadvantage of African Americans in the long wake of slavery and in the subsequent injustices of Jim Crow laws (Warner and Srole 1945; Gordon 1964; Jaynes and Williams 1989; Bean and Bell-Rose 1999; Alba and Nee 2003; Holzer 2009). Yet neither narrative seems fully to apply to new nonwhite immigrants, especially Latino newcomers, who tend not to see

Susan K. Brown is associate professor of sociology at the University of California, Irvine. **Frank D. Bean** is distinguished professor of sociology and director of the Center for Research on Immigration, Population, and Public Policy, University of California, Irvine.

We thank the organizers of the workshop (Michael Jones-Correa and James McCann), the other workshop participants, and Carole Uhlaner for helpful suggestions. Direct correspondence to: Susan K. Brown at skbrown@uci.edu, Department of Sociology, University of California, 3151 Social Science Plaza, Irvine, CA 92697; and Frank D. Bean at fbean@uci.edu, Department of Sociology, University of California, 3151 Social Science Plaza, Irvine, CA 92697.

themselves in monoracial terms (Lee and Bean 2010; Telles 2014). In part to move beyond such conceptualizations, Michael Jones-Correa (1998, 2007) recommends that students of Latino politics focus less on *ethnic* or *transnational* dynamics and more on *immigrant* politics, defined as "a liminal state of disengagement from the politics of both sending or receiving countries, even if not from politics entirely" (2007, 53–54).

Because so many Latino immigrants to the United States come as unauthorized entrants (Bean et al. 2014), their migration status needs to be taken into account explicitly in models of political incorporation. Political scientists have widely noted that the nature of initial societal membership among immigrants may matter for political incorporation (Hochschild and Mollenkopf 2009; Mollenkopf 2013). Similarly, sociologists have argued that the initial lack of legitimate and official societal membership has unleashed forces that are highly exclusionary but potentially impermanent (Bean and Brown 2015). Thus, in addition to studies of political integration as a function of individual background and experience on factors affecting voting and civic participation, we also need to assess the effects of local organizations and institutions, such as those with implications for settlement or citizenship, as well as the effects of more distal bureaucracies that establish policies and priorities and carry out enforcement (Bloemraad 2013; Ramakrishnan 2013; Jones-Correa 2013).

This paper looks at the latter kind of factors. The lack of political integration, in particular, starts with the absence of initial societal membership, together with the organizational and institutional factors that define and sustain this lack, in a process called *membership exclusion* (Bean, Brown, and Bachmeier 2015). This approach argues that the official denial of societal membership through organizational and institutional means curtails individual-level structural integration. That is, initial societal membership constitutes a necessary, if not sufficient, condition for immigrant integration, including individual-level political integration. This paper assesses this idea by investigating the extent to which unauthorized status among immigrants is associated with both general and particular forms of political knowledge, as well as with other kinds of structural integration, the dimensions of which tend to reinforce both one another and political knowledge. Thus, we hypothesize that gradations of legalization and citizenship will relate positively both to general political knowledge and to other kinds of integration. We further hypothesize that being unauthorized will be associated with low general political knowledge and the absence of mutually reinforcing forms of structural integration, although we also suggest why unauthorized status may positively be associated with particular knowledge. Empirically, we examine how unauthorized status among Latino immigrants on the one hand and different kinds of legal and citizenship status on the other separately affect general and particular political knowledge and relationships among aspects of structural integration.

IMMIGRANT-GROUP POLITICAL INCORPORATION

Thinking about the dimensionality of integration helps us understand the implications of the membership-exclusion approach for political integration. The classic assimilation perspective and variants that emphasize ethnoracial status (see Brown and Bean 2006; Bean and Brown 2015) all share the idea that different aspects of integration tend to progress together over time, even if somewhat haltingly. They thus tend to be one-dimensional (Alba and Nee 2003). More pluralist frameworks, as exemplified by European multicultural approaches, emphasize that the sociocultural aspects of integration (compared with the economic, spatial, and political aspects) may occur at different times or not at all (Fokkema and De Haas 2011; Kymlicka 1995; Montserrat and Rex 2010). Thus, the retention of specific ethnic-group values, customs, and behavioral practices is not foreclosed. Moreover, sociocultural distinctiveness is envisioned as not incompatible with other kinds of integration. Such perspectives are more multidimensional in conceptualization because they allow immigrant groups to maintain religious and family practices and other ethnic values and behaviors that are distinct from those of native mainstream groups and from those of other ethnic immigrant groups (Modood 2007; Reitz et al. 2009; Wright and Bloemraad 2012), thus fostering social diversity. Because these sociocultural practices remain distinct from other forms of structural integration, overall incorporation embodies at least two dimensions.

Exclusionary dynamics are another example of multidimensional incorporation. Political scientists often distinguish between entry dynamics (meaning kind of initial membership) and subsequent forms of political incorporation. Jennifer Hochschild and John Mollenkopf (2009) and Hochschild and her colleagues (2013) present conceptual schema that underscore how different kinds of political integration take place at different points in the overall process, especially the difference between entry and later attitudes and behaviors. They note that U.S. immigrants cannot vote until they naturalize, meaning that voting behavior cannot become a relevant aspect of political incorporation until immigrants have lived in the country long enough to become eligible to apply for citizenship. This sequence alone implies that prior membership is important for other integration outcomes. Just as one cannot vote without becoming a citizen, neither can newcomers apply for citizenship without having become legal permanent residents. The lack of social citizenship for unauthorized immigrants reaches its extreme form when such migrants are officially excluded from many arenas of social and economic participation (by dint of policy and law), so that other forms of incorporation are effectively shut off. This foundational principle undergirds the theoretical perspective of membership exclusion (Bean, Brown, and Bachmeier 2015).

Legal status provides access to opportunity (and thus social mobility), as well as partial access to some degree of a social safety net. In short, the lack of initial societal membership implies an important precondition for other forms of integration. Official boundaries that demarcate ineligibility for social citizenship in a given society not only cut off access to opportunity, they also foster stigmatization and exploitation that further hamper structural advancement (Joppke 2010; Hochschild et al. 2013; Hochschild and Mollenkopf 2009; Zolberg 1999). The nature of such exclusionary boundaries can vary from country to country, involving variously, for example, religion, colonial origins, race, residency restrictions, or citizenship (Freeman 1979; Fredrickson 1988; Pickus 1998; Solinger 1999; Alba and Silberman 2002; Bauer et al. 2005; Papademetrios 2006; Sokatch and Myers 2014). Whatever the particular basis for a strong exclusionary boundary, the presence and status of migrants falling outside the boundary results in their being seen and treated as illegitimate. This is even more strongly the case when such boundaries are institutionalized in formal law.

In the United States historically, previous instances of notable denials of social citizenship include the enslavement of African Americans in the South, Mexican Americans in Texas through the first half of the twentieth century, the forced relocation of Native Americans in the Trail of Tears, and Chinese exclusion (Lieberson 1980; Montejano 1987; Foley 1997; Lee 2002; Perdue and Green 2007; Rumbaut 2006). All of these groups were either dislocated or subjected to apartheid-like exclusions that were not officially eliminated until the civil rights legislation of the mid-1960s (Nee and Holbrow 2013). Immigrants incurring exclusions today, like these ethnoracial minorities earlier, experience social and psychological distress (Gonzales 2011; Nee and Holbrow 2013; Yoshikawa 2011), strain and tension stemming from nonmembership dampening forms of immigrant structural integration, such as educational attainment (Bean et al. 2015).

Unauthorized migrant status has constituted an ever stronger exclusionary boundary in the United States over the past three decades, since the 1986 Immigration and Reform Act criminalized the hiring of unauthorized workers (Bean, Vernez, and Keely 1989). More recent laws deemed that migrants themselves were committing illegal acts by working, thus deepening the marginalization of the Latinos who make up the bulk of the U.S. unauthorized population (Massey 2013; Tienda and Sánchez 2013; Motomura 2014). Because so many Latinos remain in marginal statuses for long periods, such legal exclusions, including the inability to get a driver's license and ineligibility for many kinds of jobs, limit individual economic mobility. Burdens also extend to the children of such immigrants, undercutting their access to higher education, heightening stress, undermining motivations to achieve, and slowing cognitive and emotional development (Bean et al. 2011; Nee and Holbrow 2013; Yoshikawa 2011). A membership-exclusion hypothesis explicitly specifies that other forms of integration, including later political incorporation, are unlikely to any appreciable degree without this earliest form of political incorporation. In this sense, membership exclusion explicitly involves a multidimensional conceptualization of integration because it posits a sharp integration divide between those with membership, for whom aspects of integration proceed in a relatively unhindered fashion, and those without such status, whose integration does not.

Unauthorized Status and Political Knowledge
Here we study political integration by focusing on both general and particular forms of political knowledge. By general political knowledge, we mean information regarding how much Latino immigrants know about certain key civic features of American national political institutions. By particular political knowledge, we mean their knowledge of a particular feature of the American economy that we would expect to be especially salient to labor migrants, who come to the United States to work, often expecting not to stay. This category applies almost universally to unauthorized Latino migrants (Bean et al. 2015). The two specific forms of particular knowledge we examine are how accurately they follow the national unemployment rate and how accurately they perceive changes in unemployment over the past year.

The latter measures are political economy variables because awareness of unemployment conditions reflects knowledge about the socioeconomic context within which political integration occurs but does not tap general civics knowledge per se. Rather, it shows awareness of the strength of the labor market and its changes resulting from government policies. Although this is different from civic knowledge, it may be particularly useful given that research shows voters often cast their ballots based on broad economic conditions, especially job availability (Delli Carpini and Keeter 1996). For unauthorized migrants, it may indicate their potential for collective political action, given that other forms of political involvement are unavailable. We thus use data on three indicators—a measure of general political knowledge and two measures of particular awareness of unemployment. These come from a recent survey of Latino immigrants, one carried out both just before and after the 2012 national U.S. elections. Specifically, we examine data on Latino immigrants' knowledge of the maximum number of terms a U.S. president can serve and of the length of a single term for those elected to the U.S. Senate, as well as the accuracy of perceptions about the national unemployment rate and its recent change. General political knowledge reflects broad familiarity with the American political system and relates to wider awareness of and participation in U.S. politics more generally (Galston 2001), thus providing a basis for gauging Latino immigrant political integration.

We do not assess other general political behaviors or perceptions and feelings about American politics. Thus we do not try to examine phenomena like voting because so many Latino immigrants, because they are not citizens, are ineligible to vote. Nor do we examine subjective feelings about politics because these may be appreciably affected by many Latinos' not being citizens and thus unable to vote. Our examination of knowledge about changes in unemployment represents an effort to tap into a secondary indicator of more concrete politically relevant knowledge that may not relate to eligibility to vote per se but reflects knowledge of economic conditions related to the reasons for migration. Although unauthorized labor migrants may be excluded from structural opportunities that would provide incentives to acquire general political civics knowledge, they may be quite sensitive to employment opportunities. In fact, research has consistently shown that the size of the flow of unauthorized migrants to the United States closely tracks the U.S. unemployment rate (Council on Foreign Relations 2009; Hanson 2006). Unauthorized migrants' politically relevant knowledge about this aspect of the economy may thus actually exceed that of legal migrants, whose positions are more secure and motives more varied. With this in mind, we thus carry out assessments of Latino immigrant political incorporation by examining how both general knowledge about American civics and awareness about important particular features of the national economic context vary with migration and citizenship status, length of time spent in the country, and key aspects of structural integration.

Why is this likely to be fruitful, given that native-born citizens have been found to have unusually low levels of political and economic knowledge? For example, only a third of the U.S. population in 2014 could approximately identify the unemployment rate (Pew Research Center 2014). Moreover, such knowledge has remained low for decades, even as levels of education have risen (Galston 2001). Although political scientists continue to discuss the implications of low levels of civic knowledge for politics in the United States, research indicates both the quality and quantity of political participation is associated with greater civic knowledge. In part because greater civic knowledge may result from more participation, it is often argued that low levels of particular civic knowledge do not preclude active and constructive political participation based on general and diffuse knowledge (Galston 2001; Popkin and Dimock 1999). Moreover, among the respondents in the 2012 Latino Immigrant National Election Study (LINES), who were foreign born, even though only 10.5 percent could correctly report the length of term served by U.S. senators, this is not much different from the responses of Latino voters overall (23.4 percent) or of African American voters (23.6 percent).[1] It thus seems reasonable to examine both how and how much general and particular political knowledge varies with migration status and indicators of structural integration.

Research Hypotheses

A membership-exclusion conceptualization of integration implies that not only will unauthorized status be associated with distinctly low levels of political knowledge, but also other kinds of integration will tend to be low and not related to political knowledge. Moreover, with structural integration suppressed, these other kinds of integration will often not be strongly connected with each other either. Membership thus constitutes a necessary condition for other integration processes to occur. Given this, we focus first on explaining variations in general political knowledge. Because the simple passage of time brings some increase in familiarity with the new society, political knowledge may vary positively with the length of time Latino immigrants (authorized and unauthorized) have lived in the United States. However, exposure without membership is less likely to open structural doors to opportunity.

We expect unauthorized migrants to show less general political knowledge than legal migrants (who have been green card holders for varying lengths of time) and naturalized citizens, but higher levels of the particular knowledge of the unemployment rate. This is likely if for no other reason than unauthorized migrants are more cut off from social and economic opportunities and cannot advance as rapidly in ways that might themselves increase political knowledge, but at the same time are more sensitive to labor market fluctuations. In short, we expect unauthorized migrants to show exceptionally low levels of general political knowledge, even after we control for differences between them and legal migrants in other factors that might be expected to boost political knowledge (such as exposure and life-course measures and indicators of economic and linguistic integration). Among legal migrants, however, we expect to find that both gradations of legalization and citizenship and higher levels of other kinds of integration will be positively related to political knowledge. Stated differently, aspects of structural integration among legal but not unauthorized migrants will be more likely to mediate relationships between exposure and life-course dynamics in the new society on the one hand and

---

1. Of course, the target population of the American National Election Studies (ANES) 2012 Time Series Study is citizens of voting age, most of whom are native-born, and whose knowledge of civics might be expected to exceed that of immigrants.

the acquisition of political knowledge on the other.

DATA, MEASURES, AND STRATEGY OF ANALYSIS

To assess these ideas, we use data from the LINES. This survey was conducted in 2012 in two waves, one in the month leading up to the election in November, and one in the six weeks after the election. Through landline and cell phone interviews, the survey targeted adult immigrants from Spanish-speaking countries in Latin America, resulting in a sample size of 855 in the preelection wave. The postelection wave involved interviews with 435 respondents from the first wave and 451 new ones, for a total of 886. Most of the interviews were conducted in Spanish, and much of the survey instrument was identical to that of the 2012 American National Election Study. The bulk of our analysis comes from the preelection wave, but the question on knowledge of the actual unemployment rate comes from the postelection wave.

We measure specific political knowledge by answers to two civics questions and two broad general economic and political knowledge questions. The latter asked about the national level of unemployment and how much it had recently changed. The former asked about how many terms a president of the United States can serve and about the length of terms U.S senators serve. In all, 56.6 percent of the respondents provided a correct answer to the presidential term question, but only 10.5 percent did to the Senate term question. Only 4.9 percent answered both questions correctly, so we coded civics knowledge as a dichotomous variable based on answering at least one question correctly.[2] In regard to knowledge about change in the unemployment rate, the respondents were queried as to whether they thought the national unemployment rate had gotten better, gotten worse, or stayed the same over the previous year. Because the unemployment rate fell by 1 percentage point between October 2011 and October 2012, from 8.8 percent to 7.8 percent (Bureau of Labor Statistics 2014), we again constructed a dichotomous variable, coding as accurate those who said that unemployment had improved versus all other answers. In this sample, 35.2 percent of respondents correctly indicated that unemployment had gotten better. On the question about exact knowledge of the unemployment rate, we accepted answers from 5 to 10 percent as knowledgeable. In all, 9.5 percent of the sample knew the approximate unemployment rate.

We measure migration status based on information obtained in the LINES survey in response to several questions. These include a question about naturalization, which was asked of everyone; a question asked of those who said no to the naturalization question about whether they "came with papers"; a question asked of those who said they did come with papers about whether "they had a green card now"; a question of those who did not come with papers about whether they "had a valid driver's license" (this question was also asked of those who did not answer the naturalization or the "came with papers" questions); and a question of those who did not have a valid driver's license about whether they had some other form of valid government picture ID. Answers to the questions in this "decision tree" enabled all immigrants to be classified as either naturalized citizens, legal permanent residents (LPRs, often called green card holders), driver's license or government picture ID immigrants, or unauthorized immigrants. We assume the driver's license immigrants have valid visas because in 2012 every state except New Mexico and Washington required verification to obtain such a license; Utah offered a driving privilege card (Wang 2013). This category also includes immigrants

---

2. Our measure of general political knowledge has three levels: no knowledge, knowledge of one political term requirement, or knowledge of both presidential term limits and the length of Senate terms. Here we collapse the knowledge category into a binary variable of no knowledge versus knowledge of at least one set of term requirements. Less than 5 percent of the sample could answer both questions, and when we estimate ordered logit models to allow effects to operate across all three values, these do not yield improvements in fit to the binary logit model. The ordered logit models predict virtually no cases in the category "knowing both kinds of term limits." We conclude that we do not lose relevant information by combining the categories.

Figure 1. Categorization of Migration or Citizenship Status

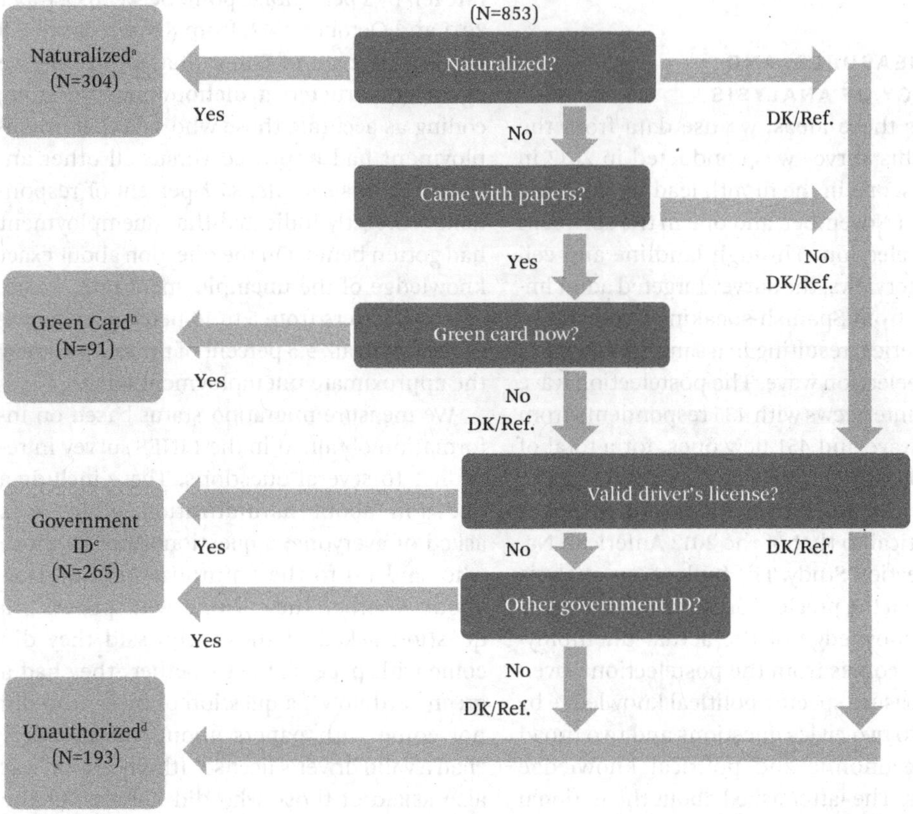

```
                         (N=853)
                        Naturalized?
   Naturalized[a]    Yes          No         DK/Ref.
   (N=304)  ←─────              │              ─────→
                                ▼
                          Came with papers?
                        Yes             No
                                       DK/Ref.
                         │
                         ▼
   Green Card[b]      Green card now?
   (N=91)   ←─── Yes              No
                                 DK/Ref.
                                  │
                                  ▼
                          Valid driver's license?
   Government    ←─── Yes      No        DK/Ref.
   ID[c]                       │
   (N=265)                     ▼
                         Other government ID?
              ←─── Yes           No
                                DK/Ref.
                                 │
                                 ▼
   Unauthorized[d]
   (N=193)
```

Source: Authors' compilation based on preelection survey questions from McCann and Jones-Correa 2012.
[a]Naturalized = Everyone who is naturalized.
[b]Green Card = Everyone who is not naturalized but who came with papers and now has legal permanent residency.
[c]Government ID = Everyone who is neither naturalized nor holds legal permanent residency but who holds either a valid driver's license or some other form of government picture identification.
[d]Unauthorized = Everyone else.

who say they possess a valid government-issued picture identification (see figure 1).

As expected, the civics knowledge score (percentage knowing the answer to at least one question) for naturalized citizens (71.5 percent) exceeds those for all of the other migration status groups (table 1), green card (60.5 percent) and driver's license holders (63.3 percent) showing similar percentages. Most significantly, only about half as many of the unauthorized migrants (35.5 percent) could answer at least one of the questions correctly. On accuracy of knowledge of the change in the unemployment rate over the past year, however, unauthorized immigrants show a higher percentage (40.2) than any of the legal groups (33.8 percent combined). This difference for an indicator of politically relevant labor market knowledge is consistent with the idea that, although immigrants may be subject to membership-exclusion forces that cut off their access to many sources of structural opportunity and general knowledge about civics, their awareness of those features of their political or economic context most salient to their reasons for migrating (such as the change in the

Table 1. Political Knowledge, U.S. Latino Immigrants, 2012

Migration-Citizenship Status	N		Percentage with Knowledge of Political Terms	SD	Percentage Knowing Change in Unemployment Rate	SD	Percentage Knowing Approximate Unemployment Rate	SD
	Preelection[a]	Postelection						
A. Naturalized	304	312	71.5	45.2	32.4	46.9	11.1	31.5
B. Green card	91	136	60.5	49.1	30.5	46.3	3.6	18.6
C. Driver's license	265	244	63.3	48.3	36.6	48.3	10.9	31.2
D. Unauthorized	193	178	35.5	48.0	40.2	49.2	9.4	29.2
Total	853	870	59.6	49.1	35.2	47.8	9.5	29.4

Source: Authors' compilation based on McCann and Jones-Correa 2012.

[a]All questions except for the approximate unemployment rate are based on the survey wave taken shortly before the 2012 election. The second wave of questions followed the election. About half the respondents in the second wave also answered the first wave of the survey, and about half of the respondents were new.

unemployment rate) can exceed that of legal immigrants. This is consistent with other research on specific awareness among unauthorized Mexicans of political issues directly relevant to their lives. For example, Carole Uhlaner (1996) finds that in 1994, 98 percent of Mexican immigrants lacking citizenship, versus 89 percent of Mexican American citizens, knew about Proposition 187, the ballot initiative in California to bar unauthorized migrants from access to social services.

We also include three other kinds of variables in the statistical models predicting political knowledge. The first set consists of indicators of socio-structural incorporation—education (as measured by years of schooling completed), household income (as measured annually in thousands of dollars), and preference for speaking English at home (scored on a 6-point scale). These variables indicate levels of structural incorporation, specifically economic incorporation. Based on the membership-exclusion theoretical considerations introduced earlier, we expect these to covary among LPR and citizen immigrants, both with each other and with political incorporation, in the cases of general and particular indicators of political knowledge (that is, by civics knowledge and by the accuracy of knowledge of change in the unemployment rate).

The second set of variables consists of two temporal exposure measures. One is the length of time the immigrant has been in the country. According to classic assimilation theory, the greater the exposure, the greater the political knowledge, both specific and general (Alba and Nee 2003). The second measure is *youthful age of arrival*. Viewed through a life-course lens, the younger a person is at arrival, the stronger the effect of exposure and the greater the integration (Gubernskaya, Bean, and Van Hook 2013). To tap this aspect of integration, we looked at seventy-five minus age of arrival.[3] Again, membership-exclusion theoretical expectations would expect these variables to vary positively with political knowledge and with structural indicators of incorporation among LPR and naturalized citizen immigrants but not unauthorized migrants. The third indicator is gender, which we simply include as a control variable. Although women show similar or lower levels of political knowledge than men, these do not vary by migration status.

The core of the membership exclusion hypothesis is that unauthorized migration status precludes (or at least severely limits) other kinds of incorporation except sociocultural facets. Accordingly, we expect unauthorized immigrants to have much less political civics knowledge than legal and naturalized immigrants, and for relationships among indicators of integration for the unauthorized to be weak and not explain much variation in political knowledge. In other words, with the possible exception of simple duration, which constitutes a strictly temporal measure of exposure, we expect other indicators—education, income, English, and life-course accentuation—not to matter much for political knowledge among unauthorized migrants. Thus, in the analyses, we first examine the zero-order and adjusted effects of migration status on the political knowledge indicators for all migrants. We then run a series of regression models separately for the group we call legal immigrants (ID holders, LPRs, and naturalized citizens) on the one hand and for unauthorized migrants on the other to ascertain whether structural and exposure factors explain knowledge variation more so among those with legal standing than among those without it. The differences in the patterns implied by the hypotheses are shown in figure 2.

EMPIRICAL FINDINGS

We have already seen that civics political knowledge for the unauthorized is disproportionately below that for legal migrants (see table 1). Only 35.5 percent of the unauthorized correctly answer either of the two civics knowledge questions (the maximum number of terms a president can serve and the length of

---

3. This numerical transposition brings into alignment the direction of any observed statistical relationship with the direction expected by theory. In this case, the expectation is that longer durations starting from youthful ages will result in additional positive effects on incorporation beyond that of simply duration, so we make the transposition to show this effect working in a positive direction.

Figure 2. Hypothesized Relationships Between Exposure and Political Knowledge

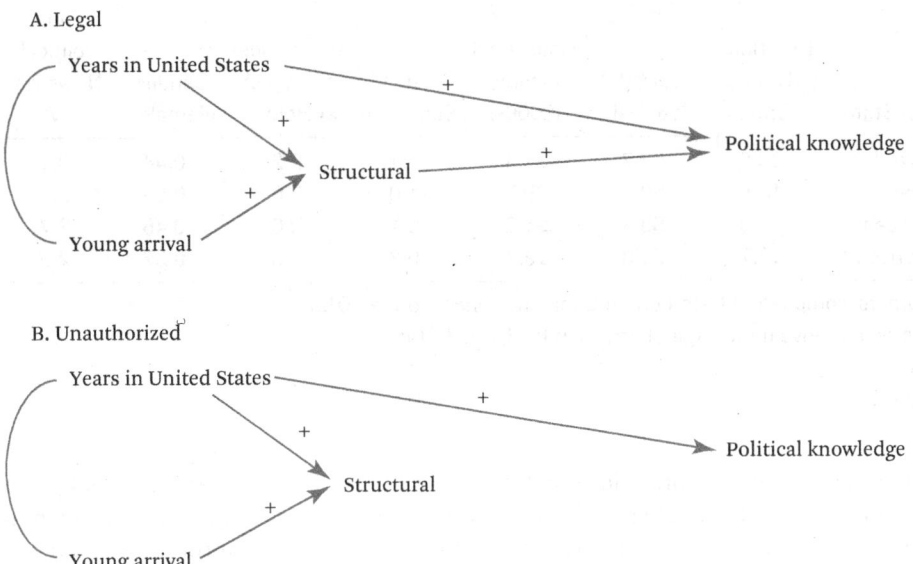

Source: Authors' compilation.
Note: For legal immigrants, structural integration mediates effects of exposure on political knowledge. For the unauthorized, structural integration does not mediate effects of exposure on political knowledge.

Senate term). Also, unauthorized immigrants fall notably below the other groups in how long they have been in the country, years of schooling, income, and English preference (see table 2). For example, unauthorized migrants report only 9.3 years of schooling on average compared with 11.1 years for the naturalized, and annual household incomes below $20,000 compared with the naturalized, whose household incomes are almost 60 percent higher ($31,400). However, in regard to knowledge of change in unemployment, the unauthorized are more aware of current unemployment trends than the other groups (40.2 percent knew the rate had dropped versus 33.8 percent for the legal and naturalized immigrants combined). As we noted earlier, knowledge of changes in the unemployment rate, though plausibly a particularly politically relevant indicator that taps into political incorporation, seems especially salient for unauthorized Mexican migrants, who are quintessential labor migrants (Bean and Stevens 2003; Bachmeier and Bean 2011). Thus, better knowledge of unemployment in their case may mostly reflect heightened sensitivity to labor market conditions, a not surprising tendency. Our conjecture that knowledge of unemployment fluctuations might vary in a direction opposite to their knowledge of civics is thus borne out. If such knowledge reflects unauthorized status and perhaps also potential for collective political action, we would not expect this indicator to necessarily show much relationship with other variables.

Legal and unauthorized immigrants differ in temporal exposure and other indicators of structural integration. We can see this clearly in table 3. For example, the group we term legals has more years of schooling (10.3 on average) than unauthorized migrants (9.3 on average). They also report greater annual household income, longer durations in the United States, but not younger ages at arrival. In addition, they also score higher on preferences for speaking English at home (or for those in the postelection wave of the survey, greater comfort in speaking English). We also present in table 3 the intercorrelations for legal immigrants compared with those for unauthorized immigrants. When these are examined separately (in the bottom two panels), we see that

Table 2. Means for Exposure, Structural Variables, and Gender

Migration-Citizenship Status	Duration in United States	Youthful Arrival[a]	Household Income ($000s)	Years of Schooling	Preference for English at Home[b]	Gender (Female)	Gets Political News via TV[c]
A. Naturalized	28.5	53.7	31.4	11.1	2.2	0.44	3.1
B. Green card	18.5	50.2	29.7	11.0	2.0	0.55	2.8
C. Driver's license	20.3	53.3	21.8	9.1	2.0	0.46	2.7
D. Unauthorized	13.7	51.3	19.7	9.3	1.8	0.57	2.5

Source: Authors' compilation based on McCann and Jones-Correa 2012.
[a]Defined as seventy-five minus age of arrival in the United States.
[b]1 to 5 scale
[c]0 to 5 scale

aspects of structural integration (education, income, and preference for English at home for legal immigrants) show tendencies to relate positively and significantly to one another and to political civics knowledge (middle panel). That is, they tend to reflect positive integration dynamics. They also relate positively to exposure measures, which is also consistent with integration dynamics. For unauthorized immigrants, however, hardly any correlations among indicators are significant, mostly those that involve exposure measures. In short, the exclusion dynamics impinging on unauthorized immigrants limit their progress to such a degree across all values of these variables that indicators of exposure, structural integration, and political knowledge do not interconnect much with one another.

We next report differences in civics knowledge across all of the migration status categories (unauthorized immigrants, ID immigrants, LPRs, and the naturalized) by successively estimating logistic regressions of political knowledge on the categories (with a dummy variable for ID immigrants omitted from the equation, making this group the reference category), followed by models including sets of selected control variables (see table 4). Without adjusting for other factors (column 1), the migration status categories show the expected direction and magnitude of relationships with political civics knowledge. For example, naturalized Latino immigrants are 46 percent more likely than ID immigrants (as indicated by an odds ratio of 1.46) to know either the number or the length of presidential or Senate terms, ID and green card holders not being significantly different from one another. Unauthorized migrants, however, are 68 percent less likely than ID holders to possess such knowledge, a highly statistically significant difference. In short, consistent with the membership-exclusion hypothesis, unauthorized immigrants are disproportionately less likely to show civic awareness than legal immigrants.

The different migration status categories, however, include persons who have spent varying lengths of time in the country and come at younger ages. When we include the number of years in the United States in the models (column 2), we see as expected that it is positively and significantly related to political civics knowledge. More important, it reduces the size of the naturalization status difference, lowering it by about one-third, from 46 percent above that of ID holders to 20 percent above, a remaining difference that is not statistically significant. In other words, once we take into account that naturalized citizens have lived longer in the country, their level of political civics knowledge and those of the other legal groups are no longer significantly different from each other. By contrast, the deficit for unauthorized immigrants remains quite large (63 percent below that of the ID holders). Including both duration and youthful arrival in the models (column 4) does not change this pattern. Neither does adding indicators of structural integration (columns 5 and 6). Whether we include income by itself, or income, educa-

Table 3. Means, Standard Deviations, and Intercorrelations for Variables

Variables	Means	SD	2	3	4	5	6	7	8	9
Total sample										
1. Political knowledge	0.67	0.61	0.03	0.13***	0.15***	0.22***	0.05	0.12***	-0.09*	0.09**
2. Unemployment change	0.35	0.48	1.00	0.03	0.05	-0.48	-0.47	-0.01	-0.09**	-0.07
3. Education	10.0	4.3		1.00	0.23***	-0.07	0.12***	0.24***	-0.04	0.13***
4. Household income ($000s)	25.6	22.8			1.00	0.14***	0.12***	0.20***	-0.15***	0.14***
5. Duration in United States	21.5	11.4				1.00	0.25***	0.11**	-0.07*	0.16***
6. Youthful arrival	52.6	11.3					1.00	0.17***	-0.04	-0.00
7. Preference for English	2.0	0.89						1.00	-0.12***	0.07*
8. Gender (female)	0.49	0.50							1.00	-0.04
9. Gets political news on TV	2.80	1.23								1.00
Legal immigrants										
1. Political knowledge	0.76	0.61	0.03	0.13**	0.14***	0.12**	0.05	0.08*	-0.05	0.06
2. Unemployment change	0.34	0.47	1.00	-0.03	0.07	-0.02	-0.02	-0.01	-0.10*	-0.12*
3. Education	10.3	4.2		1.00	0.24***	-0.12**	0.13**	0.21***	-0.03	0.12**
4. Household income ($000s)	31.0	19.7			1.00	0.09*	0.10**	0.17***	-0.16***	0.12**
5. Duration in United States	23.8	10.7				1.00	0.25***	0.06	-0.04	0.13**
6. Youthful arrival	53.0	10.8					1.00	0.16***	-0.04	0.00
7. Preference for English	2.1	0.9						1.00	-0.11**	0.02
8. Gender (female)	0.46	0.5							1.00	-0.03
9. Gets political news on TV	2.88	1.25								1.00
Unauthorized immigrants										
1. Political knowledge	0.37	0.52	0.08	0.02	0.04	0.22	-0.07	0.10	-0.12	0.09
2. Unemployment change	0.40	0.49	1.00	0.02	0.06	-0.08	-0.13	0.02	-0.08	0.13
3. Education	9.3	3.9		1.00	0.11	-0.11	0.06	0.18*	-0.01	0.10
4. Household Income ($000s)	24.3	9.8			1.00	0.08	0.16	0.25***	0.05	0.15*
5. Duration in United Stattes	13.7	6.1				1.00	0.24	0.07	-0.01	0.04
6. Youthful arrival	51.3	8.4					1.00	0.18*	-0.01	-0.10
7. Preference for English	1.8	0.8						1.00	-0.11	0.21***
8. Gender (female)	0.58	0.49							1.00	-0.05
9. Gets political news on TV	2.52	1.11								1.00

Source: Authors' compilation based on McCann and Jones-Correa 2012.
Two-tailed: *$p < .05$; **$p < .01$; ***$p < .001$

Table 4. Logistic Regressions of General Political Knowledge on Variables

Independent Variables	Models (Odds Ratios)						
	1	2	3	4	5	6	7
Migration-citizenship status							
Naturalized	1.46*	1.20	1.45*	1.20	1.10	0.95	0.94
Green card	0.89	0.93	0.91	0.93	0.85	0.78	0.78
Government ID (omitted)	—	—	—	—	—	—	—
Unauthorized	0.32***	0.37***	0.32***	0.37***	0.38***	0.39***	0.39***
Years in United States		1.02**		1.02**	1.02**	1.03**	1.03**
Youthful age of arrival			1.01	1.00	1.00	0.99	0.99
Household income ($000s)					1.01*	1.01†	1.01†
Years of education						1.06**	1.06**
English preference at home						1.08	1.08
Gender (female)						0.90	0.90
Gets political news from TV							1.06
Chi²	65.47***	73.86***	65.71***	73.86***	81.12***	93.25***	94.15***
N	853	853	853	853	853	853	853

Source: Authors' compilation based on McCann and Jones-Correa 2012.
Two-tailed: †$p < .10$; *$p < .05$; **$p < .01$; ***$p < .001$

tion, and preferring to speak English at home all at once, the deficit in unauthorized political knowledge remains large. However, these factors do explain the differences in civics knowledge among the groups of legal immigrants. As membership-exclusion theoretical considerations would suggest, the major divide in both level and pattern of political knowledge occurs between unauthorized and legal immigrants.

We also estimate models analyzing awareness of unemployment and changes in unemployment. As noted, this indicator represents politically relevant knowledge about the state of the labor market for unauthorized immigrants. In fact, the strongest awareness among Latino immigrants of the direction of recent trends in the strength of the labor market emerges for the group most likely to be labor migrants, namely the unauthorized (table 5, left side). In all of the logistic regression models, such migrants show a tendency to display greater accuracy of unemployment change than the legal groups, though not to a large enough degree to reach statistical significance compared with those holding government IDs, but it is significant when compared with all of the legal groups combined. The two migration-status groups one would expect to enjoy the most secure levels of immigrant integration in the country, the naturalized and the LPRs, are the least likely to know the recent direction of unemployment in the United States, reflecting perhaps that their life situations depend less on such matters. However, this tendency on their part is not statistically significant in either case. Also interesting is that the exclusion of the unauthorized from opportunities for structural advancement in the country appears not to affect their knowledge of the actual strength of the labor market (table 5, right side), though they are sensitive to whether the labor market is changing. This finding is consistent with research showing that unauthorized potential labor migrants in Mexico are well aware of the prospects of finding work in the United States (Massey et al. 1987).

Theoretical expectations based on consideration of membership exclusion suggest not only that unauthorized Mexican immigrants will show considerably less general political civics knowledge than legal immigrants, but also that they will experience substantially less structural integration. These dynamics imply for unauthorized migrants that measures of structural integration (for example, measures of English usage, education, and income) will

Table 5. Logistic Regressions of Knowledge of Unemployment Measures on Variables

	Models (Odds Ratios)					
	Knows Change in Unemployment Rate			Knows Actual Unemployment Rate		
Independent Variables	1	2	3	1	2	3
Migration-citizenship status						
A. Naturalized	0.87	0.84	0.80	1.14	0.82	0.84
B. Green card	0.72	0.71	0.71	0.30**	0.25**	0.24
C. Government ID (omitted)	—	—	—	—	—	
D. Unauthorized	1.11	1.16	1.19	0.82	0.88	0.89
Years in United States	1.00	0.99	0.99	0.99	0.99	1.00
Youthful age of arrival	0.99	0.99	0.99	1.01	1.00	1.00
Household income ($000s)		1.01†	1.01†		1.00	1.01
Years of education		0.99	0.98		1.08*	1.08*
English[a]		0.98	0.97		0.84	0.84
Gender (female)		0.68*	0.68*		0.60*	0.61*
Gets political news from TV[b]			1.24**			0.81†
Chi²	6.12	17.86*	29.76**	11.04†	28.61**	32.00***
N	853	853	853	870	870	870

Source: Authors' compilation based on McCann and Jones-Correa 2012.
[a]In the preelection survey, respondents were asked whether they preferred to use English at home. In the postelection survey, they were asked how comfortable they were speaking English.
[b]In the preelection survey, respondents were asked whether they got political news from television. In the postelection survey, they were asked how many programs on the election they had watched.
Two-tailed: †$p < .10$; *$p < .05$; **$p < .01$; ***$p < .001$

show little if any relationship with political civics knowledge, with each other, or with measures of exposure (such as how long people have been in the country or how young they are when they arrive). In fact, when we examine all of these relationships in series of nested regression models like those previously examined, but now for authorized and unauthorized immigrants separately, we see that this is decidedly the case (see table 6, bottom panel). We also pooled these groups and ran models testing for the statistical significance of the effect on general civics knowledge of the interaction between legal status and structural integration (the latter measured by a composite socioeconomic status variable combining education, income, and English proficiency). As expected, the interaction effect was positive and statistically significant, indicating that different patterns of incorporation relationships characterize legal and unauthorized immigrants. Among unauthorized immigrants, scarcely any exposure or structural factors show any relationship with knowledge of political civics, the one exception being temporal exposure, or the longer the immigrants have been here. This is not really surprising, because the simple passage of time inevitably results in acquisition of some familiarity with aspects of the environment. However, because unauthorized status curtails access to structural integration, specific aspects of such integration fail to emerge either singly or in combination with each other, with the result that they show little covariation.

This contrasts sharply with the patterns among the categories of legal immigrants, where both length of time in the country and facets of structural integration reveal positive relationships with the extent of political civics knowledge (table 6, top panel). The results for authorized immigrants thus in large measure conform with the model of political knowledge

Table 6. Logistic Regressions of General Political Knowledge on Variables

Structural and Control Characteristics	Models (Odds Ratios)					
	1	2	3	4	5	6
Legal migrants						
Years in United States	1.02**		1.02*	1.02*	1.03**	1.02**
Youthful age of arrival		1.02	1.01	1.01	1.00	1.00
Household income ($000s)				1.02**	1.01**	1.01*
Years of education					1.07**	1.07**
English preference at home					1.04	1.04
Gender (female)					0.98	0.98
Get political news from TV						1.05
Chi²	7.59**	2.02	8.37*	18.12***	29.67***	30.07***
Unauthorized migrants						
Years in United States	1.09**		1.10**	1.10**	1.10**	1.01**
Youthful age of arrival		0.97	0.95†	0.95†	0.95†	0.95†
Household income ($000s)				0.99	0.98	0.98
Years of education					1.00	1.00
English preference at home					1.37	1.33
Gender (female)					0.67	0.68
Get political news from TV						1.11
Chi²	11.20***	1.70	14.45**	14.95***	19.08***	19.58***

Source: Authors' compilation based on McCann and Jones-Correa 2012.
Two-tailed: †$p < .10$; *$p < .05$; **$p < .01$; ***$p < .001$

that Michael Delli Carpini and Scott Keeter formulated (1996). We see that women are less knowledgeable than men in general about civics matters, this difference coming about both through relationships between gender and other variables (especially education), although gender retains some of its own effect controlling for these (a pattern Delli Carpini and Keeter term a socialization effect). They also observe major effects on political knowledge through the structural positions individuals occupy in society (indicated here by education, English preference, and income). The results for Latino legal immigrants also show these patterns. We also find effects of both exposure and youthful arrival, the latter operating to enhance exposure effects.

Delli Carpini and Keeter also suggest that mediating effects on political knowledge may result from media exposure. Immigrants with more favorable structural positions have more access to media and thus more political knowledge. We would not expect such relationships here for unauthorized immigrants, again because of their minimal structural integration as a result of membership exclusion. But such a pattern might emerge among legal immigrants. We test for this by constructing a simple model involving exposure, structural, and behavioral (media usage) effects on political knowledge. We estimate logistic regressions for these connections consistent with an overall recursive set of relationships among the sets of variables (see table 7). We also use for these the results of the logistic regressions of political knowledge on media usage and other variables shown in model 6 of table 6,[4] simplifying the structural effects by showing results for a simple compos-

---

4. We determine an effect by simply assessing the statistical significance of the relationship. If it is notable in this sense, we depict its association in figure 3 by an arrow in the diagram running from the independent to the dependent variable.

Table 7. Regressions for Mediating Variables and Antecedent Characteristics

	Legal and Naturalized Immigrants			Unauthorized Immigrants		
Antecedent Variables[a]	Structural Composite	Political News on TV	Political Knowledge[b]	Structural Composite	Political News on TV	Political Knowledge[b]
Years in United States	0.01†	0.02**	1.02*	0.02	0.01	1.10**
Youthful arrival	0.02**	−0.01	1.01	0.02	−0.02†	0.95†
Structural	—	0.07*	1.19**	—	0.16**	1.02
Gets political news on TV	—	—	1.08	—	—	1.12
Constant	−1.22**	2.85***	0.784*	−1.20	3.73***	1.54
R²	0.053	0.025	0.038	0.015	0.074	0.117
Chi²			18.183**			17.191**
N	660	660	660	193	193	193

Source: Authors' compilation based on McCann and Jones-Correa 2012.
[a]Gender is included as an antecedent variable, but coefficients are omitted.
[b]These are odds ratios. Because political knowledge is a binary variable, we ran logistic regressions in this case and present the Nagelkerke R².

Figure 3. Relationships Among Variables

A. Legal (naturalized, green card, or government identification)

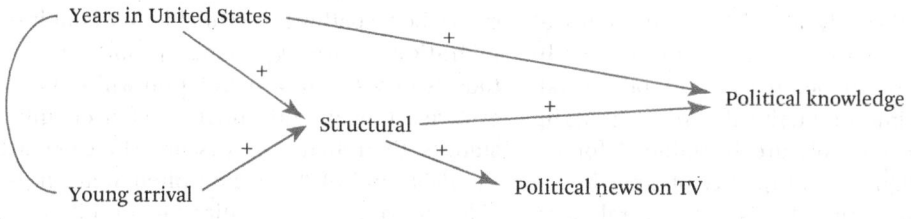

B. Unauthorized

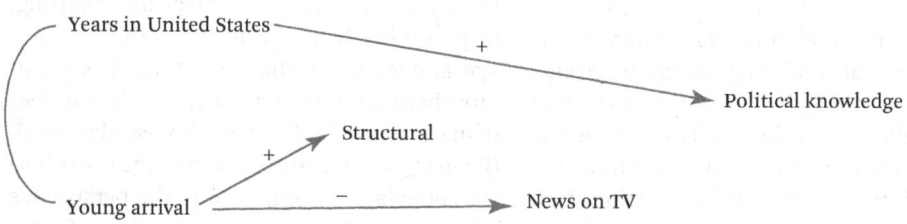

Source: Authors' compilation.

ite structural variable.[5] We find that authorized immigrants in fact show some tendency for structural position to influence political knowledge, but this does not operate much through greater access to and reliance on TV news. Rather, the structural factor exerts its own (small) direct effect on political knowledge.

The mediating effect is not large because

---

5. The composite variable combines z-scores for preferring English at home and income. We do not include education because its relationship with other variables is distorted because for Mexican immigrants, it captures both schooling effects and birth cohort effects, which often work in opposite directions.

the effect of TV news on political knowledge, though positive, is not statistically significant. We present pictorial representations of these relationships, for both the groups of legal immigrants and the group of unauthorized immigrants, in figure 3. For the legal immigrants, interlocking associations among exposure, structural, and behavioral mediating variables are extensive, as is clear from the many connections in the diagram and as we would expect among immigrants whose migration status leaves them relatively unfettered in the pursuit and experience of immigrant incorporation dynamics. Among the unauthorized immigrants, by contrast, scarcely any connections among these factors emerge. Again this is what we would expect given the strictures imposed on incorporation opportunities by what we term *membership exclusion*.

CONCLUSIONS AND POLICY IMPLICATIONS

Overall, these findings are consistent with expectations. Unauthorized Latino immigrants show significantly lower levels of political knowledge than LPRs, those with driver's licenses or official picture IDs, and the naturalized. More important, this difference holds up when even controls are introduced for exposure (quantity and quality of time in the country) and various kinds of structural incorporation. In short, those subject to severe membership exclusion distinctively lack political knowledge relative to other kinds of immigrants. Structural controls explain differences in political knowledge within the groups of legal immigrants (the LPRs, ID holders, and the naturalized) but do not account for the lower political knowledge of the unauthorized. Moreover, forms of structural integration often mediate the effects of exposure on political knowledge acquisition for legal immigrants but not for the unauthorized, further illustrating mechanisms by which membership exclusion leads to severe disadvantages in the usual kinds of individual-level political incorporation. However, unauthorized migrants, precisely because their status makes them ineligible for conventional political activity, may find recourse in collective action, as evidenced by the mass protests in 2006 to proposed legislation to criminalize their presence in the country, and by the Justice for Janitors campaigns throughout the country during the 1990s and 2000s and the janitors strike in Los Angeles at around the same time. The heightened awareness of changes in the unemployment rate observed here among the unauthorized is consistent with the possibility that factors that directly affect the lives of unauthorized migrants can spark collective protests, such actions being perhaps a sole outlet for political expression. This would be consistent with the findings later in this issue by David Sears, Felix Zavala, and Vanessa Danbold, who observed that unauthorized migrants are less attached to political parties.

What are the policy options for dealing with the stifling effects of membership exclusion? Here we have demonstrated them only for the case of political knowledge, but they are in reality broader and perhaps even more harmful, and likely to grow larger. What can be done? At present, unauthorized migrants have few pathways to legalization and wait years in line even when a pathway is available. Without immigration reform, a greater proportion of today's unauthorized population will remain excluded longer, and under harsher circumstances, than their predecessors who came in the 1960s and 1970s. If the United States provides no pathways to legalization, or if it institutes difficult or punitive pathways (those that include long wait times, large fines for having been unauthorized, sizable fees for legalizing, or prohibitively high thresholds that discourage applications), the size of the group will grow because of the relatively smaller number of natives available to do less-skilled work (Bean et al. 2014). And growth of the unauthorized population would lead to the persistence of educational and other disadvantages for Latino immigrants and their families.

REFERENCES

Alba, Richard D. 2009. *Blurring the Color Line: The New Chance for a More Integrated America*. Cambridge, Mass.: Harvard University Press.

Alba, Richard D., and Victor Nee. 2003. *Remaking the American Mainstream: Assimilation and Contemporary Immigration*. Cambridge, Mass.: Harvard University Press.

Alba, Richard D., and Roxane Silberman. 2002. "Decolonization Immigrations and the Social Origins of the Second Generation: The Case of North Africans in France." *International Migration Review* 36(4): 1169–93.

Bachmeier, James D., and Frank D. Bean. 2011. "Comparative Patterns of Schooling and Work Among Adolescents: Implications for Mexican Immigrant Incorporation." *Social Science Research* 40(6): 1579–95.

Bauer, Thomas, Barbara Dietz, Klaus F. Zimmermann, and Eric Zwintz. 2005. "German Migration: Development, Assimilation, and Labour Market Effects." In *European Migration: What Do We Know?*, edited by K. F. Zimmermann Oxford: Oxford University Press.

Bean, Frank D., James D. Bachmeier, Susan K. Brown, and Rosaura Tafoya-Estrada. 2011. "Immigration and Labor Market Dynamics." In *Just Neighbors? Research on African American and Latino Relations in the United States*, edited by Edward Telles, Mark Q. Sawyer, and Gaspar Rivera-Salgado. New York: Russell Sage Foundation.

Bean, Frank D., and Stephanie Bell-Rose. 1999. *Immigration and Opportunity: Race, Ethnicity, and Employment in the United States*. New York: Russell Sage Foundation.

Bean, Frank D., and Susan K. Brown. 2015. "Demographic Analyses of Immigration." In *Migration Theory: Talking Across Disciplines*, 3rd ed., edited by Caroline Brettell and James F. Hollifield. New York: Routledge.

Bean, Frank D., Susan K. Brown, and James D. Bachmeier. 2015. *Parents Without Papers: The Progress and Pitfalls of Mexican-American Integration*. New York: Russell Sage Foundation.

Bean, Frank D., Susan K. Brown, James D. Bachmeier, Jennifer Van Hook, and Mark A. Leach. 2014. "Unauthorized Mexican Migration and the Socioeconomic Attainment of Mexican Americans." In *Diversity and Disparities: America Enters a New Century*, edited by John R. Logan. New York: Russell Sage Foundation.

Bean, Frank D., Jennifer Lee, and James D. Bachmeier. 2013. "Immigration and the Color Line at the Beginning of the 21st Century." *Daedalus* 142(3) Summer: 123–40.

Bean, Frank D., and Gillian Stevens. 2003. *America's Newcomers: Immigrant Incorporation and the Dynamics of Diversity*. New York: Russell Sage Foundation.

Bean, Frank D., Georges Vernez, and Charles B. Keely. 1989. *Opening and Closing the Doors: Evaluating Immigration Reform and Control*. Santa Monica, Calif.: RAND Corporation and Urban Institute Press.

Bloemraad, Irene. 2013. "'The Great Concern of Government': Public Policy as Material and Symbolic Resources." In *Outsiders No More? Models of Immigrant Political Incorporation*, edited by Jennifer Hochschild, Jacqueline Chattopadhyay, and Michael Jones-Correa. New York: Oxford University Press.

Brown, Susan K., and Frank D. Bean. 2006. "Assimilation Models, Old and New: Explaining a Long-Term Process." Washington, D.C.: Migration Policy Institute. Accessed January 24, 2016. http://www.migrationinformation.org/feature/display.cfm?id=442.

Bureau of Labor Statistics. 2014. "Databases, Tables and Calculators by Subject." Modified October 27, 2014. Accessed January 25, 2016. http://data.bls.gov/timeseries/LNS14000000.

Council on Foreign Relations. 2009. *U.S. Immigration Policy*. Independent Task Force Report no. 63. New York: Council on Foreign Relations.

Delli Carpini, Michael X., and Scott Keeter. 1996. *What Americans Know About Politics and Why It Matters*. New Haven, Conn.: Yale University Press.

Fokkema, Tineke, and Hein de Haas. 2011. "Pre- and Post-Migration Determinants of Socio-Cultural Integration of African Immigrants in Italy and Spain." *International Migration* 53(6): 3–26.

Foley, Neil. 1997. *The White Scourge: Mexicans, Blacks, and Poor Whites in Texas Cotton Culture*. Berkeley: University of California Press.

Fredrickson, George M. 1988. *The Arrogance of Race: Historical Perspectives on Slavery, Racism, and Social Inequality*. Middletown, Conn.: Wesleyan University Press.

Freeman, Gary P. 1979. *Immigrant Labor and Racial Conflict in Industrial Societies: The French and British Experience, 1945–1975*. Princeton, N.J.: Princeton University Press.

Galston, William. 2001. "Political Knowledge, Political Engagement, and Civic Education." *Annual Review of Political Science* 4 (June): 217–34.

Gonzales, Roberto G. 2011. "Learning to Be Illegal: Undocumented Youth and Shifting Legal Contexts in the Transition to Adulthood." *American Sociological Review* 76(4): 602–19.

Gordon, Milton M. 1964. *Assimilation in American Life: The Role of Race, Religion, and National Origins.* New York: Oxford University Press.

Gubernskaya, Zoya, Frank D. Bean, and Jennifer Van Hook. 2013. "(Un)Healthy Immigrant Citizens: Naturalization and Activity Limitations in Older Age." *Journal of Health and Social Behavior* 54(4): 427–43.

Hanson, Gordon H. 2006. "Illegal Migration from Mexico to the United States." *Journal of Economic Literature* 44(4): 869–924.

Hochschild, Jennifer, Jacqueline Chattopadhyay, Claudine Gay, and Michael Jones-Correa. 2013. *Outsiders No More? Models of Immigrant Political Incorporation.* Oxford: Oxford University Press.

Hochschild, Jennifer, and John Mollenkopf. 2009. *Bringing Outsiders In: Transatlantic Perspectives on Immigrant Political Incorporation.* Ithaca, N.Y.: Cornell University Press.

Holzer, Harry J. 2009. "The Labor Market and Young Black Men: Updating Moynihan's Perspective." *Annals of the American Academy of Political and Social Science* 621(January): 47–69.

Jaynes, Gerald D., and Robin M. Williams. 1989. *A Common Destiny: Blacks and American Society.* Washington, D.C.: National Academies Press.

Jones-Correa, Michael. 1998. *Between Two Nations: The Political Predicament of Latinos in New York City.* Ithaca, N.Y.: Cornell University Press.

———. 2007. "Fuzzy Distinctions and Blurred Boundaries: Transnational, Ethnic, and Immigrant Politics." In *Latino Politics: Identity, Mobilization, and Representation*, edited by Rudolpho Espino, David L. Leal, and Kenneth J. Méier. Charlottesville: University of Virginia Press.

———. 2013. "Thru-Ways, By-Ways, and Cul-de-Sacs of Immigrant Political Incorporation." In *Outsiders No More? Models of Immigrant Political Incorporation*, edited by Jennifer Hochschild, Jacqueline Chattopadhyay, Claudine Gay, and Michael Jones-Correa. Oxford: Oxford University Press.

Joppke, Christian. 2010. *Citizenship and Immigration.* Malden, Mass.: Polity Press.

Kymlicka, Will. 1995. *Multicultural Citizenship: A Liberal Theory of Minority Rights.* Oxford: Oxford University Press.

Lee, Ericka. 2002. "The Chinese Exclusion Example: Race, Immigration, and American Gatekeeping, 1882–1924." *Journal of American Ethnic History* 21(3): 36–62.

Lee, Jennifer, and Frank D. Bean. 2010. *The Diversity Paradox: Immigration and the Color Line in Twenty-First Century America.* New York: Russell Sage Foundation.

Lieberson, Stanley. 1980. *A Piece of the Pie: Blacks and White Immigrants Since 1880.* Berkeley: University of California Press.

Massey, Douglas S. 2013. "America's Immigration Policy Fiasco." *Daedalus* 142(3): 5–15.

Massey, Douglas S., Rafael Alarcón, Jorge Durand, and Humberto Gonzáles. 1987. *Return to Aztlan: The Social Process of International Migration from Western Mexico.* Berkeley: University of California Press.

McCann, James A., and Michael Jones-Correa. 2012. *Latino Immigrant National Election Study, 2012.* New York: Russell Sage Foundation, Carnegie Corporation of New York, Purdue University, and Cornell University.

Modood, Tariq. 2007. *Multiculturalism: A Civic Idea.* Malden, Mass.: Polity Press.

Mollenkopf, John. 2013. "Dimensions of Immigrant Political Incorporation." In *Outsiders No More? Models of Immigrant Political Incorporation*, edited by Jennifer Hochschild, Jacqueline Chattopadhyay, Claudine Gay, and Michael Jones-Correa. Oxford: Oxford University Press.

Montejano, David. 1987. *Anglos and Mexicans in the Making of Texas, 1836–1986.* Austin: University of Texas Press.

Montserrat, Guibernau, and John Rex. 2010. *The Ethnicity Reader: Nationalism, Multiculturalism and Migration.* Cambridge: Polity Press.

Motomura, Hiroshi. 2014. *Immigration Outside the Law.* New York: Oxford University Press.

Nee, Victor, and Hilary Holbrow. 2013. "Why Asian Americans Are Becoming Mainstream." *Daedalus* 142(3): 65–75.

Papademetriou, Demetrios G. 2006. *Europe and Its Immigrants in the 21st Century: A New Deal or a Continuing Dialogue of the Deaf?* Washington, D.C.: Migration Policy Institute.

Perdue, Theda, and Michael G. Green. 2007. *The Cherokee Nation and the Trail of Tears.* New York: Viking.

Pew Research Center. 2014. "From ISIS to Unemployment: What Do Americans Know?" Washington, D.C.: Pew Hispanic Center.

Pickus, Noah M.J. 1998. *Immigration and Citizenship in the Twenty-First Century.* Lanham, Md.: Rowman & Littlefield.

Popkin, Samuel L. and Michael A. Dimock. 1999. "Political Knowledge and Citizen Competence." In *Citizen Competence and Democratic Institutions*, edited by Stephen L. Elkin and Karol E. Soltan. University Park: Pennsylvania State University Press.

Ramakrishnan, S. Karthick. 2013. "Incorporation versus Assimilation: The Need for Conceptual Differentiation." In *Outsiders No More? Models of Immigrant Political Incorporation*, edited by Jennifer Hochschild, Jacqueline Chattopadhyay, Claudiine Gay, and Michael Jones-Correa. Oxford: Oxford University Press.

Reitz, Jeffrey G., Raymond Breton, Karen Kisiel Dion, and Kenneth L. Dion. 2009. *Multiculturalism and Social Cohesion: Potentials and Challenges of Diversity*. New York: Springer.

Rumbaut, Rubén G. 2006. "The Making of a People." In *Hispanics and the Future of America*, edited by Marta Tienda and Faith Mitchell. Washington, D.C.: National Academies Press.

Sokatch, Daniel, and David N. Myers. 2014. "Israel's Dilemma: Who Can Be an Israeli?" *Los Angeles Times*, January 14, 2014. Accessed January 25, 2016. http://articles.latimes.com/2014/jan/14/opinion/la-oe-myers-israel-citizenship-arabs-20140114.

Solinger, Dorothy J. 1999. *Contesting Citizenship in Urban China: Peasant Migrants, the State, and the Logic of the Market*. Berkeley: University of California Press.

Telles, Edward E. 2014. *Race in Another America: The Significance of Skin Color in Brazil*. Princeton, N.J.: Princeton University Press.

Tienda, Marta, and Susana M. Sánchez. 2013. "Latin American Immigration to the United States." *Daedalus* 142(3): 48–64.

Uhlaner, Carole J. 1996. "Latinos and Ethnic Politics in California: Participation and Preference." In *Latino Politics in California*, edited by Aníbal Yáñez-Chávez. San Diego: Center for U.S.-Mexican Studies.

Wang, Hansi Lo. 2013. "More States Let Unauthorized Immigrants Take the Wheel." National Public Radio, June 23, 2013. Accessed January 25, 2016. http://www.npr.org/blogs/codeswitch/2013/06/23/194281121/more-states-let-unauthorized-immigrants-take-the-wheel.

Warner, W. Lloyd, and Leo Srole. 1945. *The Social Systems of American Ethnic Groups*. New Haven, Conn.: Yale University Press.

Wright, Matthew, and Irene Bloemraad. 2012. "Is There a Trade-Off Between Multiculturalism and Socio-Political Integration? Policy Regimes and Immigrant Incorporation in Comparative Perspective." *Perspectives on Politics* 10(1): 77–95.

Yoshikawa, Hirokazu. 2011. *Immigrants Raising Citizens: Undocumented Parents and Their Young Children*. New York: Russell Sage Foundation.

Zolberg, Aristide R. 1999. "Matters of State: Theorizing Immigration Policy." In *The Handbook of International Migration: The American Experience*, edited by Charles Hirschman, Philip Kasinitz, and Joshua DeWind. New York: Russell Sage Foundation.

Emigrant Politics, Immigrant Engagement: Homeland Ties and Immigrant Political Identity in the United States

ROGER WALDINGER AND LAUREN DUQUETTE-RURY

Immigrants are also emigrants, possessing social ties that link them to people and places left behind. Although this duality is inherent to the migration process, researchers typically separate the study of emigration from that of immigration. Using new survey data on Latino immigrant social and political engagement in the sending and receiving society, we assess how political attitudes and national allegiance are shaped by social and political ties acquired at home and abroad. We find that immigrants' home country social ties yield modest political consequences, whereas the more important influences sustaining connections to homeland polities stem from premigration political experiences. Both cross-border social ties and premigration political experiences reinforce homeland national identities. Furthermore, the acquisition of U.S. citizenship tends to corrode homeland attachments and Latino immigrants are more likely to shift political allegiance from home to host state once legal status is obtained.

Keywords: immigration, emigration, political engagement, cross-border ties, transnationalism

Every immigrant is an emigrant, every alien a citizen, every foreigner a national. These dualities lie at the heart of the migration process, leaving migrants caught in a dialectic of constant tension, but they are lost by the prevailing academic division of labor, which separates the study of emigration from the study of immigration. Because the students of assimilation stand with their back at the border, both the international and the inherently political nature of population movements across national boundaries fall out of view. Consequently, what they call assimilation turns out to be something different: namely, the transformation of foreigners into nationals, thus not just diffusing immigrants into a so-called mainstream, but replacing one particularism with another. Taking a similar stance, the scholars of immigrant politics suffer from a like defect, in this case, aggravated by the failure to see that the arrival of international migrants does not simply produce the familiar American dilemma, in which status citizens lack first-class citizenship. The phenomenon, rather, entails a global dilemma inseparable from the nature of population movements across boundaries itself, as status citizenship in democratic nation-states is inherently exclusionary, leaving most foreigners on the "wrong" side of the territorial boundary and all foreigners initially crossing that boundary outside the citizenry.

By contrast, the proponents of the transnational perspective, understanding that networks of goods, ideas, and most importantly people regularly and normally spill across ter-

Roger Waldinger is distinguished professor of sociology at the University of California, Los Angeles. **Lauren Duquette-Rury** is assistant professor of sociology at the University of California, Los Angeles.

Direct correspondence to: Roger Waldinger at waldinge@soc.ucla.edu, Department of Sociology, University of California, 264 Haines Hall, Los Angeles, CA 90095; and Lauren Duquette-Rury at duquette@soc.ucla.edu, Department of Sociology, University of California, 290 Haines Hall, Los Angeles, CA 90095.

ritorial lines, have demonstrated the importance and prevalence of the connections between places of origin and destination and the factors that make distant places so often interlaced. Although rightfully emphasizing the cross-state dimension, this approach is too pat, pretending that migrants can lead lives across borders, even though their alien status impedes incorporation in the receiving society, and their alien location distances them from their homeland and diminishes incentives to participate in homeland politics.

The current academic division of labor thus produces two strands of research often not in conversation with the other—one strand examines emigrant political engagement in countries of origin, and the other considers immigrant political incorporation in countries of destination. Recent research in political science, for example, is beginning to uncover factors associated with a diverse set of political practices emigrants engage in at home (Ahmadov and Sasse 2015; Burgess 2014), though the bulk of the research focuses on the propensity, incidence, and determinants of transnational absentee voting in home country elections (Escobar, Arana, and McCann 2015; Leal, Lee, and McCann 2012; Lafleur and Sánchez-Domínguez 2014). Other research has started to unpack not only when, why, and how emigrants engage in politics in the sending country, but also the diverse channels through which immigrants "remit" political opinions, attitudes, and behaviors to nonmigrant citizens as well as how individual migration experiences shift the political attitudes of migrants after return (Pérez-Armendáriz and Crow 2010; Careja and Emmenegger 2012; Rother 2009). However, this research rarely accounts for the ways in which immigrant experiences in the destination country condition home country attachments, national loyalty, and political interest and engagement.

Similarly, despite a growing body of research on immigrant political incorporation in the United States, which this issue of *RSF* aims to significantly advance (Jones-Correa 1998; Bloemraad 2006; Hochschild et al. 2013; Barreto and Muñoz 2003), few studies consider how transnational ties—be they political, social, or economic—influence immigrants' opinions on major issues, interest in politics, and formal and informal modes of political and civic engagement. The handful of studies that account for migrants' transnational ties often use dual citizenship as a limited proxy given the dearth of data on individual immigrants' transnational ties. Moreover, studies that assess how transnational ties affect immigrant political incorporation have not reached consensus. As Sarah Gershon and Adrian Pantoja (2014) explain, research is negative or positive, or as yet researchers remain unconvinced. The "pessimists" argue migrants' "divided loyalties" are incompatible with naturalization, and the time and costs associated with simultaneous participation in home and host impedes positive orientations and political activism in the destination (Huntington 2004; Staton, Jackson, and Canache 2007; Cain and Doherty 2006). Other research arrives at more optimistic conclusions. Louis DeSipio (2006) shows that transnational networks had a positive effect on citizenship acquisition, but the substantive results were minimal; additional research finds that dual citizenship and other transnational activities enhance Latino immigrants' propensity to naturalize (Jones-Correa 2001; Gershon and Pantoja 2014).

Although these studies are an important addition to our collective understanding of how transnational ties stymie or thwart political incorporation in the destination, data limitations have curtailed researchers' ability to disaggregate transnational ties into different kinds of cross-border practices. We as yet do not have a clear sense of what kinds of transnational ties explain the variation in political incorporation. Moreover, no study to our knowledge, the Sears, Zavala, and Danbold contribution to this volume notwithstanding, accounts for the extent to which immigrant premigration political socialization in the country of origin affects various forms of political orientations and allegiances to host and home. Sears and his colleagues find that premigration political experience positively affects Latino and Latina immigrant partisan self-categorization. Our paper continues to push research in a direction that acknowledges and empirically examines that every immigrant is an emigrant and that transnational ties may explain political engagement both here and there.

This paper thus demonstrates how attention to the dualities inherent in the migration process can shed new light on the ways in which international migrants from Latin America and the Hispanic Caribbean engage with polities and nations in both sending and receiving societies. As we show, these immigrants are indeed also emigrants, possessing social ties that link them to the people and places left behind. Yet these ties yield political consequences of modest effect. Our findings reveal the more important influences sustaining emigrants' connections to homeland polities stem from premigration political experiences. Both cross-border social ties and premigration political experiences sustain national identities based in the homeland left behind. We also find the acquisition of U.S. citizenship is accompanied by a decline in home country attachments as immigrants begin shifting allegiance from home to host state.

POLITICS ACROSS BORDERS

Cross-border ties typically spring from the connected survival strategies pursued by both migrants and their closest relatives at home (Waldinger 2015). Emigration is often undertaken without the goal of immigration: rather, relocating to a developed society takes place so that emigrants can gain the access to the resources that can only be found there. In turn, those gains get channeled back home to stabilize, secure, and improve the options of the kin network remaining there. Relocation to a richer state yields the potential for enjoying the fruits of its wealth. However, the emigrants are also foreigners not knowing the ropes and aliens lacking the full protections granted to citizens and therefore encounter risks and uncertainties of myriad sorts. So when trouble strikes, the emigrants turn to the stay-at-homes for help. Because assistance from the latter is often the condition of exit, the emigrants' dependency on the stay-at-homes gives the former all the more reason to attend to the needs of the latter. These intertwined survival strategies yield continuing exchanges of money, support, information, and ideas; as migrant populations grow, those exchanges broaden and deepen, producing an infrastructure that facilitates and reinforces these bidirectional flows (Mazzucato 2009).

Reinforcing the strength of those connections is that family migration is often a multistage process. Sometimes entire nuclear families move in one fell swoop; often, however, departures proceed one by one, the household head leaving first, only later followed by spouse and children. Alternatively, a young, unmarried person moves abroad and then, whether formally or informally, later sponsors the movement of the person who will become his or her spouse. Rarely does every significant other change place of residence: obligations to aging parents at home can keep remittances, letters, phone calls, and visits flowing well after roots in the host country have become deeply established.

However, these cross-border ties do not necessarily act as vectors of homeland political engagement or connection. To begin with, some migrants entirely fall out of the cross-border circuit, though generally only a minority cuts the tie altogether. As for those who remain connected, some cross-border exchanges do not involve communication—remittance sending, for example, can be done electronically—which means that some of the interactions across borders may be entirely devoid of political content. Likewise, contacts that take place long distance may not yield political information of the same quality or with the same content as exchanges occurring in person. Politics might well filter into the course of weekly communications typically focusing on other matters. In-person visits, however, will yield opportunities for the transmission of indirect information that can only be gleaned in situ, as when a visit coinciding with a homeland political campaign brings the migrant face-to-face with the politics left behind.

Moreover, migration is an implicitly and double-pronged political act. In departing home, the migrants vote with their feet, taking a step of quiet rebellion against the state of origin. Although economically induced migrations are explicitly apolitical, representing exit, not voice, a tacitly political conclusion may be behind that apolitical act. As argued by the Mexican sociologist Arturo Santamaria Gómez in words that could easily apply to countless other migrations, "the deepest experience, the most strongly felt discomfort of the migrants toward the Mexican government was the conviction that with a 'good government' they would not have had to leave their country" (1994, 165). Indeed, when interviewed during the mid-2000s by a team of Mexican political scientists, Mexican immigrants in Los Angeles repeatedly sounded this point of view: "The perception that the interviewees have of Mexican politics is in general negative, repeatedly associated with corruption, violence, poverty and incapacity to govern, independent of the political party. A very significant indicator consists of the fact that, of the 90 interviewees there was not one positive opinion about politics in Mexico" (Alarcon, Rabadan, and Ortiz 2012, 298).

Because migrant behavior often reflects widespread cynicism toward political action, institutions, and leaders, it is also often the product of childhood socialization, the lessons of which may last for a lifetime. Because not everyone leaves, but rather only those who decide to take matters into their own hands, migrants may also be less disposed from the outset to look to government or politics to provide a solution for their needs. Because moving to a richer country usually turns out better for migrants, it can reinforce the same cynical political worldview that motivated the decision to abandon home.

Though infra-political beliefs may motivate emigration, politics as such are unlikely to have been of salient importance before migration. Migrants detached from home country politics before leaving home are unlikely to reconnect once abroad. To begin with, younger, not older, people are the more likely to depart for a foreign land. Because most electoral systems bar minors from voting, many migrants are likely to leave with little if any experience in formal politics and limited prior exposure. Political conditions at home are also an influential factor: undemocratic, partially democratic, or even democratizing nations may provide limited opportunities for engagement with electoral politics, even for those eligible to vote prior to migration.

Conditions after migration are also likely to exercise a depoliticizing effect on inclinations to engage with homeland matters. Social networks linking less politically attentive migrants to those more politically engaged could transmit needed homeland political signals, but without a history of expatriate engagement, that group is small. Likewise, mobilization could occur were homeland political parties present, but their absence is the overwhelming rule. As noted, all migrants begin as aliens, which means that they start in a state of nonincorporation and it is there that many long remain. Until the migrants become citizens, they stand outside the polity, which keeps them distant from the efforts at mobilization that so often trigger political interest and knowledge. And in the event that other aliens dominate the social environment, local ties and networks are unlikely to offer the capacity needed to make politics—whether of the homeland or hostland sort—salient.

Although detached from and possibly repelled by homeland politics, migrants arrive from contemporary nation-states as nationals, emotionally tied to the putative nation, people, and land left behind. In the event that homeland national identity is wanting, the encounter with a foreign environment and treatment as unwanted foreigners convinces a migrant that he or she is the very foreign national that the native nationals perceive. As the Mexican anthropologist and sociologist Manuel Gamio noted almost a century ago in the very first work of social science on Mexican immigration, the displaced Mexican peasants then arriving in the United States had "little notion of their nationality or their country" but on arrival in the United States "learn immediately what their mother-country means, and they always think of it and speak of it with love" (1930, 128). Roughly seventy years later, studying a union local with a large Mexican immigrant workforce, the sociologist David Fitzgerald came across a myth that quelled members' interest in naturalization: the fear "that becoming a U.S. citizen requires a ritualistic rejection of Mexican nationality that includes stomping and spitting on the Mexican flag" (2004, 236).

Paradoxically, the encounter with an alien environment increases the salience of homeland national identity, thereby reducing the incentives to obtain receiving society citizenship, which is the condition of formal host society political participation. Because citizenship is tied to national identity, acquisition of a new citizenship is a matter of the heart, not just the brain. As clearly implied by the myth that Fitzgerald discovered, abandoning one's nationality and replacing it with another may seem like an act of betrayal, one in which one turns one's back on family as well as country. Because the returns to any investment in host society naturalization are variable and the expenditures in time, effort, and money significant, powerful rational reasons may also lie behind the decision to remain an alien and thereby retain one's home nationality. And of course, these considerations only apply to aliens eligible for naturalization, a condition inapplicable to the eleven million undocumented immigrants in the United States.

But because the emigrants are also immigrants, the decision to move to another country also often represents an implicit vote for that state. In particular, when crossing into the borders of the rich democracies, the migrants opt for a state organized in a way that promotes economic growth, provides the public services and investments needed for that continued productivity, and maintains public order. The combination of rules, norms, and institutions that migrants find in their new homes makes for societies that are generally more successful than those the migrants have left behind (Acemoglu, Johnson, and Robinson 2005), which is precisely why migration is usually good for the migrants.

The encounter with those rules, norms, and institutions also imparts lessons that are at least implicitly political. Because bureaucratic organizations are preferable to those that are predatory, safe streets to those that are dangerous, (reasonably) honest elections to those that are chronically stolen, the migrants come to both recognize and appreciate the social model that prevails in the new environment. Hence, though the heart may constrain the affective change needed to transfer national loyalties and the brain may recoil at the costs of doing so, no such barriers prevent migrants from perceiving the advantages of the social model that makes movement to a new country such a good idea and from preferring that arrangement to the one left behind.

EMPIRICAL ASSESSMENT

The Latino Immigrant National Election Study (LINES) provides an unparalleled opportunity to empirically assess these ideas, because the survey provides an abundance of information regarding these dualities at the core of the migrant experience. In this paper, we focus on aspects relating to interest in politics and national identity, whether linked to home or host state, as well as political attitudes related to trust and responsiveness of government. The paper analyzes responses to questions from waves 1 and 2 regarding interest in homeland politics, interest in the 2012 U.S. presidential election, attitudes about trust and responsive government, and questions regarding attachment to the United States and the home country. We present descriptive statistics of relevant variables in tables 1 and 2.

Both waves 1 and 2, conducted before and after the 2012 U.S. national elections, asked about interest in home country politics, though with differences in question wording making it difficult to interpret the diverging response patterns. In wave 1, most respondents reported that they either paid "a lot" (35 percent) or "some" (18 percent) attention to home country politics. When asked about interest in home country politics in wave 2, however, 63 percent of respondents answered "none at all" or "a little." A cross-tab of the panel of 427 respondents for which there are valid data indicates that the proportion answering "a lot" declined from 39 percent in wave 1 to 18 percent in wave 2. A look at other sources of data suggests that wave 2 may provide the more accurate view. Although not strictly comparable, because a different question was asked, most immigrants interviewed by the 2006 Latino National Survey (LNS) reported paying little to no attention to home country politics, only 15 percent reporting a lot of attention (Fraga et al. 2006). Compared with Mexicans in Mexico, the 2006 Mexican Expatriate survey reported that immigrants were far less likely to talk about or pay attention to Mexican politics (McCann, Cornelius, and Leal 2006). Almost two-thirds of the Mexican immi-

Table 1. Descriptive Statistics of Independent Variables, Pre- and Postelection Waves

Independent Variable	Preelection	Independent Variable	Preelection
Premigration voting		**Immigrant march in metro 2006**	43
Yes	57	**Consulate in metro**	35
No	43	**Education***	
Plan to return to home country		Less than high school	62
Plan to return	22	High school	20
No plan to return	70	Some college	12
Don't know	7	BA or BS or greater	7
Active in political party in home country		**Premigration voting**	
Not active	71	Yes	48
Somewhat active	19	No	52
Very active	10		
Language		**Frequency of contact with friends**	
Only English	1	Never	9
Mostly English	1	Every couple months	13
Both	26	Monthly	28
Mostly Spanish	34	Weekly	49
Only Spanish	38	**Frequency of home country visit**	
Children living in household in United States		Never	20
Yes	78	More than five years ago	24
No	22	Once in last five years	8
Legal status		Once in last three years	14
Undocumented	46	Yearly or more	34
Legal permanent resident	12	**Frequency of sending remittances**	
Naturalized citizen	42	Never	30
Born in Mexico*	45	Once a year or less	19
Born in Central America*	10	Every few months	19
Mean years lived in United States*	23	Once a month	24
Mean age*	49	More than once a month	8
Gender*		**Legal status**	
Male	45	Undocumented	37
Female	55	Legal permanent resident	20
Marital status*		Naturalized citizen	43
Not married	40		
Married	60		

Source: Author's calculations based on McCann and Jones-Correa 2012.
Note: Percentages are rounded up and totals may exceed 100 percent.
* indicates pooled results across waves 1 and 2.

grants queried that same year by a nationally representative survey undertaken by the Pew Hispanic Center agreed with the statement "I am insufficiently informed about Mexican politics to vote" (Suro and Escobar 2006).

Wave 2 included several questions regarding national identity in both home and host states. A first battery of questions asked about feelings associated with seeing the American flag as well as general feelings about the United States. Later in the survey, two identical questions were posed, this time regarding the

Table 2. Descriptive Statistics of Dependent Variables, Pre- and Postelection Waves

Preelection Wave	Home	Host	Postelection Wave	Home	Host
Government run			**Attention to home country politics**		
By a few big interests	83	45	None	28	—
For the benefit of all	17	55	Only a little	18	—
People in government			Some	18	—
Waste a lot	72	41	A lot	35	—
Waste some	13	33	**Interest in politics**		
Don't waste very much	7	12	None at all	30	—
Don't know	8	14	A little	33	—
How many in government are corrupt			Some	18	—
All	30	4	A lot	18	—
Most	41	8	**Patriotism (feelings for flag)**		
About half	16	25	Not good at all	4	1
A few	12	53	Slightly good	5	5
None	1	10	Moderately good	14	14
Trust government to do the right thing			Very good	52	56
			Extremely good	25	24
Just about always	6	22	**Patriotism (love of country)**		
Most of the time	5	18	Hate it	<1	<1
Only some of the time	61	58	Dislike it	2	1
Never	28	3	Neither like nor dislike it	6	1
Elections make governement responsive			Like it	37	53
			Love it	54	44
A good deal	56	25	**Mean warmth toward government**	36	68
Some	36	48			
Not much	8	27			

Source: Author's calculations based on McCann and Jones-Correa 2012.
Note: Percentages are rounded up and totals may exceed 100 percent.

homeland state. Most immigrants answered positively (extremely or very good, like or love) to all four questions. Nonetheless, respondents were more likely to display negative feelings toward the home country than the United States. Questions regarding the national flag, whether that of the home country or of the United States, elicited similar responses, as did the question regarding overall feeling. We also analyze a variable created by subtracting answers to the home and host country feeling thermometer to gauge a comparison between host and home country patriotism.

Both waves 1 and 2 include questions pertinent to understanding immigrants' comparative assessment of the social models found in home and host states. Wave 1 includes five questions related to government effectiveness and responsiveness in home and host states. Although the answers to these queries about "the government in Washington" versus the "government in the country of origin" do not suggest that Washington is viewed uncritically, it is nonetheless perceived in a far more positive light than the home country government. For example, 71 percent of respondents thought that "all or most" of the people in the home country government were corrupt, as opposed to only 12 percent holding that opinion when asked about Washington. Although opinion toward Washington could also lean in a negative direction, as indicated by the large proportion of respondents who thought that Washington "wastes a lot" and is run by "a few big interests," the corresponding views towards the home country were still far more critical. Wave 2 includes a number of questions measuring immigrants' warmth towards the federal and local (U.S.) governments and their home country government. As indicated by the response to these queries using the standard "feeling thermometer" on a zero (cold) to 100 (warm) gauge, respondents felt a good deal more warmth, toward both "the federal government in Washington" (69) and the "local police in your community" (68) than toward "the government in the country of origin" (36). As further indication of the low esteem in which they held home country governments, the same respondents gave an identically low rating to Romney, but a 75 to Obama.

Following the approach outlined, in the analysis to follow we principally focus on the influence of variables related to cross-border ties, premigration home country political experience, and legal status in the United States. Information about legal status and premigration voting appears in both waves of LINES. Both waves contain almost identical proportions of U.S. citizen respondents (42 versus 43 percent); however, wave 1 contains a higher proportion of undocumented respondents (46 versus 37 percent). Just under half of the respondents to wave 1 (57 percent) reported having voted prior to migration whereas just under half (48 percent) provide the same answer in wave 2. Wave 1 also includes a question about activity in a political party or some other organization prior to migration; the great majority (71 percent) report no activity; just 10 percent report having been very active.

Data on cross-border ties are only to be found in wave 2; in wave 1, we use a question regarding plans for return migration as a limited proxy. The great majority of respondents report frequent contact with persons in the home country; about half report that contact is weekly. Not surprisingly, the interviews report that visits and remittances—both much more materially demanding—occur at lower rates. Moreover, a sizeable proportion seems to have dropped out of at least one of these cross-border activities (20 percent never having visited and 49 percent never remitting or remitting yearly or less). Nonetheless, the majority remit at least every few months or more frequently and 48 percent report visiting home at least once in the past three years, yearly, or more. As other studies have shown, a very small proportion of the respondents have completely abandoned these cross-border activities; on the other hand, the proportion engaging in all three forms of cross-border activity at the most frequent is only slightly larger (Soehl and Waldinger 2010). As suggested by the polychoric correlations, sending money and visiting are more likely to be mutually exclusive alternatives, with remitting more likely to be accompanied by the sending of money. The great majority of respondents (70 percent) asked, in wave 1, about plans to return home answered no, an additional 7 percent saying that they did not know.[1]

The analysis includes a number of other, generally standard migration variables used here as controls, including years in the United States and a squared term for years, age, gender, marital status, education (the four-category recode contained in the original dataset), English language proficiency, separate indicator variables coding the respondent's metropolitan area for the presence of a consulate from the country of origin and whether the area had been the site of an immigrant rights demonstration in 2006, and dummies for Mexicans and Central Americans. The analysis of wave 1 questions also includes a variable indicating whether the respondent has a child living in the home country. The analysis of wave 2 also includes a variable concerning the respondent's principle source of news, whether in English, Spanish, or both languages.

Because the measures of interest and patriotism and most of the governmental effectiveness questions are ordinal, those analyses use ordinal logistic regression. Because the question regarding government's possible domination by big interests is binary, we use logistic regression. The tables reporting the results of the ordered logit and logistic regressions dis-

---

1. We also included an indicator for whether the respondent was a member of a hometown association, but the results were not significant.

play predicted probabilities for key variables of interest. The feeling thermometers vary on a 0 to 100 scale and hence ordinary least squares (OLS) is used; the relevant table displays the coefficients for the key variables of interest.

RESULTS

Interest in Home Country Politics

As noted, interest in home country politics appears to have declined during the course of the U.S. election, though differences in the questions used in waves 1 and 2 (attention versus interest) make definitive interpretation elusive.

We report the effects of pre- and postelection wave political interest in home and host country in table 3 and in the third column of table 4. Both wave 1 and wave 2 point to the likely importance of premigration political experience, as at both times, voting prior to migration was associated with significantly higher interests in home country politics, though point estimates differ. The analysis of wave 1 shows that prior political experience had a stronger association with interest in home country politics than a prior experience of voting: going from respondents with no prior history of political engagement to those who had

Table 3. Changes in Predicted Probabilities, Political Interest in United States and Country of Origin, Preelection Wave

	Host Country	Home Country
	"Very Interested" in Political Campaigns	"A Lot" of Interest in Politics
Plan to return to home country		
Plan to return	37	49
No plan to return	32	36
Don't know	29	24
Premigration voting		
Never voted	31	34
Voted	35	42
Active in political party in home country		
Not active	30	34
Somewhat active	38	48
Very active	39	51
Education		
Less than high school	31	36
High school graduate	27	38
Some college	36	42
B.A. or B.S. or greater	55	48
Years in United States		
Ten	28	42
Twenty	33	35
Thirty	37	24
Legal status		
Undocumented	31	37
Legal permanent resident	26	41
Naturalized citizen	37	40

Source: Author's calculations based on McCann and Jones-Correa 2012.
Note: Predicted from the ordered logit results for most positive outcomes.

Table 4. Changes in Predicted Probabilities, Political Interest and National Identity, Postelection Wave

	Host Country		Home Country		
Cross-Border Ties	Patriotism ("Extremely Good" Feelings for Flag)	Patriotism ("Loves" Country)	"A Lot" of Interest in Politics	Patriotism ("Extremely Good" Feelings for Flag)	Patriotism ("Loves" Country)
How often contact friends					
Never	25	56	23	18	52
Every couple months	20	48	14	25	54
Monthly	22	43	15	23	47
Weekly	26	40	17	31	56
How often visits					
Never	26	47	16	28	48
More than five years ago	29	39	14	27	53
Once in last five years	17	52	17	20	50
Once in last three years	23	33	14	24	50
Yearly or more	22	46	20	30	60
How often sends money					
Never	22	34	12	23	51
Once a year	29	54	22	29	48
Once a month	23	42	18	26	56
More than once a month	25	47	19	30	56
Premigration voting					
Never voted	24	45	13	23	45
Voted	25	41	21	32	63
Legal status					
Undocumented	22	39	15	23	27
Legal permanent res.	23	36	20	15	20
Naturalized citizen	27	52	16	19	22
Years in United States					
Ten	24	39	16	56	56
Twenty	24	43	17	51	51
Thirty	24	46	17	50	50
Education					
Less than high school	27	54	13	28	55
High school	18	58	15	21	48
Some college	25	52	21	33	55
College or more	25	51	30	28	57

Source: Author's calculations based on McCann and Jones-Correa 2012.
Note: Predicted from the ordered logit results for most positive outcomes

been very active increases the probability of having "a lot" of interest in home country politics from 34 percent to 51 percent.

Otherwise, however, the factors of influence seem to vary from one wave to another. Thus, education is associated with statistically significant higher levels of attention to home country politics in wave 2, especially among the college educated. In wave 1, however, the coefficients lack statistical significance, though as shown in the predicted probabilities, the association between college education and interest in home country politics is high. In wave 1, interest in home country politics declines significantly with years of settlement; in wave 2, however, years of residence in the United States yield no effect.

Both waves 1 and 2 hint at the possibility that cross-border ties may foster an interest in home country politics, though the supporting evidence is limited and inconsistent. Wave 1 respondents, uncertain whether they planned to stay in the United States or return home, were significantly less likely to report having a lot of interest in home country politics than those planning to return, though the factors making for uncertainty about settlement may be related to those diminishing interest in home country politics.

By contrast, cross-border ties, measured in wave 2, yield contradictory effects. Respondents who sent money home were more likely to report paying a lot of attention to home country politics than those who did not remit were, though among those who did remit, differences in rates appeared to not matter. Going from the lowest level of remitting (none) to the next highest (once a year) was associated with a 10 percentage point increase in the fraction reporting that they had paid a lot of attention to home country politics (0.12 to 0.22), but attention to home country politics fell off slightly at higher levels of remitting. Surprisingly, attention to home country politics was lower among those who had at least some contact as opposed to those (decidedly few) who had stopped communicating altogether. More frequent home country visitors were no more likely to pay attention to home country politics than respondents who had never returned home after migration to the United States. In neither wave 1 nor wave 2 did legal status alter interest in home country politics, thus contradicting prior studies arguing that hostland political incorporation would reinforce homeland political engagement (Guarnizo, Portes, and Haller 2003).

Patriotism
Because questions regarding patriotism only appear in wave 2, our indicators of premigration political participation are limited to premigration voting. We report the results of these models in table 4. Nonetheless, this variable has a consistently positive effect on both measures of home country patriotism, whether elicited by feelings about seeing the home country flag or by a query about overall feeling for the country. Thus, moving from no prior voting to prior voting shifts the probability of answering "extremely good" about the feelings generated by seeing the flag from 0.23 to 0.32; in regard to overall feelings, the same contrast increases the probability of answering "love" from 0.45 to 0.63. By comparison, the indicators of cross-border connectedness have weak and inconsistent effects. Respondents who report having weekly contact with home country relatives and friends were almost twice as likely as those who had entirely fallen out of contact to feel extremely good when seeing the flag (0.31 versus 0.18). However, the coefficient for weekly contact was significant only at the 0.1 level and these same respondents were no more likely to report love for the home country than those who never had any contact with home country friends. Likewise, those respondents who sent remittances more than once a month were somewhat more likely to feel extremely good when seeing the home country flag than those who never remitted, but the coefficient was significant only at the 0.1 level, its impact was slight (0.23 versus 0.30) and overall feelings about the home country entailed no such association.

By contrast, patriotic feelings toward the United States (see table 4) seem to derive from quite different sources. Not one of the variables of interest was related to feelings elicited by seeing the U.S. flag. In addition, Mexican-born respondents were less well inclined toward the United States, showing a 0.19 probability of reporting feeling extremely good when seeing the U.S. flag, as opposed to 0.27 for Central Americans and for all others. By contrast, the model more effectively predicts overall feeling for the United States (measured in five categories, going from hate to love), though with results that are not fully expected. More home country contact and more frequent remitting are associated with less patriotic feelings toward the United States. Greater home country contact has a linear, negative relationship with U.S. patriotism, because going from those with weekly home country contact to those never having home country contact changes the probability of reporting love from 0.40 to 0.56. Likewise, those who have never visited the home country report more love for the United States (0.47 versus 0.34) than those who have visited once in the past three years, though none of the other categories are significantly different from never. Surprisingly, higher remitting frequencies, as opposed to never remitting, are generally more closely associated with more patriotic feelings toward the United States, though the relationship is not linear. Last, naturalized citizens are a good deal more likely than either undocumented or green card respondents (probability of love 0.52 versus 0.36 for green card holders and 0.39 for undocumented respondents) to report patriotic feelings for the United States.

Perceptions of Government
As noted, respondents queried in LINES rated home country governments far more critically than Washington. As shown in table 5, an experience of prior voting made for a significantly warmer rating of the home country government. By contrast, only two of the indicators of home country connectedness had statistically significant coefficients—remitting ($p < .1$) and visiting ($p < .1$) and curiously only those who remitted once a year thought more favorably of the home government than did those who never remitted. Those respondents who had obtained U.S. nationality were significantly more likely to give the home country government a more negative rating than either green card holders or undocumented immigrants.

By contrast, naturalized citizens were no more likely to rate the U.S. government favorably than their undocumented or green card counterparts were, though still rating the U.S. government well above that of their home country's (58 versus 48). With the exception of those whose most recent home country visit had taken place five years prior to the survey—and who rated the U.S. government more favorably—the opinions of more frequent visitors were no different from those who never visited at all. No other variable measuring cross-border connectedness proved statistically significant.

The same variables measuring cross-border connections are weakly and inconsistently related to the indicators of governmental effectiveness and responsiveness reported in tables 6 and 7. Naturalized citizens were more likely than their undocumented counterparts to think that home country governments were run by a few big interests ($p < .1$) though more likely to think that people in government "don't waste very much" ($p < .05$). Persons with a prior history of some activism were slightly more likely to trust home country governments to do the right thing but also more likely to think that those governments were run by a few big interests rather than for the benefit of all. Persons who had voted before migrating were more inclined than nonvoters to think that home country governments would do the right thing ($p < .01$), but the probability of responding in so positive a fashion was very low ($p = .07$); those who were unsure about their return to their home country were more likely ($p < .05$) than respondents planning to settle to think that the home country government could be trusted to do the right thing, but again levels of trust were low. Cross-border variables exercised even less influence on views toward the U.S. government. Levels of trust towards the U.S. government were no different among respondents with a history of migrating before migration as opposed to those with no such history. Persons not certain whether they would emigrate again were less likely than settlers to think that people in government "don't waste very much," but more likely to think that elections make government more responsive. Paradoxically, in comparison to respondents with no history of political party ac-

Table 5. OLS Regression on Warmth Toward Governments, Postelection Wave

Cross-Border Ties	Host Country	
	Warmth Toward Home	Warm Toward Host
How often contact friends		
Every couple months	-2.709	2.100
	(6.259)	(4.555)
Monthly	.588	3.179
	(5.979)	(4.368)
Weekly	-.826	6.743
	(5.762)	(4.196)
How often visits		
More than five years ago	5.428	8.462
	(3.968)	(3.085)**
Once in last five years	3.272	2.034
	(5.045)	(3.971)
Once in last three years	7.785	2.608
	(4.581)	(3.505)
Yearly or more	6.039	1.754
	(3.865)	(3.169)
How often sends money		
Once a year	6.719	-1.166
	(3.861)	(3.036)
Once a month	-4.789	-3.573
	(3.803)	(2.861)
More than once a month	-.738	-4.212
	(3.557)	(2.718)
Premigration voting	7.079	-1.165
	(2.706)**	(2.347)
Years lived in United States	.142	-.103
	(.392)	(.305)
Years lived in United States (squared)	.003	-.002
	(.006)	(.005)
Education		
High school	-2.779	-3.310
	(3.211)	(2.727)
Some college	-5.058	-.190
	(3.747)	(2.949)
B.A. or B.S. or greater	-6.492	-6.954
	(5.403)	(3.478)*
Legal U.S. status		
Legal permanent resident	-1.875	3.758
	(4.054)	(2.937)
Naturalized	-7.141	-3.213
	(3.196)*	(2.741)
Constant^	55.097	61.182
	(9.852)***	(7.817)***
Total observations	641	614

Source: Author's calculations based on McCann and Jones-Correa 2012.
Note: Omitted categories: never (contact, visit, send money), primary education or less, no papers; R-squared for the regression feeling thermometer models for U.S. government is 0.08; ; R-squared for the regression feeling thermometer models for host government is 0.11. Standard Errors in parenthesis.
*$p < .05$; **$p < .01$; ***$p < .001$

Table 6. Changes in Predicted Probabilities, Trust in U.S. Government, Preelection Wave

	Host Country				
	Government Run "for the Benefit of All"	People in Government "Don't Waste Very Much"	How Many in Government Are Corrupt: "a Few"	Trust Government to Do Right Thing "Just About Always"	Elections Make Government "a Good Deal" More Responsive
Plan to return to home country					
Plan to return	54	6	53	18	24
No plan to return	48	6	57	22	23
Don't know	41	4	52	16	41
Premigration voting					
Never voted	51	6	56	18	22
Voted	47	6	56	22	27
Active in political party in home country					
Not active	54	6	55	19	25
Somewhat active	39	6	59	25	24
Very active	39	5	55	22	21
Level of education					
Less than high school	43	5	56	20	27
High school grad	45	6	56	20	20
Some college	62	9	56	27	22
B.A. or B.S. or greater	68	3	52	9	27
Legal status					
Undocumented	47	6	55	23	27
Legal permanent resident	44	3	59	15	20
Naturalized citizen	54	6	56	19	22
Years in United States					
Ten	44	17	57	21	25
Twenty	47	11	58	22	23
Thirty	53	8	55	19	24

Source: Author's calculations based on McCann and Jones-Correa 2012.
Note: Predicted from the ordered logit results for most positive outcomes.

Table 7. Changes in Predicted Probabilities, Trust in Home Country Government, Preelection

	Home Country				
	Government Run "for the Benefit of All"	People in Government "Don't Waste Very Much"	How Many in Government Are Corrupt: "a Few"	Trust Government to Do Right Thing "Just About Always"	Elections Make Government "a Good Deal" More Responsive
Plan to return to home country					
Plan to return	86	7	11	5	62
No plan to return	81	7	12	6	52
Don't know	80	9	13	8	53
Premigration voting					
Never voted	81	6	10	4	57
Voted	83	8	13	7	52
Active in political party in home country					
Not active	85	7	10	5	56
Somewhat active	74	7	15	7	50
Very active	85	8	15	7	52
Education					
Less than high school	80	9	14	7	49
High school graduate	84	6	10	5	58
Some college	86	6	9	5	64
B.A. or B.S. or greater	89	4	10	5	53
Legal status					
Undocumented	80	5	10	6	54
Legal permanent resident	78	7	14	8	51
Naturalized citizen	88	9	13	4	56
Years in United States					
Ten	6	7	12	6	51
Twenty	6	7	11	5	56
Thirty	5	7	11	5	58

Source: Author's calculations based on McCann and Jones-Correa 2012.
Note: Predicted from the ordered logit results for most positive outcomes.

tivism before migration were less likely than the premigration activists to think that the host country government was run "by a few big interests."

DISCUSSION AND CONCLUSION

Moving from one country to another inevitably proves a transformative experience because the simple requirements of survival force migrants to adapt to the new environment. Starting out small, subtle, and relatively costless, those changes generate rewards, which is why they are often cumulative, distancing immigrants from the people and places left behind.

Nonetheless, migrants' ties to those people and places are widespread and, though attenuating with settlement, have the power to resist time's erosive effects, largely because these cross-border connections advance the ends of both migrants and stay-at-homes. In this sample, as in others that we have examined, cross-border connections are both prevalent and persistent: not quite 2 percent of the sample has abandoned all ties to relatives and friends back home. Thus reasons are sound to suspect that these cross-border ties might serve to anchor migrants in the host country polity, just as they maintain connections to the migrant's egocentric network still at home.

However, that possibility finds little support in the analysis discussed. Although a third of the sample visit the home country at least once a year, those face-to-face contacts do very little political work. Remitting and maintaining regular contact matter somewhat more, but inconsistently, because relationships are never linear, and show irregular effects across the different outcomes of interest. Moreover, because our sample from the LINES dataset are current immigrants residing in the United States, we are unable to account for individuals who have returned to their home country. This limitation is noteworthy because it is possible that the rationale for returning to the country of origin is related to persistent feelings of warmth and allegiance to the home country or continued disenfranchisement and marginality in the United States.

Given the cross-sectional nature of the sample, we have limited traction on the question of why cross-border ties yield so little influence. That these cross border ties are not of a piece may be one source of constraint: the great majority of respondents maintain at least some connection extending across borders, but few (6 percent) keep up regular contact, visiting, and remitting. As resource-absorbing activities, remitting and visiting tend to be mutually exclusive, as indicated by their low correlation with one another. Although more compatible with regular contact, which is virtually free, respondents calling home weekly are just as likely to have never visited home since moving to the United States as they are likely to have taken a visit within the prior year. Hence, the connections linking migrants and stay at home persist but lack the coherence and consistency needed for the transmission of home country political signals, which naturally take a more erratic and episodic form.

Moreover, these respondents clearly seem to be people who opted for exit rather than voice. Based on the responses to the feeling thermometers and the questions regarding trust, it seems appropriate to say that the home country government is viewed with disdain, respondents placing it on a par with their rating of the presidential candidate who endorsed a migration policy involving self-deportation. Because most (56 percent) also think that home country governments do not pay much attention to elections, these disillusioned nationals in exile do not have much reason to attend to home country politics, especially given that the home country can do so little to resolve problems associated with immigration. By contrast, those who exercised voice prior to migration are more interested in home country matters and more approving of home country governments.

Although migrants seem detached from home country politics and disillusioned with home country governments, they are nonetheless loyal nationals, not a surprising finding because the latter is more a matter of the heart than the brain, a feeling implanted so early and so deeply that it is only extirpated with difficulty. Although powerful, those feelings bear little relationship to the prevalence and frequency of home country ties.

Moreover, immigrant national loyalties are up for grabs, as indicated by their responses to the questions regarding feelings for the United States and the U.S. flag, as well as their positive rating of the U.S. government. Acquisition of U.S. citizenship does not entirely corrode interest in home country politics or affection for the country left behind. But naturalization is associated with more positive feelings for the United States and a more negative assessment of the home country government, though we note that the causal direction here could go either way.

At the end of the day, these respondents find themselves in a liminal political situation, in the country of reception but not of it, while simultaneously of the country of origin but not in it. Still loving the country where they were born, they think little of its government and, though the matter is not raised in this survey, almost surely understand that home country governments can do little to solve the problems encountered in the place where they actually live. Although they appreciate the place of residence and even the government so busily deporting Latino immigrants, they remain excluded from its polity, as close to half are undocumented. Moreover, that barrier is unlikely to be crossed soon, because the price for comprehensive immigration reform—should it ever happen—will be paid by making the beneficiaries of legalization tread a long and arduous road to citizenship. Thus, the twinned decisions of home and host governments—the first deciding not to take care of its nationals, the second deciding not to welcome the people who are nonetheless wanted and needed—have created a natural experiment, in which millions of people spend long stretches of time with no option for formal political participation. Although highly undesirable, that condition offers ample research potential, as we have yet to understand the long-term consequences, both political and otherwise, of persistent alien status.

REFERENCES

Acemoglu, Daron, Simon Johnson, and James A. Robinson. 2005. "Institutions as a Fundamental Cause of Long-Run Growth." In *Handbook of Economic Growth*, vol. 1, edited by Philippe Aghion and Steven N. Durlauf. Philadelphia, Pa.: Elsevier.

Ahmadov, Anar K., and Gwendolyn Sasse. 2015. "A Voice Despite Exit: The Role of Assimilation, Emigrant Networks, and Destination in Emigrants' Transnational Political Engagement." *Comparative Political Studies* 49(1): 1–37.

Alarcon, Rafael, Luis Escala Rabadan, and Olga Odgers Ortiz. 2013. *Mudando el hogar al norte: trayectorias de integración de los inmigrantes mexicanos en Los Ángeles*. Tijuana, Mexico: El Colegio de la Frontera Norte.

Barreto, Matt A., and José Muñoz. 2003. "Reexamining the 'Politics of In-Between': Political Participation Among Mexican Immigrants in the United States." *Hispanic Journal of Behavioral Sciences* 25 (November): 427–47.

Bloemraad, Irene. 2006. *Becoming a Citizen: Incorporating Immigrants and Refugees in the United States and Canada*. Berkeley: University of California Press.

Burgess, Katrina. 2014. "Unpacking the Diaspora Channel in New Democracies: When Do Migrants Act Politically Back Home?" *Studies in Comparative International Development* 49(1): 13–43.

Cain, Bruce E., and Brendan J. Doherty. 2006. "The Impact of Dual Nationality on Political Participation." In *Transforming Politics, Transforming America: The Political and Civic Incorporation of Immigrants in the United States*, edited by Taeku Lee, S. Karthick Ramakrishnan, and Ricardo Ramírez. Charlottesville: University of Virginia Press.

Careja, Romana, and Patrick Emmenegger. 2012. "Making Democratic Citizens: The Effects of Migration Experience on Political Attitudes in Central and Eastern Europe." *Comparative Political Studies* 45(7): 875–902.

DeSipio, Louis. 2006. "Transnational Politics and Civic Engagement: Do Home Country Political Ties Limit Latino Immigrant Pursuit of US Civic Engagement and Citizenship?" In *Transforming Politics, Transforming America: The Political and Civic Incorporation of Immigrants in the United States*, edited by Taeku Lee, S. Karthick Ramakrishnan, and Ricardo Ramírez (Charlottesville: University of Virginia Press, 2006).

Escobar, Cristina, Renelinda Arana, and James A. McCann. 2015. "Expatriate Voting and Migrants' Place of Residence." *Migration Studies* 3(1): 1–31.

Fitzgerald, David. 2004. "Beyond 'Transnationalism':

Mexican Hometown Politics at an American Labour Union." *Ethnic and Racial Studies* 27(2): 228-47.

Fraga, Luis R., John A. Garcia, Rodney Hero, Michael Jones-Correa, Valerie Martinez-Ebers, and Gary M. Segura. 2006. Latino National Survey (LNS), 2006. ICPSR20862-v6. Ann Arbor, MI: Inter-university Consortium for Political and Social Research [distributor], 2013-06-05. doi:10.3886/ICPSR20862.v6.

Gamio, Manuel. 1930. *Mexican Immigration to the United States: A Study of Human Migration and Adjustment.* Chicago: University of Chicago Press.

Gershon, Sarah A., and Adrian D. Pantoja. 2014. "Pessimists, Optimists, and Skeptics: The Consequences of Transnational Ties for Latino Immigrant Naturalization." *Social Science Quarterly* 95(2): 328-42.

Gómez, Arturo Santamaría. 1994. *La política entre México y Aztlán: Relaciones Chicano Mexicanas del 68 a Chiapas 94.* Universidad autónoma de Sinaloa.

Guarnizo, Luis, Alejandro Portes, and William J. Haller. 2003. "Assimilation and Transnationalism: Determinants of Transnational Political Action among Contemporary Migrants." *American Journal of Sociology* 108(6): 1211-48.

Hochschild, Jennifer, Jacqueline Chattopadhyay, Claudine Gay, and Michael Jones-Correa, eds. 2013. *Outsiders No More? Models of Immigrant Political Incorporation.* New York: Oxford University Press.

Huntington, Samuel P. 2004. *Who Are We?: The Challenges to America's National Identity.* New York: Simon and Schuster.

Jones-Correa, Michael. 1998. *Between Two Nations: The Political Predicament of Latinos in New York City.* Ithaca, N.Y.: Cornell University Press.

———. 2001. "Under Two Flags: Dual Nationality in Latin America and Its Consequences for Naturalization in the United States." *International Migration Review* 35(4): 997-1029.

Lafleur, Jean-Michel, and María Sánchez-Domínguez. 2014. "The Political Choices of Emigrants Voting in Home Country Elections: A Socio-Political Analysis of the Electoral Behaviour of Bolivian External Voters." *Migration Studies* 3(2): 1-27.

Leal, David L., Byung-Jae Lee, and James A. McCann. 2012. "Transnational Absentee Voting in the 2006 Mexican Presidential Elections." *Electoral Studies* 31(3): 540-49.

Mazzucato, Valentina. 2009. "Informal Insurance Arrangements in Ghanaian Migrants' Transnational Networks: The Role of Reverse Remittances and Geographic Proximity." *World Development* 37(6): 1105-14.

McCann, James, Wayne Cornelius, and David Leal. 2006. "Mexico's 2006 Voto Remoto and the Potential for Transnational Civic Engagement Among Mexican Expatriates." Paper prepared for the annual meeting of the American Political Science Association. Philadelphia (August 31-September 3, 2006).

McCann, James A., and Michael Jones-Correa. 2012. Latino Immigrant National Election Study, 2012. New York: Russell Sage Foundation, Carnegie Corporation of New York, Purdue University, and Cornell University.

Pérez-Armendáriz, Clarisa, and David Crow. 2010. "Do Migrants Remit Democracy? International Migration, Political Beliefs, and Behavior in Mexico." *Comparative Political Studies* 43(1): 119-48.

Rother, Stefan. 2009. "Changed in Migration? Philippine Return Migrants and (Un)Democratic Remittances." *European Journal of East Asian Studies* 8(2): 245-74

Soehl, Thomas, and Roger Waldinger. 2010. "Making the Connection: Latino Immigrants and Their Cross-Border Ties." *Ethnic and Racial Studies* 33(9): 1489-510.

Suro, Roberto, and Gabriel Escobar. 2006. "Survey of Mexicans Living in the US on Absentee Voting in Mexican Elections." Washington, D.C. Pew Hispanic Center.

Staton, Jeffrey K., Robert A. Jackson, and Damarys Canache. 2007. "Dual Nationality Among Latinos: What Are the Implications for Political Connectedness?" *Journal of Politics* 69(2): 470-82.

Waldinger, Roger. 2015. *The Cross-Border Connections: Immigrants, Emigrants, and their Homelands.* Cambridge, Mass.: Harvard University Press.

Healthy Skepticism or Corrosive Cynicism? New Insights into the Roots and Results of Latino Political Cynicism

MELISSA R. MICHELSON

The degree to which citizens and residents trust the government is crucial for the maintenance of democracy and a stable civil society. Trust in government generates willingness to conform to rules and regulations, as well as to work within the democratic system rather than turning to more confrontational or even violent political action. The degree to which immigrants trust the government has symbolic importance, reflecting how well we are staying true to our history as a melting pot and to our history as a nation of immigrants. Residents need to feel safe to contact authorities in case of emergency, without threat of deportation or other negative reprisals related to their immigration status. Existing research finds that Latinos in the United States are increasingly cynical, threatening various negative consequences for the political system. The health of our democracy thus demands a good understanding of the causes and consequences of Latino immigrant trust in government (or lack thereof). This article compares Latino trust in government in the context of the 2012 presidential election campaign—one in which outreach to Latino citizens in pursuit of their votes signaled that they were important and powerful members of the polity—to Latino trust in government in the context of the 2006 immigration marches—one in which Latinos found themselves taking to the streets to protest anti-Latino and anti-immigrant legislation. Latino political trust is sensitive to this shifting context, suggesting that how U.S. society treats Latino immigrants has powerful effects on their political socialization and attitudes.

Keywords: trust in government, Latino immigrants, 2012 election, immigration marches, Latino political attitudes

Political trust matters. The degree to which individuals trust the government is an indicator of the health of civic society and their willingness to support and comply with public policies. Political trust influences the degree to which elected officials are able to govern effectively and the likelihood that the public will believe that the country's resources are being spent wisely rather than wasted. Beyond its importance as an indicator of general civic health, feelings of political trust among traditionally marginalized or underrepresented ethnoracial groups serve as a measure of a healthy democracy—the degree to which members of these communities trust the government is a proxy for how well they are being incorporated into civil society and feel like full members of the polity.

Rogers Smith (1997, 2004) and other scholars have shown how citizenship and inclusion in the U.S. polity has traditionally been defined in terms of race and gender classifications. Throughout U.S. history, immigration and naturalization policies have been explicitly de-

Melissa R. Michelson is professor of political science at Menlo College.

My thanks to James McCann, Michael Jones-Correa, Mark Hugo Lopez, and Annie Franco for their valuable help; all errors, of course, remain my own. Direct correspondence to: Melissa R. Michelson at melissa.michelson @menlo.edu, Menlo College, 1000 El Camino Real, Atherton, CA 94027.

signed to maintain the United States as a white Protestant nation and to materially privilege the white population (Haney-López 1996; Lipsitz 1998; King 2000). These ascriptive understandings, in turn, have affected the development of political thought within ethnoracial communities, as well as approaches to and engagement with political and collective action (García Bedolla and Michelson 2012; Lavariega Monforti and Michelson 2014). In sum, for many people the terms *American* and *voter* conjure up images of (non-Latino) whites.

When citizens are invited to participate in the electoral process—when they are mobilized to vote—they are given an explicit message of inclusion and political power. Theoretically, this should also influence feelings of trust in government, as those who feel empowered should also feel more trusting of the political system. An opportunity to test this theory arises from the shifting political environment of the last decade, because Latinos have experienced polar extremes in terms of societal messages about their degrees of belonging and political power. In 2006, Latinos were told that they did not belong. In 2012, they were told that they had the power to determine the outcome of the presidential election. In 2006, Latinos were marching in the streets in protest of harsh anti-immigrant legislation passed by the House of Representatives. In 2012, Latinos found Democrats and Republicans walking in *their* streets, asking for their support in the presidential election, and many undocumented immigrants had applied to be part of the Deferred Action for Childhood Arrivals (DACA) program announced by President Obama in July 2012, a program that deferred the threat of deportation and allowed participants to obtain two-year work permits. In sum, Latinos were much more likely to feel a sense of belonging in the United States in the fall of 2012 than in 2006. This should be particularly true for citizens, who were not only being told by media and campaigns that they belonged, but also that they were politically powerful.

This paper tests the hypothesis that Latinos would be more likely to say that they trust the government in the fall of 2012 than in 2006. In addition, in contrast to earlier findings from previous scholarship, citizens are hypothesized to be more trusting than noncitizens, reflecting the sense of empowerment generated via election campaign rhetoric.

THE IMPORTANCE OF POLITICAL TRUST

Political trust is generally understood as "a basic evaluative orientation toward the government founded on how well the government is operating according to people's normative expectations" (Hetherington 1998, 791). For decades, respondents to surveys have been asked the same basic question meant to measure this trust: "How much of the time do you trust the government to do what is right—just about always, most of the time, some of the time, or never?" Political trust by citizens and residents is crucial for the maintenance of democracy and a stable civil society, and is a powerful predictor of individual political behavior. Rima Wilkes notes, "Trust in government is essential to the health of democratic societies. Trust increases communication between citizens, facilitates the building of democratic organizations, reduces transaction costs and helps to minimise conflict. It also affects tax compliance, electoral choices and policy preferences. Trust matters" (2014, 2).

Low levels of trust lead to decreased compliance with laws, regulations, and judicial decisions, or even active resistance, and make it more difficult for government to take action to address domestic policy concerns (Levi 1998; Scholtz and Lubell 1998; Tyler 1998; Hetherington 1998; Chanley, Rudolph, and Rahn 2001).

The degree to which immigrants trust the government is particularly important because it reflects how well we are staying true to our history as a melting pot and as a nation of immigrants. How well are we incorporating new members of the polity, and how welcome do they feel? On March 31, 2014, the *New York Times* published a story about the tendency of young Latinos—the future voting core of America and the likely key to victory in the 2016 election—to resist registering to vote because of their cynicism about both political parties. Noting the lack of comprehensive immigration reform (or the promise that some might be approved in the near future), or even passage of a narrower piece of immigrant-related legislation like a DREAM Act, combined with the extremely high rate of deportations imposed by the Obama administration, Latinos in the United States were said to be becoming increasingly cynical, generating negative consequences for the political system.[1]

Reflecting the importance of political trust, scholars for decades have noted with alarm the decreasing trust of Anglo (non-Latino white) Americans. As low as Anglos score on surveys of political trust, African Americans score even lower. In contrast, multiple studies have shown that Latinos are more trusting of government than Anglos (Guzmán 1970; Garcia 1973; de la Garza et al. 1992; Putnam 2001). Sergio Wals (2011) finds that Mexican immigrants with higher levels of trust in the Mexican government are more likely to be trusting of the U.S. government. Early studies of Mexican American youth found that youths become increasingly distrustful as they reach adolescence (Garcia 1973), that those who identify as Chicano are more cynical than those who identify as Mexican American (Gutierrez and Hirsch 1973), and that those living in cities with more Mexican American political influence are more trusting (Buzan 1980). Using data from the 1980s and 1990s, scholars find that Mexican American citizens are more cynical than noncitizens of Mexican descent (Michelson 2001), that Puerto Ricans born in the mainland United States are less trusting than Puerto Ricans born on the island of Puerto Rico (de la Garza 1995; Michelson 2003a), and that Mexican American adults who are more acculturated or see more discrimination against those of Mexican descent are more cynical than those who are less acculturated or see less discrimination (Michelson 2003b). As Roger Waldinger and Lauren Duquette-Rury discuss elsewhere in this volume, many other variables predict Latino immigrants' feelings of trust (or cynicism) in the U.S. government, including plans to return and the degree to which an individual voted or was involved with a political party in their home country. Recent examinations of Latino cynicism clarify that Latino trust in government (or the lack thereof) is a function of their acculturation into a racialized subculture. In other words, as Latinos become acculturated they also become more likely to believe that the government is racist, ethnocentric, or anti-immigrant (Michelson 2007; Lavariega Monforti and Michelson 2014).

LATINO CYNICISM AMID THE 2006 IMMIGRATION MARCHES

In 2006, Latinos across the country were taking to the streets to protest the Sensenbrenner bill (HR 4437). As Amalia Pallares and Nilda Flores-González note, "In 2006, hundreds of thousands of people took to the streets to protest a congressional bill that would have criminalized undocumented immigrants and those who assisted them. More than 250 massive marches, or megamarches, as they were popularly called, were held throughout the country in cities large and small during March and April, culminating in simultaneous marches on May 1 that drew an estimated 3.5 to 5 million people" (2010, xv). The 2006 Latino National Survey (LNS), a random-digit dialing sample of 8,634 self-identified Latino residents of the United States conducted from November 17, 2005, through August 4, 2006, was in the field amid this political environment of threat and racism.[2] Consistent with previous survey research, LNS respondents are quite trusting of the government, particularly when compared with national surveys of the general pop-

---

1. The Development, Relief, and Education for Alien Minors (DREAM) Act would provide a pathway to regularization of the immigration status of undocumented youth who graduate from college or serve in the military; the exact list of eligibility requirements has shifted over time as various concerns about the original DREAM Act have been addressed.

2. The Latino National Survey was conducted from November 2005 and August 2006, with a New England extension conducted in late 2007 and early 2008, for a total of 9,834 respondents (8,634 in the original survey and 1,200 in the New England extension). To focus on Latino political attitudes from the appropriate time period, this study uses only the original LNS dataset.

ulation. In the 2008 American National Election Study (ANES), only 5 percent of respondents said they trust the government "just about always." In fact, not since 1966 have more than 9 percent of ANES respondents to this question given the most trusting response. In contrast, 12.3 percent of respondents to the LNS said that they trust the government "just about always." In addition, 19.3 percent said they trust the government most of the time, 49.8 percent trust the government some of the time, and 18.6 percent never trust the government.

Michael Dawson's (1994) theory of linked fate posits that individuals who share a strong group identity believe that their personal fate is tied to that of the collective; in other words, that the success of individuals and the group are linked. The 2006 LNS data indicate that the path to cynicism is the result of a lack of a feeling of belonging. A strong feeling of linked fate inoculates Latinos against the corrosive effect of acculturation by providing a sense of belonging with the Latino community. As Lavariega Monforti and Michelson note, "Cynicism is not just a result of being exposed to the 'harsh reality' of racism and discrimination in this country, or to the political attacks on immigrants such as those experienced by the Latino community in 2006. Rather, cynicism (or trust) is a reflection of a sense of belonging and community, of social capital and interpersonal trust" (2014, 106).

Using a survey of Texans conducted in the summer of 2012, Benjamin Knoll, Rene Rocha, and Robert Wrinkle (2013) find that levels of Secure Communities enforcement affects feelings of trust in government. Their survey of Anglos and Latinos in Texas revealed that foreign-born Latinos are more trusting of government in low-enforcement areas than are U.S.-born Latinos and Anglos, but that Latinos become less trusting as enforcement increases. Their finding about Secure Communities enforcement is consistent with the LNS data: Latinos who are signaled by the local government that they do not belong, through increased enforcement of Secure Communities, are more cynical; low enforcement signals to foreign-born Latinos that they are more welcome, generating increased trust.

LATINO POLITICAL POWER AND THE 2012 ELECTION

Although racism and anti-immigrant sentiment continue to be widespread in the United States, recent demographic trends and political events have served to alter the political context in such a way as possibly to reduce Latino cynicism. In 2012, Latinos found themselves courted by politicians on both sides of the aisle and repeatedly reminded of their potential political power. In such a context, previous findings about predictors of political trust may no longer be relevant or may work in different ways.

Latinos have been characterized as a sleeping giant for decades; in the weeks leading up to the 2012 presidential election evidence from both major political parties suggested that they believed 2012 would be the year that the giant finally awoke. As Gabriel Sanchez notes, "2012 was undoubtedly big for Latinos" (2013). According to Eric Rodriguez of the National Council of La Raza, outreach to Latinos in 2012 was notable in two ways: for the massive outreach to Latino eligible and registered voters, and for the four interviews provided by presidential candidates to Spanish-language news media outlets, including a bilingual presidential debate (2013). The cover story of the March 5, 2012, issue of *Time* featured an array of Latino faces titled, "Yo Decido. Why Latinos will pick the next President."

A *Yahoo!News* story on September 24, 2012, titled "Vota por mi! Why the Latino vote is crucial in 2012," noted the Spanish news media participation by Obama and Romney, commenting, "The bilingual events were yet another reminder of how crucial the Latino vote will be in this election." The story notes that this "is why both candidates are aggressively courting Latino voters," including high-profile speaking roles for prominent Latinos at both party conventions, endorsements from well-known Latino entertainers, Spanish-language advertisements that included President Obama signing off with "soy Barack Obama y apruebo este mensaje," and Republican spots featuring Romney's bilingual son. "Obama even appeared on a popular local Miami radio station with a Cuban-American host who calls himself

The Pimp with the Limp" (Tapper, Coolidge, and Pham 2012). The power of the Latino vote in 2012 was also emphasized by Obama's July 2012 announcement of the DACA program, widely seen as an election-year move meant to attract Latino support and soften criticism of his administration's lack of progress on comprehensive immigration reform.

The degree to which both parties courted the Latino vote in 2012 is also reflected in the increased level of spending on Spanish-language television advertisements in 2012 compared to previous presidential election campaigns. Although not all Latinos speak Spanish or get their news from Spanish-language television, such spending is a good indicator of outreach to Latino voters because Spanish-language ads are the only advertising specifically targeted to Latino voters. According to the ad tracking firm Kantar Media CMAG, spending in 2012 was eight times what was spent in 2008, which was itself a record year; spending on Spanish-language ads increased from $3 million to nearly $50 million between the 2000 and 2008 campaigns (Abrajano 2010; Hajnal and Lee 2011; Kantar Media 2012).

At the same time that Latinos (especially likely voters) were courted and empowered in 2012, however, other aspects of the political context at the time might be expected to maintain and exacerbate Latino cynicism. Even as the Latino community welcomed and praised the DACA program, they noted its timing (June 15, 2012) as a blatant effort to court the Latino vote in advance of the November election. Obama was widely criticized as the "Deporter in Chief," and was pressed multiple times during the 2012 campaign by Univision news anchor Jorge Ramos for his failure to deliver on 2008 campaign promises for comprehensive immigration reform. More about this aspect of the 2012 political context is discussed by Garcia-Rios and Barreto elsewhere in this volume. These aspects of the 2012 context notwithstanding, I hypothesize that Latinos in 2012 felt more included and powerful as compared to 2006, and that this will be reflected in increased expressions of trust in government.

DATA AND HYPOTHESES

This paper uses data from three national surveys: the 2005–2006 LNS and two conducted just prior to the November 2012 presidential election, the Latino Immigrant National Election Study (LINES) and the ANES. The LINES preelection wave was conducted from October 4 through November 5, 2012, and includes 855 respondents. The LINES postelection wave was conducted from November 12 through December 20, 2012, and includes 886 respondents, 435 from the preelection phase and 451 fresh respondents. All respondents are adult immigrants from Spanish-speaking countries of Latin America. Interviews were conducted by telephone in both English and Spanish, including a mix of landlines and cellular numbers (for more information, see McCann and Jones-Correa 2012). Data collection for the ANES 2012 Time Series Study began in early September and continued into January 2013. Preelection interviews were conducted with study respondents during the two months prior to the 2012 elections and were followed by postelection reinterviewing beginning November 7, 2012. It includes 1,007 Latino respondents (for more information, see ANES 2013).

An important feature of the LINES data and ANES data is the timing: just before the 2012 presidential election. This allows for comparisons with and hypotheses related to the context of Latino political power with the 2006 LNS, which also asked a nationwide sample of Latinos about their feelings of trust in government. The major hypotheses investigated here are that Latino trust in government in 2012 will be stronger than in 2006, and that in 2012 Latino citizens will be more trusting than noncitizens, reflecting the context of a presidential election that highlighted citizens' ability to vote and their potential power to decide the outcome of that election, whereas noncitizens could not and likely were negatively impacted by the continued delay of comprehensive immigration reform:

H_1: Latinos surveyed in 2012 will be more trusting of government than will Latinos surveyed in 2006.

H$_2$: Latino citizens surveyed in 2012 will be more trusting of government than will Latino citizens surveyed in 2006.

H$_3$: Latino citizens surveyed in 2012 will be more trusting of government than will Latino noncitizens.

These hypotheses are explored with models that include a variety of independent variables found in previous scholarship to be important predictors of trust in government among Latinos. Consistent with that scholarship, the models include tests of the following subhypotheses:

H$_4$: Latino trust in government will be negatively correlated with perceived discrimination against Latinos and personal experiences of discrimination.

H$_5$: Latino trust in government will be positively correlated with preference for an American identity (rather than a Latino or Hispanic or country-of-origin identity).

H$_6$: Latino trust in government will be positively correlated with feelings of linked fate with the Latino community.

H$_7$: Latino trust in government will be positively correlated with support for blending in to the host culture of the United States rather than maintaining a distinct culture.

Additional predictors of trust in government found to be important in previous scholarship are also included: language of interview, English-language fluency, partisanship, approval of the president (Barack Obama), trust in government in the country of origin, and gender, as well as standard sociodemographic variables of age, education, and income.[3]

Many surveys, including those examined here, ask respondents whether they were contacted before the election and asked to vote. For example, the 2012 LINES survey asked, "Did anyone from one of the political parties call you up or come around and talk to you about the campaign this year?" Respondents were also asked, "Other than someone from the two major parties, did anyone (else) call you up or come around and talk to you about supporting specific candidates in this last election?" Although these self-reports might initially seem a good source of information about the extent of mobilization efforts, they are known to be highly unreliable (Vavreck 2007; Michelson 2014). Thus, they are not included in this analysis.

Dependent Variables

The analysis here focuses on answers to the standard *trust* item, as well as an alternative item, *big interests*. The LINES and ANES items are worded as follows. *Trust*: "How much of the time do you think you can trust the government in Washington to do what is right—just about always, most of the time, or only some of the time?" *Big interests*: "Would you say the government in Washington is pretty much run by a few big interests looking out for themselves or that it is run for the benefit of all the people?" These questions were also asked in the 2006 LNS, albeit with different wording for *big interests*. LNS respondents were asked to agree or disagree with the statement, "Government is pretty much run by just a few big interests looking out for themselves, and not for the benefit of all the people." Response categories for the single *trust* item also varied. "Never" was included in the LNS and in the ANES alternate question. "Never" is not included in the LINES *trust* item wording or the ANES standard wording for face-to-face interviews but is recorded as a volunteered response; ANES respondents interviewed via the Internet did not have this response option. In the comparisons that follow, parallel questions are used as often as possible and tables indicate when the question wording (or response categories) differed for each group of respondents.

---

3. Some respondents switched languages between the pre- and post-LINES surveys. Because the trust question was asked during the preelection interview, this analysis uses language used in the preelection interview. Unfortunately, although the ANES was conducted in both English and Spanish the language of interview is not included in the dataset. An alternative measure, self-reported language use at home, is thus used to explore both datasets.

LINES includes an additional two questions that are traditionally used in ANES analyses to construct a trust-in-government index (see Wilkes 2014), these questions (*waste* and *corrupt*) are not included in the LNS and thus no comparisons between 2006 and 2012 levels of trust in government are possible with those items, but they are used to construct a trust in government index to test my secondary hypotheses. The question wordings for those additional questions are as follows. *Waste*: "Do you think that people in government in Washington waste a lot of the money we pay in taxes, waste some of it, or don't waste very much of it?" *Corrupt*: "How many of the people running the government in Washington are corrupt? All, most, about half, a few, or none?" To construct the index, responses to all four trust questions were recoded on a scale of 0 to 100, summed, and scaled to create an index that ranges from 0 to 100.

RESULTS

The most basic hypothesis examined here is that Latinos were more trusting in 2012 than they were in 2006. This is tested by comparing responses to the 2006 LNS and 2012 LINES and ANES surveys, noting the different response categories available to respondents in each survey. Results are shown in table 1. Trust in government is notably higher among LINES respondents than among LNS respondents. Note that the LNS and ANES include both first-generation (foreign-born) and U.S.-born respondents, whereas LINES respondents are all first-generation. LINES respondents are the most trusting, 21.7 percent giving the most trusting response versus only 12.3 percent of all LNS respondents and 14.6 percent of all first-generation LNS respondents. Respondents to the ANES, in contrast, are less likely to give the most trusting response but are also less likely to give the least trusting response. For example, they are more likely to say that they trust the government "most of the time" when asked the standard question, and less likely to say never when asked the revised question, 7.4 percent for Latinos interviewed face-to-face and 8.0 percent for Latinos interviewed via the Internet, compared with 18.6 percent of LNS respondents. Overall, there is some support for H_1 when comparing the LNS to the LINES, but less when comparing the LNS to the ANES.

H_1 was further explored with comparisons of responses to the *big interests* question. Results are shown in table 2. In 2006, only 30.5 percent of Latinos responding to the LNS, and only 33.9 percent of first-generation respondents, said that they disagreed with the question and believed that government was run for the benefit of all people. There is mixed evidence of increased trust when comparing this with responses to the more neutral question wording used in the LINES and the ANES. Whereas 54.5 percent of LINES respondents gave the trusting response to the question, only 28.2 percent of ANES Latino respondents gave this response, a level of trust statistically indistinguishable from the 2006 LINES proportion.

Digging deeper into the data, respondents are divided into subgroups based on nativity and citizenship, as appropriate to each dataset. These comparisons are shown in tables 3 and 4.

Table 3 examines trust in government among first-generation respondents only. Findings are similar to those from table 1: LINES respondents are notably more trusting than LNS respondents, particularly when looking at the percentage of respondents giving the most trusting response. ANES respondents, however, are less likely than LNS respondents to say that they are very trusting. At the same time, LNS respondents are much more likely to say that they never trust the government compared to ANES respondents. Table 4 examines first-generation Latino responses to the *big interests* item. In 2006, responses to this item were quite cynical, only 33.9 percent of first-generation LNS respondents disagreeing with the question; a very similar 34.5 percent of 2012 ANES respondents also gave the trusting answer to this question. In the 2012 LINES survey, by contrast, 54.5 percent of respondents gave the trusting answer. In sum, changes over time are not consistent, though this may in part be an artifact of the shifting question wording.

Previous scholarship has found that citizens are less trusting of the government, reflecting increased awareness of the American

Table 1. Latino Trust in Government, Standard Question

	2006 LNS			2012 ANES			
				Standard Response Categories		Revised Response Categories	
	ALL	First Generation	2012 LINES	F2F	Internet	F2F	Internet
	N=8,634	N=6,184	N=783	(N=223)	(N=281)	(N=245)	(N=251)
Just about always	12.3	14.6	21.7	4.5	6.8	Always 2.0	Always 1.2
Most of the time	19.3	16.8	17.9	27.4	32.4	20.4	15.5
Only some of the time	49.8	49.2	57.9	61.0	60.9	About half the time 29.0	About half the time 35.9
						Some of the time 41.2	Some of the time 39.4
Never	18.6	19.3	2.6 {Vol.}	7.2 {Vol.}	N/A	7.4	8.0

Source: Author's compilation based on ANES 2012, McCann and Jones-Correa 2012, Fraga et al. 2013.

Note: Figures in percentages. "Never" is not included in the LINES trust item wording or the ANES standard wording for face-to-face interviews but is recorded as a volunteered response; ANES respondents interviewed via the Internet did not have this response option. LNS data includes respondents from the original 2005–2006 survey only (N=8,634); all LINES respondents are first generation. ANES includes 1,007 Latino respondents, half of which were asked each version of the trust in government question. Data used to generate this figure is shown in table 1A.

Table 2. Latino Trust in Government, Big Interests Question

	2006 LNS		2012 LINES	2012 ANES
	All (N=7,663)	First Generation (N=5,336)	(N=725)	(N=979)
	Government is pretty much run by just a few big interests looking out for themselves, and not for the benefit of all the people.		Would you say the government in Washington is pretty much run by a few big interests looking out for themselves or that it is run for the benefit of all the people?	
Agree/big interests	69.5	66.1	45.5	71.8
Disagree/all the people	30.5	33.9	54.5	28.2

Source: Author's compilation based on ANES 2012, McCann and Jones-Correa 2012, Fraga et al. 2013.

Note: Figures in percentages. LNS data includes respondents from the original 2005–2006 survey only (N=8,634); all LINES respondents are first generation.

Table 3. First-Generation Latinos Who Trust the Government

| | LNS (2006) | | | LINES (2012) | | | ANES (2012) | | | |
| | | | | | | | All, Standard Response Categories | | All, Alternative Response Categories | |
	All	Citizens	Noncitizens	ALL	Citizens	Noncitizens	F2F (N=63)	Internet (N=119)	F2F (N=76)	Internet (N=109)
	N=6,184	N=2,342	N=3,842	N=783	N=319	N=464				
Just about always	14.6	12.1	16.1	21.7	25.1	19.4	9.5	10.1	Always 5.3	Always 1.8
Most of the time	16.8	18.9	15.6	17.9	16.9	18.5	36.5	35.3	22.4	22.0
Only some of the time	49.2	52.4	47.3	57.9	53.9	60.6	52.4	54.6	About half the time 32.9	About half the time 39.5
									Some of the time 34.2	Some of the time 27.5
Never	19.3	16.6	21.0	2.6 {Vol.}	4.1 {Vol.}	1.5 {Vol.}	1.6 {Vol.}	N/A	5.3	9.2

Source: Author's compilation based on ANES 2012, McCann and Jones-Correa 2012, Fraga et al. 2013.

Note: Figures in percentages. "Never" is not included in the LINES *trust* item wording or the ANES face-to-face standard wording but is recorded as a volunteered response. ANES respondents interviewed via the Internet did not have this response option. LNS data includes first generation respondents from the original 2005–2006 survey only (N=8,634); all LINES respondents are first generation.

Table 4. First-Generation Latinos Who Trust the Government, Big Interests Question

	2006 LNS (N=5,336)	2012 LINES (N=725)	2012 ANES (N=359)
	Government is pretty much run by just a few big interests looking out for themselves, and not for the benefit of all the people.	Would you say the government in Washington is pretty much run by a few big interests looking out for themselves or that it is run for the benefit of all the people?	
Agree/big interests	66.1	45.5	65.7
Disagree/all the people	33.9	54.5	34.5

Source: Author's compilation based on ANES 2012, McCann and Jones-Correa 2012, Fraga et al. 2013.
Note: Figures in percentages.

Table 5. Latino Citizens and Noncitizens Who Trust the Government, Standard Question

	LNS Noncitizens (N=3,842)	LNS Citizens (N=4,792)	LINES Noncitizens (N=464)	LINES Citizens (N=319)
Just about always	16.1	9.2	19.4	25.1
Most of the time	15.6	22.3	18.5	16.9
Only some of the time	47.3	51.8	60.6	53.8
Never	21.0	16.7	1.5 {Vol.}	4.1 {Vol.}

Source: Authors' compilation based on McCann and Jones-Correa 2012, Fraga et al. 2013.
Note: "Never" is not included in the LINES *trust* item wording but is recorded as a volunteered response.

Table 6. Latino Citizens and Citizens Who Trust the Government, Big Interests Question

	LNS Noncitizens (N=3,232)	LNS Citizens (N=4,431)	LINES Noncitizens (N=429)	LINES Citizens (N=296)
	Government is pretty much run by just a few big interests looking out for themselves, and not for the benefit of all the people.		Would you say the government in Washington is pretty much run by a few big interests looking out for themselves or that it is run for the benefit of all the people?	
Agree/big interests	64.3	73.3	42.7	49.7
Disagree/all the people	35.7	26.7	57.3	50.3

Source: Authors' compilation based on ANES 2012, McCann and Jones-Correa 2012, Fraga et al. 2013.
Note: Figures in percentages.

norm of cynicism or exposure to discrimination and racism. Here, I hypothesize that this will be reversed given the supportive context of 2012. Because the ANES only includes citizens, this hypothesis is tested using the LNS and LINES data only.

As shown in table 5, trust among noncitizen Latinos shows little movement over time, 16.1 percent of 2006 LNS respondents and 19.4 percent of 2012 LINES respondents giving the most trusting answer. In contrast, trust among citizens differs by a large and statistically significant amount, from 9.2 percent in 2006 to 25.1 percent in 2012, supporting H_2. Table 6 illustrates similar movement for responses to the *big interests* question, though again these results must be interpreted with caution given the item wording differences. In addition, trust in 2012 among Latino citizens is higher than trust among non-Latino citizens, 19.4 percent and 25.1 percent giving the most trusting response. Responses to the *big interests* item differ in the opposite direction, however, 57.3 percent of noncitizens and 50.3 percent of citizens giving the trusting response. In sum, evidence is mixed for H_3.

Secondary Hypotheses

As noted, previous scholarship has devised and tested various models of trust in government among Latinos, using as predictors measures of discrimination, identity, linked fate, and support for acculturation into mainstream U.S. society. In addition to testing my major hypothesis about shifting trust among Latinos over time, I used the LINES data to test findings based on previous surveys of Latinos. However, in part because of the panel structure of the data, not all items relevant to these hypotheses were asked of all LINES respondents. Measures of discrimination, linked fate, and support for acculturation were all asked only of postelection respondents. To examine the effect of these variables on feelings of political trust, the Amelia II package in R was used to impute missing data (Honaker, King, and Blackwell 2013).

Two measures of perceived discrimination are used to explore trust among Latinos: one about personal experiences, and one about the degree to which respondents believe that discrimination against Latinos and Hispanics exists in the United States. The two items have been found in previous surveys to generate notably different reported levels of discrimination among Latino respondents (Fraga et al. 2010, 71–72). In general, Latinos are much more likely to report discrimination against Latinos as a group than personal experiences based on their ethnicity; both measures are used here to test H_4. The importance of preference for an American identity is included to test H_5. H_6 is tested with inclusion of responses to questions about linked fate; respondents were asked, "Do you think that what happens generally to Hispanic people in this country will have something to do with what happens in your life?" Those who answered yes were further asked whether they thought it would affect them a lot, some, or not very much. These two items are combined to generate a measure of linked fate ranging from 1 = none to 4 = a lot. To test H_7, the multivariate models include responses to questions about the importance of blending in, "How important is it for Hispanics to: Change so that they blend into the larger American society?" and maintaining a distinct culture, "How important is it for Hispanics to: Maintain their distinct cultures?" Given that very few (N = 7 and N = 4) LINES respondents chose the "not at all important" response to each item, in the analysis those responses are recoded with the adjacent response ("not very important").

Secondary Hypotheses Results

Two multivariate models were estimated, as shown in table 7, one with the basic trust in government question, *trust*, as the dependent variable, and one using a trust index constructed from all four trust questions (*trust*, *big interests*, *waste*, and *corrupt*). Reflecting previous scholarship, the models include variables indicating language of interview, use of Spanish at home, partisanship, approval of President Barack Obama, trust in the government of the country of origin, gender, age, education, and income. In addition, data is weighted to be nationally representative. Few respondents declined to answer the *trust* item; more responses are missing (and thus more are imputed) for the trust index.[4]

Controlling for other variables, citizenship is not a statistically significant predictor of political trust among LINES respondents, disconfirming H_3. As shown in model 1, political trust is stronger among supporters of President Obama, older respondents, respondents with lower levels of household income, and among those who trusted the government in their country of origin. Model 2 predicts levels of trust as measured by the four-item index. Again, citizenship is not a statistically significant predictor of trust; respondents who see less discrimination against Latinos, who support the president, and whose interviews were conducted in Spanish have stronger scores on the trust-in-government index.

---

4. Seventy responses to *trust* are imputed; 332 responses to *trust index* are imputed.

Table 7. Multivariate Ordered Logit Models of Latino Trust in Government

	Model 1 (Trust, 3 Categories)		Model 2 (Trust Index)	
	Coefficient	SE	Coefficient	SE
Citizen	.181	.218	.249	3.459
Years in United States	-.005	.012	-.164	.137
Discrimination against Hispanics	-.163	.097	-3.350*	1.108
Discrimination, personal	-.057	.107	.165	1.131
American identity	-.026	.327	-6.752	3.630
Linked fate	.116	.108	-.179	1.214
Blend in	.138	.212	.103	2.363
Distinct	.010	.186	1.212	1.789
Spanish interview	.259	.387	9.939*	4.333
Democrat	-.089	.210	.778	2.441
Approve President Obama	.567*	.143	6.695*	1.493
Female	.075	.197	-1.188	2.366
Age	.023*	.011	.177	.099
Education	.021	.027	-.161	.263
Income	-.221*	.099	-1.445	1.112
Trust government, country of origin	.260*	.124	4.771	2.114
Cut_1	3.189	1.245	—	
Cut_2	4.260	1.254	—	
Constant	—		23.313	12.615
N	666		670	

Source: Author's compilation based on McCann and Jones-Correa 2012.
Note: Data is weighted to be nationally representative. Missing data is imputed using the Amelia II package in R.
*$p < .05$ (two-tailed)

DISCUSSION

Much changed for Latinos in America between 2006 and 2012. In 2006, marchers felt compelled to take to the streets in massive numbers to protest the racism and anti-immigrant sentiment expressed by the Sensenbrenner bill. Although the size of the megaprotests was a sign of power and solidarity, that they were seen as necessary was also a reminder of Latinos' lack of traditional political power (Beltrán 2010). In 2012, in contrast, Latinos received frequent reminders of their power to determine the outcome of the presidential election through the traditional and conventional power of voting. Citizens in particular were told that they were an important component of the American political system. This paper explores the hypothesis that this shifting political context led Latinos, particularly Latino citizens, to become more trusting of the government, reversing a decades-long trend of findings that Latino trust decreases with acculturation into the U.S. system. Additional variables in the models sought to confirm findings from previous research.

Overall, and most significantly, the main hypothesis is confirmed by the LINES data: Latinos surveyed in 2012 were much more likely to say that they trust the government than were Latinos surveyed in 2006, and the difference is particularly large when comparing responses from U.S. citizens. This is a marked change from previous findings. When signaled by elites and media that they were welcome and that they were important, Latino immigrants said they were more trusting of the government.

Given the limitations of cross-sectional survey data, alternative explanations exist for these observed shifts. One is that Latinos were responding in 2012 to the candidacy of Barack Obama and the control of the presidency by the Democratic Party; previous research has shown a strong link between which political party controls the presidency and how partisans feel about the government (Keele 2005). Not all Latinos are Democrats; in fact, 37 percent of Latino voters supported Republican Ronald Reagan in 1984, and 40 percent supported Republican George W. Bush in 2004. However, shifting levels of trust may nevertheless reflect the change in who controls the presidency. This is tested by examining the timing of the shift in Latino trust in government over time, from 2000 to 2012, encompassing both George W. Bush's Republican and Obama's Democratic administrations. A second alternative explanation is that the observed shift is part of a broader shift in public trust in government—that Latinos shifted their opinions in sync with non-Latinos in response to broader contextual shifts in the political environment. This is tested by examining shifts in public trust in government for the same 2000 to 2012 period for a variety of ethnoracial groups.

BROADER TRENDS IN TRUST IN GOVERNMENT

As noted, public opinion surveys have measured trust in government for decades, allowing for examination of shifts over time, although longitudinal data on Latinos (and blacks) is elusive because of the small number of Latino respondents included in most national surveys. For example, although the ANES has collected data on trust in government since 1958, no Latinos are included before 1978, and the total number of Latino respondents from 1978 to 2008 is 2,290, almost a quarter of those from 2008 alone. Combining data from a variety of sources, including the LNS, the ANES, the Pew Hispanic Center, and the Pew Research Center for the People & the Press, reveals a clear divergence in patterns of Latino (and black) trust in government from white trust in government, as shown in figure 1.

Figure 1. White, Black, and Latino Trust in Government, 2000–2012

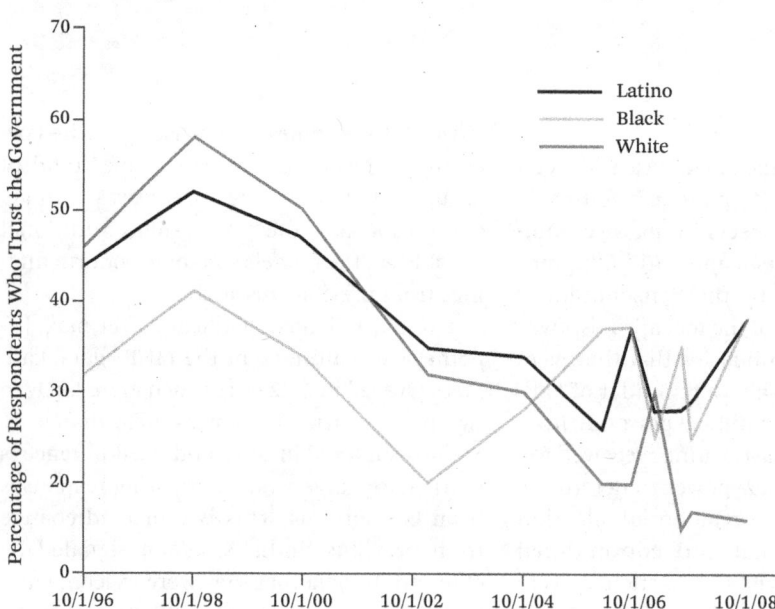

Source: Author's compilation based on ANES 2010, ANES 2012, Pew Research Center 2015.
Note: Data points indicate the percentage of respondents saying that they trust the government always or most of the time.

Table 8. Trust in Government, 2000–2012

	2000	2002	2004	2006	2008	2012
White Democrats	49.8	50.6	37.7	22.7	33.6	20.9
	(N=518)c	(N=433)c	(N=308)c	(N=959)a	(N=214)c	(N=698)c
White Independents	39.0	50.7	48.4	23.3	28.6	10.9
	(N=141)c	(N=67)c	(N=62)c	(N=288)a	(N=63)c	(N=256)c
White Republicans	42.4	62.2	59.6	44.3	26.1	13.3
	(N=530)c	(N=534)c	(N=376)c	(N=742)a	(N=234)c	(N=824)c
Latino Democrats	44.4	58.5	42.2	29.3	32.1	42.6
	(N=54)c	(N=41)c	(N=45)c	(N=3,970)b	(N=137)c	(N=498)d
Latino Independents	50.0	50.0	20.0	29.0	33.3	26.8
	(N=16)c	(N=4)c	(N=10)c	(N=3,146)b	(N=30)c	(N=112)d
Latino Republicans	37.1	67.7	51.4	43.1	42.9	40.0
	(N=35)c	(N=31)c	(N=35)c	(N=1,518)b	(N=42)c	(N=110)d

Source: Author's compilation based on ANES 2010, ANES 2012, McCann and Jones-Correa 2012, Fraga et al. 2013, Pew Research Center 2015.
Note: Cell entries indicate percentage of respondents saying that they trust the government always or most of the time. Partisans include leaners.
a 2006 Pew Survey (in Pew 2015).
b 2006 Latino National Survey (in Fraga et al. 2013).
c The table gives data by year. The ANES data for 2000–2008 is from the cumulative datafile (ANES 2010) and ANES data for 2012 is from ANES 2012.
d 2012 LINES.

White distrust in government shows a fairly steady increase over time, particularly since 2002. In contrast, Latino (and black) distrust increases from 2002 to 2006 and then stays fairly constant in 2008, then drops in 2010 and 2012.

Although not conclusive, these trends are consistent with the explanation offered here, that Latino trust in government is responsive to the political climate and to signals of belonging issued by policymakers and policies. Black and Latino trust are moving together, but white trust follows a different trajectory. This suggests that changes in the political climate including the election of the first black president in U.S. history and the related attentiveness to black and Latino voters by both political parties is affecting black and Latino attitudes toward the government. Further discussion of black public opinion and political trust is beyond the scope of this paper. For Latinos, the long-term trends and subgroup differences (citizens versus noncitizens) provide suggestive evidence that Latino trust is responsive to shifts in the political environment.

Trust in government is responsive to which party controls the presidency (Keele 2005), but trust among Latinos (and blacks) may also reflect minority empowerment. Unfortunately, there is limited data available on how nonwhite trust in government by party affiliation varies over time, due to small sample sizes in most public opinion surveys. Some trends are still visible, as shown in table 8, but note that for many of the cell entries these percentages are based on fairly small numbers of responses. Focusing on the larger cell sizes, Latino Republicans and Independents held about the same level of trust between 2006 and 2012, but Latino Democrats became more trusting, indicating that minority empowerment is not the mechanism driving increased trust. White Republicans and Independents became less trusting between 2006 and 2012 while white Democrats were more trusting in 2008 but less trusting in 2012.

Table 9. Latino Feelings of External Political Efficacy

	ANES (N=510)	LINES Citizens (N=324)	LINES Noncitizens (N=483)	LNS Citizens (N=4,465)	LNS Noncitizens (N=3,305)
		Public officials don't care much what people like me think.			
Disagree	17.7	27.2	27.2	—	
		People like me don't have any say about what the government does.		People like me don't have any say in what the government does.	
Disagree	35.5	41.2	28.9	44.9	40.7

Source: Author's compilation based on ANES 2012, McCann and Jones-Correa 2012, Fraga et al. 2013.
Note: All figures in percentages.

TRUST AND POLITICAL EFFICACY

A considerable body of work finds that trust in government is closely related to feelings of external political efficacy, although the concepts differ. Stephen C. Craig defines trust as "the anticipated quality of government outputs," and external efficacy as "the degree to which an individual perceives his political actions as being (potentially) successful" (1979, 229). In other words, while trust is about the quality of government action, external efficacy is about government responsiveness. This suggests that the increased outreach to Latino voters between 2006 and 2012 should be reflected not just in feelings of trust but also in feelings of empowerment. In fact, heightened feelings of external political efficacy between 2006 and 2012 may be the mechanism through which trust increased among Latino citizens.

There are two traditional measures of external efficacy; respondents are asked whether they agree or disagree with the following items: "Public officials don't care much what people like me think" (*dontcare*), and "People like me don't have any say about what the government does" (*nosay*). While both items were included in the 2012 ANES and LINES, only *nosay* was included in the LNS, although with slightly different wording ("People like me don't have any say in what the government does.")

Given that feelings of political trust increased among Latinos between 2006 and 2012 due to increased outreach by politicians and heightened feelings of belonging, it follows that feelings of external political efficacy should also have increased, particularly among Latino citizens. Using responses to the *nosay* item in the three surveys generates some evidence that this is the case, as shown in table 9. In 2006, citizens reported slightly stronger feelings of external political efficacy than did noncitizens, 44.9 percent versus 40.7 percent, a statistically significant difference of 4.2 percentage points (S.E. = 1.1). Among respondents in 2012 (LINES), citizens reported much stronger feelings of external political efficacy, 41.2 percent versus 28.9 percent, a statistically significant difference of 12.1 percentage points (S.E. = 3.4). However, looking again at the 2012 data, there is no difference in how citizens and noncitizens responded to the *dontcare* item. At the same time, Latino respondents to the ANES and LINES reported somewhat weaker feelings of external political efficacy (in 2012) than did respondents to the LNS (in 2006). In sum, there is some evidence that the same contextual factors generating increased trust between 2006 and 2012 also led to increased feelings of external efficacy among Latino citizens, but the efficacy data is incomplete and inconsistent.

CONCLUSION

The degree to which members of ethnoracial minority groups feel that they belong to the broader polity has important effects on their method and degree of acculturation. The depiction in 2012 of Latinos as deciders, as American voters, combined with outreach that respected their culture—including Spanish-language television advertisements and candidate appearances on Spanish-language television—sent a clear message to Latinos: *you belong*. This support and inclusion led Latinos to be less cynical about their government despite the continued inability of Congress to pass comprehensive immigration reform, or even a DREAM Act, and the continued high level of deportations suffered by the Latino community under the Obama administration.

The wake of the 2012 elections brought renewed attention to the power of the Latino vote. Media and elites recognized the contribution of Latino voters to Obama's landslide victory and predicted how this might influence future contests. A postmortem analysis of why Republican nominee Mitt Romney did so poorly noted the need to reach out to Latino voters to keep the party competitive. Speculation abounded regarding how this demonstration of Latino political power—and the likelihood that the growing Latino electorate would continue to be decisive—would affect immigration policy reform. Regardless of how these trends play out, evidence from the LINES and LNS surveys in the two very different political contexts of 2006 and 2012 suggests that the way U.S. society treats Latino immigrants has powerful effects on their political socialization and attitudes.

REFERENCES

Abrajano, Marissa M. 2010. *Campaigning to the New American Electorate: Advertising to Latino Voters*. Stanford, Calif.: Stanford University Press.

American National Election Studies (ANES). 2010. Time Series Cumulative Data File dataset. Ann Arbor: University of Michigan; Palo Alto: Stanford University. Accessed February 29, 2016. http://www.electionstudies.org/.

———. 2012. The ANES 2012 Time Series Study dataset. Ann Arbor: University of Michigan; Palo Alto: Stanford University. Accessed February 26, 2016. http://www.electionstudies.org/.

———. 2013. *User's Guide and Codebook for the Preliminary Release of the ANES 2012 Time Series Study*. Ann Arbor: University of Michigan; Palo Alto: Stanford University.

Beltrán, Cristina. 2010. *The Trouble with Unity: Latino Politics and the Creation of Identity*. New York: Oxford University Press.

Buzan, Bert C. 1980. "Chicano Community Control, Political Cynicism and the Validity of Political Trust Measures." *Western Political Quarterly* 33(1): 108–20.

Chanley, Virginia A., Thomas J. Rudolph, and Wendy M. Rahn. 2001. "The Origins and Consequences of Public Trust in Government: A Time Series Analysis." *Public Opinion Quarterly* 64(3)(Fall): 239–56.

Citrin, Jack. 1974. "Comment: The Political Rele-

APPENDIX

Table A1. Data for Figure 1

	Latino	Black	White	Source
10/31/12	38	38	16	ANES
10/4/11	29	25	17	PRC
8/21/11	28	35	15	PRC
3/1/11	28	25	30	PRC
9/6/10	37	37	20	PRC
3/21/10	26	37	20	PRC
10/15/08	34	28	30	ANES
1/09/07	35	20	32	PRC
10/15/04	47	34	50	ANES
10/15/02	52	41	58	ANES
10/15/00	44	32	46	ANES

Source: Author's compilation based on ANES 2010, ANES 2012, Pew Research Center 2015.

vance of Trust in Government." *American Political Science Review* 68(3): 973–88.

Citrin, Jack, and Donald Philip Green. 1986. "Presidential Leadership and the Resurgence of Trust in Government." *British Journal of Political Science* 16 (October): 431–53.

Craig, Stephen C. 1979. "Efficacy, Trust, and Political Behavior: An Attempt to Resolve a Lingering Conceptual Dilemma." *American Politics Research* 7(2): 225–39.

Dawson, Michael C. 1994. *Behind the Mule: Race and Class in African-American Politics*. Princeton, N.J.: Princeton University Press.

Fraga, Luis Ricardo, John A. Garcia, Rodney E. Hero, Michael Jones-Correa, Valerie Martinez-Ebers, and Gary M. Segura. 2010. *Latino Lives in America: Making It Home*. Philadelphia, Pa.: Temple University Press.

———. 2013. Latino National Survey (LNS), 2006. ICPSR20862-v6. Ann Arbor, MI: Inter-university Consortium for Political and Social Research. doi: 10.3886/ICPSR20862.v6.

de la Garza, Rodolfo O. 1995. "The Effects of Ethnicity on Political Culture." In *Classifying By Race*, edited by Paul E. Peterson. Princeton, NJ: Princeton University Press.

de la Garza, Rodolfo O., Louis DeSipio, F. Chris Garcia, John Garcia, and Angelo Falcón. 1992. *Latino Voices: Mexican, Puerto Rican and Cuban Perspectives on American Politics*. Boulder, Colo.: Westview Press.

Garcia, F. Chris. 1973. *Political Socialization of Chicano Children: A Comparative Study with Anglos in California Schools*. New York: Praeger.

García Bedolla, Lisa, and Melissa R. Michelson. 2012. *Mobilizing Inclusion: Transforming the Electorate Through Get-out-the-Vote Campaigns*. New Haven, Conn.: Yale University Press.

Gutierrez, Armando, and Herbert Hirsch. 1973. "The Militant Challenge to the American Ethos: 'Chicanos' and 'Mexican Americans.'" *Social Science Quarterly* 53(1): 830–49.

Guzmán, Ralph. 1970. "The Political Socialization of the Mexican American People." Ph.D. diss., University of California, Los Angeles.

Hajnal, Zoltan L., and Taeku Lee. 2011. *Why Americans Don't Join the Party: Race, Immigration, and the Failure (of Political Parties) to Engage the Electorate*. Princeton, N.J.: Princeton University Press.

Haney-López, Ian F. 1996. *White by Law: The Legal Construction of Race*. New York: New York University Press.

Hetherington, Marc. 1998. "The Political Relevance of Political Trust." *American Political Science Review* 92(4)(December): 791–808.

Honaker, James, Gary King, and Matthew Blackwell. 2013. "Amelia II: A Program for Missing Data." Version 1.7.2. Accessed January 24, 2016. http://cran.r-project.org/web/packages/Amelia/vignettes/amelia.pdf.

Kantar Media. 2012. "Spanish-Language Election Ad Spending 8 Times Higher in 2012 than 2008." http://kantarmediana.com/cmag/press/spanish-language-ad-spending-8-times-higher-2012-2008.

Keele, Luke. 2005. "The Authorities Really Do Matter: Party Control and Trust in Government." *Journal of Politics* 67(3): 873–86.

King, Desmond. 2000. *Making Americans: Immigration, Race, and the Origins of the Diverse Democracy*. Cambridge, Mass.: Harvard University Press.

Knoll, Benjamin R., Rene R. Rocha, and Robert Wrinkle. 2013. "Immigration Enforcement and Political Orientations Among Foreign and Native-Born Latinos." Paper delivered at the 2013 annual meeting of the Western Political Science Association, Hollywood, Calif. (March 28–30, 2013).

Lavariega Monforti, Jessica, and Melissa R. Michelson. 2014. "Multiple Paths to Cynicism: Social Networks, Identity, and Linked Fate Among Latinos." In *Latino Politics en Ciencia Política*, edited by Tony Affigne, Evelyn Hu-DeHart and Marion Orr. New York: New York University Press.

Levi, Margaret. 1998. "A State of Trust." In *Trust and Governance*, edited by Valerie Braithwaite and Margaret Levi. New York: Russell Sage Foundation.

Lipsitz, George. 1998. *The Possessive Investment in Whiteness: How White People Benefit from Identity Politics*. Philadelphia: Temple University Press.

McCann, James A., and Michael Jones-Correa. 2012. Latino Immigrant National Election Study, 2012. New York: Russell Sage Foundation, Carnegie Corporation of New York, Purdue University, and Cornell University.

Michelson, Melissa R. 2001. "Political Trust Among Chicago Latinos." *Journal of Urban Affairs* 23(3–4): 323–34.

———. 2003a. "Boricua in the Barrio: Political Trust Among Puerto Ricans." *Centro: Journal of the Center for Puerto Rican Studies* 15(1): 138–51.

———. 2003b. "The Corrosive Effect of Assimilation: How Mexican-Americans Lose Political Trust." *Social Science Quarterly* 84(4): 918–33.

———. 2007. "All Roads Lead to Rust: How Acculturation Erodes Latino Immigrant Trust in Government." *Aztlán: A Journal of Chicano Studies* 32(2) (Fall): 21–46.

———. 2014. "Memory and Voter Mobilization." *Polity* 46(4): 591–610.

Pallares, Amalia, and Nilda Flores-González. 2010. *¡Marcha!: Latino Chicago and the Immigrant Rights Movement*. Chicago: University of Illinois Press.

Pew Research Center. 2015. "Beyond Distrust: How Americans View Their Government." November 23, 2015. Washington, D.C. Accessed February 29, 2016. http://www.people-press.org/2015/11/23/beyond-distrust-how-americans-view-their-government/.

Putnam, Robert D., principal investigator. 2001. *2000 Social Capital Community Benchmark Survey*. Cambridge, Mass.: Harvard University, John F. Kennedy School of Government, Saguaro Seminar. Accessed January 26, 2016. http://ropercenter.cornell.edu/2000-social-capital-community-benchmark-survey/.

Rodriguez, Eric. 2013. "In 2012, Hispanic Voter Turnout versus Voting Power." *NCLRblog.org*, June 20, 2013. Accessed January 26, 2016. http://blog.nclr.org/2013/06/20/in-2012-hispanic-voter-turnout-vs-voting-power/.

Sanchez, Gabriel R. 2013. "The Untapped Potential of the Latino Electorate." *LatinoDeciscions.com*, January 15, 2013. Accessed January 26, 2016. http://www.latinodecisions.com/blog/2013/01/15/the-untapped-potential-of-the-latino-electorate/.

Scholtz, John T., and Mark Lubell. 1998. "Trust and Taxpaying: Testing the Heuristic Approach to Collective Action." *American Journal of Political Science* 42(2): 398–417.

Tapper, Jake, Richard Coolidge, and Sherisse Pham. 2012. "Vota por mi! Why the Latino vote is crucial in 2012." *Yahoo!News*, Accessed January 26, 2016. http://news.yahoo.com/blogs/power-players/vota-por-mi-why-latino-vote-crucial-2012-112648435.html.

Tyler, Tom R. 1998. "Trust and Democratic Governance." In *Trust and Governance*, edited by Valerie Braithwaite and Margaret Levi. New York: Russell Sage Foundation.

Vavreck, Lynn. 2007. "The Dangers of Self-Reports of Political Behavior." *Quarterly Journal of Political Science* 2: 325–43.

Wals, Sergio C. 2011. "Does What Happens in Los Mochis Stay in Los Mochis? Explaining Postmigration Political Behavior." *Political Research Quarterly* 64(3): 600–11.

Wilkes, Rima. 2014. "Trust in Government: A Micro–Macro Approach." *Journal of Trust Research* 4(2): 113–31. doi: 10.1080/21515581.2014.889835.

Politicized Immigrant Identity, Spanish-Language Media, and Political Mobilization in 2012

SERGIO I. GARCIA-RIOS AND MATT A. BARRETO

Social identity theorists have long studied identity as one of the prime determinants of behavior. However, political scientists have had a hard time identifying consistent patterns between ethnic identity and political participation, especially among immigrants. In this paper, we take a more complex approach and explore whether a sense of immigrant linked fate is salient in explaining political participation among immigrants and, further, what may have caused immigrant identity to become so politicized. Specifically, we look at the issue of immigration reform in 2011 and 2012, and the manner in which both positive and negative messages were a catalyst for a politicized immigrant identity, and the resulting mobilizing effects. Using the 2012 Latino Immigrant National Election Study data, we argue that exposure to Spanish-language news media and feelings of immigrant-linked fate created a politicized immigrant identity among Latino immigrants, which resulted in greater political participation and civic engagement. Rather than seeing immigrants as low-resourced and unengaged in American politics, our theory of politicized immigrant identity explains that Latino immigrants draw on their identity as immigrants and as Americans to participate in their new homeland.

Keywords: immigrant identity, Spanish-language media, linked fate, Latino politics, 2012 election

In December 2005, Republican Congressman Jim Sensenbrenner introduced House Resolution 4437, which was viewed as one of the strictest anti-immigration bills introduced in the U.S. Congress in modern times. In response, millions of immigrants and their allies took to the streets in protest in the spring of 2006 and suddenly immigration reform was thrust on to the national stage as a major policy issue. In the years since, the immigration issue has only grown more important to both immigrant-rights advocates and their opponents. Indeed, a steady drum beat of high-profile issues have created the space for immigration to become a major political issue in the Latino community: attempts to pass a comprehensive immigration bill in 2006–2007, then candidate Barack Obama's promise that he would get immigration reform passed in 2009, Arizona's controversial anti-immigration racial profiling law in 2010, sit-ins by DREAMers in 2011, record deportations by the Obama administration, Mitt Romney's infamous self-deport policy, and finally the executive administrative order known as DACA (Deferred Action for Childhood Arrivals) in 2012. Indeed, the polling firm Latino Decisions reports that immigration reform became the top issue for Latino voters in 2012, a shift from 2008 when the economy was the top issue. According to new research on the

Sergio I. Garcia-Rios is assistant professor of government and Latino studies at Cornell University. **Matt A. Barreto** is professor of political science and Chicana/o studies at the University of California, Los Angeles.

Direct correspondence to: Sergio I. Garcia-Rios at garcia.rios@cornell.edu, Cornell University, 308 White Hall, Ithaca, NY 14853; and Matt A. Barreto at barretom@ucla.edu, University of California, 4289 Bunche Hall, Los Angeles, CA 90095.

Latino vote in 2012, both Loren Collingwood, Matt Barreto, and Sergio Garcia-Rios (2014) and Barreto and Collingwood (2015) argue that the anti-immigrant rhetoric on the Right, and pro-immigrant response from the Left framed the entire election climate for Latinos. Likewise, Leonie Huddy and her colleagues report in this issue that perceived hostility by Republicans strongly affected Latino immigrant partisan identity as Democrats in 2012. In this paper, we ask what effect exposure to immigration messaging had on political engagement and participation among Latino immigrants. Did the discussion of immigration as a political issue influence a politicized immigrant identity that contributed to immigrant political participation, or did it leave them frustrated and disenchanted with the political system?

Social identity theorists have long studied identity as one of the prime determinants of behavior. However, political scientists have had a hard time identifying consistent patterns between ethnic identity and political participation, especially among immigrants. We take a more complex approach and explore whether a sense of ethnic linked fate among Latino immigrants is salient in explaining political participation and, further, what may have contributed to immigrant identity becoming so politicized. Specifically, we look at the issue of immigration reform in 2011 and 2012, the manner in which both positive and negative messages were catalysts for a politicized immigrant identity, and the resulting mobilizing effects. Using the 2012 Latino Immigrant National Election Study (LINES) survey data, we argue that exposure to Spanish-language news media and feelings of immigrant linked fate created a politicized immigrant identity among Latino immigrants, which resulted in greater political participation and civic engagement. Rather than seeing immigrants as low-resourced and unengaged in American politics, our theory of politicized immigrant identity explains that Latino immigrants draw on their identity as immigrants and as Americans to participate in their new homeland.

IDENTITY THEORY AND IMMIGRANTS

The social psychologists Henri Tajfel and John Turner argue that human interaction ranges on a spectrum from being purely interpersonal on the one hand to purely intergroup on the other (Tajfel 1978; Tajfel and Turner 1979). They maintain that moving from the interpersonal to the intergroup end of the spectrum changes how people see themselves and each other. Drawing on his own social cognition work (Tajfel and Wilkes 1963), Tajfel argues that the mere process of making salient "us and them" distinctions changes the way people see each other. The motivating principle underlying competitive intergroup behavior was a desire for a positive and secure self-concept (Turner 1975; Ethier and Deaux 1994; Ullah 1987). Therefore, if people are motivated to have a positive self-concept, they should be motivated to think of their groups as good groups. Striving for a positive social identity, group members are motivated to think and act in ways that achieve or maintain a positive distinctiveness between ones' own group and relevant out-groups. Thus, ethnic identification is one of the prime bases for participation in social movements (Simon et al. 1998).

However, although social identity theory suggests that upholding a positive distinctiveness is a natural instinct, doing so is difficult for Latin American immigrants, who are usually pushed from their country of origin and pulled into the United States precisely because of their lack of resources (Staudt and Garcia-Rios 2011). For Latino immigrants in America today, identities are complex and dynamic. The very act of migration implies the confrontation of a new set of norms and expectations that shape how immigrants see themselves and, consequently, how they act. For instance, the acquisition of English opens an important door into American culture, particularly thorough English-language media. Conversely, the Spanish-language media reflects the immigrant experience and reinforces ties to the home country (Suro 1994). Although English-language media prevails in terms of availability, Spanish-language media has been increasing exponentially in recent years. Given the dual challenge of learning a new culture and preserving their culture and identity, immigrants choose to criss-cross between media outlets. A study by the Pew Hispanic Center shows that about two-thirds of first generation

Latinos watch at least some of their news in English, more than those who report using English at work. Moreover, an overwhelming 78 percent of all Latinos say that the Spanish-language media is "very important to the economic *and political* development of the Hispanic population" (Suro 2004, 2.)

Given the increase in Spanish media availability and Spanish-language news outlets, as well as the increased politization of Latino identity, we hold that the choice of news consumption has political implications. How you get your news not only shapes how you see the world but, as social identity theory suggests, also affects how Latino immigrants see themselves and act politically.

CURRENT THEORIES OF IMMIGRANT POLITICAL ENGAGEMENT

One of the most commonly accepted theories in studies of political participation is that of resource mobilization. Those with more stake in the system, more income, education, or age, are more likely to participate. From *The American Voter* to Steven Rosenstone and John Hansen (1993) to the latest research on participation, political scientists have demonstrated unequivocally that higher-resourced individuals participate more. The implication then is that communities with fewer resources are unengaged and perhaps even disengaged from American politics. When it comes to studies of immigrant communities, this is a common explanation given for the comparatively low levels of participation by Latino and Asian immigrants.

Primarily because of lower levels of education, income, English-language skills, and exposure to American political institutions, immigrant voters have consistently demonstrated low levels of political participation. In addition to a lack of resources, naturalized Latinos are rarely, if ever, the target of voter mobilization drives, further decreasing their awareness of campaign issues and likelihood to turn out (Cassel 2002; de la Garza et al. 1992; de la Garza 1996; de la Garza, Menchaca, and DeSipio 1994; DeSipio 1998; DeSipio and de la Garza 1992; Guerra 1992; Mollenkopf, Olson, and Ross 2001; Pachon 1991; Shaw, de la Garza, and Lee 2001). Wendy Tam Cho argues that naturalized citizens are likely to participate less than native-born citizens because they have had less exposure to the U.S. political system. Her data analysis of a 1984 public opinion survey in California leads her to conclude that "the lower participation rate among minorities is now largely dependent upon being foreign-born and not being able to speak English" (1999, 1150). Examining data from 1996, Loretta Bass and Lynn Casper also find that among naturalized citizens, "the odds of voting are 26 percent lower than those of native-born citizens" (2001, 504). Like Tam Cho, they argue that because naturalized citizens are newer to American politics and less "integrated into U.S. institutions and social customs" (504), they are less likely to cast a ballot. However, this premise is based on two assumptions: that immigrant identity suggests lower levels of acculturation and that lack of exposure to English is a negative and demobilizing factor.

Early models of political participation found a significant relationship between socioeconomic variables and the propensity to vote (Campbell et al. 1960; Verba and Nie 1972; Wolfinger and Rosenstone 1980). In particular, age, education, income, and marital status were found to be strong predictors of an individual's likelihood of voting. Given that many immigrants, particularly those from Latin America, come to this country for economic opportunities, they typically have not demonstrated high levels of these socioeconomic status (SES) indicators, and as a result have typically not had high levels of participation.[1] Further, previous research into Latino immigrants noted that they were detached from American politics and often more interested in happenings in their home country. An additional "resource" for navigating the political system that increases the likelihood of Latino turnout is English-language proficiency. As a result of these trends, candidates and campaigns typically ignored immigrant communities (see Stevens and Bishin 2011). Given the

---

1. Again, the historical exception here was the politically charged Cuban immigrant communities, who needed higher resource levels to escape Cuba for the United States.

importance of mobilization and recruitment to political participation, foreign-born citizens often found themselves uninformed, unaware, and uninvolved in elections (Shaw, de la Garza, and Lee 2000).

Although these assumptions have proven true in data analyses in the 1990s and early 2000s, we argue that today, both of these premises are misguided. It is true that recently arrived Latino immigrants have less knowledge of U.S institutions and processes. Models of political economy, however, suggest several reasons why better-informed citizens are more likely to turn out and that less-informed voters might have an incentive to delegate their vote to better-informed citizens by abstaining (Feddersen and Pesendorfer 1996, 1999; Gerber and Green 2000). Thus, given the rapidity of demographic and political changes, Spanish media outlets have begun to fill the knowledge and information gap. With these changes in mind, we offer a new theoretical framework for understanding foreign-born political engagement. In doing so, we draw on existing research by Barreto and José Muñoz (2003), and confirmed by David Sears, Felix Danbold, and Vanessa Zavala in this issue, that foreign-born Latinos are eager to engage politics, and that this eagerness extends to noncitizens.

HOW IMMIGRATION BECAME A POLITICAL IDENTITY

Over the last decade, immigrant communities gained a higher profile in American politics. Rather than seeing immigrants as stuck "in between" homeland and new home, scholars are beginning to find evidence that immigrants are participating in politics at higher rates (Voss and Bloemraad 2011). Research on Latino immigrants in California best exemplifies this new trajectory and establishes a theory of politicized immigrant identity that we draw heavily on. The anti-immigrant environment in California in the mid-1990s gave way to a new cohort of politically active immigrants (Pantoja, Ramírez, and Segura 2001; Milkman 2011). One of the main proponents of this theory, Ricardo Ramírez, has documented extensively that Latino immigrants reacted with frustration and political engagement when faced with policies and rhetoric that negatively targeted immigrants in California (2013). In *Mobilizing Opportunities* (2013), Ramírez argues that the contentious political environment, coupled with a steadfast coverage of the immigration issue by Spanish-language media and the growth of Latino advocacy groups, resulted in heightened levels of naturalization and political participation among California Latinos, in particular immigrants. Through a series of published articles and book chapters, Ramírez and his colleagues changed the way scholars think about Latino immigrant participation (see Fraga and Ramírez 2004; Barreto, Ramírez, and Woods 2005; Barreto, Ramírez, Fraga, and Guerra 2009; Ramírez 2013).

Notably, Taeku Lee (2008) has warned scholars not to oversimplify the politics-to-identity link, rejecting those analyses that put in a single dummy variable for race and attempt to assign some sort of group-based identity politics. We wholeheartedly agree. Rather than assuming that all immigrants will carry this identity-to-politics link, we need to be able to account for context, exposure to different stimuli, and strength of ethnic identity, as Lee (2008) recommends. New research on Latino political mobilization continues to focus on how the immigration issue can mobilize or demobilize. Francisco Pedraza argues that how welcoming or unwelcoming a state or locality is to immigrants can greatly affect how Latino immigrants view and engage the political system (2014). When confronted with a hostile political environment in which immigrants seem to be under attack, Pedraza finds lower levels of political trust; Gabriel R. Sanchez (2006) finds that perceived discrimination leads to increased political participation. Perhaps because their numbers have grown, Latino immigrants appear to be mobilizing together to push back against anti-immigrant rhetoric and policy. Indeed, this has been a relatively new finding of those studying the 2006 immigration rallies. For example, Barreto and his colleagues (2009) find that Latinos who said immigration was their top issue of concern were the most likely to have a favorable view of the 2006 immigration rallies. They argue that the immigration rallies laid the groundwork for a sense of immigrant linked fate—which they call *solidaridad*—because so many immigrants felt targeted: "HR 4437 became a common enemy, because its expansive reach mobilized multiple constituencies and provided the basis for *solidaridad*, or solidarity, even among disparate groups" (Barreto, Manzano, Ramírez, and Rim 2009, 747). Similarly, but using the 2006 Latino National Survey and date of interview as a quasi-experiment, Chris Zepeda-Millán and Sophia Wallace (2013) find clear evidence that exposure to the immigration marches had a lasting effect on Latino racial identity. Although it may seem obvious, immigration created a bridge to political participation during the 2006 immigration rallies that we believe continues today. Likewise, research on the rallies by Zepeda-Millán (2014) finds that group identity was cued as a result of the 2006 rallies, and that the anti-immigrant sentiment spurred participation and mobilization.

Thinking about participation in 2012, we argue that two factors spurred the creation of an immigrant political identity that motivated civic and political engagement. The first was the constant attention to undocumented immigrant rights by both the DREAM Act activists and the Spanish-language news media (Barreto and Garcia-Rios 2012). In particular, we identify Univision news anchor Jorge Ramos as a leading figure in promoting a politicized immigrant identity. Ramos was joined in this effort by coanchor Maria Elena Salinas, as well as by dozens of Spanish-language radio and print news journalists who kept attention on this issue of critical importance to their audience (see Subervi-Vélez 2008). The second factor at play in 2012 was the often harsh anti-immigrant rhetoric from politicians and political candidates for office. This took the form of negative statements about immigrants from Republican candidates trying to court the far Right conservative vote, and was most visible during the lengthy 2012 Republican presidential primary. We discuss each of these two factors in turn.

To understand why immigration continued to be a salient issue to Latinos in 2012, we can start with expectations created by Barack Obama in 2008. As a presidential candidate, Obama told Latino audiences that passing comprehensive immigration reform would be his top priority. He promised immigrants that he would get legislation passed in 2009, in his first year in office. In an effort to gain trust from Republicans that his administration would enforce immigration laws, and ultimately win their support for a bipartisan immigration bill, the Obama administration increased resources and attention to interior deportations. However, when it became clear that comprehensive immigration legislation would not be moving forward in Congress, the Immigration and Customs Enforcement (ICE) did not slow deportations. To the contrary, they picked up the pace and began deporting even more immigrants, an overwhelmingly majority of whom were Latino. Under the Obama administration, the number of Latino immigrants deported reached record highs. ICE officials liked to say that they were targeting known criminals, but the facts on the ground proved otherwise. Latino journalists such as Pilar Marrero, Jorge Ramos, Maria Elena Salinas, and José Diaz-Balart began reporting—daily—the stories of everyday working immigrants who were being deported. Many who were deported had young U.S.-born children. In some instances, parents were apprehended and sent to detention centers during the day while their children were in school. Young adults were also being deported, the so-called DREAMers. Children who were brought to the United States at a young age, raised in America, but did not have documentation were sometimes detained or deported as they prepared to enroll in college or even join the U.S. military. For Spanish-language media, the deportations were a real crisis facing their audience, and therefore they covered the story in depth. As immigrants were reading the newspaper or watching Univision in 2011 and 2012, they became very informed about how the political system was taking its toll on immigrant communities.

While Obama was being criticized for his deportation policy, on the other side of the aisle Republicans oscillated between pushing for positive reforms (McCain, Rubio), being accused of hate-speech against immigrants (King, Sessions), or willfully ignoring and obstructing reform (Boehner, Cantor). As immigrant rights advocates pushed for passage of the DREAM Act and comprehensive immigration reform, many Republicans protested, calling immigrants criminals, job-stealers, and un-American. For example, Georgia Republican Congressman Paul Broun said, "these illegal aliens are criminals and we need to treat them as such" (Foley 2013). Iowa Republican Congressman Steve King compared immigration policy to corralling animals, saying we should electrify the border fence with Mexico just like we do with livestock. As a follow-up, Mr. King said, "They came here on their own, they came here to live in the shadows. There's no moral calling for us to solve the problem they created for themselves" (Le 2013). Dozens more examples abound as Republicans at all levels of office, backed by the Tea Party, came out with aggressive negative statements about immigrants.

Perhaps the most salient to the 2012 context was the way in which the Republican presidential candidates called to make English the official language and to stop making government services or forms available in Spanish. They vowed to veto the DREAM Act and encourage more states to follow Arizona's lead in encouraging police to stop and question immigrants for proof of legal status. And then of course there was Mitt Romney's infamous self-deport policy statement when asked how he would deal with the estimated 11 million undocumented immigrants. Throughout 2012, Latino immigrants were exposed to constant anti-immigrant, anti-Latino comments by politicians seeking to be their representatives (DeFrancesco Soto 2012). The *USA Today* editorial board questioned why Republican presidential candidates were "hellbent on proving who can be the harshest and least thoughtful on the subject of illegal immigrants" (2011). U.S. Senator Marco Rubio "told his party to tone down its hard-edged stance on immigration" (Fox News Latino 2011). Spanish media in particular covered these issues as key to their audience, leading the *Washington Times* to proclaim in a headline that "Spanish-language media 'obsessed' on immigration issue." Stephan Dinan (2012) explains in a lengthy article about the role of Spanish-language media:

> For Hispanic voters getting their news from Spanish-language press, the view is very different—and decidedly unsympathetic to the Republican Party.... Spanish-language reports zeroed in on an immigration battle, which saw Kansas Secretary of State Kris Kobach win passage of a strict enforcement plank in the document. While the English press this week has wondered about which Republicans would mention Medicare, and who would play the attack-dog role for the GOP, Spanish-langauge media have been focused on what hasn't been addressed: immigration. That is not good news for Mitt Romney, whose position—the strictest enforcement stance of any major political party nominee in history—does not go over well with Hispanic voters.

In a comprehensive analysis of Spanish-language media, Federico Subervi-Vélez and Xavier Medina Vidal (2015) detail the growing importance of Spanish news coverage with respect to elections. The authors note that 2012 was a watershed year for the Latino media, in large part due to their strong coverage of the immigration issue. Later in this issue, Leonie Huddy, Lilliana Mason, and Nechama Horwitz discuss strong evidence that group identity was related to immigrant political participation in 2012. As a result of perceived anti-immigrant discrimination among Republicans, many Latino immigrants increased their strong Democratic partisanship, and ultimately their political engagement in 2012, as Huddy and her colleagues report.

In response to both the Obama deportation policy and the obstruction by Republicans in Congress, young undocumented immigrants began political protests in the nation's capital and across the country. The DREAM movement was ever-present in 2011 and 2012 and provided a space that bridged immigrant identity and politics, and allowed immigrant political and civic engagement to build. Further, a synergy was evident between the DREAM movement and Spanish-language media: print, radio, and television all covering and promoting the political engagement of the DREAMers. In addition to pure reporting, Spanish-language media also played an implicit and explicit role in political mobilization, especially in encouraging Latino immigrants to vote. In a comprehensive review of the role of Spanish- and English-language political media, Subervi-Vélez (2008) argues that research "should pay more attention to the intersection between media and Latinos when assessing political socialization and mobilization of Latinos." In one of the most sophisticated tests of the Spanish media hypothesis, Jennifer Merolla and her colleagues (2012) implement a series of control-treatment experiments in which they expose Hispanic and non-Hispanic respondents to media primes about immigration. Across four tests, conducted in 2007, they find consistent evidence that Latinos report higher levels of interest in political engagement, as well as validated political action (sending a letter to a public official) after being exposed to media information about immigration. Although this study was only measuring exposure to English-language media, it does demonstrate quite powerfully that immigration coverage can be a mobilizing force for Latinos. We agree, and attempt to focus our theory of Latino immigrant mobilization, in part, on the critical role of Spanish-language news media.

Implicitly, Spanish-language media played a mobilizing role by its constant coverage of "the Latino vote." Print, radio, and television all devoted extensive news stories to the 2012 election and to the role Latinos could play as a growing and influential electorate. Simply from reports about the election, Latino immigrants who consume Spanish-language media were constantly reminded that they could be an important voting bloc. Explicitly, Spanish-language media such as Univision, Entravision, and impreMedia partnered with Latino advocacy groups such as NALEO, NCLR, and Mi Familia Vota to promote public service announcements telling Latinos to get out and vote. This effort, Ya es hora—ve y vota, was first launched in 2008. By 2012, it was an extensive campaign to get out the Spanish-speaking Latino vote. In a postelection review, the *New York Times* described the effort by Spanish-language media and advocacy groups as critical to the Latino vote: "But how Latinos got that message—the relentless call to register, to vote, to participate—was as important as the message itself: Hispanic television and grass-roots groups working together generated a civic campaign they called *Ya Es Hora*. Now is the time" (Alvarez 2012).

In countless households, Latinos tuned their television sets to Univision and heard Jorge Ramos, the host of *Al Punto*, the Spanish version of *Meet the Press*, discuss the candidates' positions on issues critical to them. They switched on Spanish-language radio and heard myriad reasons their vote could spur change. And if voters in some battleground areas needed a ride to the polls, television and radio stations owned by Entravision Communications, Univision's largest affiliate, offered those, too. The drumbeat lasted for months.

Univision, which reaches 96 percent of all Hispanic households, and Telemundo, the second-largest network, and their affiliates ran information about the election and the issues regularly, not just on newscasts but also on their most popular news programs. They sponsored hundreds of public service announcements, giving Latinos local information on where to register and vote. The effort, by and large, was nonpartisan.

These accounts were echoed by journalists themselves in the Spanish-language media. In a discussion about the Latino vote following the 2012 election, Pilar Marrero, head political writer for impreMedia newspapers explained that Spanish-language news had a unique connection to the Latino immigrant community—most of the journalists themselves are immigrants—and have a strong commitment to covering issues related to immigration politics accurately and thoroughly:

> Since the mid-1990s, *La Opinion* and the rest of the Spanish language media has been intensely covering the latest "anti-immigrant" era that has dominated public policy since that time. But that attention has been particularly intense over the last few years, and particularly during the Obama Administration and the drive to pass immigration reform and the increase in deportations promoted by the administration.
>
> Our work has been not only to chronicle what's happening in our immigrant communities and the policies that drive those realities, but to move away from the partisan Democrat versus Republican rhetoric and to

connect the dots between the actions on both sides and the policies that are affecting people on the ground.

The reason we have an impact in that community and its political participation and opinions is because we reflect their reality and the policies that affect it. Those communities are pretty much invisible in other media or they are covered only from the point of view of the "other."[2]

Thus, naturalized citizens seeing the immigration debate unfold before their eyes were more attuned to politics in 2012 than in years past. In particular, those consuming Spanish-language media were getting an extra dose of immigrant identity and politics. In some ways, this is consistent with research by Benjamin Bishin and Casey Klofstad (2012) among Cuban communities in Miami that finds a strong immigrant-politics link to political activism. Rather than rejecting politics, as Sears, Danbold, and Zavala report in this issue, many Latino immigrants in 2012 were actively engaged, demonstrating moderate to high levels of party crystallization. Even among those not declaring an immediate party preference, Sears and his colleagues find Latino immigrants leaning toward political parties at higher rates than anticipated, suggesting well-formed political ideologies and attitudes that map on to the political parties, perhaps as a consequence of the heightened attention to immigration issues in 2012.

OUR EXPECTATIONS

As stated, social identity theorists suggest that individuals are strongly driven to maintain a positive self-image and that threats to one's group will catalyze actions on political participation that depend on the level of identification with the group. Given the political discourse during the 2012 presidential campaign, we form the following hypothesis:

H_1: Latino immigrants with a politicized immigrant identity will be more likely to participate in nonelectoral activities.

We operationalize politicized immigrant identity as those respondents who have high degrees of both immigrant linked fate and interest in politics. Although we expect politicized identity to serve as a mobilizer, it will not necessarily translate into actual votes. To this end, we expect the Spanish-language news to serve as a funnel to translate mobilization into intention to vote.

H_2: Latino immigrants who are heavy consumers of Spanish-language TV news will have a higher interest in voting and campaign activity in 2012.

We operationalize heavy consumers of Spanish-language news as those respondents who are Spanish dominant and said they pay a great deal of attention to national politics on television.

These expectations are driven by our theory as described. First, we think that ethnic linked fate will be most relevant in nonelectoral participation, consistent with research by Sanchez (2006), Natalie Masuoka (2006), and Attiya Kai Stokes (2003), each of which find that group commonality and linked fate matter greatly for nonelectoral participation but are insignificant when it comes to, or even negatively associated with, voting. We emphasize politicized immigrant identity in the first models for nonelectoral participation. Although we shift the focus to Spanish-language media in models 2 and 3, we continue to control for linked fate. However, we do move the theoretical focus to the importance of the Spanish-language news media in tables 2 and 3 because we believe the explicit attention on the 2012 election by Univision and Telemundo should be associated with electoral participation. This is consistent with the research by Subervi-Vélez (2008) and Barreto, DeFrancesco, and Merolla (2011), which both suggest exposure to Spanish-language television can mobilize voter turnout.

OUR FINDINGS

We use the 2012 Latino Immigrant National Election Study developed by James McCann and Michael Jones-Correa (2012) to model immigrant political behavior. Funded by the Russell Sage Foundation, the LINES is a com-

---

2. Pilar Marrero, May 8, 2014, personal correspondence.

panion to the American National Election Study (ANES) in which Latino immigrants—regardless of their citizenship status—are asked many of the core questions from the ANES, as well as immigrant-specific demographic questions. The ANES now maintains a Latino oversample, but only about 30 percent of respondents are immigrants and all are naturalized citizens. The LINES offers an important correction to the ANES by extending the respondent pool to include all adult residents within the Latino community.

As stated, the first part of our analysis is concerned with testing the extent to which a politicized Latino identity will mobilize immigrants. For this model, we use an index of civic participation as our outcome variable; this index includes participating in a rally, attending a political meeting, signing a petition, and donating money. The index ranges from 0 to 6. Further, we operationalize politicized identity as a high degree of linked fate with other Latinos—a unique question presented to Latino immigrant respondents on the LINES. We do not, however, expect all those with immigrant linked fate to be politicized, so we also rely on a measure of interest in politics and interest in the 2012 election, which we combine into a scale of 2 to 8. To isolate those with a politicized immigrant identity, we interact linked fate with political interest to test our first hypothesis of politicized immigrant identity.

To further assess how the immigration narrative in 2012 affected immigrant political participation, we have included a key independent variable for immigration policy preference, which ranges from less welcoming (Make all unauthorized immigrants felons and send them back to their home country) to more welcoming (Allow unauthorized immigrants to remain in the United States and eventually qualify for U.S. citizenship, without penalties). We expect those who have the strongest support for a pathway to citizenship to also be the most likely to engage in nonelectoral politics.

Building on the extant literature in Latino politics, our first model includes control variables for language spoken at home, whether the respondent has naturalized, percentage of life lived in the United States, and whether the respondent is of Mexican origin. Finally, we control for traditional SES indicators and gender.[3] Given the nature of our outcome variable—a count of nonelectoral participation—we use an ordered logistic regression and test using a Poisson count model. Results are entirely consistent.

Table 1 shows the results of the first set of models: a base model with all main variables, and another with an interaction of linked fate and political interest, our measure of politicized immigrant identity.

In the base model, both political interest and linked fate are positive and significantly related to political participation among Latino immigrants, that is they both have an independent direct effect on participation. However, once we include the interaction term, we see that the direct effect of these variables is muted and no longer significant for linked fate, and that the interaction item is statistically significant. Therefore, interest in politics translates into greater civic engagement, especially for Latino immigrants who also have a high sense of linked fate identity. The results support our first hypothesis.

Second, we see significant results for our immigration policy item. Immigrants who support a path to citizenship for the undocumented were more likely to participate in 2012 than those who supported deportation of the undocumented. Again, this is supporting evidence of how immigration became a mobilizing issue for Latino immigrants in 2012. People who felt strongly about this issue were indeed more likely to get involved in politics across a variety of types of participation. Finally, in looking to model fit statistics, mostly the Bayesian information criterion (BIC) score, we see model improvement in the second model with the interaction item for linked fate and interest in politics.

Our second set of models use vote intention as the outcome variable. This variable measures presidential vote interest in a scale of 1

---

3. Because of sample size considerations, we have used multiple imputation to regain missing cases for socioeconomic control variables, which allow us to employ a larger sample size.

Table 1. Predictors of Nonelectoral Civic Participation Among Latino Immigrants in 2012

	Base Model		Politicized Identity Model	
	Coef	SE	Coef	SE
Political interest	0.151***	0.044	0.078*	0.036
Linked fate	0.265***	0.069	−0.194	0.224
Interest X linked fate			0.098**	0.030
Path to citizenship	0.204*	0.095	0.199*	0.092
Attention to political news	0.105	0.133	0.090	0.137
Spanish at home	−0.371***	0.119	−0.360***	0.119
Naturalized citizen	−0.272	0.235	−0.272	0.234
Mexican	0.081	0.221	0.072	0.221
High school graduate	0.421	0.271	0.489*	0.255
Some college or more	0.622**	0.270	0.620***	0.269
Age eighteen to thirty-four	−0.052	0.309	−0.018	0.308
Age thirty-five to forty-four	−0.011	0.269	−0.001	0.270
Age forty-five to fifty-four	0.302*	0.152	0.289*	0.144
Income $20K to $40K	−0.195	0.242	−0.186	0.241
Income $40K and higher	0.091	0.324	0.144	0.323
Missing income	−0.477*	0.237	−0.474*	0.236
Female	0.023	0.194	0.039	0.194
Percentage of life in United States	0.551*	0.256	0.548*	0.255
Cut 1	−0.568	0.876	−0.996	0.897
Cut 2	0.670	0.876	0.241	0.896
Cut 3	1.557	0.877	1.137	0.897
Cut 4	2.261	0.881	1.854	0.899
Cut 5	2.982	0.889	2.592	0.907
Cut 6	3.646	0.903	3.269	0.919
Observations	453.		453	
Log-likelihood	−639.46		−619.56	
Maximum likelihood R^2	0.159		0.263	
BIC	1466.53		1421.25	

Source: Authors' calculations based on McCann and Jones-Correa 2012.
*$p < .1$; **$p < .05$; ***$p < .01$

to 5 (5 = extremely interested in casting a vote) and was asked across all respondents regardless of citizenship status. To our knowledge, this is the first attempt to measure explicit interest in voter participation among noncitizens. We think it holds much promise in understanding Latino immigrant political engagement (see Jones-Correa 2001). Beyond interest in politics, in this model we focus specifically on attention to political television news to assess whether the efforts of Spanish media effectively boosted vote intention. We also include our original interest in politics variable used in the first set of models as a control measure to ensure that our new political attention variable accounts just for exposure to TV news and not overall interest in politics. To ensure that we capture Spanish-language TV news watchers, we include an interaction between Spanish-dominant household and how much attention the respondent pays to news about national politics on television.[4] Al-

---

4. We also considered using a direct measure of Spanish-language news consumption, but this question was asked only of the postelection sample and is not present for all respondents. Further, the question on the post-

Table 2. Predictors of Interest in Voting in 2012 Election Among Latino Immigrants

	Base Model		Spanish TV Model	
	Coef	SE	Coef	SE
Political interest	0.141**	0.071	0.137*	0.072
Attention to political news	0.0736	0.109	-0.711*	0.422
Spanish at home	-0.151	0.123	-0.738**	0.331
Spanish X political news			0.189*	0.099
Path to citizenship	0.331**	0.141	0.323**	0.141
Linked fate	0.135	0.083	0.137	0.083
Naturalized	-0.550**	0.248	-0.569**	0.250
Mexican	0.0656	0.234	0.103	0.235
High school graduate	0.372	0.288	0.359	0.288
Some college or more	1.004***	0.304	1.015***	0.304
Age eighteen to thirty-four	-0.881***	0.327	-0.923***	0.327
Age thirty-five to forty-four	-0.36	0.287	-0.402	0.289
Age forty-five to fifty-four	-0.024	0.276	-0.0418	0.278
Income $20K to $40K	0.113	0.252	0.145	0.252
Income $40K and higher	0.356	0.360	0.471	0.363
Missing income	-0.264	0.277	-0.247	0.278
Female	-0.0805	0.203	-0.0811	0.204
Percentage of life in United States	0.371	0.520	0.384	0.521
Cut 1	-1.660*	0.918	-4.165***	-1.600
Cut 2	-0.862	0.905	-3.360**	-1.588
Cut 3	0.692	0.901	-1.79	-1.577
Cut 4	1.915**	0.906	-0.559	-1.575
Observations	434		434	
Log-likelihood	-486.17		-468.42	
Maximum likelihood R^2	0.141		0.156	
BIC	1001.68		985.10	

Source: Authors' calculations based on McCann and Jones-Correa 2012.
*$p < .1$; **$p < .05$; ***$p < .01$

though access to Spanish-language television can vary by geography, access is less of an issue today with Univision and Telemundo covering more than two hundred media markets (Medina Vidal 2012). As with the first set of models for nonelectoral participation, we also include the respondents' immigration policy preference, higher values representing support for a path to citizenship for the undocumented. All other additional controls used in the first set of models are also included.

The results for our 2012 vote interest model are shown in table 2. As in the base model, neither attention to politics nor Spanish dominant seem to predict a higher interest in voting by themselves. Political interest does continue to show a significant and positive relationship, as in the first set of models, as we should expect. We also continue to see a mobilizing effect from those who support immigration reform with a path to citizenship, being more likely to express interest in voting. However,

election sample about Spanish-language news did not measure how closely respondents followed news about politics on television, but rather was a question about how often they rely on Spanish- rather than English-language media. We feel our interaction item much more accurately captures exposure to Spanish TV political news.

once we include our interaction term to assess the actual effect of Spanish-language TV news attention we find several significant relationships. First, the direct effects of exposure to political news and speaking only Spanish are both negatively related to interest in voting. However, these direct effects are typically interpreted as the absence of the interacted item. For example, in the Spanish-language TV news model we see that paying attention to news when Spanish at home is not present holds a negative relationship. This means that English-speaking households that watch a great deal of television news are demobilized. Further, speaking Spanish mostly at home is also negative on its own, when attention to television news is not present, suggesting that Spanish-dominant households not watching Univision or Telemundo are not being mobilized. Consistent with research by Subervi-Vélez (2008), it is only the confluence of attention to TV political news in Spanish-dominant households that produces heightened interest in voting—what we call the Jorge Ramos effect.[5]

Although not all immigrants are eligible to vote, anyone can get involved by volunteering for a campaign, helping canvass door-to-door and get out the vote, or affiliating with a candidate by wearing a campaign button or attending a campaign rally. Because it mirrors the ANES, the LINES asked its sample of Latino immigrants if they participated in any of these campaign-specific activities. These are typically reserved for only die-hard political activists, but the LINES dataset reveals that 25 percent of Latino immigrants participated in one or more campaign acts. Participation among naturalized U.S. citizens was slightly higher (28 percent), but nearly one in five noncitizen immigrants (19 percent) took part in a campaign, consistent with the Barreto and Muñoz findings (2003). Thus, in our third set of models, we examine a four-item index of campaign activity,[6] and once again look toward the effect of Spanish TV news as a possible source of mobilization.

Table 3 presents the results of our regression predicting participation in campaign activity. High levels of political interest continue to motivate participation; however, independent of political interest, immigrants who are Spanish dominant and pay serious attention to political news on television are significantly more likely to become involved in campaign activity. As in the earlier findings, Spanish-dominant immigrants not watching a great deal of TV news are statistically less likely to become involved in campaign activity; however, the interaction term reveals that Spanish-language political news clearly mobilized Latino immigrants in 2012. The Jorge Ramos effect was present not only in heightened interest in voting but also in directly engaging with campaigns—an empirical finding consistent with the theory Subervi-Vélez (2008) established about the political engagement fostered by Spanish-language media.

We also find support for immigrant identity and campaign activity, the variable linked fate showing a positive and significant relationship with participation in the interaction model.

Interpreting the Size of the Effects

The substantive effects of immigrant identity and Spanish-language news media are best illustrated in the form of predicted probabilities. Figure 1 portrays the predicted number of acts a Latino immigrant will engage in from our nonelectoral participation scale. The x-axis represents degree of political interest and two

---

5. Although we cannot specifically isolate Univision news anchor Jorge Ramos in these data (no question was asked about which show respondents watched), Ramos has the highest ratings of any nightly news anchor in America—in English or Spanish. Univision reaches 96 percent of Hispanic households and has a 72 percent unduplicated audience, which means that 72 percent of their viewers are not reached by any other network. Between Univision and Telemundo, Univision carries a 3-to-1 advantage in viewers. Further, Ramos has 1.3 million Twitter followers, against 346K for Ilia Calderon (Univision), 336K for Maria Elena Salinas (Univision), and 134K for José Diaz-Balart (Telemundo). Thus, we are fairly confident in calling Ramos a leading voice in Spanish-language TV news.

6. The campaign activities were as follows: asked others to vote for or against a candidate, attended a campaign rally or event, wore a campaign button or posted a yard sign, and volunteered directly for a campaign.

Table 3. Predictors of Campaign Activity During 2012 Election Among Latino Immigrants

	Base Model		Spanish TV Model	
	Coef	SE	Coef	SE
Political interest	0.213**	0.078	0.209***	0.069
Attention to political news	0.199	0.117	-0.532	0.399
Spanish at home	-0.213*	0.105	-0.801**	0.332
Spanish X political news			0.179*	0.083
Path to citizenship	0.060	0.145	0.054	0.140
Linked fate	0.094	0.072	0.103*	0.052
Naturalized	-0.178	0.243	-0.196	0.233
Mexican	-0.719***	0.226	-0.704***	0.219
High school graduate	0.609*	0.279	0.591**	0.268
Some college or more	0.218	0.275	0.210	0.264
Age eighteen to thirty-four	-0.127	0.317	-0.165	0.307
Age thirty-five to forty-four	-0.090	0.283	-0.141	0.274
Age forty-five to fifty-four	-0.111	0.274	-0.138	0.264
Income $20K to $40K	-0.199	0.250	-0.167	0.241
Income $40K and higher	-0.272	0.342	-0.164	0.333
Missing income	-0.130	0.291	-0.128	0.281
Female	-0.219	0.201	-0.225	0.194
Percentage of life in United States	0.551	0.521	0.529	0.502
Cut 1	0.919	0.907	-1.560	1.570
Cut 2	3.327	0.921	0.851	1.574
Cut 3	4.413	0.944	1.938	1.585
Observations	449		449	
Log-likelihood	-399.62		-331.13	
Maximum likelihood R^2	0.178		0.191	
BIC	917.96		986.91	

Source: Authors' calculations based on McCann and Jones-Correa 2012.
*p < .1; **p < .05; ***p < .01

lines are plotted for immigrants who say they have no sense of linked fate (blue, dashed line, light blue confidence band in background) and for immigrants who say they have a high degree of linked fate with other immigrants (red, solid line, light red confidence band in background). Latino immigrants with no sense of linked fate demonstrate only a modest and nonsignificant increase in political participation across values of political interest, from an estimated 1.02 acts to 1.65. However, among Latino immigrants with a strong sense of linked fate, increased political interest is strongly associated with increased political engagement. In fact, those with linked fate and political interest are estimated to take part in 3.08 acts, more than three times the rate of those who have no sense of linked fate (at 0.81 acts). The combination of a linked fate identity and heightened political interest create the politicized immigrant identity we hypothesized and result in very high levels of political engagement among Latino immigrants in 2012. These results support and reinforce the research of Huddy and her colleagues in this issue, who find in-group identity to be positively associated with political participation among Latino immigrants.

In figure 2, we explore how exposure to Spanish-language TV news is associated with higher levels of interest in voting. Here, the x-axis represents how closely respondents followed television news coverage of politics and the election, and the two lines depict English-

Figure 1. Predicted Political Acts

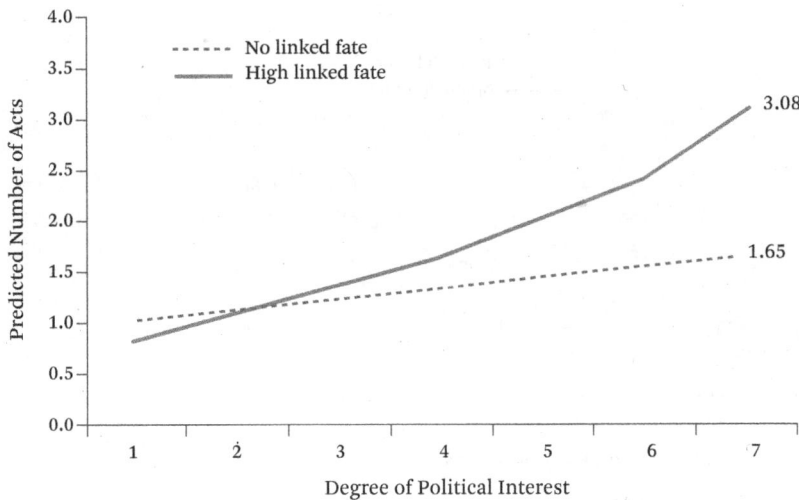

Source: Author's calculations based on McCann and Jones-Correa 2012.

Figure 2. Predicted Vote Interest

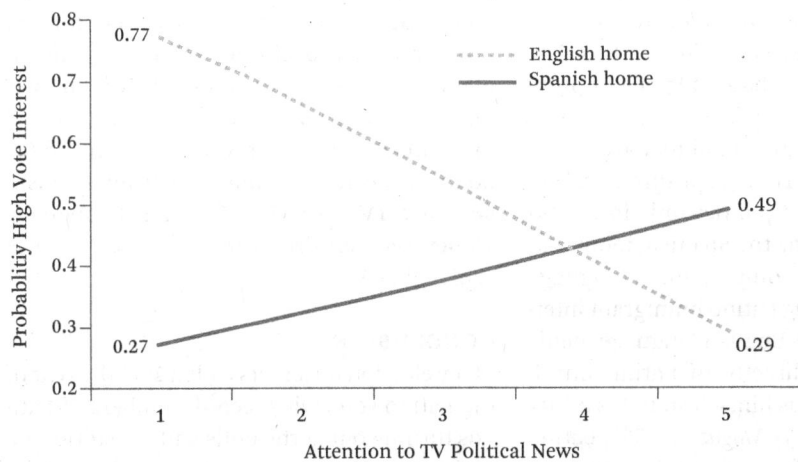

Source: Author's calculations based on McCann and Jones-Correa 2012.

dominant (orange, dashed line) and Spanish-dominant (purple, solid line) respondents. For English-dominant immigrants, increased attention to TV news actually decreased interest in voting in 2012 by almost 50 percentage points. This could be the result of a mostly negative news environment about politics and the lack of any empowering messages for immigrants. As Spanish-language journalist Pilar Marrero said, "Those communities are pretty much invisible in other media or they are covered only from the point of view of the 'other'" In contrast, Spanish-dominant immigrants who paid close attention to political news on television had a statistically significant increase in reporting the highest level of interest in voting. This finding is consistent with the *New York Times* account of Spanish-language television in 2012: "In countless households, Latinos tuned their television sets to Univision and heard Jorge Ramos, the host of *Al Punto*, the Spanish version of *Meet the Press*, discuss

Figure 3. Predicted Campaign Acts

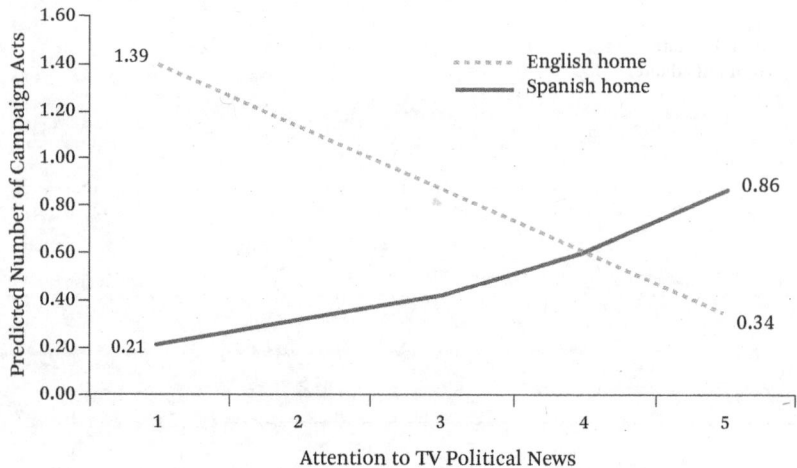

Source: Author's calculations based on McCann and Jones-Correa 2012.

the candidates' positions on issues critical to them." Comparing respondents who said they were paying very close attention to TV news about politics and the election in 2012, Spanish-dominant respondents had a 49 percent probability of being extremely interested in voting; English-dominant were 20 points lower, at 29 percent probability. Thus, exposure to television news coverage of politics only increased voting intensity among the Spanish dominant, presumably because only Spanish-language media was stimulating Latino immigrant interest in voting, whereas English-language media was not speaking directly to Latino immigrants. As Jorge Ramos himself stated in a 2014 interview with *New York Magazine*, "The Latino community expects from us much more than just news. They expect from us leadership. And they expect from us somehow to represent them" (Cherlin 2014).

Finally, we see the same effect for participation in campaign activity in figure 3. The gap in campaign involvement between English-dominant (dashed line) and Spanish-dominant (solid line) immigrants is large when attention to political news is not considered. English-dominant and fully bilingual immigrants have, potentially, many more opportunities to get involved and participate in campaigns. Campaigns are presumably less likely to reach out and try to include the least acculturated, Spanish-dominant immigrants. However, once we incorporate attention to TV news into the model, this trend reverses. Spanish-dominant immigrants who closely followed political news on television were more likely than their English-dominant counterparts to get involved in campaigns, growing from an estimated 0.2 political acts to 0.86 political acts for Spanish-language TV news viewers. English-language TV news viewers dropped from 1.39 acts to 0.34 acts (figure 3).

CONCLUSION

Many election observers called 2012 the year of the Latino vote, with record numbers of Latinos turning out at the polls and a historic vote in favor of Obama. However, a closer read indicates that it may have been the election year of the Latino immigrant. Immigration was front and center as a campaign issue from the Republican primary debates that pushed the candidates further to the Right to embrace anti-immigrant positions, to the executive order issued by Obama in June 2012 offering relief from deportation to nearly one million DREAMers. We argue that Latino immigrants found themselves constantly referencing their immigrant identity during the 2012 election cycle, and that this became a way of psychological engagement and political mobilization. This was further reinforced by the Jorge Ramos effect, whereby Spanish-language media played an important role in engaging, informing, and mobilizing Latinos in 2012. Leading journalists such as Ramos, Maria Elena Salinas, Pilar Marrero and more highlighted what was at stake for immigrant communities in 2012. Their reporting on immigration issues was relentless and offered a perspective to Latino immigrants that was missing in English media. The result was a Latino immigrant community that was highly informed and highly engaged in the 2012 election. Not only was interest in voting high, but our analysis also demonstrates high levels of nonelectoral participation, such as attending a protest or writing a letter to an elected official. In addition, we find heightened levels of participation in campaigns, especially among those who closely followed Spanish-language political news.

The LINES dataset provides an opportunity to test many of our deeply held notions about political participation among an immigrant community that is largely absent in the ANES. Among Latinos, the 2012 ANES face-to-face component offers only 125 foreign-born respondents, all of whom are U.S. citizens and eligible to vote, as per ANES sample frame standards. In contrast, the LINES contains a total of 1,304 interviews with Latino immigrants, about 40 percent of whom are naturalized citizens. Thus the data allow us to test and extend our analyses of political participation to Latino immigrants living in the United States, citizens and noncitizens alike, and the data reveal an actively engaged Latino immigrant community in America. As the Latino immigrant population continues its path of incorporation in America, these findings suggest a politically aware immigrant community poised to participate fully in the politics of the nation.

REFERENCES

Alvarez, Lizette. 2012. "For Latino Groups, Grass-Roots Efforts Paid Off in Higher Number of Voters." *New York Times*, November 27, 2012. Accessed January 26, 2016. http://www.nytimes.com/2012/11/28/us/politics/for-latino-groups-grass-roots-efforts-paid-off-in-higher-number-of-voters.html.

Barreto, Matt A., and Loren Collingwood. 2015. "Group-Based Appeals and the Latino Vote in 2012: How Immigration Became a Mobilizing Issue." *Electoral Studies* 40 (December): 490–99.

Barreto, Matt, Victoria DeFrancesco, and Jennifer Merolla. 2011. "Multiple Dimensions of Mobilization: The Impact of Direct Contact and Political Ads on Latino Turnout in the 2000 Presidential Election." *Journal of Political Marketing* 10(4): 303–27.

Barreto, Matt, and Sergio I Garcia-Rios. 2012. "El poder del voto latino en Estados Unidos en 2012." *Foreign Affairs* 12(4): 16–19.

Barreto, Matt, Sylvia Manzano, Ricardo Ramírez and Kathy Rim. 2009. "Immigrant Social Movement Participation: Understanding Involvement in the 2006 Immigration Protest Rallies." *Urban Affairs Review* 44(5): 736–64.

Barreto, Matt A., and José Muñoz. 2003. "Reexamining the 'Politics of In-Between': Political Participation Among Mexican Immigrants in the United States." *Hispanic Journal of Behavioral Sciences* 25 (November): 427–47.

Barreto, Matt, Ricardo Ramírez, Luis Fraga, and Fernando Guerra. 2009. "Why California Matters: How California Latinos Influence the Presidential Election." In *The Latino Vote in the 2004 Presidential Election*, edited by Rodolfo de la Garza, Louis DeSipio, and David Leal. South Bend, Ind.: University of Notre Dame Press.

Barreto, Matt, Ricardo Ramírez, and Nathan Woods. 2005. "Are Naturalized Voters Driving the California Latino Electorate? Measuring the Impact of IRCA Citizens on Latino Voting." *Social Science Quarterly* 86(4): 792–811.

Bass, Loretta, and Lynne Casper. 2001. "Differences in Registering and Voting Between Native-Born and Naturalized Americans." *Population Research and Policy Review* 20(6): 483–511.

Bishin, Benjamin G., and Casey Klofstad. 2012. "The Political Incorporation of Cuban Americans: Why Won't Little Havana Turn Blue?" *Political Research Quarterly* 65(3): 586–99.

Campbell, Angus, Philip Converse, Warren Miller, and Donald Stokes. 1960. *The American Voter*. New York: John Wiley & Sons.

Cassel, Carol A. 2002. "Hispanic Turnout: Estimates from Validated Voting Data." *Political Research Quarterly* 55(2): 391–408.

Cherlin, Reid. 2014. "Talking TV Ratings, Immigration, and Salsa Sales with Univision Anchor Jorge Ramos." *New York Magazine*, May 3, 2014. Accessed January 28, 2016. http://nymag.com

/daily/intelligencer/2014/05/jorge-ramos-on-ratings-and-immigration.html.

Collingwood, Loren, Matt Barreto, and Sergio Garcia-Rios. 2014. "Revisiting Latino Voting: Cross-Racial Mobilization in the 2012 Election." *Political Research Quarterly* 67(3): 632–45.

DeFrancesco Soto, Victoria. 2012. "Anti-Immigrant Rhetoric Is Anti-Latino." *The Nation*, February 24, 2012.

DeSipio, Louis. 1998. *Counting on the Latino Vote: Latinos as a New Electorate*. Charlottesville: University of Virginia Press.

DeSipio, Louis, and Rodolfo O. de la Garza. 1992. "Making Them Us: The Political Incorporation of Culturally Distinct Immigrants and Non-Immigrant Minorities in the United States." In *Nations of Immigrants: Australia, the United States, and International Migration*, edited by Gary Freeman and James Jupp. Melbourne: Oxford University Press.

Dinan, Stephen. 2012. "Spanish Language Media 'Obsessed' on Immigration Issue." *Washington Times*, August 30, 2012. http://www.washingtontimes.com/news/2012/aug/30/spanish-language-media-obsessed-on-immigration-iss/.

Ethier, Kathleen A., and Kay Deaux. 1994. "Negotiating Social Identity When Contexts Change: Maintaining Identification and Responding to Threat." *Journal of Personality and Social Psychology* 67(2): 243–521.

Feddersen, Timothy J., and Wolfgang Pesendorfer. 1996. "The Swing Voter's Curse." *American Economic Review* 86(3): 408–24.

———. 1999. "Abstention in Elections with Asymmetric Information and Diverse Preferences." *American Political Science Review* 93(2): 381–98.

Foley, Elise. 2013. "Paul Broun: Republicans 'Getting Soft' on Immigration." *Huffington Post*, March 22, 2013. Accessed February 29, 2016. http://www.huffingtonpost.com/2013/03/22/paul-broun-republians-immigration_n_2932324.html.

Fox News Latino. 2011. "Rubio Tells GOP to Shift Tone on Immigration." November 15, 2011. Accessed January 28, 2016. http://latino.foxnews.com/latino/politics/2011/11/15/rubio-tells-gop-to-ease-up-on-immigration/.

Fraga, Luis Ricardo, and Ricardo Ramírez. 2004. "Demography and Political Influence: Disentangling the Latino Vote." *Harvard Journal of Hispanic Policy* 16: 69–96.

de la Garza, Rodolfo O. 1996. *Ethnic Ironies: Latino Politics in the 1992 Elections*. Boulder, Colo.: Westview Press.

de la Garza, Rodolfo O., Louis DeSipio, F. Chris Garcia, John Garcia, and Angelo Falcon. 1992. *Latino Voices: Mexican, Puerto Rican, and Cuban Perspectives on American Politics*. Boulder, Colo.: Westview Press.

de la Garza, Rodolfo O., Martha Menchaca, and Louis DeSipio, eds. 1994. *Barrio Ballots: Latino Politics in the 1990 Elections*. Boulder, Colo.: Westview Press.

Gerber, Alan S., and Donald P. Green 2000. "The Effects of Canvassing, Telephone Calls, and Direct Mail on Voter Turnout: A Field Experiment." *American Political Science Review* 94(3): 653–63.

Guerra, Fernando. 1992. "Conditions Not Met: California Elections and the Latino Community." In *From Rhetoric to Reality: Latino Politics in the 1988 Elections*, edited by Rodolfo O. de la Garza and Louis DeSipio. Boulder, Colo.: Westview Press.

Jones-Correa, Michael. 2001. "Institutional and Contextual Factors in Immigrant Naturalization and Voting." *Citizenship Studies* 5(1): 41–56.

Le, Van. 2013. "Steve King: Immigrants 'Came Here to Live in the Shadows'; We Have No Moral Calling to Resolve Immigration." *America's Voice*, July 10, 2013. Accessed February 29, 2016. http://americasvoice.org/blog/steve-king-immigrants-came-here-to-live-in-the-shadows-we-have-no-moral-calling-to-resolve-immigration/.

Lee, Taeku. 2008. "Race, Immigration and the Identity-to-Politics Link." *Annual Review of Political Science* 11: 457–78.

Masuoka, Natalie. 2006. "Together They Become One: Examining the Predictors of Panethnic Group Consciousness Among Asian Americans and Latinos." *Social Science Quarterly* 87(5): 993–1011.

McCann, James A., and Michael Jones-Correa. 2012. Latino Immigrant National Election Study, 2012. New York: Russell Sage Foundation, Carnegie Corporation of New York, Purdue University, and Cornell University.

Medina Vidal, D. Xavier. 2012. "*Voces del Capitolio*: Spanish Language Media in the Statehouse." Ph.D. diss., University of California, Riverside.

Merolla, Jennifer, Adrian Pantoja, Ivy Cargile, and Juana Mora. 2012. "From Coverage to Action: The Immigration Debate and Its Effects on Participation." *Political Research Quarterly* 66(2): 322–35.

Milkman, Ruth. 2011. "LA's Past, America's Future? The 2006 Immigrant Rights Protests and Their Antecedents." In *Rallying for Immigrant Rights: The Fight for Inclusion in 21st Century America*, edited by Kim Voss and Irene Bloemraad. Berkeley: University of California Press.

Mollenkopf, John, David Olson, and Tim Ross. 2001. "Immigrant Political Incorporation in New York and Los Angeles." In *Governing American Cities: Interethnic Coalitions, Competition, and Conflict*, edited by Michael Jones-Correa. New York: Russell Sage Foundation.

Pachon, Harry. 1991. "U.S. Citizenship and Latino Participation in California." In *Racial and Ethnic Politics in California*, edited by Byran O. Jackson and Michael B. Preston. Berkeley, Calif.: Institute of Governmental Studies Press.

Pantoja, Adrian, Ricardo Ramírez, and Gary M. Segura. 2001. "Citizens by Choice, Voters by Necessity: Patterns in Political Mobilization by Naturalized Latinos." *Political Research Quarterly* 54(4): 729–50.

Pedraza, Francisco I. 2014. "The Two-Way Street of Acculturation, Discrimination, and Latino Immigration Restrictionism." *Political Research Quarterly* 67(4): 889–904.

Ramírez, Ricardo. 2013. *Mobilizing Opportunities: The Evolving Latino Electorate and the Future of American Politics*. Charlottesville: University of Virginia Press.

Rosenstone, Steven J., and John M. Hansen. 1993. *Mobilization, Participation, and Democracy in America*. New York: Macmillan Press.

Sanchez, Gabriel R. 2006. "The Role of Group Consciousness in Latino Public Opinion." *Political Research Quarterly* 59(3): 435–46.

Shaw, Daron, Rodolfo O. de la Garza, and Jongho Lee. 2000. "Examining Latino Turnout in 1996: A Three-State, Validated Survey Approach (California, Florida, Texas)." *American Journal of Political Science* 44(2): 338–46.

Simon, Bernd, Michael Lowery, Stefan Stürmer, Ulrike Weber, Peter Freytag, Corinna Habig, Claudia Kampmeier, and Peter Spahlinger. 1998. "Collective Identification and Social Movement Participation." *Journal of Personality and Social Psychology* 74(3): 646–58.

Staudt, Kathleen, and Sergio I. Garcia-Rios. 2011. "Economic Policy Matters: Incentives that Drive Mexicans Northward." In *Crossing and Controlling Borders—Immigration Policies and their Impact on Migrants' Journeys*, edited by Mechthild Baumann, Astrid Lorenz, and Kerstin Rosenow. Leverkusen, DE: Budrich UniPress.

Stevens, Daniel, and Benjamin G. Bishin. 2011. "Getting Out the Vote: Minority Mobilization in a Presidential Election." *Political Behavior* 33(3): 113–38.

Stokes, Atiya Kai. 2003. "Latino Group Consciousness and Political Participation." *American Politics Research* 31(4): 361–78.

Subervi-Vélez, Federico A., ed. 2008. *The Mass Media and Latino Politics: Studies of U.S. Media Content, Campaign Strategies and Survey Research: 1984–2004*. New York: Routledge.

Subervi-Vélez, Federico A., and Xavier Medina Vidal. 2015. "Latino Politics and the Media." *Oxford Bibliographies*, March 30, 2015.

Suro, Roberto. 1994. *Remembering the American Dream: Hispanic Immigration and National Policy*. New York: Twentieth Century Fund Press.

Tajfel, Henri E. 1978. *Differentiation Between Social Groups: Studies in the Social Psychology of Intergroup Relations*. Oxford: Oxford University Press.

Tajfel, Henri E., and John C. Turner. 1979. "An Integrative Theory of Intergroup Conflict." In *The Social Psychology of Intergroup Relations*, edited by William G. Austin and Stephen Worchel. Monterey, Calif.: Brooks-Cole.

Tajfel, Henri E., and A. L. Wilkes. 1963. "Classification and Quantitative Judgement." *British Journal of Psychology* 54(2): 101–14.

Tam Cho, Wendy K. 1999. "Naturalization, Socialization, Participation: Immigrants and (Non-)Voting." *Journal of Politics* 61(4): 1140–55.

Turner, John C. 1975. "Social Comparison and Social Identity: Some Prospects for Intergroup Behaviour." *European Journal of Social Psychology* 5(1): 5–34.

Ullah, Philip. 1987. "Self-Definition and Psychological Group Formation in an Ethnic Minority." *British Journal of Social Psychology* 26(1): 17–23.

USA Today. 2011. "Editorial: Immigration Rhetoric Disconnected From Reality." *USA Today* Editorial Board, September 26, 2011. Accessed January 28, 2016. http://usatoday30.usatoday.com/news/opinion/editorials/story/2011-09-26/illegal-immigration-GOP-debate/50560658/1.

Verba, Sidney, and Norman Nie. 1972. *Participation in America: Political Democracy and Social Equality*. New York: Harper and Row.

Voss, Kim, and Irene Bloemraad. 2011. *Rallying for Immigrant Rights: The Fight for Inclusion in 21st*

Century America. Berkeley: University of California Press.

Wolfinger, Raymond E., and Steven J. Rosenstone. 1980. *Who Votes?* New Haven, Conn.: Yale University Press.

Zepeda-Millán, Chris. 2014. "Weapons of the (Not So) Weak: Imigrant Mass Mobilization in the U.S. South." *Critical Sociology*, May 27, 2014. doi: 10.1177/0896920514527846.

Zepeda-Millán, Chris, and Sophia J. Wallace. 2013. "Racialization in Times of Contention: How Social Movements Influence Latino Racial Identity." *Politics, Groups, and Identities* 1(4): 510–27.

PART II
The Social Dimensions of Political Engagement

A Different Hue of the Gender Gap: Latino Immigrants and Political Conservatism in the United States

KATHARINE M. DONATO AND SAMANTHA L. PEREZ

Using the 2012 Latino Immigrant National Election Study, we investigate gender differences in the liberal-conservative identification of Latino immigrants. We assess differences between Latino immigrant men and women in ideological ratings and consider two explanations for a different hue of the gender gap in political ideology. One emphasizes women's greater social conservatism compared with men; the second considers whether and how gender differences in political ideology shift with longer U.S. residence. We find that Latinas are more politically conservative than Latinos, net of other factors, and that relationships between different social issue predictors, or length of U.S. residence, and liberal-conservative self-identification are gendered.

Keywords: gender, political conservatism, Latino immigrants

In recent history, gender gaps in U.S. politics have become commonplace. Although not viewed as a politically salient characteristic for much of the twentieth century, gender is now treated by political pundits, media analysts, and scholars alike as a key attribute that differentiates political attitudes and voting behavior. Generally speaking, compared with men, women are more likely to vote, support Democratic candidates, and hold different views on domestic and foreign issues. As a result, since the 1980s, many studies have examined the extent and determinants of the gender gap in the United States and other industrialized nations (see Verba, Burns, and Schlozman 1997; Kaufmann and Petrocik 1999; Inglehart and Norris 2000; Arceneaux 2001; Kaufmann 2002, 2006; Paxton, Kunovich, and Hughes 2007; Clark and Clark 2008).

Although prior studies have suggested a number of explanations for these gender differences, large-scale and sustained growth in the immigrant population may complicate such explanations in the United States. Not only have immigrants increased in their share of the U.S. population since 1960, from approximately 5 to 13 percent in 2012, the foreign-born population has grown by 31 percent, from thirty-one to forty-one million, since 2000. Alongside this trend is growth in the Hispanic-Latino population. In 2010, 16 percent (50.5 million) of the U.S. population was of Hispanic

---

Katharine M. Donato is professor of sociology at Vanderbilt University. **Samantha L. Perez** is a doctoral student in sociology at Vanderbilt University.

We are grateful to the Russell Sage Foundation (RSF) for its support of this project, and to participants attending the RSF Conference on the Latino Immigrant National Election Study in May 2014 for their thoughtful comments. In addition, we appreciate the generous support received from Vanderbilt University's College of Arts and Science. Direct correspondence to: Katharine M. Donato at katharine.donato@vanderbilt.edu, Vanderbilt University, Department of Sociology, PMB 351811, Nashville, TN 37235; and Samantha L. Perez at samantha.l.perez@vanderbilt.edu, Vanderbilt University, Department of Sociology, PMB 351811, Nashville, TN 37235.

or Latino origin, up from 13 percent (35.3 million) in 2000 (U.S. Census Bureau 2011). These changes have occurred during a period of gender-balanced U.S. immigration, although immigrant gender composition varies substantially by national origin (Donato et al. 2011; Donato and Gabaccia 2015).

In this paper, we focus on Latino U.S. immigrants and examine the relationship between gender and political ideology. Using the 2012 Latino Immigrant National Election Study (LINES), a new dataset about Latino immigrant political behavior and participation, we investigate gender differences in the liberal-conservative identification of Latino immigrants. We carefully assess differences between Latino immigrant men and women in ideological ratings and consider two possible explanations for a different hue of the gender gap in political ideology. One explanation emphasizes women's greater moral conservatism. The second considers whether and how gender differences in political ideology shift with longer U.S. residence. As a whole, our analysis is part of a growing body of scholarship aimed at understanding how the Latino gender gap in U.S. politics varies across race, ethnicity, and nativity (Conway 2008; Bejarano, Manzano, and Montoya 2011; Bejarano 2013).

LITERATURE REVIEW

This section reviews studies on the gender gap in U.S. politics and focuses on those that examine the Latino gender gap and its determinants. We begin by presenting relevant findings from the Pew Hispanic's 2011 National Survey of Latinos (NSL). Paul Taylor and his colleagues (2012) report that Latinos nationwide have more liberal political views than the U.S. general population, but that Latinos hold more conservative beliefs on some social issues, such as abortion and homosexuality. Nativity further nuances these findings, with foreign-born Hispanics more likely than their U.S.-born counterparts to describe their views as conservative (35 versus 28 percent, respectively), and with U.S.-born Hispanics more likely than the foreign born to report being liberal or very liberal (34 versus 27 percent, respectively). Although this report published no gender differences, other work describes Latina immigrant women as being more politically conservative than their male counterparts (Bejarano 2013). As we see in the following section, this is a different hue of the gender gap and contrasts with the modern gender gap that Cal Clark and Janet Clark (2008) and others describe.

Gender Gap in Political Behavior and Ideology

Although gender was not viewed as central to understanding political behavior early in the twentieth century, political scientists began to reevaluate women's role in politics in the 1980s (Tolleson-Rinehart 1992). A robust literature examines the gender gap in political beliefs, voting behavior, and partisanship toward different policy issues in the United States and elsewhere (see Verba, Burns, and Schlozman 1997; Kaufman and Petrocik 1999; Inglehart and Norris 2000; Arceneaux 2001; Kaufman 2002, 2006; Paxton, Kunovich, and Hughes 2007; Clark and Clark 2008). In the United States, a significant gender gap in voting first appeared in the 1980 presidential election, with more women than men favoring the Democratic presidential candidate Jimmy Carter (CAWP 2012). Since then, gender differences in voting and other political behavior have "become a permanent part of the American political landscape" (Clark and Clark 2008, 3). Compared with men, women are more likely to vote, support Democratic candidates, and hold liberal views on policy issues.

A number of factors explain the gender gap in U.S. politics. One is related to modernization. As national economies modernize and develop, women complete higher levels of education and increasingly participate in the formal sector of the economy. These changes accompany cultural shifts about gender, which are associated with a rise in feminism, and together they have political consequences that include, in some nations, a gender gap in political behavior and attitudes (Manza and Brooks 1998; Inglehart and Norris 2003; Paxton, Kunovich, and Hughes 2007). For example, in the United States, rising numbers of women in the workforce led to a "cumulative net shift among women" supporting Democratic presidential candidates (Manza and Brooks 1998, 1259).

A gender gap in politics may also arise from shifts in men's behavior and attitudes rather than women's. For example, if men are increasingly identifying as politically conservative or shifting from being Democrats to Independents, or if they are less likely to turn out and vote in elections, these shifts may help explain the gender gap. In fact, a recent Pew Research Center (2012) study shows that although women are more likely than men to identify as Democrats, this gender gap has not shifted since 1990. What has changed in recent years is men's identification as Independents. Since 1990, men have increasingly identified as Independents and been more likely than women to do so.

Using data from the American National Election Studies (ANES), Barbara Norrander and Clyde Wilcox (2008) document that since 1972 men have become more conservative than women, and that among women ideological polarization is higher than in the past. Since the 1970s, ideological differences between working, middle-, and upper-class men have disappeared. However, during the same period, women with high levels of education have become more polarized from those with less education. Highly educated women are both more liberal and more numerous than their counterparts with less education. Interestingly, cultural conflicts between religious social conservatives and more educated secular liberals explain some of the ideological identity differences between women and men. Although women and men respond similarly to some cultural issues, women's ideological identity was more likely than men's to be based on attitudes about abortion, and men's identity was more likely based on class concerns, though this latter finding holds less now than in the past.

Latino Gender Gap

Susan Welch and Lee Sigelman (1992) were the first to examine Latino gender differences in political attitudes, using national data to compare them with blacks and whites. The authors found that Latinas were more ideologically liberal and more supportive of the Democratic party than men, but that the Latino gender gap was smaller than that for blacks and whites. Not long after, Lisa Montoya (1996) expanded on their work by examining the gender gap among Latino immigrants from Mexico, Puerto Rico, and Cuba. Using data from the 1989 Latino National Political Survey, she found relatively small differences between men and women in political ideology, party identification, and presidential voting.

Recent work by Christina Bejarano and by Bejarano, Sylvia Manzano, and Celeste Montoya (2013, 2011) focuses on the Latino gender gap in U.S. politics and considers how the gender gap varies by race and ethnicity and by immigrant generational status. Both studies use data from the 2006 Latino National Survey to examine generational differences in Latino political ideology. Findings are that, with longer U.S. residence, a gender gap emerges among immigrants in their propensity to maintain close ties with their origins. This finding is consistent with studies by Sherri Grasmuck and Patricia Pessar (1991), Pierrette Hondagneu-Sotelo (1994), and Cecilia Menjívar (2000), who report that Dominican, Mexican, and Central American women spouses preferred to remain in the United States, but their male husbands preferred to return to origin communities. Also important for our purposes is that men's and women's responses about political ideology differ across generations. Relative to foreign-born Latinos—that is, the first generation—those in subsequent generations are more likely to identify as politically liberal. Moreover, with respect to a gender gap in political ideology, although immigrant Latinas rated themselves as more conservative than immigrant Latinos, by the fourth generation Latinas shifted to the left of men and reported their political ideology as liberal.

Explaining the Latino Immigrant Gender Gap

Only a few studies interrogate the Latino gender gap in political behavior and attitudes (Bejarano, Manzano, and Montoya 2011; Bejarano 2013). This work focuses largely on generational differences, asking how Latinos and Latinas born outside of the United States differ from the U.S. born. As a result, it tells us little about explanations for the nontraditional gender gap, whereby Latina immigrants are more politically conservative than men, and specifically whether and under what conditions this form of the gender gap shifts such that Latinas become more liberal than Latinos. Therefore, in line with Bejarano's work, we begin by expecting that Latina immigrants will be more politically conservative than their Latino counterparts.

H_1: We expect that political ideology identification among Latino immigrants varies significantly by gender. Latina immigrants will be more politically conservative than men.

In our analysis here, we provide two possible explanations for this nontraditional gender gap in ideology among Latino immigrants. The first is about moral and social conservatism; it holds that women immigrants are more conservative than men on moral and social issues such as support for abortion or homosexuality. Presumably because of childhood socialization and adult experiences that are gendered along traditional and patriarchal lines, such differences in morally conservative views will help explain the gender gap in ideology. Therefore, we expect that effects for attitudes toward abortion, homosexuality, and other social issues depend on gender. Women's conservative attitudes will increase women's political conservatism, whereas men's attitudes will not. This leads to two hypotheses:

H_{2a}: We expect that attitudes toward abortion or homosexuality will significantly predict political conservatism net of gender and other variables.

H_{2b}: We expect that effects for attitudes toward abortion or homosexuality will be conditioned by gender.

The second explanation captures political assimilation that occurs over time, and assesses whether and how Latino immigrants shift their ideological positions with more time spent in the United States. This theory holds that the gender gap in ideology is related to a carryover of attitudes from immigrants' origin countries and length of U.S. residence. That political attitudes shift over time is an idea consistent with Zoltan Hajnal and Taeku Lee (2011), who document how partisanship among Latinos and Asian Americans changed with longer U.S. residence, but do not consider whether and how these assimilative effects are different for women than for men.

Grasmuck and Pessar (1991), Hondagneu-Sotelo (1994), and Menjívar (2000) describe strong gendered preferences among Latino immigrants to return to their countries of origin: with more time in the United States, Dominican, Mexican, and Central American women reported wanting to remain in the United States, whereas their husbands remained committed to eventually returning to their origin communities. Many of these women made economic contributions to their households, making traditional gender scripts more difficult to follow. In addition, compared with newly arrived Latina and Latino immigrants, Latinas with longer stays in the United States typically have greater access than men to schools and community organizations. These contacts may help socialize and teach immigrant women about political ideological identification and policy issues linked to being a Democrat versus a Republican, but in ways that are different from their male counterparts, whose understanding about what liberalism and conservatism mean may derive largely from connections to the workplace. Michael Jones-Correa (1998) shows that political socialization is gendered among Latino immigrants: the men in his sample oriented their politics toward their country of origin as women became involved in U.S. organizations. Thus, with more time in the United States, Latina immigrants may increasingly adopt U.S.-based political perspectives and, similar to U.S.-born women, become more liberal than men in ideological identification. Latino men, on the other hand, may become more conservative.

H_{3a}: We expect that length of U.S. residence will significantly predict political conservatism net of gender and other variables.

H_{3b}: We expect that effects for length of U.S. residence will be conditioned by gender.

Data and Methods

We examine whether and how gender differentiates Latino immigrants' political ideology and explanations for this variation. To do so, we use data from the 2012 Latino Immigrant National Election Study, a nationally representative pre- and postelection telephone survey of immigrants from Spanish-speaking Latin American countries. Although similar to the 2012 ANES and using many comparable measures, the LINES sample is composed of 1,304 foreign-born Latino adults. The majority are not citizens; as a result, approximately 95 percent of the sample completed their interview in Spanish.

The preelection sample has 855 respondents, and the postelection wave has 886 respondents. Of those surveyed postelection, 435 respondents participated in the preelection survey and 451 respondents were new, surveyed only after the election. Because some key variables for this analysis are available only in the postelection data collection, we restrict our analytic sample to the 886 postwave respondents.

Following Rebekah Young and David Johnson (2010), we use multiple imputation procedures to recover missing data on the independent and dependent variables. To do so, we first created a series of replicate datasets that assigned imputed values for missing values. We separately analyzed each imputed dataset, and then pooled the replicate datasets to generate a single set of mean parameter estimates. We therefore used the multiple imputation by chained equation approach, to generate ten replicates using a series of univariate regressions. To maximize the size of our analytic sample, we imputed values for the following variables: age; naturalization; years of education; income; year of U.S. arrival; marital status; country of birth; feelings toward abortion, gays and lesbians, and the police; perceived discrimination variables; and liberal-conservative ranking.[1] With multiple imputation, we recovered relevant values for the complete postelection sample (N=886).[2]

Dependent Variable

Our dependent variable is liberal-conservative ideological ranking; it is measured by asking respondents how they would describe themselves. Respondents answered with one of the seven response categories: 1 = extremely liberal, 2 = liberal, 3 = slightly liberal, 4 = moderate, 5 = slightly conservative, 6 = conservative, and 7 = extremely conservative. If respondents did not answer this question the first time it was asked, they were then asked what they would consider themselves if they had to choose between liberal and conservative.[3]

Although prior studies suggest that liberal-conservative self-identification has been a poor predictor of party identification and policy stances (see Campbell et al. 1960), recent work suggests that partisanship among U.S. voters is now more strongly related to liberal-conservative identification (Lewis-Beck et al.

---

1. Values of these original variables had the following share (percentage) missing: age, 10.5; naturalized, 32.9; years of education, 3.8; income, 20.2; year of U.S. arrival, 4.6; marital status, 3.9; country of birth, 32.5; feelings toward abortion, 4.1; feelings toward gays and lesbians, 42.6; feelings toward people on welfare, 38.3; feelings toward police, 34.4; discrimination against Hispanics, 34.5; discrimination against immigrants, 34.9; discrimination against blacks, 36.7; discrimination against gays and lesbians, 39.7; discrimination against women, 36.7; and liberal-conservative ranking, 38.8.

2. In a sensitivity test, we compared the results described with those from regression models using the original data without imputed dependent variable values and found comparable results (available from authors on request).

3. In Spanish, respondents were asked, "En estos dias, se escucha mucho hablar de liberales y conservadores. En donde se ubicaria usted? Se considera sumamente liberal, liberal, algo liberal, moderado o mitad de comino, algo conservador, conservador o sumamente conservador, o no ha pensado mucho al respecto?" If respondents selected moderate, don't know, or haven't thought much about it, they were then asked, "Si tuviera que elegir, se consideria liberal o conservador?"

2008; Bafumi and Shapiro 2009). Because of rising polarization among U.S. voters, self-reported ideological orientations and political partisanship are more overlapping than in the past. Yet, among immigrants, little is known about whether liberal-conservative self-reporting correlates with party identification or policy stances. Therefore, to help justify our use of liberal-conservative self-identification as a dependent variable, we examined its relationship to difference in support for Obama and Romney as presidential candidates in 2012. Net of controls, we find a robust negative relationship between liberal-conservative identification and the difference in support; the more conservative Latino immigrant respondents are, the smaller the difference in support for the two presidential candidates. Table A1 presents coefficients from these models.[4]

Independent Variables

In addition to gender (coded 1 = women, 0 = men), we focus on a set of variables that assess social conservatism. The first is respondents' feelings toward abortion. We recoded this into a series of dummy variables: always permitted = 1 if respondents reported that abortion should always be permitted and 0 = otherwise (reference category); permitted only after need = 1 if respondents felt that abortion should be permitted only after need was clearly established and 0 = otherwise; permitted if rape or incest = 1 if they believed that abortion should be permitted only in cases of rape, incest, or danger to the woman's life and 0 = otherwise; and abortion should never be permitted = 1 and 0 = otherwise. The second set of variables are feeling thermometers that measure favorability toward gays and lesbians, people on welfare, and the police, using a scale from 0 to 100, 0 indicating least favorable and 100 most favorable. For each variable, we collapsed responses into three dummy variables: less favorable where 1 = less than 40 and 0 = other; middle-of-the-road where 1 = 40 to 59 and 0 = other; and more favorable where 1 = 60 up through 100 and 0 = other. In the regressions, more favorable is the reference category.

The final group of indicators of social conservatism capture perceived discrimination toward Hispanics, immigrants, and—more generally—five different groups. For perceived discrimination against Hispanics and immigrants, we recoded responses into three categories: a lot or great deal, moderate or a little, and none. To measure overall perceived discrimination, we created a summary index that ranges from 0 to 5 and summed respondents' responses to questions about whether they perceive discrimination against Hispanics, immigrants, blacks, gays and lesbians, and women. We then recoded this summary index: if respondents perceived discrimination against four or five of these groups, we coded a dummy variable as 1 = a lot or great deal and 0 = other. If they perceived two or three, we coded a second dummy variable as 1 = moderate and 0 = other; if they perceived one or less, we coded a third dummy as 1 = little and 0 = other.

Finally, to assess an assimilation explanation for the gender gap in political ideology, we use a variable that captures years since arriving in the United States as an indicator of assimilation. This information is available in continuous years, and for the respondents in our sample, it ranges from less than one year up to seventy-four years. We recoded this information into a set of four dummy variables: zero to five years (the reference category); six to ten years; eleven to fifteen years; sixteen or more years.

Control Variables

We include a variety of control variables. Age is in continuous years, and marital status is a dummy variable where 1 = currently married, 0 = other. We recode education into a dummy variable where 1 = some college or greater and 0 = less than college. We enter income in its original ordinal form whereby 0 =< $20,000; 1

---

4. Although we do not examine whether differences in support vary between immigrants and U.S. natives, we expect less difference among Latino immigrants than for U.S. natives. This is because a sizable share is estimated to be in the United States without authorization (see Bean and Brown, this issue), thus unable to vote in presidential elections or predict when they may be able to do so in the future. Relatedly, immigrants may not have a sharp sense of what liberal or conservative means in the U.S. context, a point we return to in the discussion.

= $20 to $39,999; 2 = $40 to $59,999; and 3 = $60,000 or more. Being naturalized is also a dummy variable (1 = naturalized and 0 = not naturalized), and national origin is a set of dummy variables representing Mexican, Cuban, South American, Central American, and Dominican born.[5]

ANALYTIC STRATEGY

We begin by describing the extent to which gender differences in liberal-conservative ideological rankings exist within categories of key independent variables.[6] We then present ordinary least squares (OLS) regression models that examine whether and how gender affects ideological rankings (model 1), and how the gender effect shifts after controlling for other variables (model 2). To determine whether gender effects differ for those with strong versus weak opinions about abortion; more versus less favorable feelings about gays and lesbians, people on welfare, and the police; a lot versus little perceived discrimination toward Hispanics, immigrants, and overall; and for those with shorter versus longer U.S. residence, we introduce interaction terms between gender and these items (model 3). The interactions indicate whether indicators of social conservatism and assimilation vary significantly by gender net of relevant explanatory variables. Effects for attitudes toward abortion, feelings toward different groups, and perceived discrimination varying by gender is support for the social conservatism hypothesis. If the effect for length of U.S. residence varies by gender, this is support for our assimilation hypothesis.

RESULTS

Table 1 displays how liberal-conservative self-identification rankings vary by key independent variables for the total sample, men, and women. The first row describes baseline gender differences in political ideological rankings, ranging from one through seven. Consistent with prior studies, women were significantly more conservative than men (4.4 versus 4.1).

With respect to feelings about abortion, the only significant gender difference was for respondents who believed that abortion should be permitted only for rape or incest. Among these respondents, women were significantly more conservative than men (4.7 versus 4.3). Women whose feelings toward gays and lesbians were less favorable were significantly more conservative than men (4.9 versus 4.6, respectively). Regarding feelings about people on welfare and the local police, women were also more conservative than men. Women who had more favorable and middle-of-the-road feelings toward people on welfare were more conservative (4.4 versus 4.1 and 4.4. versus 4.0, respectively). Similarly, those who felt more favorably and those with middle-of-the-road feelings were also more conservative than men (4.5 versus 4.2 and 4.5 and 4.0, respectively).

Women were also more conservative among those who perceived moderate discrimination against Hispanics (4.7 versus 4.1), high or moderate levels of discrimination against immigrants (4.3 versus 4.1 and 4.6 versus 4.2, respectively), and a lot or a little discrimination overall (4.7 versus 4.1 and 4.7 versus 4.3, respectively). Finally, significant gender differences appear among those who have lived in the United States between eleven and fifteen years, and more than fifteen years. For both groups, women were more conservative (4.3 versus 3.8 and 4.5 versus 4.2, respectively).

Table 2 presents three OLS regression models that predict liberal-conservative ranking and include feelings toward abortion. Model 1 includes only the effect for gender, and its direction is consistent with the significant difference found in table 1. Women are significantly more conservative in political ideology than men. In addition, controlling for other variables, including those for feelings toward abortion, model 2 shows that, net of these effects, women are more conservative than men. Overall, we see that older respondents are more, and that those with at least some college are less, conservative. More income also increases conservatism rankings. Feelings toward abortion affect liberal-conservative self-

---

5. Table A2 presents more information about variable operationalization.

6. Table A3 presents statistics that describe gender differences in the variables used in this analysis.

Table 1. Average Self-Reported Liberal-Conservative Ranking

	Total	Men	Women
Average ranking on liberal-conservative scale (1–7)	4.3	4.1	4.4***
Moral conservatism: feelings toward			
Abortion			
Should always be permitted	3.8	3.8	3.9
Should be permitted after need is established	4.0	3.9	4.1
Should only be permitted for rape/incest	4.5	4.3	4.7**
Should never be permitted	4.5	4.5	4.5
Gays and lesbians			
More favorable (0–39)	3.9	3.8	4.0
Middle-of-the-road (40–59)	4.2	4.1	4.3
Less favorable (60–100)	4.8	4.6	4.9*
People on welfare			
More favorable (0–39)	4.3	4.1	4.4**
Middle-of-the-road (40–59)	4.3	4.0	4.4**
Less favorable (60–100)	4.4	4.5	4.3
Local police			
More favorable (0–39)	4.4	4.2	4.5**
Middle-of-the-road (40–59)	4.3	4.0	4.5**
Less favorable (60–100)	3.9	3.9	3.8
Moral conservatism: perceived discrimination			
Against Hispanics			
A lot/great deal	4.2	4.1	4.2
Moderate/a little	4.4	4.1	4.7***
None	4.7	4.8	4.6
Against immigrants			
A lot/great deal	4.2	4.1	4.3*
Moderate/a little	4.4	4.2	4.6**
None	4.6	4.5	4.7
Overall (0–5)			
A lot/great deal (4 or 5)	4.4	4.1	4.7***
Moderate (2 or 3)	4.3	4.2	4.3
Little (0 or 1)	4.5	4.3	4.7*
Assimilation: years in the United States			
0–5	4.2	3.9	4.4
6–10	4.0	4.0	3.9
11–15	4.0	3.8	4.3**
16+	4.4	4.2	4.5**
N	886	392	494

Source: Authors' compilation based on McCann and Jones-Correa 2012.
*$p < .1$; **$p < .05$; ***$p < .01$

identification in expected ways. Respondents with more restrictive views of abortion—that is, those who believe it should only be allowed for rape or incest or it should never be permitted—were significantly more politically conservative than those who had a more permissive stance.

Model 3 adds interactions between gender and feelings toward abortion. Results show that the interaction coefficients are not statis-

Table 2. Regression Models Predicting Self-Reported Liberal-Conservative Ranking (Feelings Toward Abortion)

	Model 1	Model 2	Model 3
Sociodemographic characteristics			
Female	0.331***	0.298***	0.325
	(.116)	(.113)	(.235)
Age		0.013**	0.012**
		(.005)	(.005)
Married		0.187	0.189
		(.118)	(.119)
Some college or more		−0.344**	−0.343**
		(.144)	(.144)
Income		0.120*	0.123*
		(.070)	(.070)
Naturalized		−0.122	−0.123
		(.137)	(.138)
Years in the United States (continuous)		0.007	0.008
		(.006)	(.006)
National origin (ref=Mexican)			
Cuban		0.034	0.043
		(.241)	(.243)
South American		0.159	0.162
		(.231)	(.230)
Central American		−0.047	−0.045
		(.175)	(.175)
Dominican		−0.041	−0.047
		(.284)	(.283)
Feelings toward abortion (ref=always be permitted)			
Should be permitted after need is established		0.155	0.166
		(.178)	(.247)
Should only be permitted for rape or incest		0.658***	0.631***
		(.149)	(.215)
Should never be permitted		0.735***	0.843***
		(.172)	(.267)
Interactions			
Female*need			−0.023
			(.352)
Female*only			0.055
			(.294)
Female*never			−0.189
			(.339)
Intercept	3.979***	2.760***	2.750***
	(.088)	(.262)	(.277)
N	886	886	886
R^2	0.012	0.095	0.096

Source: Authors' compilation based on McCann and Jones-Correa 2012.
*$p < .1$; **$p < .05$; ***$p < .01$

tically significant predictors of liberal-conservative ranking. However, in this model, the coefficients for feelings toward abortion represent the effects of these feelings among men. Therefore, male respondents with more restrictive views of abortion were significantly more conservative.

Table 3 presents two panels with selected coefficients from regression models predicting liberal-conservative ranking with six indicators of social conservatism. Panel A displays models that include feeling thermometers for gays and lesbians, people on welfare, and local police. Model 1 includes only the predictor for female and shows that women are more politically conservative than men. The two sets of models that follow show the effects for feelings toward one of the three groups, net of other factors, and effects for the interactions between gender and each of the feeling thermometer variables, respectively.

With respect to feelings about abortion, model 2a shows that net of these and other variables, the gender effect remains. In addition, respondents who had middle-of-the-road and less favorable feelings toward gays and lesbians were significantly more conservative. Model 2b adds interactions between gender and feelings toward gays and lesbians, and by doing so asks whether and how effects for support for gays and lesbians are conditioned by gender. Although we expected that Latina immigrants would be more conservative about supporting gays and lesbians than comparable Latinos, coefficients for the interaction terms are not significant. Instead, men with less favorable views of gays and lesbians are significantly more politically conservative (b = 0.735, $p < 0.01$). In addition, the effect for women with more favorable attitudes toward abortion, seen in the female coefficient (b = 0.352, $p < 0.10$), suggests that they are also more politically conservative. Thus, women are more conservative in political ideology than men, and some evidence indicates that effects for support of gays and lesbians on liberal-conservative self-identification varies somewhat by gender.

The next set of models includes feelings toward people on welfare. Once again, net of other factors, the effect for female remains, and those with less favorable views of people on welfare are more politically conservative. After adding interactions between gender and feelings toward people on welfare, we find that women with less favorable views of people on welfare are less (not more) conservative. Moreover, the significant female effect (b = 0.585, $p < 0.10$) suggests that women with more favorable feelings toward people on welfare self-report as more conservative. These findings contrast with the one finding for men: those with less favorable views of people on welfare are significantly more conservative.

The final set of models in panel A contains feelings toward local police. Model 4a shows that the gender effect remains, net of feelings toward local police, with women more conservative than men. Furthermore, similar to model 3b on the effects for women, model 4b suggests that liberal-conservative ranking is conditioned by gender and feelings toward local police. Women who hold less favorable views of local police are significantly less conservative (b = -0.702, $p < 0.10$), and those who hold more favorable views of the police are significantly more conservative. Therefore, findings from the three models that include feelings toward gays and lesbians, people on welfare, and local police suggest that women are sometimes more likely than men to be morally or socially conservative, but not in predictable ways.

Panel B shows coefficients from OLS regression models predicting liberal-conservative ranking, and includes variables for perceived discrimination against Hispanics, immigrants, and an overall summary measure of discrimination. Model 2a includes perceived discrimination against Hispanics and shows that women are more conservative than men, net of controls and key predictors. In addition, respondents who perceived some or little to no discrimination against Hispanics were significantly more conservative than those who perceived a great deal. In model 2b, we include interactions for gender and perceived discrimination against Hispanics but find that these are not statistically significant. Furthermore, we lose the effect for women who perceive a lot of discrimination (-0.105 is not significant). The model has only one gendered effect: it appears in the effect for none or little perceived

Table 3. Selected Coefficients Regression Models Predicting Self-Reported Liberal-Conservative Ranking: Six Indicators of Social Conservatism

Panel A	Model 1	Gays and Lesbians		People on Welfare		Local Police	
		Model 2a	Model 2b	Model 3a	Model 3b	Model 4a	Model 4b
Female	0.331***	0.361***	0.352*	0.367***	0.585*	0.356***	0.379***
	(.116)	(.113)	(.211)	(.116)	(.185)	(.115)	(.140)
Feelings toward: (ref= more favorable)							
Middle-of-the-road		0.276**	0.277	−0.031	0.083	−0.147	−0.239
		(.135)	(.210)	(.127)	(.194)	(.129)	(.188)
Less favorable		0.754***	0.735***	0.235	0.575***	−0.507	−0.171
		(.145)	(.219)	(.161)	(.230)	(.212)	(.316)
Interactions							
Female*middle-of-the-road		−0.002		−0.222		0.183	
		(.267)		(.251)		(.260)	
Female*less favorable		0.038		−0.768***		−0.702*	
		(.291)		(.322)		(.407)	
Intercept	3.979***	3.115***	3.119***	3.115***	3.077***	3.356***	3.322***
	(.088)	(.267)	(.293)	(.267)	(.296)	(.266)	(.275)
N	886	886	886	886	886	886	886
R^2	0.012	0.090	0.090	0.062	0.069	0.067	0.072

Panel B	Model 1	Discrimination Against Hispanics		Discrimination Against Immigrants		Discrimination Summary Index	
		Model 2a	Model 2b	Model 3a	Model 3b	Model 4a	Model 4b
Female	0.331***	0.387***	-0.105	0.384***	0.520	0.412***	0.172
	(.116)	(.116)	(.430)	(.115)	(.445)	(.116)	(.174)
Perceived discrimination (ref=a lot)							
Moderate/a little		0.234**	0.059	0.245**	0.178	0.278**	0.016
		(.119)	(.176)	(.122)	(.178)	(.127)	(.196)
None/little (overall)		0.543**	0.703*	0.252	0.159	0.416***	0.238
		(.240)	(.362)	(.250)	(.369)	(.157)	(.220)
Interactions							
Female*some discrimination			0.376		0.147		0.531**
			(.232)		(.237)		(.253)
Female*none/little discrimination			-0.353		0.197		0.369
			(.461)		(.471)		(.297)
Intercept	3.979***	3.138***	3.229***	3.171***	3.206***	3.071***	3.245***
	(.088)	(.268)	(.281)	(.263)	(.268)	(.267)	(.285)
N	886	886	886	886	886	886	886
R^2	0.012	0.066	0.071	0.063	0.064	0.069	0.075

Source: Authors' compilation based on McCann and Jones-Correa 2012.
Notes: Controls for age, marital status, level of education, income, citizenship, years in the United States, and whether respondent is Cuban, South American, Central American, or Dominican.
*$p < .1$; **$p < .05$; ***$p < .01$

Table 4. Selected Coefficients for Regression Models Predicting Liberal-Conservative Rank

	Model 1	Model 2	Model 3
Female	0.331***	0.354***	0.917*
	(.116)	(.116)	(.521)
Years in the United States (ref = 0–5 years)			
6–10		−0.258	0.291
		(.327)	(.440)
11–15		−0.145	−0.033
		(.296)	(.398)
16+		0.060	0.320
		(.282)	(.368)
Interactions			
Female*6–10			−1.213*
			(.649)
Female*11–15			−0.303
			(.578)
Female*16+			−0.599
			(.544)
Intercept	3.975***	3.391***	3.173***
	(.088)	(.342)	(.377)
N	886	886	886
R^2	0.012	0.061	0.069

Source: Authors' compilation based on McCann and Jones-Correa 2012.
Notes: Controls for age, marital status, level of education, income, citizenship, years in the United States, and whether respondent is Cuban, South American, Central American, or Dominican.
*p < .1; **p < .05; ***p < .01

discrimination, which is really the effect for men. Here it is significant, but only at the .10 level (b = 0.703).

The second set of models in panel B includes perceived discrimination against immigrants. Model 3a shows, again, that women are more conservative than men, controlling for characteristics including perceived discrimination against immigrants. In contrast, respondents who perceived moderate levels of discrimination were significantly more conservative than those who perceived a lot of discrimination. However, perceiving little discrimination against immigrants was not a significant predictor of liberal-conservative ranking, and model 3b describes no significant effects for interactions between gender and perceived discrimination.

Using a summary index to measure overall discrimination, the final set of models reveal that respondents who perceived at least some or little to no discrimination were more politically conservative. When we add interactions for gender and perceived discrimination (model 4b), the only gender effect we see is that women who perceive moderate levels of discrimination are more conservative. Thus, these models suggest that gender differences in perceived discrimination against individual groups do not predict liberal-conservative ranking, the exception being for women who perceive moderate levels of overall discrimination.

Table 4 presents another set of regression models predicting liberal-conservative rankings. To assess whether variation in political ideology is related to a gendered process of assimilation, we include several dummy variables for years of U.S. residence. The gender coefficient in this model is significant with and without controls. Interestingly, model 2 shows no significant effects for length of U.S. residence. Yet after entering gender*duration interaction terms, we see that effects for length of U.S. residence vary significantly by gender.

Figure 1. Predicted Liberal-Conservative Rankings

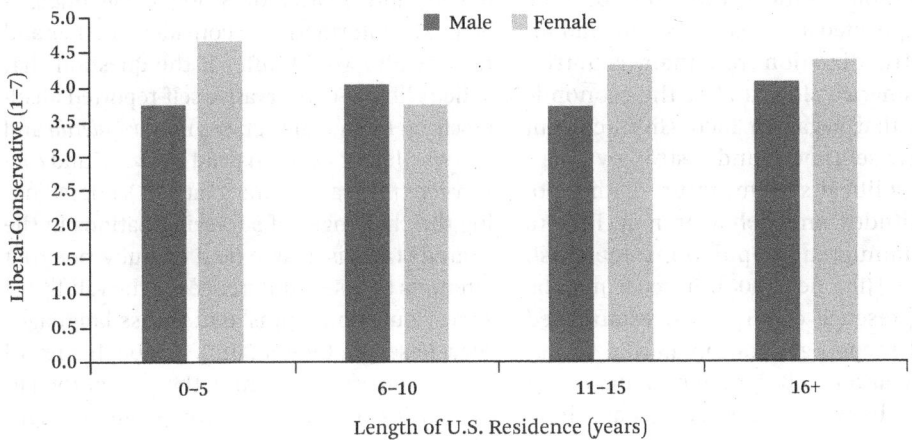

Source: Authors' compilation based on McCann and Jones-Correa 2012.
Note: Derived from table 4, model 3.

Women who have been residing in the United States for six to ten years are significantly less conservative (b = -1.213, $p < 0.10$). However, we also see a positive effect ($p < 0.10$) for being female, suggesting that newly arrived women (those with fewer than six years of U.S. residence) are more politically conservative (b = 0.917).

To better visualize these effects, we generated predicted ideological ratings in figure 1, which offers a visual representation of model 3 from table 4. Examining gender differences in the height of the bars within each duration category, we see that women who have been in the United States for longer are less conservative than when they first arrive, the largest drop corresponding to six to ten years of U.S. residence. In contrast, men with longer U.S. residence seem to become more conservative as the years go by, except the eleven to fifteen year span (where we see a slight dip). Our results, then, suggest a process of gendered political assimilation among Latino immigrants. Net of other factors, among recent arrivals, men are more liberal than women, but as the years living in the United States accumulate, this difference shifts and narrows.

DISCUSSION

In this paper, we find that Latino immigrants illustrate a different hue of the gender gap in political ideology: Latinas are more politically conservative than Latinos. This gender gap appears to be a consequence of both gendered differences in moral conservatism and gendered political assimilation. Thus, feelings toward abortion, gays and lesbians, people on welfare, and local police, as well as perceived discrimination, are related to liberal-conservative self-identification. Not only are immigrant women born in Latin American countries more politically conservative, this gap holds only for recently arrived immigrants. After living in the United States for at least five years, Latinas report themselves as more liberal, and after fifteen years, Latino men view themselves as more conservative. Thus, this analysis complicates our understanding about Latino political behavior and attitudes. It suggests that we have much more to learn before predicting where Latinos will ultimately fall on the political spectrum.

Although beyond the scope of this paper, this analysis raises a number of important questions for future research. First, to what extent do these findings hold for other race and ethnic groups in the United States? Second, if immigration is a rupture that substantially transforms the lives of both women and men and challenges traditional gender roles, then what other gendered political consequences might it have? Since the early 1990s and passage of restrictive immigration policies, antiterrorism legislation, and the welfare reform act, crossing the Mexico-U.S. border without authorization has become more complicated and costly (Donato and Armenta 2011). Migration from many countries in Latin America slowed after the economic downturn that began in 2006. Given current xenophobic sentiment and a strongly polarized U.S. political system, future Latino political attitudes and behavior may link to whether immigrant populations replenish themselves (Jiménez 2008). If so, it may be that the presence of large and established first- and second-generation Latino immigrant populations will tighten national-origin boundaries between Latino groups and have gendered consequences for political identity and behavior.

Our results also raise questions about the mechanisms that produce them. For example, why should the effects of length of residence depend on gender? Do women become more politically liberal over time because they primarily engage with schools, which are nonprofit institutions, while men become more conservative because they primarily engage with for-profit self-interested institutions? Although consistent with our results, we have no way to assess this because the data used in the analysis are cross-sectional and ill suited to address the task.

Finally, these findings suggest that future research must explicitly consider how liberal-conservative self-identification is complex, nuanced, and gendered. Along these lines, it would be informative to consider whether and how results would differ if the question that solicits liberal-conservative self-reported ideology from Latino immigrants used *izquierda* and *derecha* (left or right) instead of *liberal* and *conservador* (liberal or conservative). Understanding the challenges of surveying Latinos in the United States is a large field of study, one that attempts to assess differences in the validity of survey questions translated across languages (Pew Research Center 2015). Although a priori there is no reason to think that use of the latter indicator explains why women's self-identification differs from men, it is possible that immigrants may interpret conservative and liberal differently than natives.

Latino immigrant ideological self-identification is important because Latino immigrants and their offspring will represent a large segment of the future political landscape in the United States. Yet they are not a monolithic group. These immigrants hail from a diverse set of national origins (even if Mexicans currently outnumber all others), and they and their children represent different and, at times, overlapping interests. Exactly what these differences mean for the Latino electorate in the United States is not yet clear, but the results in this paper suggest they are likely to include salient gendered consequences.

APPENDIX

Table A1. Regression Models Predicting Difference in Presidential Candidate Ranking

	Model 1	Model 2
Sociodemographic characteristics		
Female	2.563	6.409
	(3.815)	(4.184)
Liberal-conservative ranking (1–7)	−3.535***	−4.431**
	(1.348)	(1.792)
Age		−0.342
		(.236)
Married		3.688
		(4.356)
Some college or more		0.373
		(6.004)
Income		−1.686
		(3.082)
Naturalized		−15.382***
		(5.917)
Years in the United States (continuous)		0.805***
		(.252)
National origin (ref=Mexican)		
Cuban		−18.314
		(13.597)
South American		−19.717*
		(11.508)
Central American		4.510
		(5.614)
Dominican		19.835**
		(9.794)
Interactions		
Female*liberal-conservative ranking		
Intercept	150.862***	156.527***
	(5.990)	(11.872)
N	435	435
R^2	0.016	0.11

Source: Authors' compilation based on McCann and Jones-Correa 2012.
*$p < .1$; **$p < .05$; ***$p < .01$

Table A2. Operationalization of Variables

Variables	Operationalization
A. Dependent variable	
Self-reported liberal-conservative ranking	Scale from 1–7, 1 = extremely liberal and 7 = extremely conservative
B. Independent variables	
Sociodemographic characteristics	
Female	Coded 1 for female, 0 otherwise
Age	Age at time of survey, from eighteen to ninety-five
Married	Coded 1 for married (spouse present or absent), 0 otherwise
Some college or more	Coded 1 for some college and BA/BS or great, 0 otherwise
Income	Coded 0 = <$20k, 1 = $20–39,999k, 2 = $40–59,999k, 3 =$60k+
Naturalized	Coded 1 for naturalized citizen, 0 otherwise
Years in the United States (continuous)	Time in the United States, calculated 2012 (year of survey) – year of arrival to United States
National origin (set of dummy variables)	
Mexican (reference)	Coded 1 if country of birth is Mexico, 0 otherwise
Cuban	Coded 1 if country of birth is Cuba, 0 otherwise
South American	Coded 1 if country of birth is Argentina, Bolivia, Chile, Colombia, Ecuador, Peru, Uruguay or Venezuela, 0 otherwise
Central American	Coded 1 if country of birth is Costa Rica, El Salvador, Guatemala, Honduras, or Nicaragua, 0 otherwise
Dominican	Coded 1 if country of birth is Dominican Republic, 0 otherwise
Feelings toward abortion (set of dummy variables)	
Should always be permitted (reference)	Coded 1 if respondent indicated that abortion should always be permitted, 0 otherwise
Should be permitted if need clearly established	Coded 1 if respondent indicated that abortion should be permitted if need is clearly established, 0 otherwise
Should only be permitted for cases of rape or incest	Coded 1 if respondent indicated that abortion should only be permitted for cases of rape/incest, 0 otherwise
Should never be permitted	Coded 1 if respondent indicated that abortion should never be permitted, 0 otherwise
Feelings toward gays and lesbians (set of dummy variables)	
More favorable (reference)	Coded 1 if respondent rated gays and lesbians between 60–100 on 100 pt scale, 0 otherwise
Middle-of-the-road	Coded 1 if respondent rated gays and lesbians between 40–59 on 100 pt scale, 0 otherwise
Less favorable	Coded 1 if respondent rated gays and lesbians between 0–39 on 100 pt scale, 0 otherwise
Feelings towards people on welfare (set of dummy variables)	
More favorable (reference)	Coded 1 if respondent rated people on welfare between 60–100 on 100 pt scale, 0 otherwise
Middle-of-the-road	Coded 1 if respondent rated people on welfare between 40–59 on 100 pt scale, 0 otherwise
Less favorable	Coded 1 if respondent rated people on welfare between 0–39 on 100 pt scale, 0 otherwise

Table A2. (cont.)

Variables	Operationalization
Feelings towards local police (set of dummy variables)	
More favorable (reference)	Coded 1 if respondent rated local police between 60–100 on 100 pt scale, 0 otherwise
Middle-of-the-road	Coded 1 if respondent rated local police between 40–59 on 100 pt scale, 0 otherwise
Less favorable	Coded 1 if respondent rated local police between 0–39 on 100 pt scale, 0 otherwise
Perceived discrimination against Hispanics	
A lot/great deal	Coded 1 if respondents perceived that level of discrimination against Hispanics was "a lot" or "a great deal"; 0 otherwise
Moderate/a little	Coded 1 if respondents perceived that level of discrimination against Hispanics was "a little" or "a moderate amount"; 0 otherwise
None	Coded 1 if respondents perceived that level of discrimination against Hispanics was "none at all"; 0 otherwise
Perceived discrimination against immigrants	
A lot/great deal	Coded 1 if respondents perceived that level of discrimination against immigrants was "a lot" or "a great deal"; 0 otherwise
Moderate/a little	Coded 1 if respondents perceived that level of discrimination against immigrants was "a little" or "a moderate amount"; 0 otherwise
None	Coded 1 if respondents perceived that level of discrimination against immigrants was "none at all"; 0 otherwise
Perceived overall discrimination	
A lot/great deal	Coded 1 if respondent perceived discrimination against 4 or 5 of the following 5 groups: blacks, gays and lesbians, Hispanics, immigrants, and women; 0 if otherwise
Moderate/a little	Coded 1 if respondent perceived discrimination against 2 or 3 of the following 5 groups: blacks, gays and lesbians, Hispanics, immigrants, and women; 0 if otherwise
Little	Coded 1 if respondent perceived discrimination against 0 or 1 of the following 5 groups: blacks, gays and lesbians, Hispanics, immigrants, and women; 0 if otherwise
Years in the United States (set of dummy variables)	
0–5 years	Coded 1 if 0–5 years, 0 otherwise
6–10 years	Coded 1 if 6–10 years, 0 otherwise
11–15 years	Coded 1 if 11–15 years, 0 otherwise
16+	Coded 1 if 16 or more, 0 otherwise

Source: Authors' compilation.

Table A3. Independent Variables

	Total	Men	Women
Sociodemographic characteristics			
Percent female	55.8		
Mean age	49.5	48.8	50.0
Percent married	61.1	66.8	56.5***
Percent some college or greater	19.6	20.4	19.0
Income			
Percent <$20k	50.1	41.8	56.7***
Percent $20–$39,999k	33.6	35.5	32.2
Percent $40–$59,999k	10.1	13.8	7.1***
Percent $60k+	6.2	8.9	4.1***
Naturalized citizen	41.2	42.1	40.5
Mean years in the United States	23.7	24.0	23.4
National origin			
Mexican	67.2	68.6	66.0
Cuban	7.1	5.4	8.5*
South American	6.9	7.7	6.3
Central American	13.5	14.0	13.2
Dominican	5.2	4.3	5.9
Moral conservatism: feelings toward			
Abortion			
Should always be permitted	20.0	21.7	18.6
Should be permitted after need is established	17.2	20.9	14.2***
Should only be permitted for rape or incest	37.3	35.5	38.7
Should never be permitted	25.6	21.9	28.5**
Gays and lesbians			
More favorable	30.1	29.9	30.4
Middle-of-the-road	40.9	41.1	40.7
Less favorable	29.0	29.1	29.0
People on welfare			
More favorable	43.9	43.4	44.3
Middle-of-the-road	38.0	37.5	38.5
Less favorable	18.1	19.1	17.2
Local police			
More favorable	67.4	69.9	65.4
Middle-of-the-road	23.4	21.7	24.7
Less favorable	9.3	8.4	9.9
Moral conservatism: perceived discrimination			
Against Hispanics			
A lot/great deal	52.8	45.7	58.5***
Moderate/a little	41.5	48.5	36.0***
None	5.6	5.9	5.5
Against immigrants			
A lot/great deal	59.5	52.8	64.8***
Moderate/a little	34.2	40.6	29.2***
None	6.3	6.6	6.1

Table A3. (*cont.*)

	Total	Men	Women
Overall (0–5)			
A lot/great deal (4 or 5)	48.4	41.3	54.1***
Moderate (2 or 3)	32.3	33.9	31.0
Little (0 or 1)	19.3	24.7	15.0***
Assimilation: years in the United States			
0–5	4.7	4.9	4.7
6–10	7.9	7.4	8.3
11–15	16.6	16.1	17.0
16+	70.8	71.7	70.0
N	886	392	494

Source: Authors' compilation based on McCann and Jones-Correa 2012.
*$p < .1$; **$p < .05$; ***$p < .01$

Table A4. Regression Models Predicting Ranking, Feeling Thermometers

		Gays and Lesbians		People on Welfare		Federal Government		Local Police	
	Model 1	Model 2a	Model 2b	Model 3a	Model 3b	Model 4a	Model 4b	Model 5a	Model 5b
Sociodemographic characteristics									
Female	0.331***	0.361***	0.352*	0.367***	0.585*	0.355***	0.354**	0.356***	0.379***
	(.116)	(.113)	(.211)	(.116)	(.185)	(.115)	(.139)	(.115)	(.140)
Age		0.009*	0.009*	0.014**	0.014*	0.014**	0.014**	0.014**	0.014**
		(.005)	(.005)	(.005)	(.005)	(.005)	(.006)	(.005)	(.005)
Married		0.193	0.194	0.199	0.196	0.203*	0.202*	0.159	0.165
		(.120)	(.120)	(.121)	(.121)	(.122)	(.122)	(.121)	(.120)
Some college or more		-0.429***	-0.428***	-0.460***	-0.478***	-0.470***	-0.470***	-0.489***	-0.490***
		(.146)	(.147)	(.150)	(.150)	(.151)	(.151)	(.150)	(.149)
Income		0.098	0.098	0.087	0.091	0.079	0.078	0.082	0.087
		(.071)	(.071)	(.072)	(.073)	(.073)	(.074)	(.072)	(.072)
Naturalized citizen		-0.101	-0.102	-0.109	-0.108	-0.103	-0.103	-0.097	-0.098
		(.139)	(.139)	(.141)	(.141)	(.141)	(.141)	(.141)	(.141)
Years in the United States (continuous)		0.005	0.005	0.005	0.005	0.005	0.005	0.005	0.005
		(.006)	(.006)	(.006)	(.006)	(.006)	(.006)	(.006)	(.006)
National origin (ref=Mexican)									
Cuban		0.015	0.015	-0.06	-0.07	-0.042	-0.041	-0.071	-0.082
		(.252)	(.252)	(.263)	(.260)	(.268)	(.269)	(.260)	(.256)
South American		0.139	0.137	0.149	0.126	0.178	0.182	0.186	0.139
		(.230)	(.230)	(.241)	(.237)	(.241)	(.241)	(.241)	(.244)
Central American		-0.073	-0.073	-0.061	-0.069	-0.065	-0.065	-0.076	-0.062
		(.177)	(.178)	(.178)	(.180)	(.179)	(.179)	(.177)	(.177)
Dominican		-0.07	-0.069	-0.083	-0.071	-0.068	-0.069	-0.103	-0.091
		(.284)	(.282)	(.294)	(.294)	(.290)	(.290)	(.288)	(.286)

Feelings toward: (ref=more favorable)							
Middle-of-the-road	0.276**	0.277	-0.031	0.083	0.146	0.154	-0.147	-0.239
	(.135)	(.210)	(.127)	(.194)	(.136)	(.206)	(.129)	(.188)
Less favorable	0.754***	0.735***	0.235	0.575***	-0.02	-0.059	-0.507	-0.171
	(.145)	(.219)	(.161)	(.230)	(.225)	(.324)	(.212)	(.316)
Interactions								
Female*middle-of-the-road		-0.002		-0.222		-0.017		0.183
		(.274)		(.251)		(.265)		(.260)
Female*less favorable		0.038		-0.768***		0.075		-0.702*
		(.291)		(.322)		(.435)		(.407)
Intercept	3.979***	3.115***	3.115***	3.119***	3.077***	3.206***	3.208***	3.356***	3.322***
	(.088)	(.267)	(.267)	(.293)	(.296)	(.263)	(.268)	(.266)	(.275)
N	886	886	886	886	886	886	886	886	886
R^2	0.012	0.090	0.090	0.062	0.069	0.060	0.060	0.067	0.072

Source: Authors' compilation based on McCann and Jones-Correa 2012.

*$p < .1$; **$p < .05$; ***$p < .01$

Table A5. Regression Models Predicting Ranking, Perception of Discrimination

	Against Hispanics			Against Immigrants		Overall	
	Model 1	Model 2a	Model 2b	Model 3a	Model 3b	Model 4a	Model 4b
Sociodemographic characteristics							
Female	0.331***	0.387***	-0.105	0.384***	0.520	0.412***	0.172
	(.116)	(.116)	(.430)	(.115)	(.445)	(.116)	(.174)
Age		0.013**	0.013**	0.013**	0.013**	0.013**	0.012**
		(.005)	(.005)	(.005)	(.005)	(.005)	(.005)
Married		0.170	0.166	0.171	0.169	0.162	0.154
		(.122)	(.122)	(.122)	(.123)	(.123)	(.122)
Some college or more		-0.455***	-0.465***	-0.469***	-0.469***	-0.460***	-0.476***
		(.149)	(.149)	(.148)	(.148)	(.147)	(.148)
Income		0.091	0.096	0.086	0.085	0.099	0.094
		(.073)	(.073)	(.072)	(.073)	(.072)	(.072)
Naturalized citizen		-0.119	-0.111	-0.095	-0.091	-0.103	-0.105
		(.141)	(.141)	(.141)	(.141)	(.140)	(.140)
Years in the United States (continuous)		0.006	0.006	0.005	0.005	0.006	0.006
		(.006)	(.006)	(.006)	(.006)	(.006)	(.006)
National origin (ref=Mexican)							
Cuban		-0.126	-0.073	-0.115	-0.119	-0.145	-0.136
		(.262)	(.265)	(.265)	(.265)	(.258)	(.258)
South American		0.112	0.143	0.114	0.117	0.075	0.073
		(.245)	(.243)	(.245)	(.243)	(.242)	(.236)
Central American		-0.055	-0.067	-0.044	-0.050	-0.014	-0.03
		(.178)	(.180)	(.177)	(.177)	(.176)	(.176)
Dominican		-0.072	-0.085	-0.065	-0.061	-0.05	-0.036
		(.287)	(.281)	(.284)	(.283)	(.276)	(.277)

	(1)	(2)	(3)	(4)	(5)	(6)
Perceived discrimination (ref=a lot/great deal)						
Moderate/little		0.234**	0.059	0.245**	0.178	0.016
		(.119)	(.176)	(.122)	(.178)	(.196)
None/little (overall)		0.543**	0.703*	0.252	0.159	0.238
		(.240)	(.362)	(.250)	(.369)	(.220)
Interactions						
Female*moderate/little			0.376		0.147	0.531**
			(.232)		(.237)	(.253)
Female*none/little			-0.353		0.197	0.369
			(.461)		(.471)	(.297)
Intercept	3.979***	3.138***	3.229***	3.171***	3.206***	3.245***
	(.088)	(.268)	(.281)	(.263)	(.268)	(.285)
N	886	886	886	886	886	886
R^2	0.012	0.066	0.071	0.063	0.064	0.075

Source: Authors' compilation based on McCann and Jones-Correa 2012.

$*p < .1; **p < .05; ***p < .01$

Table A6. Regression Models Predicting Ranking, Years in the United States

	Model 1	Model 2	Model 3
Sociodemographic characteristics			
Female	0.331***	0.354***	0.917*
	(.116)	(.116)	(.521)
Age		0.013***	0.013***
		(.005)	(.005)
Married		0.206*	0.207*
		(.121)	(.122)
Some college or more		−0.462***	−0.484***
		(.150)	(.148)
Income		0.075	0.071
		(.072)	(.071)
Naturalized		−0.118	−0.118
		(.134)	(.135)
National origin (ref=Mexican)			
Cuban		−0.034	−0.033
		(.268)	(.267)
South American		0.168	0.16
		(.240)	(.235)
Central American		−0.054	−0.036
		(.177)	(.175)
Dominican		−0.099	−0.067
		(.283)	(.274)
Years in the United States (ref = 0–5 years)			
6–10		−0.258	0.291
		(.327)	(.440)
11–15		−0.145	−0.033
		(.296)	(.398)
16+		0.060	0.320
		(.282)	(.368)
Interactions			
Female*6–10			−1.213*
			(.649)
Female*11–15			−0.303
			(.578)
Female*16+			−0.599
			(.544)
Intercept	3.975***	3.391***	3.173***
	(.088)	(.342)	(.377)
N	886	886	886
R^2	0.012	0.061	0.069

Source: Authors' compilation based on McCann and Jones-Correa 2012.
*$p < .1$; **$p < .05$; ***$p < .01$

REFERENCES

Arceneaux, Kevin. 2001. "The 'Gender Gap' in State Legislative Representation: New Data to Tackle an Old Question." *Political Research Quarterly* 54(1): 143-60.

Bafumi, Joseph, and Robert Y. Shapiro. 2009. "A New Partisan Voter." *Journal of Politics* 71(1): 1-24.

Bejarano, Christina E. 2013. *The Latino Gender Gap in US Politics*. New York: Routledge.

Bejarano, Christina E., Sylvia Manzano, and Celeste Montoya. 2011. "Tracking the Latino Gender Gap: Gender Attitudes Across Sex, Borders, and Generations." *Politics & Gender* 7(4): 521-49.

Campbell, Angus, Philip E. Converse, Warren E. Miller, and Donald E. Stokes. 1960. *The American Voter*. New York: John Wiley & Sons.

Center for the American Woman and Politics (CAWP). 2012. "The Gender Gap: Voting Choices in Presidential Elections." Fact Sheet. New Brunswick, N.J.: Rutgers University, Eagleton Institute of Politics. Accessed December 18, 2014. http://www.cawp.rutgers.edu/fast_facts/voters/gender_gap.php.

Clark, Cal, and Janet Clark. 2008. *Women at the Polls: The Gender Gap, Cultural Politics, and Contested Constituencies in the United States*. Cambridge: Cambridge University Press.

Conway, M. Margaret. 2008. "The Gender Gap: A Comparison Across Racial and Ethnic Groups." In *Voting the Gender Gap*, edited by Lois Duke Whitaker. Chicago: University of Illinois.

Donato, Katharine M., Joseph T. Alexander, Donna R. Gabaccia, and Johanna Leinonen. 2011. "Variations in the Gender Composition of Immigrant Populations: How They Matter." *International Migration Review* 45(3): 495-526.

Donato, Katharine M., and Amada Armenta. 2011. "What We Know About Unauthorized Migration." *Annual Review of Sociology* 37: 529-43.

Donato, Katharine M., and Donna Gabaccia. 2015. *Gender and International Migration: Slavery to Present*. New York: Russell Sage Foundation.

Grasmuck, Sherri, and Patricia R. Pessar. 1991. *Between Two Islands: Dominican International Migration*. Berkeley: University of California Press.

Hajnal, Zoltan L., and Taeku Lee. 2011. *Why Americans Don't Join the Party: Race, Immigration, and the Failure (of Political Parties) to Engage the Electorate*. Princeton, N.J.: Princeton University Press.

Hondagneu-Sotelo, Pierrette. 1994. *Gendered Transitions: Mexican Experiences of Immigration*. Oakland: University of California Press.

Inglehart, Ronald, and Pippa Norris. 2000. "The Developmental Theory of the Gender Gap: Women's and Men's Voting Behavior in Global Perspective." *International Political Science Review* 21(4): 441-63.

Jiménez, Tomás R. 2008. "Mexican Immigrant Replenishment and the Continuing Significance of Ethnicity and Race." *American Journal of Sociology* 113(6): 1527-67.

Jones-Correa, Michael. 1998. "Different Paths: Gender, Immigration and Political Participation." *International Migration Review* 32(2): 326-49.

Kaufmann, Karen M. 2002. "Culture Wars, Secular Realignment, and the Gender Gap in Party Identification." *Political Behavior* 24(3): 283-307.

———. 2006. "The Gender Gap." *PS: Political Science & Politics* 3 (July): 447-53.

Kaufmann, Karen M., and John R. Petrocik. 1999. "The Changing Politics of American Men: Understanding the Sources of the Gender Gap." *American Journal of Political Science* 43(3): 864-87.

Lewis-Beck, Michael S., William G. Jacoby, Helmut Norpoth, and Herbert F. Weisberg. 2008. *The American Voter Revisited*. Ann Arbor: University of Michigan Press.

Manza, Jeff, and Clem Brooks. 1998. "The Gender Gap in U.S. Presidential Elections: When? Why? Implications?" *American Journal of Sociology* 103(5): 1235-66.

McCann, James A., and Michael Jones-Correa. 2012. Latino Immigrant National Election Study, 2012. New York: Russell Sage Foundation, Carnegie Corporation of New York, Purdue University, and Cornell University.

Menjívar, Cecilia. 2000. *Fragmented Ties: Salvadoran Immigrant Networks in America*. Oakland: University of California Press.

Montoya, Lisa J. 1996. "Latino Gender Differences in Public Opinion: Results from the Latino National Political Survey." *Hispanic Journal of Behavioral Sciences* 18(2): 255-76.

Multiple Imputation in Stata, Part 1. UCLA: Statistical Consulting Group. Accessed October 13, 2014. http://www.ats.ucla.edu/stat/sas/notes2/.

Norrander, Barbara, and Clyde Wilcox. 2008. "The Gender Gap in Ideology." *Political Behavior* 30(4): 503-23.

Paxton, Pamela, Sheri Kunovich, and Melanie M.

Hughes. 2007. "Gender in Politics." *Annual Review of Sociology* 33: 263–84.

Pew Research Center. 2012. *Partisan Polarization Surges in Bush, Obama Years*. Section 9: "Trends in Party Affiliation." Washington, D.C.: Pew Research Center for the People & the Press. Accessed January 30, 2016. http://www.people-press.org/2012/06/04/section-9-trends-in-party-affiliation/.

———. 2015. "The Unique Challenges of Surveying U.S. Latinos." Washington D.C.: Pew Research Center. Accessed January 30, 2016. http://www.pewresearch.org/2015/11/12/the-unique-challenges-of-surveying-u-s-latinos/.

Taylor, Paul, Mark Hugo Lopez, Jessica Hamar Martinez, and Gabriel Velasco. 2012. "When Labels Don't Fit: Hispanics and Their Views of Identity." Washington, D.C.: Pew Hispanic Center. Accessed January 30, 2016. http://www.pewhispanic.org/files/2012/04/PHC-Hispanic-Identity.pdf.

Tolleson-Rinehart, Sue. 1992. *Gender Consciousness and Politics*. New York: Routledge.

U.S. Census Bureau. 2011. "The Hispanic Population: 2010." Washington, D.C.: Government Printing Office. http://www.census.gov/prod/cen2010/briefs/c2010br-04.pdf

Verba, Sidney, Nancy Burns, and Kay Lehman Schlozman. 1997. "Knowing and Caring About Politics: Gender and Political Engagement." *Journal of Politics* 59(4): 1051–72.

Welch, Susan, and Lee Sigelman. 1992. "A Gender Gap Among Hispanics? A Comparison with Blacks and Anglos." *Western Washington Quarterly* 45(1): 181–99.

Young, Rebekah, and David R. Johnson. 2010. "Imputing the Missing Y's: Implications for Survey Producers and Survey Users." Proceedings of the AAPOR Conference Abstracts.

Religion and the Political Engagement of Latino Immigrants: Bridging Capital or Segmented Religious Assimilation?

DAVID L. LEAL, JEROD PATTERSON, AND JOE R. TAFOYA

This paper uses the Latino Immigrant National Election Study (LINES) to better understand the relationship between religion and immigrant political and civic engagement. Over the last half century, both American religion and the immigration landscape have changed in important ways. The LINES, which includes a number of religious questions from the American National Election Study and a rare focus on Latino newcomers, provides the opportunity to better understand the contemporary relationship between the two. We find that measures of religious belongings, beliefs, and behaviors (the Three Bs) are not generally associated with the civic and political engagements of Latino immigrants. We posit that such null results may be explained by the varying religious experiences of immigrants—some developing bridging social capital through religious institutions, but others experiencing what might be called segmented religious assimilation.

Keywords: migration, immigrants, religion and politics, segmented assimilation, social capital, Latino politics

The goal of this article is to better understand how religion shapes the political engagement of the Latino first generation. The Latino Immigrant National Election Study (LINES) is a unique dataset that provides rare perspectives on Latino immigrants, an understudied population. Although a growing number of surveys now include enough Latino respondents to allow separate analysis, such as the American National Election Studies (ANES), the share of foreign-born respondents is typically low. This is especially the case for the study of religion and politics, as few surveys include the range of questions necessary to understand contemporary dynamics. The LINES combines a large sample of Latino immigrants with a number of religion questions from the ANES. We can therefore explore how the religious belongings, behaviors, and beliefs of the Latino first generation influence their engagement in civic affairs and electoral politics.

Understanding religion is increasingly important to the study of American politics—although this is not often recognized—because of the considerable, and intertwined, transformations of demography and religion. As is well known, the 1965 Immigration Act brought from across the globe large numbers of people previously barred from migration. Less noted, however, is that these individuals brought new religious traditions, theologies, practices, symbols, and interpretations to America, thereby

---

David L. Leal is professor of government at the University of Texas at Austin. **Jerod Patterson** is a doctoral candidate in the Department of Government at the University of Texas at Austin. **Joe R. Tafoya** is a doctoral candidate in the Department of Government at the University of Texas at Austin.

Direct correspondence to: David L. Leal at dleal@austin.utexas.edu, The University of Texas at Austin, Department of Government, 158 W 21st St., A1800, Austin, TX 78712; Jerod Patterson at jerod@pattersonconsultants.com; and Joe R. Tafoya at jrtafoya@utexas.edu.

disrupting established patterns of religious life. Immigrants not only founded new churches but also joined, and diversified, existing denominations.

This would come to have implications for politics and policy. Many of these churches, while traditionally conservative, recognized that immigrants from the developing world were not only joining congregations but also potential targets of evangelization. These immigrants and their children are increasingly seen as the future of many denominations, which has caused institutional reassessments of policies such as immigration reform. The Southern Baptist Convention (2011), for example, has adopted resolutions supporting comprehensive immigration reform with a path to legal status for unauthorized immigrants.

These changes are overlapping with longer-standing transformations in American religious identity and practice. For much of American history, denominational affiliation was a key dividing line with political, social, and economic implications. This was reflected in the title of Will Herberg's (1955) classic book *Protestant, Catholic, Jew*. Changes were nevertheless emerging that would complicate traditional categories, including the fundamentalist and modernist split within Protestantism and the concomitant development of different beliefs and practices within traditions and denominations. Scholars realized that old categorizations no longer described the reality of religion in American life (Kellstedt et al. 1996; Layman 1997, 2001; Green 2007; Olson and Warber 2008; Smidt, Kellstedt, and Guth 2009) and that religion was fundamentally restructuring (Wuthnow 1990).

The concepts of belief (such as biblical literalism) and behavior (such as church attendance) were therefore added to belonging (denomination). These Three Bs better captured the "new religion gaps" (Green 2007) and allowed scholars to understand how contemporary religion was shaping politics. For instance, conservatives and liberals from different denominations are increasingly working together to achieve political and policy goals. To add to the complexity, religious orientations may also have different political effects by race and ethnicity (McDaniel and Ellison 2008; Leal and Patterson 2013), and many Americans are now moving away from any religious affiliation (Campbell, Green, and Layman 2013; Corral, Leal, and Tafoya 2015).

Demographic trends are generating renewed research across the social sciences on minority populations, and the Latino and Asian American religious experiences are the subject of increased attention. For Latinos, scholars have explored such topics as religion and civic activism (Espinosa, Elizondo, and Miranda 2005), the role of faith during the migration journey (Hagan 2008), the activism of Latino faith-based organizations (Wilson 2008), the role of religion in the farmworkers movement (Prouty 2006), historical accounts (Sandoval 2006), the place of Latinos in American religion and Catholicism (Stevens-Arroyo 1980; Díaz-Stevens and Stevens-Arroyo 1998; Matovina and Riebe-Estrella 2002; Matovina 2012), Latino ministry (Dahm 2004), and Latino theology (De La Torre and Aponte 2001). While space considerations preclude a more detailed discussion of this literature, it can be found in the previous work of the first two authors of this article (Leal 2010; Leal and Patterson 2013, 2014).

Although Catholicism has long been a core component of Latino cultures, it is less so every year. In 2006, the Pew Forum on Religion & Public Life (2007) found that 68 percent of Latinos were Catholic, a figure that had declined to 55 percent by 2013 (Pew Research Center 2014). Many of these former Catholics are now attending evangelical and Pentecostal congregations, but the number of Latino "Nones" also increased (from 8 percent to 18 percent). At the same time, the large number of migrants from Mexico, Central America, the Dominican Republic, and other Spanish-speaking nations in the Western Hemisphere has augmented Catholic numbers. Even if many ultimately change religious identities in the United States or become converts before the migration experience, the American Catholic population would have shrunk over the last two decades without "the infusion of millions of Latino Catholics" (Keysar 2014, 11). The paradox is that while Latinos are decreasingly Catholic, American Catholicism is increasingly Latino.

These changes in Latino religious affiliation are particularly clear across the generations.

The 2006 Pew survey found that while foreign-born Latinos were 74 percent Catholic, their native-born counterparts were 58 percent. The 2013 Pew survey notes that 60 percent of the foreign born are Catholic—a 14 percentage-point drop in seven years—and that 50 percent of the second generation and 45 percent of the third generation are Catholic (Pew Forum 2007; Pew Research Center 2014). The figures vary slightly in different surveys, but the trends are clear.

Although the religion and politics literature addresses a wide and growing range of topics, this paper is interested more specifically in the role of religion in shaping Latino immigrant political engagement.

This paper summarizes what we know about immigrants and religion by examining the literature on how religion can shape Latino political engagement. In particular, the debate between Verba, Schlozman, and Brady (1995) and Jones-Correa and Leal (2001) raised the question of whether Catholicism enhances or dampens Latino political participation. We contribute to this discussion by asking how religious measures—and particularly Catholicism—are associated with variables for electoral and civic participation among the Latino first generation. We discuss the variables in the 2012 LINES and how they allow for (and in some instances, limit) new research on these topics. The paper also presents models that add to our understanding of how religion shapes the political engagement of Latino immigrants and how the results—which predominantly show little association between religion and politics—can be interpreted in multiple ways.

IMMIGRANTS AND RELIGION

We might begin by remembering the words of Koheleth that "there is nothing new under the sun" (Ecclesiastes 1:9). Indeed, research on religion and immigration probes a question that is perhaps as old as humanity itself. As the Psalmist so poignantly reflected on the central crisis of the Hebrew people's Babylonian exile, "How can we sing the songs of Zion while in a foreign land?" (Psalms 137:4)

Research demonstrates the important role of religion in the lives of immigrants and immigrant communities (for example, Leonard et al. 2005; Foley and Hodge 2007; Chen and Jeung 2012). In surveying this research, a logical starting point would be why, in theoretical terms, religion matters to the immigrant experience. Thomas Tweed (2006) offers a potential explanation, arguing that religion is inherently spatial: "As spatial practices, religions are active verbs linked with unsubstantial nouns by bridged prepositions: *from, with, in, between, through*, and most important *across* . . . religions designate where we are from, identify whom we are with, and prescribe how we move across" (79). Religion enables, in Tweed's view, "homemaking"—"It draws boundaries around us and them; it constructs collective identity and, concomitantly, imagines degrees of social distance" (111). In his terms, it enables both "dwelling" and "crossing," that is, "finding a place and moving across space" (59). In essence, religion shares the central concerns of the immigrant experience: singing the songs of home while coming to terms with a new life in a foreign land.

As the exilic Psalm suggests, religion is a powerful and multifunctional force. In broad terms, it can reinforce ethnic identities and provide a space within which ethnic differences may be expressed, while also promoting participation in, or assimilation into, a new host country. Research supports this dual role (see, for example, Dolan 1975; Yang 1999; Yang and Ebaugh 2001; Cherry 2013) while revealing important complexities. This is why scholars have approached the question of religion and immigration from different angles.

Over the past half century, beginning at least with Herberg's (1955) seminal work, our understanding of religion and immigration has grown steadily and respect has increased for religion's explanatory power. Social scientists have addressed issues such as the functional effects of religion in promoting or inhibiting civic participation (Verba, Schlozman, and Brady 1995; Putnam 2001; Jones-Correa and Leal 2001), the role of religion in political reasoning (Lee and Pachon 2007), and group and identity politics (Chen and Jeung 2012). Scholars have also given greater nuance to such matters as the relationship between religion and ethnicity, and how religion facilitates involvement in the social and political life of a new host country. For example, this may depend on the relative strength and relatedness of ethnic and religious identities (Greeley 1971; Abramson 1973; Hammond and Warner 1993) or majority-minority status in home and host countries (Yang and Ebaugh 2001).

In addition, many religious dynamics are transnational, so that we cannot easily divide home country and American religion. Some immigrants are pre-acculturated before the journey by transnational congregational networks, which not only helps facilitate border crossing but can also change religious practices in the home nation and thereby prepare the immigrant for reception in the United States (Levitt 2002). Religious capital is therefore an important part of the migration experience, but religions are global networks and the directional arrows of personal and institutional change point in all directions.

Religion and Latino Political Participation
Research has also provided insight into the degree with which religion and communities of faith promote or inhibit participation in the social and political life of host countries among foreign-born populations and subsequent generations. More general works on civic participation have found church attendance to promote greater involvement (Verba, Schlozman, and Brady 1995; Putnam 2001). Sidney Verba and his colleagues (1995) identify the importance of civic skills and civic resources to civic participation, but they also note the unique role of religious institutions in providing the opportunity to access such skills. Although socioeconomic status (SES) and organizational resources are conceptually distinct, they note that "those with high levels of educational attainment are likely to be slotted into the kinds of prestigious and lucrative jobs and organizational affiliations that provide further political resources" and the only organization that can "provide a counterbalance to this cumulative resource process" is religion (Verba, Schlozman, and Brady 1995, 18).

Verba and his colleagues (1995) analyze time-based nonelectoral activities, voting, political contributions, and political discussion, finding that SES factors and not racial-ethnic measures are statistically significant. However, SES is developed by a variety of organizational experiences, particularly that of religion. They argue that unfortunately for Latinos, Catholicism was less likely to develop the same level of politically relevant civic skills as many Protestant denominations did. Because Latinos were predominantly Catholic at the time of the Citizens Participation Study (though the authors acknowledge a growing Protestant share), Verba and his colleagues posit that Catholicism served to dampen Latino political participation.

Michal Jones-Correa and David Leal (2001) argue that if Catholicism helped explain disparities in political participation across groups, then it should also shape participation within groups. They compare Latino and Anglo (non-Hispanic white) electoral and nonelectoral participation, finding that Catholic affiliation never reduced Latino participation—and in fact served to increase several types of engagement. By contrast, attendance at religious services was consistently significant, thus suggesting that the associational role of churches—regardless of denomination—was also important. Jones-Correa and Leal observe that "while churches play an important part in American civic life in general, in the absence of other civic associations they play a disproportionate role in the civic and political lives of Latinos" (2001, 763). In addition, religious institutions may be particularly important to immigrant communities: "As they did for previous waves of immigrants before them, Catholic churches may serve as ethnic associations as much as they do religious institutions" (764).

For Anglos, however, religious denomination was consistently insignificant across four political participation models. Although Catholicism may have once shaped Irish, Italian, and Polish American political participation, "it is not likely to be true today. For most Anglos, the difference among churches is simply denominational, not ethnic. Political appeals in Latino Catholic parishes might have a resonance they do not have in Anglo Catholic parishes" (Jones-Correa and Leal 2001, 764).

Louis DeSipio (2007), examining the 2000 Hispanic Churches in American Public Life (HCAPL) survey, notes that Catholic voter turnout was one-third higher than that of non-Catholics, which is inconsistent with the demobilization argument. He also finds that Catholics were slightly more likely than Protestants to report that their churches had become more involved in political and social questions. However, Catholics were less likely than Protestants to believe that a political candidate's faith and morals were important considerations in their vote choice.

Joanne Ibarra and David Leal (2013) replicate the Jones-Correa and Leal (2001) models using the 2006 Latino National Survey (LNS) and the 2008 ANES (with Latino oversample). None of the models indicate that Latino Catholics incur a mobilization penalty, though only the LNS found that Catholicism was positively associated with Latino political participation (voter registration and voter turnout in the 2004 presidential election). In the ANES findings, the religious variables—denomination, born-again status, religious importance, and church attendance—were consistently insignificant. For both Anglos and Latinos, religion did not shape voting, an index of nonelectoral participation, or campaign contributions.

Jongho Lee and Harry Pachon (2007) find no evidence that denomination or church attendance shaped political participation. Using the 2004 *Washington Post/Univision*/Tomas Rivera Policy Institute survey of 1,600 registered Latino voters, they test whether religious variables affected presidential vote preference, intensity of vote preference, interest in the presidential campaign, and whether they were contacted to register or to vote. Although evangelicals were more likely to support George W. Bush, no religious tradition variable was statistically significant in the other models. These null results support neither the Verba, Scholzman, and Brady (1995) nor the Jones-Correa and Leal (2001) findings because they suggest that religion was not an important factor (aside from vote direction) in 2004.

Research by sociologists and other scholars tends to support the argument that religious institutions can provide important, politically relevant skills to immigrants. Cristina Mora (2013) observes that Catholic churches provide opportunities for civic engagement for Mexican immigrants. First, participating in small groups allows immigrants the opportunity to build skills and develop networks. Second, churches provide links to nonreligious civic groups. This qualitative paper provides additional evidence that is consistent with the majority of the quantitative literature discussed previously. In addition, the edited volume by Vargas-Ramos and Stevens-Arroyo (2012) includes multiple chapters—using both qualitative and quantitative methods and across a variety of settings—that counter the argument that Catholicism demobilizes Latino populations.

Researchers have also addressed such questions for additional faiths and ethnic groups. Peggy Levitt's study of Boston-area immigrant groups, including Hindus and Muslims, finds that "even when religious institutions did not have explicit political agendas, people learned about fundraising, organizing and leadership by participation, which they applied to other settings" (2008, 778). Moreover, the greatest accumulation of civic skills occurred among those whose congregations were in close proximity to a native-born congregation, as interaction between the two offered a kind of intermediary education in U.S. political and civic life. Levitt ominously observed that "in contrast, members of stand-alone congregations, with few U.S. ties, were *on their own*" (780, emphasis added).

A recurring theme in this literature is the important role of the church not only as an institution in promoting the civic skills necessary for participation but also as a source of organizational support for participation. This is especially true of Catholic churches. For example, Matt Barreto and his colleagues (2009) find the Catholic Church played a central role in disseminating information about the immigrant rights marches, and Catholic identification was a strong predictor of participation in, or support for, these marches. Similarly, Kraig Beyerlein and Mark Chaves (2003) note that Catholic churches, more than other congregations, organized demonstrations and marches and lobbied elected officials. Cecilia Menjívar (2003) observes the same among Salvadoran immigrants as Catholic churches encourage immigrants to work collectively to transform their communities. In contrast, evangelical

Christian churches attended by Salvadorans place greater emphasis on individual salvation.

DATA AND MODELS

The LINES survey addresses each of the three traditional approaches to measuring religion in survey research: believing, behaving, and belonging. For religious belief, the LINES asked respondents two relevant questions: "Do you consider religion to be an important part of your life, or not?" and "Would you say your religion provides [some/quite a bit/a great deal] of guidance in your day-to-day living?" One might also include in this category the follow-up question for Christian respondents about whether they identify as born-again or evangelical Christians.

For the most part, the LINES follows the lead of the ANES in its religious questions. However, some deviations are notable. The first of these concerns religious belief. The LINES does not include a question on the literal interpretation of scripture, which is included in the ANES. This is a common question on several surveys, including not only the ANES but also the Cooperative Congressional Election Study (CCES), the General Social Survey (GSS), and many Pew studies.

Questions about biblical literalism reflect the role of an interpretive community in articulating a religious worldview that translates religious teachings and texts into a particular vision for social and political life (Fish 1980; McDaniel and Ellison 2008). This question is often used in research as a proxy for religious traditionalism, and the LINES does not include another such measure. However, the literalism question is primarily appropriate for Protestant traditions more so than for Catholicism.

We would also have liked a variable for charismatic or Pentecostal beliefs. A vibrant, charismatic spirituality can be found not only among Pentecostals but also increasingly among Catholics. This is especially the case in Latin America. In 1970, Pentecostals and charismatics represented no more than 4 percent of Latin America's population. According to the World Christian Database, by 2005 their numbers had increased to more than 25 percent (Pew Forum 2006). Not only is charismatic spirituality qualitatively different from non-charismatic spirituality, but its political implications are also debated.

The LINES also includes questions about religious behavior. Here, the survey follows the ANES closely and includes questions on the frequency of prayer and church attendance: "Outside of attending religious services do you pray?" and "Do you ever attend religious services, apart from occasional weddings, baptisms, or funerals?" Response options account for variation in frequency. These are helpful measures, particularly the church attendance question, which have shown predictive power in estimating social and political behaviors.

The LINES includes questions on religious affiliation. Here we find another departure from the ANES and certainly the most problematic feature of the LINES's religious measures. Like the ANES, the LINES asks respondents, "Do you mostly attend a place of worship that is Protestant, Catholic, Jewish, or something else?" or for those who do not attend religious services, "Do you consider yourself to be" any of these religious affiliations. Although the LINES stops here, the ANES offers respondents an opportunity to further define their religious affiliation. This is important for several reasons. First, because a growing number of Protestants do not identify as such (or even understand the term), only asking respondents whether they are Protestant, Catholic, Jewish, or something else will underrepresent Protestants. Many contemporary Protestants instead identify as "just Christian" or evangelical or sometimes with a denominational moniker.

A similar problem exists with the something else option in the LINES, which groups religious others and the unaffiliated, and unfortunately risks also including Protestants who do not identify with this term (an issue of growing concern to survey researchers). We can create an estimate of the Latino immigrant Nones, but the measure is not ideal.

Analysis

Our paper examines the religious, demographic, and socioeconomic determinants of Latino immigrant political engagement. This is not an exact replication of the Jones-Correa and Leal (2001) paper, as the LINES contains additional variables that are specifically relevant to immigrant populations. We are guided by the expectation that if Catholic churches boost electoral participation because they serve as community centers that can uniquely connect Latinos to political information as well as political mobilization efforts, the political and civic effects might be even stronger among immigrants.

The first measure is a dummy variable for whether the respondent voted in the 2012 presidential election. This question was only asked of naturalized citizens. We also analyze the Campaign Activity Battery (four questions) and the Civic Participation Battery (four questions). These questions were asked of all respondents, as nonelectoral participation is not limited to citizens or legal permanent residents (see Leal 2002). We also create an index variable (from 0 to 4) and dummy variable (whether the respondent participated in any activity) for each of the batteries.

The campaign measures that we use include whether a campaign attempted to mobilize the respondent, attending a campaign rally, wearing a campaign button, and working for a political campaign.[1] The civic participation measures include whether the respondent attended a civic rally, attended a civic meeting, signed an Internet petition, or signed a paper petition.[2]

To our knowledge, these analyses have not been previously conducted specifically for Latino immigrants. A variety of studies have examined the importance of religion for immigrant political engagement, but not in the manner found in this paper.

The independent variables are standard demographic measures (education, income, gender), national-origin groups measures (Mexican, Cuban, and Central American), and variables specifically applicable to immigrants (took the survey in Spanish, was brought to the United States before age sixteen, and the percentage of life lived in the United States). See appendix A for descriptive statistics for all the independent and dependent variables. In addition, a correlation matrix of the independent variables (not included) indicates that multicollinearity should not be a concern.

For each model, we first run regression models using the variables by themselves and then using the weight variable provided by the LINES (wgtrake). It was based on education, gender, and age.

Imputation

The LINES survey contains considerable missing data, both of the normal individual nonresponse variety and also because some questions were not asked of the respondents in the supplement to the second-wave survey. We therefore conduct three types of analysis for most questions: the first two use the unweighted and weighted survey data (as described), and the third uses AMELIA II in R to impute all missing data (Honaker, King, and Blackwell 2012). In this way, we provide evidence for scholars with different views of the value and propriety of weighting datasets and imputing missing data (for encouraging perspectives on imputing independent and dependent variables, see Graham 2009; Young and Johnson 2010; Hollenbach et al. 2014). As we will show, regardless of whether the weight measure is used or the data are imputed, the key religious results do not vary, which adds to our confidence in the findings.[3]

---

1. We do not include contributing money to a political campaign in the index, as the more general literature on political participation finds that it is uniquely shaped by disposable income.

2. We similarly do not include in the index the questions for giving money to a religious or a nonreligious organization.

3. Our imputation of LINES data started with our specifying the models of interest for Amelia II. The procedure assumes, as do we, that data are missing at random and then generates observations based on every parameter in the model, including the dependent variable. We tasked Amelia II with generating five imputation datasets, each with respondent identification numbers as unique cases with which to create unique values. Dependent variables were treated in a manner consistent with their nominal characteristics. Specifically, Amelia II generated integer values for whatever rate of civic or campaign participation it predicted respondents to have based on observed characteristics. The same prediction occurred for whether naturalized Latino citizens voted for presi-

Modeling

The voter turnout dependent variable, a simple dummy variable, was modeled using logit regression. Our index measures for civic and campaign participation denote counts of activities reported by the respondents. In both the LINES and the ANES, rates of participation are heavily skewed to the 0 or 1 counts. The skewed nature of these dependent variables means that ordinary least squares (OLS) is an inadequate method of estimation. The go-to approach for estimating count data is Poisson regression, but our dependent variables show overly dispersed variance (higher than mean) and an excess of 0 observations, both of which violate traditional assumptions. Under these conditions, a zero-inflated negative binomial regression is ideal but unavailable when estimating subpopulation parameters, imputed data, or models with too few observations. We therefore chose negative binomial regression as the next best procedure, which addresses excessive variance. We make no assumptions about the data-generating process for 0 (no participation) observations. They serve as our base for understanding the characteristics of respondents who reportedly engaged in political and civic activities.

In addition, we collapse the two index measures into two dummy variables for whether the respondent participated in any civic or campaign activity. These models are analyzed using logit analysis.

For ease of interpretation, all coefficients are presented as odds ratios (for Logit regressions) or incidence rate ratios (for the negative binomial regressions). Values greater than 1 represent positive associations between the independent and dependent variables, and values less than one represent negative associations.

Last, because of considerable second-wave attrition in the LINES, a second survey firm was engaged to increase the sample size. We were concerned that respondents in these two different samples would potentially yield different responses to survey questions. To address this, we tested the possibility that respondents represent separate data-generating processes. First, Amelia II, in addition to treating respondent identification numbers as unique, allowed us to consider each survey firm as a unique cross-section and generated imputations of missing observations therein. The generated datasets were then analyzed using generalized negative binomial regression, which enables users to assign a cross-section variable to test whether estimates for each differ. We applied this test to the models for the civic and campaign index measures. In each case, the auxiliary test for differences in models across cross-sections did not find statistically significant differences. That is, the data collected across the two survey firms in the second wave of the LINES are not apparently significantly different in the count models we specified.

Religious Affiliation

Examining both pre- and postwave respondents, we see that the basic religious affiliations of the LINES respondents are both different than and similar to those reported by most surveys. Using the sample weights, 61 percent identified as Catholic, 8.9 percent as unaffiliated, 13.1 percent as Other, and the remaining 17 percent as Protestant (table A1).

We can compare these responses with those of the Pew Research Center's 2013 survey, which found that the Latino foreign born are 60 percent Catholic, 16 percent evangelical Protestant, 4 percent mainline Protestant, 15 percent unaffiliated, and 4 percent Other. The share of Catholics, one of our main measures of interest, is therefore almost identical in both surveys. The differences among the other categories likely reflect the variations in how the religious affiliation question was asked by the LINES and the Pew.

---

dent in 2012. The program stacked the five datasets into one export and was analyzed by Stata's *mi estimate* protocol. The procedure was informed of the size and shape of the stacked dataset, as well as identifying variables for respondents, datasets, and variables with imputed observations. This entire process yielded a complete data frame and highly reliable parameters that range across multiple datasets.

Table 1. Models for 2012 Voter Turnout

	Voted Odds Ratio (SE)	Weighted Odds Ratio (SE)	Imputed Odds Ratio (SE)
Constant	0.020	−0.004	0.144
	(0.065)	(0.012)	(0.186)
Female	2.590	1.772	1.464
	(1.504)	(1.063)	(0.343)
Age	1.065**	1.052	1.024**
	(0.031)	(0.036)	(0.011)
Education	1.070	1.194*	1.009
	(0.108)	(0.120)	(0.040)
Income	1.620	1.443	1.297*
	(0.535)	(0.411)	(0.158)
Cuban	1.186	0.301	2.358
	(1.660)	0.455	(1.360)
Mexican	1.882	1.135	1.369
	(1.734)	(1.384)	(.544)
Central American	0.690	0.675	1.324
	(0.662)	(0.795)	(0.639)
Catholic	0.592	1.997	0.655
	(0.611)	(1.914)	(0.282)
Unaffiliated	0.860	3.533	0.777
	(1.116)	(4.860)	(0.584)
Religious other	0.033***	0.107*	0.142**
	(0.041)	(0.133)	(0.099)
Church attendance	1.122	10.210	1.082
	(0.231)	(0.220)	(0.094)
Religious importance	2.113	2.604	1.981**
	(1.813)	(2.416)	(0.598)
Born again	0.521	0.616	0.464**
	(0.421)	(0.496)	(0.160)
Party in country of origin	0.856	0.671	1.166
	(0.594)	(0.552)	(0.540)
Percentage of life in the United States	1.021	0.777	0.782
	(2.055)	(1.570)	(0.636)
Child immigrant	1.068	0.948	1.210
	(1.037)	(0.981)	(0.545)
Spanish	1.168	3.430	2.822*
	(1.844)	(3.559)	(1.396)
Observations	123	123	541
Pseudo R^2 / Prob > F	0.27	0.26	0.046

Source: McCann and Jones-Correa 2012.
Odds Ratios (OR) and Incidence Rate Ratios (IRR)
*$p < .10$; **$p < .05$; ***$p < .01$

RESULTS

Voter Turnout

The first set of regressions examines voter turnout in the 2012 presidential election (see table 1). These models, in combination with the subsequent models for electoral and civic participation, allow us to contribute to the Verba, Schlozman, and Brady (1995) and Jones-Correa and Leal (2001) debate by examining how a variety of religious factors are associated with political engagement. As noted, Verba, Schlozman, and Brady (1995) argue that fewer civic skills were associated with Catholic Church membership, which could help explain relatively low levels of Latino electoral participation. Jones-Correa and Leal (2001), however, find no evidence to support a Catholic demobilization argument. In fact, they note that the Catholic variable was positively associated with some forms of engagement and insignificant for the rest. They argue that churches serve as accessible community centers, where both political learning and recruitment can take place, and this role might be particularly consequential for immigrants.

The first model is for reported turnout—among naturalized citizens—in the 2012 presidential elections. As with most surveys, the reported turnout is likely higher than is the case, but the votes are not validated (consistent with ANES practice). The number of observations is relatively small because we are modeling a subset of the dataset, and missing data take their standard toll. Nevertheless, the model provides some unique evidence about the association of religion with Latino immigrant electoral participation.

The first column includes the basic regression model (using odds ratios), the second column model incorporates the weight measure, and the model in the third column analyzes the data as imputed by Amelia II in R. Across all three models, the Catholic and church attendance variables are statistically insignificant. Catholicism and more regular church attendance do not demobilize Latino immigrants, but neither do they encourage it. The findings therefore fall between the argument that religion bolsters or dampens minority political engagement. The only consistently statistically significant religious factor is the reporting of an Other religious affiliation; these individuals are much less likely to report voting in 2012.

Only a relatively few other variables are statistically significant in the models. In terms of SES, age is positively associated with the vote in two models (unweighted and imputed), and income and education are only statistically significant for one instance each. We conclude that the standard SES model does not appear to apply to voting among the foreign born.

We do not include a model for specific vote choice in 2012, as the number of observations was too low—below one hundred (it was relevant only to the naturalized, and it was asked only on the postelection wave). Nevertheless, a separate model (not shown) indicates that no religious variable was statistically significant and that the dominant effect was party identification.

Campaign Participation

We next examine the campaign participation batteries. As noted previously, the items in each battery have been combined into index and dummy variables. We model the unweighted measures (first two columns), the weighted measures (second two columns), and the imputed measures (last two columns). Table 2 indicates that few religious effects were present.

No religious variables are statistically significant in the first four models (unweighted and weighted). In addition, the Catholic measure is statistically insignificant in all models, and the church attendance variable is only statistically significant in the campaign index model with all missing data imputed. In addition, the other religious variables are almost entirely insignificant across the models. The one exception is the measure for the importance of religion, which is statistically significant only in the imputed models.

We also see that education (positive) is statistically significant across almost all models, as the SES theory of political engagement might predict. Women are also less likely to vote than men are, although neither age nor education was generally associated with voter turnout. Also, the variables that take into account features of the immigrant experience (such as percentage of life in the United States, immigrating to the United States as a child, or taking the survey in Spanish) are not significant in any of the models.

We also modeled (without the survey weights or missing data imputation) the individual variables that comprise the campaign index as well as an additional measure for financial contributions. These are not shown because of space considerations, but they indicate that Catholicism and church attendance are never statistically significant. The other re-

Table 2. Models for Campaign Participation

	Index IRR (SE)	Dummy Odds Ratio (SE)	Index, Weighted IRR (SE)	Dummy, Weighted Odds Ratio (SE)	Index, Imputed IRR (SE)	Dummy, Imputed Odds Ratio (SE)
Constant	0.213 (0.178)	0.041** (0.057)	0.193** (0.151)	0.048** (0.071)	0.144*** (0.057)	0.101** (0.076)
Female	0.743* (0.118)	0.632* (0.164)	0.728** (0.106)	0.547* (0.153)	0.837** (0.069)	0.889 (0.133)
Age	1.005 (0.007)	1.020 (0.012)	1.002 (0.006)	1.011 (0.014)	1.002 (0.004)	1.006 (0.008)
Education	1.067*** (0.025)	1.148*** (0.046)	1.075*** (0.020)	1.177*** (0.051)	1.058** (0.025)	1.088*** (0.025)
Income	0.950 (0.072)	1.013 (0.128)	0.936 (0.057)	0.962 (0.120)	1.021 (0.066)	1.060 (0.073)
Cuban	1.539 0.519	0.809 0.583	1.628 (0.500)	0.869 (0.666)	1.180 (0.306)	0.835 (0.333)
Mexican	0.711 (0.178)	0.689 (0.306)	0.737 (0.162)	0.677 (0.321)	0.896 (0.153)	0.772 (0.172)
Central American	1.149 (0.322)	1.500 (0.775)	1.106 (0.268)	1.590 (0.870)	1.067 (0.174)	1.039 (0.358)
Catholic	1.178 (0.336)	1.890 (0.933)	1.194 (0.360)	1.988 (1.097)	1.292 (0.234)	1.697 (0.563)
Unaffiliated	0.937 (0.392)	2.043 (1.348)	1.130 (0.431)	2.674 (2.003)	1.552 (0.428)	2.791* (1.338)
Religious other	0.784 (0.288)	0.792 (0.469)	0.837 (0.332)	0.822 (0.568)	0.999 (0.260)	1.075 (0.491)
Church attendance	1.052 (0.055)	1.108 (0.094)	1.074 (0.063)	1.141 (0.101)	1.057** (0.034)	1.059 (0.066)
Religious importance	1.011 (0.237)	1.177 (0.426)	0.979 (0.245)	1.115 (0.467)	1.491*** (0.159)	1.701*** (0.230)
Born again	1.056 (0.202)	0.813 (0.257)	1.158 (0.205)	0.937 (0.319)	1.153 (0.19)	1.125 (0.203)
Party in country of origin	1.097 (0.196)	1.130 (0.322)	1.150 (0.205)	1.200 (0.383)	1.078 (0.193)	1.381 (0.464)
Percentage of life in the United States	1.606 (0.830)	1.297 (1.081)	1.128 (0.538)	0.809 (0.732)	1.785 (0.793)	2.244 (1.082)
Child immigrant	0.842 (0.227)	1.067 (0.443)	0.953 (0.259)	1.143 (0.523)	0.877 (0.218)	0.968 (0.209)
Spanish	1.223 (0.610)	1.727 (1.379)	1.517 (0.746)	2.374 (0.072)	0.859 (0.171)	0.741 (0.219)
Observations	309	309	309	309	1,304	1,304
Pseudo R^2 / Prob > F	0.07	0.09	0.07	0.11	0.0000	0.0001

Source: McCann and Jones-Correa 2012.
Odds Ratios (OR) and Incidence Rate Ratios (IRR)
*$p < .10$; **$p < .05$; ***$p < .01$

ligious variables were largely insignificant, showing only a few scattered instances of statistical significance.[4]

Taken together, the campaign models provide additional evidence that religion is neither positively nor negatively associated with Latino immigrant political participation. More generally, we see relatively few variables at work in any given model, which suggests that political engagement may be differently structured for immigrants and the native born (a proposition we test using 2012 ANES data).

Civic Engagement

Table 3 includes the models for civic participation. Again, we see relatively few religious variables at work, and none that is consistently significant. Most important, the Catholic and church attendance variables are always insignificant. In addition, the other religious measures show only scattered, inconsistent effects. Most notable is that in the imputed models, the religiously unaffiliated (the Nones) and those who found religion important are both more likely to engage in civic activities.

The most consistently significant measures are those that involve the immigrant experience. The greater the percentage of life lived in the United States, the more likely the respondent is to participate in four of the six models. In addition, identifying with a political party in the respondent's nation of origin is associated with greater civic activity in five of the six models. The SES measures, by contrast, are largely insignificant (although income was the most notable among this group).

When we model the individual variables that make up the index measure, plus two questions about donating to a religious or nonreligious organization, we see no consistent religious effects. One difference in these models is that the role of education is more noticeable because it is statistically significant in four of the six models, whereas it was significant only once in the index and dummy variable models.

We therefore see that religion does not appear to shape the civic engagement of Latino immigrants. On the one hand, this suggests that religion is not providing a boost to civic activism among immigrants. On the other hand, it is not negatively associated with such engagement. As we will suggest, however, these null findings could mask disparate effects—some immigrants join churches that promote a bridging social capital that promotes greater civic and political engagement, while others become members of isolated congregations and consequently experience a form of segmented religious assimilation.

ANES Comparisons

Last, we created comparison models using similar dependent and independent variables from the 2012 ANES (see table A3 for descriptive statistics). The former included voter turnout, an index of campaign activities, and an index of civic participation activities (for the specific measures, see table A2). We ran these models for the Latino native-born sample as well as the Anglo (non-Hispanic white) sample (see tables 4 and 5).

For native-born Latinos, the role of religion is more evident than in the LINES models. The Catholic variable is statistically significant and positive in the two index models, whereas the church attendance variable is statistically significant and positive in the voter turnout model. Among Anglos, the Catholic variable is not significant, although the church attendance measure is positively associated with voter turnout and campaign participation.

Taken together, these ANES findings are consistent with Jones-Correa and Leal (2001). These authors note that Catholicism was never negatively, and sometimes positively, associated with Latino political engagement. For Anglos, by contrast, church attendance mattered in a way that denomination did not. They posit that such results spoke to the different roles played by churches in the lives of Latinos and Anglos.

---

4. The born again were more likely to attend a campaign rally but less likely to wear a campaign button, the Other religious were also less likely to wear a campaign button, and those who thought religion was important were less likely to donate to a campaign.

Table 3. Models for Civic Participation

	Index IRR (SE)	Dummy Odds Ratio (SE)	Index, Weighted IRR (SE)	Dummy, Weighted Odds Ratio (SE)	Index, Imputed IRR (SE)	Dummy, Imputed Odds Ratio (SE)
Constant	0.154**	0.035**	0.186	0.186	0.137***	0.148**
	(0.143)	(0.051)	(0.243)	(0.243)	(0.068)	(0.106)
Female	1.134	1.016	1.167	1.097	0.932	0.865
	(0.203)	(0.268)	(0.247)	(0.318)	(0.117)	(0.117)
Age	0.991	0.991	0.992	0.997	0.986**	0.974***
	(0.008)	(0.012)	(0.009)	(0.013)	(0.005)	(0.006)
Education	1.027	1.031	1.034	1.028	1.050*	1.018
	(0.028)	(0.041)	(0.030)	(0.046)	(0.023)	(0.023)
Income	1.121	1.230*	1.112	1.242	1.100*	1.202*
	(0.091)	(0.152)	(0.085)	(0.164)	(0.054)	(0.098)
Cuban	1.513	3.354*	1.253	2.942	1.770	2.151*
	0.784	2.455	(0.560)	(2.212)	(0.664)	(0.907)
Mexican	1.281	2.288*	1.144	1.970	1.664**	2.013**
	(0.431)	(1.134)	(0.454)	(1.005)	(0.379)	(0.526)
Central American	1.447	2.106	1.418	2.031	1.822	1.825*
	(0.546)	(1.194)	(0.628)	(1.066)	(0.624)	(0.524)
Catholic	0.753	0.830	0.745	0.706	1.329	1.350
	(0.247)	(0.425)	(0.262)	(0.408)	(0.412)	(0.458)
Unaffiliated	1.274	2.091	1.630	2.442	2.186**	2.694***
	(0.552)	(1.419)	(0.723)	(1.837)	(0.753)	(0.974)
Religious other	.607	0.775	0.631	0.639	0.900	0.875
	0(.250)	(0.478)	(0.286)	(0.444)	(0.364)	(0.357)
Church attendance	1.023	1.046	1.053	1.065	1.059	1.060
	(0.062)	(0.092)	(0.073)	(0.102)	(0.043)	(0.065)
Religious importance	1.096	1.318	0.983	1.154	1.404***	1.561**
	(0.271)	(0.492)	(0.285)	(0.476)	(0.161)	(0.270)
Born again	0.898	1.002	0.927	0.958	0.928	1.074
	(0.200)	(0.326)	(0.220)	(0.360)	(0.143)	(0.179)
Party in country of origin	1.782***	1.984**	1.547*	1.635	1.442*	1.752***
	(0.354)	(0.582)	(0.359)	(0.533)	(0.279)	(0.312)
Percentage of life in the United States	3.228**	6.460**	2.562	3.276	2.371**	6.192***
	(1.862)	(5.684)	(1.738)	(3.086)	(0.976)	(3.425)
Child immigrant	1.000	0.812	1.094	0.970	1.007	0.692
	(0.281)	(0.343)	(0.343)	(0.441)	(0.182)	(0.178)
Spanish	1.095	1.490	1.021	1.578	0.637**	0.631
	(.558)	(1.227)	(0.677)	(1.400)	(0.107)	(0.195)
Observations	308	308	308	308	1,304	1,304
Pseudo R^2 / Prob > F	0.05	0.06	0.06	0.05	0.0000	0.0000

Source: McCann and Jones-Correa 2012.
Odds Ratios (OR) and Incidence Rate Ratios (IRR)
*$p < .10$; **$p < .05$; ***$p < .01$

Table 4. ANES 2012 Models, Native-Born Latinos

	Vote OR (SE)	Campaign Participation Index IRR (SE)	Civic Participation Index IRR (SE)
Constant	0.163***	0.022***	0.104**
	(0.112)	(0.015)	(0.040)
Female	1.671*	1.033	1.285
	(0.500)	(0.311)	(0.223)
Age	1.018**	1.004	0.998
	(0.009)	(0.009)	(0.005)
Education	1.347	1.207	1.803***
	(0.283)	(0.229)	(0.178)
Income	1.073***	0.995	1.007
	(0.026)	(0.020)	(0.014)
Cuban	2.610	0.977	0.755
	2.475	(0.965)	0.341
Mexican	0.606	1.947**	1.008
	(0.193)	(0.640)	(0.176)
Catholic	0.700	2.167**	2.316***
	(0.285)	(0.752)	(0.559)
Unaffiliated	1.168	1.645	2.837***
	(0.634)	(0.999)	(0.886)
Religious other	0.675	0.731	3.596***
	(0.452)	(0.523)	(1.559)
Church attendance	1.382***	1.143	1.088
	(0.132)	(0.113)	(0.058)
Born again	0.717	1.514	1.955**
	(0.279)	(0.534)	(0.507)
Spanish	0.672	0.699	0.175***
	(0.337)	(0.314)	(0.069)
Internet sample	1.623*	1.525	1.072
	(0.468)	(0.422)	(0.174)
Observations	592	593	592
Pseudo R^2 / Prob > F	0.0000	0.0009	0.0000

Source: McCann and Jones-Correa 2012.
Odds Ratios (OR) and Incidence Rate Ratios (IRR)
*$p < .10$; **$p < .05$; ***$p < .01$

CONCLUSIONS

This paper used the unique LINES as well as the 2012 ANES to better understand the implications of religion for the political engagement of Latino immigrants. To date, the lack of survey data on Latino immigrants means that we have little quantitative evidence about the political implications of the Latino immigrant presence in American religion. Given this lack of previous research, it would be premature to draw strong conclusions from our results. Nevertheless, we hope that future researchers will continue to examine the religious profile of Latino immigrants and to study the role of religion in Latino and immigrant communities (for discussion, see Leal 2002, 2010; Barvosa-Carter 2004; DeSipio 2007; Matovina 2012).

More specifically, the paper contributes to the Verba, Schlozman, and Brady (1995) and Jones-Correa and Leal (2001) debate by examining the determinants of electoral, nonelectoral, and civic engagement. The various mod-

Table 5. ANES 2012 Models, Non-Hispanic Whites

	Vote OR (SE)	Campaign Participation Index IRR (SE)	Civic Participation Index IRR (SE)
Constant	0.096***	0.069***	0.580***
	(0.030)	(0.022)	(0.088)
Female	1.108	0.804	0.958
	(0.131)	(0.092)	(0.051)
Age	1.038***	1.014***	1.000
	(0.004)	(0.004)	(0.002)
Education	1.649***	1.230***	1.315***
	(0.119)	(0.071)	(0.036)
Income	1.051***	0.993	1.006*
	(0.008)	(0.009)	(0.004)
Catholic	1.071	1.102	1.053
	(0.200)	(0.155)	(0.077)
Unaffiliated	0.858	1.042	0.932
	(0.169)	(0.193)	(0.078)
Religious other	0.440***	1.005	1.146
	(0.118)	(0.229)	(0.148)
Church attendance	1.106**	1.081**	0.998
	(0.044)	(0.038)	(0.017)
Born again	0.897	0.920	1.060
	(0.158)	(0.140)	(0.079)
Internet sample	1.311*	1.025	1.092
	(0.179)	(0.131)	(0.065)
Observations	3,108	3,102	3,102
Pseudo R² / Prob > F	0.0000	0.0000	0.0000

Source: McCann and Jones-Correa 2012.
Odds Ratios (OR) and Incidence Rate Ratios (IRR)
*p < .10; **p < .05; ***p < .01

els, using different weighting and imputing approaches, found consistent results—almost no religious effects among Latino immigrants. In particular, there is no support for the theory that Catholicism or church attendance shapes the political or civic activism of the first generation. As we note, although this suggests that religious beliefs, belongings, and behaviors are not enhancing the involvement of immigrants in politics, neither are they reducing it. The results are inconsistent both with the theories of Verba, Schlozman, and Brady (1995) about the demobilization potential of Catholicism and with the findings of Jones-Correa and Leal (2001) about the unique electoral benefits of Catholicism to Latinos.

By contrast, the ANES models indicate that religious denomination and service attendance play a role in the political engagement of native-born Latinos and Anglos. For the former, Catholicism shapes civic and campaign activities, while attendance is associated with voter turnout. For Anglos, it is church attendance that matters, not denomination. These results are broadly consistent with those of Jones-Correa and Leal (2001), but taken together suggest that religion plays different political and civic roles for immigrants and native-born Latinos.

How do we understand these largely statistically insignificant LINES religious effects? Any fair assessment will encompass three potential explanations: issues with the survey data that led to null results; actual null results, which are nevertheless important to researchers; and mixed effects that appear as null results.

First, no dataset is without its quirks. This may particularly be the case for understudied and more difficult to study populations, which present sampling challenges. In our examination of religion and participation among Latino immigrants, the LINES manifested its share of such problems. Although the two-wave design may be a positive feature for some research questions, the drop off in wave 2 respondents required supplemental respondents in the second wave. Unfortunately, several questions from the first wave were not asked of these fresh respondents,[5] and the survey also has nontrivial missing data of the standard variety. However, the main religious results do not change when we impute the missing data, which adds to our confidence in the findings.

We also have questions about potential differences that may result from the use of two survey firms, as discussed. For example, slightly more than half of the respondents (51 percent) contacted by Latino Decisions preferred to take the survey in Spanish. In the second-wave surveys, conducted by Interviewing Services of America, about 95 percent preferred to take the survey in Spanish. This suggests nonrandom drop off, which was addressed through a new sample generated by the second firm. This could have introduced potential biases or inefficiencies into the dataset. Nevertheless, as we discussed, the results do not appear to change whether we take into account the separate survey efforts in the second wave, which is encouraging.

For the religion question, the LINES could have benefited from more appropriate questions that better capture the relevant dimensions of Latino and immigrant religion. For example, the emergence of charismatic spirituality is one of the most notable features of Christianity in Latin America and the United States, among both Catholics and Protestants. The LINES has no question to assess this important fissure. The contemporary rise of nondenominational Christianity is shared among Latino populations, yet the LINES asked respondents to choose between Catholic and Protestant labels. Other survey work finds that many Protestants do not identify with this label and may erroneously fall into an Other category without more appropriate response options. It is also difficult to assess the religiously unaffiliated due to a question-branching scheme that conflates church attendance with religious affiliation. Religion and politics scholarship understands these as different politically relevant aspects of religion. To be fair, much of the religion module was adopted from the ANES, but one might ask why the LINES retained Jewish as a response option for a study of Latino immigrants yet did not find a way to better assess charismatics, nondenominational Christians, or the unaffiliated.

Second, the null findings could reflect religious measures that are not, in fact, associated with the dependent variables. Although many scholars automatically discount null findings, academia is increasingly aware of the danger that doing so poses to scholarship. Annie Franco, Neil Malhotra, and Gabor Simonovits (2014) explain how null findings are an important part of the scientific process (see also Mervis 2014). Unfortunately, the tendency in social science is to not publish or even submit statistically insignificant results, which Franco and colleagues see as a "pernicious form of publication bias." This serves to obscure a large swath of scientific results that would otherwise help advance the scholarly conversation. At the very least, it does nothing to discourage future researchers from replicating such past work. At worst, write Franco and colleagues, "if future researchers conduct similar studies and obtain significant results by chance, then the published literature on the topic will erroneously suggest stronger effects" (2014, 1504).

Third, we might see the results in the models as reflecting the complexity of religion in immigrant communities. Rather than positing a single effect, we might instead see the immi-

---

5. These include variables that are especially relevant to studying immigrant populations, such as the number of family members at home, identification with the country of origin, and the desire to eventually return home. Some of our models would have benefited from these questions, but we did not include them because the result would be a further loss of observations (in addition to those generated by the usual missing data).

grant interaction with religion as varying. In Levitt's (2008) study of immigrants in Boston, although churches helped connect individuals to politics, the crucial factor was whether a church facilitated the interaction of immigrants with the native born. Churches that could provide this bridging social capital were more effective in promoting political engagement. By contrast, "members of stand-alone congregations, with few U.S. ties, *were on their own*" (780, emphasis added).

The results in this paper might be seen as evidence for such a complex understanding of the religious profile of Latino immigrants. Perhaps some are experiencing a form of segmented religious assimilation, which not only fails to help them adapt but contributes to an isolation associated with downward mobility. More generally, Stephen Warner sought to "remind students of assimilation (and of ethnic and racial minorities) that religion is a factor that they must take into account in their models" (1998, 103). We similarly hope that researchers of religion and assimilation will see that each literature has much to offer the other.

Although we cannot draw such conclusions without contextual parish-level data, we hope that this paper will help inspire more detailed survey and data collection efforts. They will be necessary if we are to better understand the interlocking, contemporary phenomena of immigrant growth and religious dynamism. The LINES allows us to bring some unique evidence to bear on the subject, but we also hope it will prove to be only one of many surveys that researchers will examine. Only from such collective efforts can we best understand the important and emerging topics at the intersection of Latino politics, immigration, and religion.

APPENDIX

Table A1. LINES Descriptive Statistics

	Min	Max	Mean	SD
Female	0	1	0.558	0.497
Age	18	95	48.760	14.934
Education	1	16	6.457	3.689
Income	0	7	1.753	1.111
Cuban	0	1	0.071	0.257
Mexican	0	1	0.668	0.471
Central American	0	1	0.138	0.345
Catholic	0	1	0.611	0.488
Religiously unaffiliated	0	1	0.089	0.284
Religious other	0	1	0.131	0.337
Church attendance	0	1	3.344	1.640
Religious importance	0	1	0.541	0.499
Born again	0	1	0.316	0.465
Party in country of origin	0	1	0.292	0.455
Percentage of life in United States	0	1	0.481	0.200
Child immigrant	0	1	0.237	0.425
Spanish language interview	0	1	0.663	0.473
Voted in 2012 election	0	1	0.741	0.434
Civic participation index	0	6	0.998	1.113
Civic participation dummy	0	1	0.582	0.494
Attended a rally	0	1	0.090	0.287
Attended a civic meeting	0	1	0.198	0.399
Signed an online petition	0	1	0.036	0.187

Table A1. (cont.)

	Min	Max	Mean	SD
Signed a paper petition	0	1	0.046	0.210
Donated to religious organization	0	1	0.440	0.497
Donated to nonreligious organization	0	1	0.188	0.391
Campaign participation index	0	5	0.489	0.744
Campaign participation dummy	0	1	0.380	0.486
Mobilized for campaign	0	1	0.297	0.457
Attended campaign rally	0	1	0.041	0.198
Wore campaign button	0	1	0.105	0.307
Contributed to candidate	0	1	0.028	0.166

Source: McCann and Jones-Correa 2012.

Table A2. ANES Descriptive Statistics, Native-Born Latinos

	Min	Max	Mean	SD
Female	0	1	0.499	0.500
Age	17	90	37.707	15.734
Education	1	4	1.684	0.833
Income	0	28	12.003	7.680
Cuban	0	1	0.030	0.172
Mexican	0	1	0.626	0.484
Catholic	0	1	0.394	0.489
Religiously unaffiliated	0	1	0.263	0.441
Religious other	0	1	0.046	0.209
Church attendance	0	5	2.004	2.062
Born again	0	1	0.270	0.444
Spanish language interview	0	1	0.105	0.307
Voted in 2012 election	0	1	0.670	0.471
Civic participation index	0	8	1.003	1.581
Online respondent	0	1	0.677	0.468
Attended a rally	0	1	0.066	0.249
Attended a civic meeting	0	1	0.128	0.335
Signed an online petition	0	1	0.224	0.417
Signed a paper petition	0	1	0.188	0.391
Called radio/TV to express	0	1	0.043	0.203
Messaged on social media	0	1	0.204	0.404
Letter to print outlet	0	1	0.036	0.186
Contacted member of Congress	0	1	0.114	0.318
Campaign participation index	0	3	0.182	0.498
Mobilized for campaign	0	1	0.026	0.160
Attended campaign rally	0	1	0.035	0.184
Wore campaign button	0	1	0.120	0.326

Source: ANES 2012.

Table A3. ANES Descriptive Statistics, Non-Hispanic Whites

	Min	Max	Mean	SD
Female	0	1	0.515	0.500
Age	18	90	49.357	17.318
Education	1	4	2.080	1.031
Income	0	28	15.175	7.842
Catholic	0	1	0.225	0.417
Religiously unaffiliated	0	1	0.243	0.429
Religious other	0	1	0.046	0.209
Church attendance	0	5	2.024	2.047
Born again	0	1	0.283	0.451
Voted in 2012 election	0	1	0.796	0.403
Civic participation index	0	8	1.251	1.507
Online respondent	0	1	0.652	0.476
Attended a rally	0	1	0.048	0.215
Attended a civic meeting	0	1	0.193	0.395
Signed an online petition	0	1	0.254	0.435
Signed a paper petition	0	1	0.250	0.433
Called radio/TV to express	0	1	0.030	0.171
Messaged on social media	0	1	0.217	0.412
Letter to print outlet	0	1	0.041	0.197
Contacted member of Congress	0	1	0.219	0.414
Campaign participation index	0	3	0.210	0.545
Mobilized for campaign	0	1	0.030	0.171
Attended campaign rally	0	1	0.052	0.222
Wore campaign button	0	1	0.128	0.334

Source: ANES 2012.

REFERENCES

Abramson, Harold J. 1973. *Ethnic Diversity in Catholic America*. New York: John Wiley & Sons.

American National Election Studies (ANES). 2012. The ANES 2012 Time Series Study dataset. Ann Arbor: University of Michigan; Palo Alto: Stanford University. Accessed February 26, 2016. http://www.electionstudies.org/.

Barreto, Matt, Sylvia Manzano, Ricardo Ramírez, and Kathy Rim. 2009. "Immigrant Social Movement Participation: Understanding Involvement in the 2006 Immigration Protest Rallies." *Urban Affairs Review* 44(5): 736–64.

Barvosa-Carter, Edwina. 2004. "Politics and the U.S. Latina and Latino Religious Experience." In *Introduction to the U.S. Latina and Latino Religious Experience*, edited by Hector Avalo. Boston, Mass.: Brill Academic Publishers.

Beyerlein, Kraig, and Mark Chaves. 2003. "The Political Activities of Religious Congregations in the United States." *Journal for the Scientific Study of Religion* 42(2): 229–46.

Campbell, David E., John C. Green, and Geoffrey C. Layman. 2013. "The Politics of Irreligion: The Political Causes of Growing Secularism in America." Paper presented at the annual meeting of the American Political Science Association. Chicago (October 17).

Chen, Carolyn, and Russell Jeung. 2012. *Sustaining Faith Traditions: Race, Ethnicity, and Religion among the Latino and Asian American Second Generation*. New York: New York University Press.

Cherry, Stephen. 2013. *Faith, Family, and Filipino American Community Life*. New Brunswick, N.J.: Rutgers University Press.

Corral, Alvaro, David L. Leal, and Joe Tafoya. 2015. "Declining Religiosity Among Latinos, Anglos, and African Americans: Implications for American Politics." Paper presented at the annual meeting of the American Political Science Association. San Francisco (September 3–6, 2015).

Dahm, Charles W. 2004. *Parish Ministry in a Hispanic Community*. Mahwah, N.J.: Paulist Press.

De La Torre, Miguel A., and Edwin David Aponte. 2001. *Introducing Latino/a Theologies*. Maryknoll, N.Y.: Orbis Books.

DeSipio, Louis. 2007. "Power in the Pews? Religious Diversity and Latino Political Attitudes and Behaviors." In *From Pews to Polling Places: Faith and Politics in the American Religious Mosaic*, edited by J. Matthew Wilson. Washington, D.C.: Georgetown University Press.

Díaz-Stevens, Ana-María, and Anthony Stevens-Arroyo. 1998. *Recognizing the Latino Resurgence in U.S. Religion*. Boulder, Colo.: Westview Press.

Dolan, Jay. 1975. *The Immigrant Church: New York's Irish and German Catholics 1815–1865*. Baltimore, Md.: Johns Hopkins University Press.

Espinosa, Gastón, Virgilio Elizondo, and Jesse Miranda, eds. 2005. *Latino Religions and Civic Activism in the United States*. New York: Oxford University Press.

Fish, Stanley. 1980. *Is There a Text in this Class? The Authority of Interpretive Communities*. Cambridge, Mass.: Harvard University Press.

Foley, Michael W., and Dean R. Hodge. 2007. *Religion and the New Immigrants: How Faith Communities Form Our Newest Citizens*. New York: Oxford University Press.

Franco, Annie, Neil Malhotra, and Gabor Simonovits. 2014. "Publication Bias in the Social Sciences: Unlocking the File Drawer." *Science* 345(6203): 1502–05.

Graham, John W. 2009. "Missing Data Analysis: Making It Work in the Real World." *Annual Review of Psychology* 60: 549–76.

Greeley, Andrew M. 1971. *Why Can't They Be Like Us? America's White Ethnic Groups*. New York: E.P. Dutton.

Green, John C. 2007. *The Faith Factor: How Religion Influences American Elections*. Westport, Conn.: Praeger.

Hagan, Jacqueline Maria. 2008. *Migration Miracle: Faith, Hope, and Meaning on the Undocumented Journey*. Cambridge, MA: Harvard University Press.

Hammond, Phillip E., and Kee Warner. 1993. "Religion and Ethnicity in Late-Twentieth-Century America." *Annals of the American Academy of Political and Social Science* 527: 55–66.

Herberg, Will. 1955. *Protestant, Catholic, Jew: An Essay in American Religious Sociology*. Garden City, N.Y.: Doubleday.

Hollenbach, Florian, Nils W. Metternich, Shahryar Minhas, and Michael D. Ward. 2014. "Fast & Easy Imputation of Missing Social Science Data." arXiv:1411.0647 [stat.AP]. Accessed January 31, 2016. http://arxiv.org/abs/1411.0647.

Honaker, James, Gary King, and Matthew Blackwell.

2012. "Amelia II: A Program for Missing Data." Accessed January 31, 2016. http://gking.harvard.edu/amelia.

Ibarra, Joanne D., and David L. Leal. 2013. "Latinos, Religion, and Political Engagement: Revisiting the Catholic Demobilization Hypothesis." Paper Presented at the Annual Meeting of the Western Political Science Association. Hollywood, Calif. (May 27–30, 2013).

Jones-Correa, Michael A., and David L. Leal. 2001. "Political Participation: Does Religion Matter?" *Political Research Quarterly* 54(4): 91–123.

Kellstedt, Lyman A., John C. Green, James L. Guth, and Corwin E. Smidt. 1996. "Grasping the Essentials: The Social Embodiment of Religion and Political Behavior." In *Religion and the Culture Wars*, edited by John C. Green, James L. Gurth, Corwin E. Smidt, and Lyman E. Kellstedt. Lanham, Md.: Roman and Littlefield.

Keysar, Ariela. 2014. "Filling a Data Gap: The American Religious Identification Survey (ARIS) Survey." *Religion* 44(3): 383–95. doi: 10.1080/0048721X.2014.903648.

Layman, Geoffrey C. 1997. "Religion and Political Behavior in the United States: The Impact of Beliefs, Affiliation, and Commitment from 1980 to 1994." *Public Opinion Quarterly* 61: 288–316.

———. 2001. *The Great Divide: Religion and Cultural Conflict in American Party Politics*. New York: Columbia University Press.

Leal, David L. 2002. "Political Participation by Latino Non-Citizens in the United States." *British Journal of Political Science* 32(2): 353–70.

———. 2010. "Religion in Latino Political and Civic Lives." In *Religion and Democracy in the United States Danger or Opportunity?*, edited by Alan Wolfe and Ira Katznelson. Princeton, N.J.: Princeton University Press.

Leal, David L., and Jerod Patterson. 2013. "House Divided? Evangelical Catholics, Mainstream Catholics, and Attitudes Toward Immigration and Life Policies." *The Forum: A Journal of Applied Research in Contemporary Politics* 11(4): 561–87.

———. 2014. "The Politics of Conversion: Do Changes in Religious Affiliation Shape Partisanship?" Paper presented at the annual meeting of the Midwest Political Science Association. Chicago (April 2–6, 2014).

Lee, Jongho, and Harry Pachon. 2007. "Leading the Way: An Analysis of the Effect of Religion on the Latino Vote." *American Politics Research* 35(2): 252–68.

Leonard, Karen I., Alexa Stepick, Manuel A. Vanquez, and Jennifer Holdaway, eds. 2005. *Immigrant Faiths: Transforming Religious Life in America*. Lanham, Md.: AltaMira Press.

Levitt, Peggy. 2002. "Two Nations Under God? Latino Religious Life in the United States." In *Latinos: Remaking America*, edited by Marcelo M. Suárez-Orozco and Mariela M. Páez. Berkeley: University of California Press.

———. 2008. "Religion as a Path to Civic Engagement." *Ethnic and Racial Studies* 31(4): 766–91.

Matovina, Timothy. 2012. *Latino Catholicism: Transformation in America's Largest Church*. Princeton, N.J.: Princeton University Press.

Matovina, Timothy, and Gary Riebe-Estrella, eds. 2002. *Horizons of the Sacred: Mexican Traditions in U.S. Catholicism*. Ithaca, N.Y.: Cornell University Press.

McCann, James A., and Michael Jones-Correa. 2012. Latino Immigrant National Election Study, 2012. New York: Russell Sage Foundation, Carnegie Corporation of New York, Purdue University, and Cornell University.

McDaniel, Eric, and Christopher Ellison. 2008. "God's Party? Race, Religion, and Partisanship over Time." *Political Research Quarterly* 61: 180–91.

Menjívar, Cecilia. 2003. "Religion and Immigration in a Comparative Perspective: Catholics and Evangelical Salvadorans in San Francisco, Washington, D.C., and Phoenix." *Social Religion*, 64(1): 21–45.

Mervis, Jeffery. 2014. "Why Null Results Rarely See the Light of Day." *Science* 345 (6200): 992.

Mora, G. Cristina. 2013. "Religion and the Organizational Context of Immigrant Civic Participation: Mexican Catholicism in the US." *Ethnic and Racial Studies*, v36: 1647–65.

Olson, Laura R., and Adam L. Warber. 2008. "Belonging, Behaving, and Believing: Assessing the Role of Religion on Presidential Approval." *Political Research Quarterly* 61(2): 192–204.

Pew Forum on Religion & Public Life. 2006. "Spirit and Power: A 10-Country Survey of Pentecostals." Washington, D.C.: Pew Research Center. Accessed February 22, 2016. http://www.pewforum.org/2006/10/05/spirit-and-power/

———. 2007. "Changing Faiths: Latinos and the

Transformation of American Religion." Washington, D.C.: Pew Research Center. Accessed January 31, 2016. http://www.pewforum.org/files/2007/04/hispanics-religion-07-final-mar08.pdf.

———. 2009. "Faith in Flux: Changes in Religious Affiliation in the U.S." Washington, D.C.: Pew Research Center. Accessed January 31, 2016. http://www.pewforum.org/files/2009/04/fullreport.pdf.

Pew Research Center. 2014. *The Shifting Religious Identity of Latinos in the United States*. Washington, D.C.: Pew Research Center. Accessed January 31, 2016. http://www.pewforum.org/files/2014/05/Latinos-Religion-07-22-full-report.pdf.

Prouty, Marco G. 2006. *Cesar Chavez, the Catholic Bishops, and the Farmworkers' Struggle for Social Justice*. Tucson: University of Arizona Press.

Putnam, Robert. 2001. *Bowing Alone: The Collapse and Revival of American Community*. New York: Simon & Schuster.

Sandoval, Moises. 2006. *On the Move: A History of the Hispanic Church in the United States*. New York: Orbis Books.

Smidt, Corwin E., Lyman A. Kellstedt, and James L. Guth. 2009. "The Role of Religion in American Politics: Explanatory Theories and Associated Analytical and Measurement Issues." In *Oxford Handbook of Religion and American Politics*, edited by Corwin E.Smidt, Lyman A. Kellstedt, and James L. Guth. Oxford: Oxford University Press.

Southern Baptist Convention. 2011. "On Immigration and the Gospel." Accessed January 31, 2016. http://www.sbc.net/resolutions/1213.

Stevens-Arroyo, Anthony M. 1980. *Prophets Denied Honor: An Anthology on the Hispano Church of the United States*. New York: Maryknoll.

———. 1998. "The Latino Religious Resurgence." *Annals of the American Academy of Political and Social Science* 558: 163–76.

Tweed, Thomas. 2006. *Crossing and Dwelling: A Theory of Religion*. Cambridge, Mass.: Harvard University Press.

Vargas-Ramos, Carlos, and Anthony M. Stevens-Arroyo, eds. 2012. *Blessing La Política: The Latino Religious Experience and Political Engagement in the United States*. New York: Praeger.

Verba, Sidney, Kay Schlozman, and Henry E. Brady. 1995. *Voice and Equality: Civic Volunteerism in American Politics*. Cambridge, Mass.: Harvard University Press.

Warner, R. Stephen. 1998. "Approaching Religious Diversity: Barriers, Byways, and Beginnings." *Sociology of Religion* 59(3): 193–215.

———. 2007. "The Role of Religion in the Process of Segmented Assimilation." *Annals of the American Academy of Political and Social Science* 612: 102–15.

Wilson, Catherine E. 2008. *The Politics of Latino Faith: Religion, Identity, and Urban Community*. New York: New York University Press.

Wuthnow, Robert. 1990. *The Restructuring of American Religion: Society and Faith Since World War II*. Princeton, N.J.: Princeton University Press.

Yang, Fenggang. 1999. *Chinese Christians in America: Conversion, Assimilation, and Adhesive Identities*. University Park: Pennsylvania State University Press.

Yang, Fenggang, and Helen Rose Ebaugh. 2001. "Religion and Ethnicity Among New Immigrants: The Impact of Majority/Minority Status in Home and Host Countries." *Journal for the Scientific Study of Religion* 40(3): 367–78.

Young, Rebekah, and David R. Johnson. 2010. "Imputing the Missing Y's: Implications for Survey Producers and Survey Users." *Proceedings of the AAPOR Conference Abstracts*, 6242–6248. Accessed January 31, 2016. https://www.amstat.org/sections/srms/proceedings/y2010/Files/400142.pdf.

# PART III
Political Participation and Partisanship

Latino Electoral Participation: Variations on Demographics and Ethnicity

JAN LEIGHLEY AND JONATHAN NAGLER

Using the 2012 Latino Immigrant National Election Study, the 2012 American National Election Study, and the 2012 Current Population Survey, we document the demographic factors that influenced Latino (native-born and immigrant) voter turnout and participation in the 2012 presidential election. We estimate multivariable models of turnout and participation, including standard demographic characteristics (education, income, age, gender, marital status) as explanatory variables. Our findings indicate that the relationships between these characteristics and participation are much less consistent across these datasets than the conventional wisdom would suggest. Understanding these results likely requires survey data—with large sample sizes—including information on the resources (including education and income) available to immigrants in their home countries to better understand the lingering influences of immigrants' experiences in their countries of origin on voter turnout.

Keywords: Latino, voter turnout, political participation, immigrants, socioeconomic status, country of origin, 2012 presidential election, party contact

In the early stages of the 2016 presidential primaries in the United States, the increasing size and political presence of Latinos—and Latino immigrants—has clearly been reflected in candidates' campaign rhetoric and strategies. Because immigrants and immigration policy are central to the campaign dialogue at this stage, it is especially important to understand the possible, or even likely, political responses of Latinos, both foreign- and native-born. Although scholars have repeatedly emphasized the increasing electoral relevance of Latinos (see, most recently, Barreto and Segura 2014), studies of Latino turnout and political participation present a complex and unclear picture of the factors that influence Latino political engagement.

This complexity contrasts with Sidney Verba, Kay Schlozman, and Henry Brady's (1995) seemingly simple description of how to think about why individuals participate: because they can, because they want to, or because they are asked. Surely individual resources such as money, time, and skills are important for understanding political engagement in contemporary democratic politics (most recently, see Leighley and Nagler 2014). Yet a challenge to understanding broad patterns of political engagement is that traditional demographic models such as Verba,

Jan Leighley is professor of political science at American University. **Jonathan Nagler** is professor of politics at New York University and co-principal investigator of the NYU Social Media and Political Participation Laboratory.

Thanks to the Russell Sage Foundation for survey and conference support and to Elad Zippory for research assistance. Direct correspondence to: Jan Leighley at leighley@american.edu, American University, Department of Government, 4400 Massachusetts Ave., N.W., Washington, D.C. 20016; and Jonathan Nagler at jonathan.nagler@nyu.edu, New York University, Department of Politics, 19 W. 4th St., New York, NY 10012.

Schlozman, and Brady's may be less applicable for a community that is distinctive in terms of immigration status and experience, language skills, and social integration (Junn 2010). Sergio Garcia-Rios and Matt Barreto, for example, emphasize in this volume the critical role of immigrant identity in predicting political engagement but suggest that identity is independent of the important role of resources in understanding immigrant participation.

The study of Latino voter turnout has shifted over the past several decades from comparisons of whether Latinos vote more or less than whites to more recent studies focusing on factors distinctive to Latinos or to Latino turnout in specific elections (see, for example, Wolfinger and Rosenstone 1980, in contrast to Abrajano and Panagopoulos 2011; Barreto 2005; Barreto, Segura, and Woods 2004; Bueker 2013). These new studies have not clearly resolved the extent to which the standard demographic variables repeatedly associated with citizens' decisions to vote in presidential elections likewise influence Latinos' decisions to cast a ballot.

Latino political mobilization around immigration issues has also shifted some attention to Latino political activity other than voting. These studies point to the importance of political issues and community organizations in mobilizing Latinos to take action, and in modes of participation not requiring citizenship or voter registration status (see, for example, Leal et al. 2008; Levin 2013; Mohamed 2013; in this volume, see both Garcia-Rios and Barreto and Waldinger and Duquette-Rury). Yet these studies, too, offer an unclear picture as to how the basic resources of Latinos—such as education, income, and age—influence their political engagement.

In this chapter, we use the 2012 Latino Immigrant National Election Study (LINES) and the 2012 American National Election Study (ANES) to document the demographic factors that influenced Latino voter turnout and political participation in the 2012 presidential election, and to assess the extent to which demographic resources such as education, income, and age are similar or different in their effects on Latino native-born and immigrant engagement. To put these findings in broader context, we also compare them with similar analyses for non-Hispanic whites in the 2012 presidential election.

LATINO TURNOUT: U.S.-BORN AND FOREIGN-BORN

Although demographic factors remain central in discussions of voter turnout in studies focused on mass political behavior in the United States (Leighley and Nagler 2014), studies focusing on specific racial and ethnic groups report inconsistent findings regarding the importance or meaning of the demographic correlates of turnout. Most studies of specific racial and ethnic groups, for example, find that education is an important predictor of turnout in elections, presidential and otherwise, but many report that income is not associated with greater likelihood of voting (Barreto 2005; Bueker 2013; Jang 2009; Pantoja, Ramírez, and Segura 2001; Parkin and Zlotnik 2011; Shaw, de la Garza, and Lee 2000; Tam Cho 1999).[1] The studies that tend to report statistically significant (and positive) estimates of the effects of education and income on Latinos' decisions to vote are typically based on surveys with large sample sizes (Bass and Casper 2001; Cassel 2002; Jackson 2003). Whether null findings regarding income (and sometimes education) based on smaller, typically more local or regionally based samples emerge solely due to sample size or for other reasons associated with the sample, survey administration or local political context is not clear.

Benjamin Highton and Arthur Burris (2002) analyze Latino turnout using the 1996 Current Population Survey (CPS), estimating a demographic model of turnout separately for Cuban Americans, Puerto Ricans, and Mexican Americans (sample sizes of 204, 654, and 1,958, respectively). They find education to be a significant predictor of turnout for each group, but income to be a significant predictor for only Mexican Americans. Other variables included in the model include residential stability, for-

---

1. See Leal (2002) regarding nonelectoral political participation being unrelated to education and income but related to information, identity, and English language proficiency.

eign born, and years in the United States, along with state dummies. Highton and Burris also note the importance of including how long individuals have been in the United States in models estimating the importance of nativity, and show that lower immigrant turnout, compared with native born, is modified or reduced when conditioning on years of residence in the United States. "Citizens who have lived in the country for longer periods of time," they conclude, "have had more experience with the American political system and have higher levels of political information and understanding. All these factors facilitate turnout" (2002, 301).

Many studies of Latino turnout tend to emphasize *nondemographic* factors associated with the social and political context, immigration experience or cultural characteristics and resources. These characteristics include English language use (Johnson, Stein, and Wrinkle 2003; Parkin and Zlotnik 2011; Pearson-Merkowitz 2012a, 2012b; Tam Cho 1999); length of time in United States (Highton and Burris 2002; Ramakrishnan and Espenshade 2001); and the political environment in which one naturalizes (see, for example, Ramakrishnan and Espenshade 2001). The importance of political environment is underscored by Barreto's (2005) and Adrian Pantoja, Ricardo Ramírez, and Gary Segura's (2001) findings that Latino foreign-born turnout is higher than Latino native-born turnout. Some studies also include Spanish-language ballot access and interview language in models, though the precise nature of the effects of these variables is quite variable in what is expected, how it is modeled, and the significance of the estimates (Johnson, Stein, and Wrinkle 2003; Parkin and Zlotnik 2011; Ramakrishnan and Espenshade 2001).

Recent research has, importantly, pointed to a decidedly nondemographic factor associated with Latino voter turnout: political mobilization. As in the case of studies of turnout focusing on Anglo-dominant samples based on self-reports (for example, ANES-based survey data; see Rosenstone and Hansen 1993), Latinos who report being contacted to vote are more likely to also report having voted (Pantoja, Ramírez, and Segura 2001; Ramírez 2005). More rigorous causal inferences on the importance of mobilization, of course, can be drawn from studies relying on field experiments (see, most recently, García Bedolla and Michelson 2012; Michelson 2003, 2005, 2006; Michelson and García Bedolla 2014; Stevens and Bishin 2011; Matland and Murray 2012). These studies find that Latinos who are mobilized are more likely to vote than those who are not mobilized, but also suggest that political parties are less likely to contact Latinos (than whites) and that nonparty mobilization may be less effective in mobilizing Latino turnout than party mobilization is (Stevens and Bishin 2011).

Studies of Latino immigrant turnout point to potentially distinctive influences on those Latino immigrants who have become citizens and are eligible to vote. Barreto (2005) argues that the political environment at the time of naturalization influences the level of subsequent political engagement of Latino immigrants who become eligible to vote and observes that these contextual influences vary across states (Florida, California, and Texas). As a result of these differences, naturalized Latinos may participate as much as or more than native-born Latinos (see also Pantoja, Ramírez, and Segura 2001).

Finally, studies of Latino participation beyond voter turnout are few in number (Valdez 2011; Wrinkle et al. 1996). The assumption might be made that the same factors predicting Latino turnout should be relevant to other types of participation such as attending meetings or contacting officials, but this may not be the case for Latino immigrants. In a study of Latino noncitizen participation, David Leal (2002) concludes that education, income, and length of stay in the United States were not significant predictors of Latino immigrant participation, but that political identity, English skills, and age were. Ines Levin (2013) concludes that immigrants who have gained citizenship status are no more likely to engage in community activities such as belonging to political groups or engaging in problem-solving. However, these citizens are more likely to contact government officials than are immigrants who have not completed the naturalization process.

Leal, Jerod Patterson, and Joe Tafoya report elsewhere in this issue mixed findings for the effects of education on turnout, civic participation, and campaign participation of immigrants, but no effects of income on these types of participation. However, their analyses and discussion focus primarily on the influence of religion, as opposed to demographics, on participation.

The analyses here seek to use the most recent and comprehensive data on Latino immigrants to reflect on the sources identified in the previous literature as important to understanding both turnout and other types of political participation. We examine the similarities and differences in the correlates of citizen and noncitizen participation of Latino immigrants, with comparisons to native-born Latinos and whites. We do not speak directly to the role of party or nonparty mobilization, the mobilizing effects of issues, or the importance of group identity. The focus on demographics to the exclusion of these important factors is motivated in part by the importance of documenting the distinctively different role of demographics to understanding Latino immigrant turnout and nonelectoral participation as an important first step toward understanding more fully Latino political engagement.

DATA AND SAMPLES

We use data from the 2012 LINES, the 2012 ANES, and the 2012 U.S. Census Bureau CPS. The LINES survey is a representative survey of immigrants from Latino-speaking countries, while the ANES is a nationally representative survey of U.S. citizens, including both foreign-born and native-born Latinos. The CPS is a monthly survey conducted by the Census Bureau that includes questions about voter turnout in its November survey. Together, these survey data allow us to study the turnout of native-born and foreign-born Latino citizens as well as the nonelectoral participation of native-born and foreign-born Latino citizens and noncitizens; it also allows us to compare our findings to the turnout and political participation of non-Hispanic white citizens.

Although the large sample size of the LINES survey allows questions regarding immigrants to be addressed more fully than previous studies have allowed (as demonstrated in other papers in this volume), the number of survey respondents eligible to vote remains quite small. The LINES postelection wave, which provides the measure of self-reported turnout, has 886 respondents, of whom only 327 are eligible to vote based on citizenship status.

Our measure of self-reported voter turnout is based on individuals' responses to the LINES question asking whether they had voted in the November election. Only individuals who responded "I am sure I voted" were coded as voting; those who responded "I did not vote," "I thought about voting this time, but didn't," or "I usually vote, but didn't this time" were coded as not voting.[2]

The same question wording, set of response categories, and final coding details are used for the ANES 2012 self-reported turnout measure, where we restrict the sample to three groups: U.S.-born Latinos, foreign-born Latinos, and whites. Using subsamples of U.S.-born Latinos and foreign-born Latinos in the ANES allows us to assess whether the determinants of turnout are the same for these two groups, and allows a comparison of both of

---

2. Self-reported voter turnout measures undoubtedly overestimate actual voter turnout. Since a primary goal of this paper is to compare empirical findings across the LINES and ANES samples, it is important to use the same type of measure available in both datasets. In relying on the self-reported turnout measure, it is important that the misreporting rates of Latinos and whites do not differ to draw appropriate conclusions regarding turnout differences across these two groups. We compared misreporting rates between Hispanics and the entire electorate using the 2008 Cooperative Congressional Election Survey (CCES). The sample includes 32,800 respondents, including 2,000 self-identified Hispanic respondents. For the entire sample, 79.7 percent of reported voters were validated as having voted. For Hispanic voters, 76.3 percent were validated as having voted. The misreporting rate as measured by the proportion of reported voters who were verified as being not registered, or verified as not voting, was 12.5 percent for all respondents and 13.2 percent for Hispanics. Thus we think our results for Hispanics presented using the LINES and ANES data can safely be compared with results based on reported vote for other non-Hispanic samples. [All values computed by the authors from the CCES cumulative file using the supplied weight variable.]

these groups to Latino immigrant behavior as documented in the LINES study.

In both the LINES and ANES data, we use a measure of nonvoting participation that indicates whether the respondent reports engaging in any one of five activities over the course of the election year: trying to influence another's vote; attending a campaign rally, speech, or dinner in support of a particular candidate; wearing a button or displaying a sign or sticker; doing campaign work; or contributing to a political candidate.

The demographic variables we examine in both datasets are coded the same to facilitate comparison. Our education measure has four categories: less than high school, high school graduate, some college, and college degree or higher. Income is coded into four categories: less than $20,000, $20,000 to 40,000, $40,000 to 80,000, and more than $80,000. Age is coded into four groups for presenting descriptive statistics: eighteen through thirty-four, thirty-five through forty-four, forty-five through fifty-four, and fifty-five and older.

THE DEMOGRAPHICS OF TURNOUT AND ELECTORAL PARTICIPATION

Table 1 reports the turnout and electoral participation rates (as appropriate) for five subsamples: LINES noncitizens, LINES citizens, ANES Latino foreign-born citizens, ANES native-born Latinos, and ANES (non-Hispanic) whites.[3] Of course, turnout is not reported for the noncitizen group. The ANES data suggest that Latino foreign-born citizens report voting at about the same rate as white respondents—84.3 percent compared to 85.5 percent—and that U.S.-born Latinos report voting at slightly lower levels, 78.9 percent. In contrast, only 72 percent of (LINES) Latino immigrant citizens report having voted. The discrepancy between turnout of Latino immigrant citizens across the two samples could be because of the different sampling frames used, or other survey administration differences between LINES and the ANES.[4] We also note that although all calculations are reported using weights for education and age, the LINES citizens were substantially more likely to be in the lowest income group than ANES foreign-born citizens were: 46.9 percent of the LINES citizens were in the lowest income group, compared to only 30.7 percent of ANES foreign-born Hispanics in the lowest income group.

The two (LINES and ANES) immigrant groups, however, report participating in nonvoting campaign-related activities at about the same level as U.S.-born Latinos and whites. This contrasts with the substantially lower reported nonvoting participation rate of 34.3 percent reported by (LINES) noncitizens. This could be because though these noncitizens are eligible to engage in these participatory acts, someone who is not eligible to vote themselves may simply be much less likely to attend a campaign rally or try to convince someone else how to vote.[5]

Table 2 includes the self-reported turnout rates for LINES citizens and for ANES Latino foreign-born citizens, Latino native-born citizens, and white citizens, by education, income, age, and gender. The clear pattern of increasing education level being associated with higher turnout rates that is observed for whites does not hold for the other samples, although

---

3. Throughout the paper, we use the term *whites* to refer to the non-Hispanic white subsample. See issue appendix for details on the weights used for each group: non-Hispanic whites, Hispanic immigrant citizens, and Hispanic native-born citizens.

4. We note that calculating turnout using the CPS from 2012 would yield estimates of 52.3 percent for Latino naturalized citizens, and 64.1 percent for non-Hispanic whites. Thus respondents in LINES seem to overreport turnout in ways similar to ANES respondents, or persons more likely to vote are more likely to respond to both surveys. The difference in turnout between Latino immigrant citizens and non-Hispanic whites based on the CPS data is 12.8 percent, which is similar to the difference in turnout between these two groups when using LINES and ANES data (13.5 percent).

5. However, Leal and Patterson (this volume) report immigrants' participation in civic (noncampaign) activities to be lower than the 34 percent of LINES noncitizens who engage in political participation other than voting.

Table 1. Self-Reported Turnout and Participation

	LINES Latino Immigrant Noncitizens	LINES Latino Immigrant Citizens	ANES Latino Foreign-Born Citizens	ANES Latino U.S.-Born Citizens	ANES White Citizens
Turnout		72% (351)	84.3% (124)	78.9% (260)	85.5% (2757)
Participation	34.3% (508)	46.0% (360)	43.2% (176)	45.4% (305)	45.9% (3259)

Source: Authors' calculations using ANES 2012, McCann and Jones-Correa 2012.
Note: Cell entries are the (weighted) proportion of each sample in the row who repeat voting (row 1) or participating (row 2); values in parentheses are the number of respondents of each sample in the row.

Table 2. Self-Reported Turnout by Demographic Characteristics

	LINES Latino Immigrant Citizens	ANES Latino Foreign-Born Citizens	ANES Latino U.S.-Born Citizens	ANES White Citizens
Education				
Less than high school	73.5% (184)	73.5% (39)	54.1% (26)	71.1% (150)
High school graduate	70.4% (63)	82.1% (38)	85.2% (74)	82.4% (636)
Some college	68.1% (60)	86.2% (32)	77.7% (91)	86.5% (875)
College graduate	77% (35)	100% (32)	92.9% (66)	91.6% (1070)
Income				
Less than $20,000	68.0% (132)	81.2% (43)	63.6% (70)	75.2% (416)
$20,000–$40,000	77.9% (78)	79.4% (35)	81.2% (49)	82.9% (494)
$40,000–$80,000	68.0% (49)	86.9% (43)	88.5% (73)	86.8% (813)
$80,000 and above	71.6% (22)	94.2% (21)	91.0% (62)	91.5% (884)
Gender				
Men	70.0% (158)	83.2% (79)	79.5% (149)	85.7% (1363)
Women	74.0% (193)	85.4% (65)	78.1% (111)	85.3% (1394)
Age				
Eighteen to thirty-four	57.8% (31)	83.0% (12)	92.0% (91)	73.2% (480)
Thirty-five to forty-four	77.5% (52)	85.9% (23)	85.1% (40)	86.0% (398)
Forty-five to fifty-four	69.5% (66)	89.7% (39)	68.7% (46)	87.9% (517)
Fifty-five and older	80.7% (177)	79.8% (70)	76.3% (83)	92.0% (1343)

Source: Authors' calculations using ANES 2012, McCann and Jones-Correa 2012.
Note: Cell entries are the (weighted) proportion of each sample in the row who report voting; values in parentheses are the number of respondents of each sample in the row.

in each group high school graduates and those who failed to graduate from high school vote less than college graduates. Across the four groups, U.S.-born Latinos with less than a high school education report voting substantially less than the others.

A positive relationship between income and voter turnout is confirmed for three groups, Latino immigrant citizens being the exception. Although the poorest (LINES) Latino immigrants report voting at slightly higher rates than the poorest Latinos born in the United States (68 percent compared to 63.6 percent), these immigrant citizens do not seem to benefit from additional income, because the level of turnout in this group at the highest level of income increases only to 71.6 percent (compared to reported turnout over 90 percent for each of the other samples).

The LINES immigrant citizens and ANES Latino foreign-born citizens are also distinctive in reported turnout rates by gender, where they are the only groups to report slightly higher turnout rates for women than for men—though the difference in turnout between men and women is small in all samples.

The self-reported turnout rates by age category are more complex for the three Latino subsamples than for the white citizen (ANES) sample. Conventional wisdom is that turnout increases as individuals age, and presumably gain more experience with democratic politics, but this is documented only for the white citizens. For (ANES) Latino foreign-born citizens and U.S.-born citizens, the youngest age group reports quite high levels of turnout. The lowest turnout among youth is reported by (LINES) immigrant citizens (57.8 percent).[6]

Table 3 reports levels of electoral participation other than turnout for LINES noncitizens, LINES citizens, ANES Latino foreign-born citizens, ANES Latino native born, and ANES whites, by education, income, age, and gender. Here, the expected pattern of higher levels of education being associated with greater levels of participation is confirmed for each group. Although Latino immigrant noncitizens with the least education report the least participation, Latino immigrant citizens (LINES and ANES) report participating at higher levels than U.S.-born Latinos and whites. The same positive pattern between income and turnout is observed for every group except for (ANES) Latino foreign-born citizens.

Women in the (LINES) citizen and noncitizen groups report participating less than men, as do women in the white citizen sample. Gender differences are minimal or not observed for the (ANES) Latinos, whether foreign born or U.S. born. Age is distinctive for its clear positive association with self-reported turnout for white citizens, in contrast to the other samples.

MULTIVARIABLE MODELS OF TURNOUT AND NONVOTING PARTICIPATION

We now turn to estimating multivariable models of turnout and participation, seeking to understand better the associations between each demographic characteristic and turnout or participation while conditioning on the other characteristics. These findings are important because they provide the first precise estimates of the similarities and differences of the effects of demographic characteristics on turnout and participation for Latino immigrants and for native-born Latinos with direct comparisons to white citizens. Our demographic model of turnout includes the standard measures used in studies of voter turnout: education, income, age, gender, and marital status.

Table 4 presents estimates for the demographic model of turnout estimated for the four citizen groups (LINES citizens, ANES Latino foreign-born citizens, ANES Latino U.S.-born citizens, and ANES white citizens). As predictors of turnout, we include respondents' level of education and income, as well as age and gender, and a dummy variable indicating whether the respondent is married. We also include variables for whether the respondent lives in the South, California, Florida, or Texas. Using these three state variables is a minimal way to include state-fixed effects in the model. We do not have enough observations to include fixed effects for each state. But these

---

6. The sample size in the lowest age group is quite small for ANES foreign-born citizens, which of course makes the turnout estimate much less reliable.

Table 3. Participation by Demographic Characteristics

	LINES Latino Immigrant Noncitizens	LINES Latino Immigrant Citizens	ANES Latino Foreign-Born Citizens	ANES Latino U.S.-Born Citizens	ANES White Citizens
Education					
Less than high school	28.6% (331)	40.9% (187)	42.8% (51)	39.8% (30)	35.2% (216)
High school graduate	35.3% (94)	46.1% (64)	30.6% (47)	44.3% (89)	40.1% (787)
Some college	44.2% (46)	45.4% (61)	55.5% (40)	50.2% (107)	49.3% (1019)
College graduate	60.0% (25)	50.0% (37)	56.3% (35)	47.3% (74)	53.1% (1200)
Income					
Less than $20,000	35.4% (240)	38.3% (134)	44.4% (50)	40.6% (85)	37.0% (549)
$20,000–$40,000	35.6% (128)	41.5% (81)	35.7% (46)	46.7% (61)	43.6% (607)
$40,000–$80,000	41.0% (45)	49.2% (51)	38.4% (53)	45.3% (85)	49.6% (915)
$80,000 and above	47.8% (9)	60.2% (22)	72.0% (24)	49.9% (67)	51.8% (993)
Gender					
Men	36.3% (222)	50.2% (162)	43.2% (92)	46.5% (169)	49.5% (1627)
Women	31.9% (286)	42.4% (198)	43.2% (84)	44.2% (136)	42.2% (1632)
Age					
Eighteen to thirty-four	38.5% (101)	47.6% (32)	35.8% (19)	47.8% (106)	36.8% (613)
Thirty-five to forty-four	31.4% (136)	34.9% (55)	34.3% (28)	39.6% (44)	43.5% (456)
Forty-five to fifty-four	36.3% (121)	45.9% (66)	50.0% (43)	36.4% (53)	44.8% (602)
Fifty-five and older	37.3% (114)	49.1% (179)	47.6% (86)	50.1% (102)	53.7% (1565)

Source: Authors' calculations using ANES 2012, McCann and Jones-Correa 2012.
Note: Cell entries are the (weighted) proportion of each sample in the row who report participating; values in parentheses are the number of respondents of each sample in the row.

three states capture where a large number of Hispanics reside, and thus allow us to condition on any state-based fixed effects on turnout.[7] We see in table 4 that, as expected, higher levels of education, income, and age, as well as being married, are associated with higher re-

7. State-based fixed effects would capture any specific characteristics of the state—such as a more competitive state-wide election or laws that impose fewer hurdles to voting—that could raise or depress the level of turnout in the state relative to other states. This is especially important in studying Latino turnout as Latinos tend to be overrepresented in noncompetitive states such as Florida and Texas.

Table 4. Demographic Model of Turnout

	LINES Latino Immigrant Citizens	ANES Latino Foreign-Born Citizens	ANES Latino U.S.-Born Citizens	ANES White Citizens
Education	0.007	0.583**	0.458**	0.450***
	(0.157)	(0.262)	(0.227)	(0.073)
Income	0.321*	0.105	0.378*	0.226***
	(0.181)	(0.267)	(0.199)	(0.066)
Age	0.018*	−0.017	0.034***	0.038***
	(0.011)	(0.020)	(0.013)	(0.004)
Woman	0.265	0.013	0.357	−0.055
	(0.302)	(0.484)	(0.394)	(0.129)
Married	−0.191	0.391	0.879**	0.307**
	(0.317)	(0.511)	(0.430)	(0.140)
South	−0.950*		1.183	−0.042
	(0.571)		(1.124)	(0.181)
California	−0.053		0.032	0.515*
	(0.375)		(0.482)	(0.295)
Texas	0.433		−1.854	−0.604**
	(0.580)		(1.152)	(0.277)
Florida	1.290*		−0.679	0.124
	(0.692)		(1.346)	(0.345)
Constant	−0.470	0.871	−2.176***	−1.849***
	(0.867)	(1.388)	(0.825)	(0.321)
Observations	264	139	252	2,573
LR	0.110	0.109	1.22e−05	0
Log likelihood	−147.5	−56.22	−90.83	−834.7

Source: Authors' calculations using ANES 2012, McCann and Jones-Correa 2012.
Note: Cell entry is the logit coefficient; standard errors in parentheses.
*p < .1; **p < .05; ***p < .01

ported turnout for white citizens.[8] In contrast to our expectations based on recent research, women are no more likely to report voting than men are for any of the four groups.

Our two primary indicators of socioeconomic status, education and income, are significant and estimated to be positive for both white and Latino U.S.-born citizens. In contrast, only education is significantly and positively associated with reported turnout for (ANES) Latino foreign-born citizens, and only income is positively associated with reported turnout for (LINES) immigrant citizens. These different findings might well reflect differences in the sampling frames or survey administration of LINES and ANES as much as any "real" difference in the predictors of turnout for these two samples, though this is a finding that likely requires additional investigation.[9]

In addition to these standard demographic

[8]. We also estimated each of the multivariable models including age at time of immigration. The coefficient for this variable was never significant, and did not substantially alter any of the other results. These results are available from the authors.

[9]. We also estimated the turnout model with each of the demographic variables and all four contextual variables (South, Florida, Texas, California) using data from the CPS. In this model education was a strong predictor of

characteristics, we also include whether the respondent lives in the South, California, Florida, or Texas in three of the models.[10] Including these variables in the model estimated for the ANES foreign-born citizens is not possible due to high multicollinearity among these variables (owing to the ANES foreign-born Latino respondents being drawn disproportionately from these three states). The only group for which living in the South is estimated to be significant at even the 10 percent level is for the (LINES) Latino immigrant citizens. Latino immigrant citizens living in the South are less likely to report voting than Latino immigrants living outside the South are. These immigrants are also significantly more likely to report voting if they live in Florida, again the only group for which this state context seems to influence reported turnout rates.

Although none of the contextual measures are significant for U.S.-born Latinos, both living in California and living in Texas is significantly related to turnout for white citizens. Whites living in California are significantly more likely to report voting, whereas whites living in Texas are significantly less likely. These distinctive results for Latinos and whites might reflect the different mobilization contexts of each of these states for these two groups, a point to which we return to in the conclusion.

Table 5 presents our estimates for the impact of these demographic characteristics on nonvoting participation. The additional benefit of these analyses is that they provide more detailed information regarding the correlates of participation of Latino noncitizen immigrants. Recent studies have emphasized the importance of immigration as a political issue as a mobilizer of Latino political engagement, but the question remains as to whether the socioeconomic correlates of participation enhance the political engagement of noncitizens.

As reported in table 5, the demographic correlates of nonvoting participation are significant and as expected for white citizens. Education, income, age, and being married are all positively associated with nonvoting participation, and being a woman is negatively associated with nonelectoral participation, conditional on values of the variables included in the model. However, examining the first three columns of table 5, we see that few of these demographic characteristics are systematically associated with nonvoting participation for Latino immigrants, whether citizen or not. For (LINES) noncitizens, only education significantly predicts participation, but for foreign-born Latino citizens, education and age significantly predict participation. For (LINES) immigrant citizens and (ANES) U.S.-born Latinos, none of the demographic predictors are significantly associated with participation.

These systematic estimates of the demographic correlates of turnout and nonvoting participation suggest that theories that posit the importance of socioeconomic status are more relevant to Latinos for voter turnout rather than nonvoting participation. For nonvoting participation, it appears that factors other than demographic resources might provide a different path to political engagement. We provide some additional data as to these alternative possibilities next.

IF NOT—OR ONLY—DEMOGRAPHICS, THEN WHAT?

Our focus thus far has been on Verba, Schlozman, and Brady's (1995) first explanation of why individuals participate—because they can. Given somewhat mixed evidence for the systematic importance of education and income as predictors of turnout and nonvoting participation for Latinos (whether immigrants or not), we now turn briefly to two other explanations that Verba, Schlozman, and Brady noted (and many others since then have recognized): individuals participate because they want to, or because they are asked.

Investigating these explanations fully is be-

---

voting among naturalized Latino citizens and U.S.-born Latino citizens. However, income was not a strong predictor, nor was it statistically significant for naturalized Latino citizens. This could reflect fundamental differences in sampling design between the CPS and LINES, or it could simply reflect the fragility of estimates from LINES based on only 264 respondents (for the full model results from the CPS, see table A1).

10. We use the standard eleven-state measure of the South.

Table 5. Demographic Model of Nonvoting Participation

	LINES Latino Immigrant Noncitizens	LINES Latino Immigrant Citizens	ANES Latino Foreign-Born Citizens	ANES Latino U.S.-Born Citizens	ANES White Citizens
Education	0.536***	0.038	0.308**	0.190	0.237***
	(0.131)	(0.135)	(0.156)	(0.141)	(0.043)
Income	0.115	0.242	0.136	0.127	0.091**
	(0.145)	(0.157)	(0.165)	(0.120)	(0.040)
Age	0.013	0.006	0.024**	0.002	0.017***
	(0.009)	(0.010)	(0.012)	(0.007)	(0.002)
Woman	−0.124	−0.324	0.028	0.053	−0.253***
	(0.226)	(0.269)	(0.320)	(0.245)	(0.075)
Married	−0.227	−0.205	0.040	−0.081	0.201**
	(0.227)	(0.278)	(0.354)	(0.252)	(0.082)
South	0.281	−0.426		−1.126**	0.007
	(0.415)	(0.598)		(0.572)	(0.108)
California	−0.125	0.596*		−0.048	−0.089
	(0.280)	(0.333)		(0.303)	(0.134)
Texas	−0.347	0.465		0.817	−0.147
	(0.431)	(0.615)		(0.591)	(0.185)
Florida	0.327	0.946		0.528	0.209
	(0.650)	(0.648)		(0.694)	(0.188)
Constant	−1.994***	−1.094	−2.474***	−0.839	−1.843***
	(0.593)	(0.777)	(0.904)	(0.530)	(0.199)
Observations	386	268	170	295	3017
LR	0.00358	0.234	0.0914	0.327	0
Log likelihood	−239.4	−177.2	−112.8	−198.6	−2022

Source: Authors' calculations using ANES 2012, McCann and Jones-Correa 2012.
Note: Cell entry is the logit coefficient; standard errors in parentheses.
*$p < .1$; **$p < .05$; ***$p < .01$

yond the scope of this paper, but we do think it is important to take advantage of the unique details regarding motivation and mobilization that the LINES data provides, to reflect on whether these are fruitful strategies to pursue in future research. Most conventional studies of how motivation influences participation focus on positive attitudinal orientations toward participation of citizens, attitudes such as political interest or political engagement. Although the empirical patterns reflected in these studies support arguments that motivated individuals are more likely to participate, the causal inferences drawn by predicting behavior by attitudes both measured at the same time in cross-sectional surveys are especially limited.

The LINES dataset provides an opportunity to investigate whether individuals' orientations or previous experience frames subsequent behavior by relying on immigrants' self-reported political engagement in their country of origin. It also provides an opportunity to advance two contrasting hypotheses about these relationships. On the one hand, we might expect that individuals who were politically engaged in their country of origin will be more likely to participate in the United States, the implication being that such individuals have a preference, personality, or worldview that values political engagement. On the other hand, we might expect that individuals who were politically engaged in their country of origin do not increase their overall level of engagement

Table 6. Self-Reported Turnout

	LINES Immigrant Citizens
Active in politics in country of origin	
Very active (N=17)	66.50%
Somewhat active (N=30)	80.70
Not active (N=122)	79.00
Voted in country of origin	
Sometimes (N=75)	80.90
Did not vote (N=92)	76.50
Think government in country of origin pays attention to elections	
Good deal (N=14)	96.20
Some (N=58)	73.10
Not much (N=93)	80.80
Voted in country of origin while in United States	
Yes (N=21)	91.80
No (N=148)	76.40
Interested in politics in country of origin	
A lot (N=63)	93.20
Some (N=30)	73.70
Little (N=24)	60.90
None (N=52)	68.30

Source: Authors' calculations using McCann and Jones-Correa 2012.
Note: Table entries are the (weighted) proportion of each sample in the row who report voting.

by also participating in U.S. politics, but instead continue their engagement in country-of-origin politics and are therefore less likely to engage in U.S. political matters. Roger Waldinger and Lauren Duquette-Rory discuss elsewhere in this issue the complexities of the relationships between home country and host country political orientations and experiences. Their analysis suggests that home country political engagement of immigrants sometimes "carries over" to the United States (host country) with respect to political orientations such as political trust and confidence in elections. The most relevant (for our purposes) carry-over they document is that individuals who were active in political parties in the home country are more interested in elections in the United States. But this leaves the question of whether individuals who were politically engaged in the home country are more likely to participate in the host country.

We provide some initial data on these arguments, using the self-reported turnout rates of (LINES) immigrant citizens by their level of engagement in their country of origin, in table 6. These data provide some support for the argument that individuals who voted in their country of origin are more likely to vote in the United States, once they achieve citizenship: 81 percent of individuals who reported voting in their country of origin report voting in the United States, compared to 77 percent of those who did not vote in their country of origin. More broadly, however, individuals reporting that they were somewhat active in politics in the country of origin are not substantially more likely to report voting than their non-active country-of-origin counterparts (81 percent compared to 79 percent).

On our second point as to whether continued engagement in the country of origin depresses political engagement in the United

Table 7. Reported Party and Nonparty Contact

	LINES Immigrant Noncitizens	LINES Immigrant Citizens	ANES Latino Foreign-Born Citizens	ANES Latino U.S.-Born Citizens	ANES White Citizens
Contacted by party	12.9% (510)	41.4% (361)	44.2% (176)	35.4% (305)	44.8% (3259)
Contacted by other than party	10.3% (511)	18.0% (358)	17.0% (176)	18.3% (305)	20.0% (3254)

Source: Authors' calculations using ANES 2012, McCann and Jones-Correa 2012.
Note: Cell entries are the (weighted) proportion of each sample in the row who report being contacted; values in parentheses are the number of respondents of each sample in the row.

States, we have more consistent evidence. Individuals who report continuing to vote in the country of origin while in the United States are more likely to report voting in the U.S. than are individuals who report not continuing to vote (92 percent compared to 76 percent). Those who report being very interested in the politics of their country of origin also report voting in the United States at substantially higher levels than those with less interest (93 percent compared to 74 percent and lower).

Together, these bivariate patterns suggest that immigrants who enter the United States with political interest and engagement are more likely to vote in the United States, but that continued political interest in their country of origin does not detract from their political engagement in the United States.[11] As Waldinger and Duquette-Rory suggest in this volume, the linkages between home and host country political experiences and attitudes are surely complex, yet our evidence on self-reported political participation suggests a more direct linkage.

Similar challenges of establishing rigorous causal inferences in studying attitudinal motivations and participation are associated with studying mobilization and participation. Numerous field studies have provided more rigorous evidence regarding the effectiveness of being mobilized to vote on individuals' probability of voting. These studies have pointed to the effectiveness of both party and nonparty mobilization of Latinos. Given the limited utility of including mobilization measures in cross-sectional models of turnout, we did not include such measures in the multivariable models. However, we do think it important to describe the mobilization environments reported by our different Latino and white samples, and whether such patterns are associated with self-reported turnout.

Table 7 presents the percentage of each sample that reports being contacted by either a party or a nonparty group. The dramatic difference observed in comparing the groups is the substantially lower mobilization rate for (LINES) immigrant noncitizens, where only 13 percent report being contacted by a party, and 10 percent report being contacted by a nonparty group. This group thus has dramatically lower levels of mobilization by parties. This is, of course, what we would expect because parties rely so heavily on voter registration files for voter contact efforts and are unlikely to reach out to people not eligible to vote.

However, the noncitizen group also had substantially lower contact rates by nonparty groups. U.S.-born Latinos report the lowest party-contact rate among citizens, whereas foreign-born Latinos report party-contact rates comparable to those of whites. This suggests

---

11. Of course, these are only bivariate patterns and ignore differences across countries of origin, as well as other individual-level characteristics that might be associated with voter turnout (such as other attitudinal orientations or experiences, among others).

that immigrants who naturalize may be more likely to be reached by traditional party mobilization efforts than U.S.-born Latinos are.

CONCLUSION AND DISCUSSION

Demographics are at the heart of theories of political behavior, especially voter turnout. Our interest in documenting the importance of demographic characteristics such as education, income, age, gender, and marital status for Latinos in the United States was motivated in part by challenges to the conventional wisdom regarding the demographic bases of voter turnout for Latinos in the United States. As the Latino population grows in size and political presence, understanding whether Latino electoral behavior is explained by the same factors explaining the behavior of other groups is critical to understanding electoral politics in the United States.

The availability of a new dataset focusing on Latino immigrants, along with a large oversample of Latinos in the 2012 ANES, provides a unique opportunity to document both similarities and differences between white citizens and U.S.-born Latinos, and foreign-born Latino citizens. Although relying on two different datasets introduces the possibility that some differences reflect survey-specific factors rather than actual differences in reported behavior across these groups, we nonetheless think it important that the ANES data suggest that white citizens and Latino foreign-born citizens report voting at the same rate—and a higher rate than that reported by Latino U.S.-born citizens.

Reconciling this finding with the much lower self-reported voter turnout rate of 72 percent by Latino immigrant citizens from LINES must be considered in future studies of Latino voter turnout. That the self-reported nonvoting participation rates of Latino immigrant citizens from LINES are approximately the same as those reported by each of the ANES subsamples—Latino foreign-born citizens, Latino U.S.-born citizens, and white citizens—suggests that LINES does not systematically underestimate participation levels but still does not reconcile the two estimates.

Perhaps our most notable finding is how poorly the demographic characteristics that are central to predicting whites' political engagement in the United States fare in predicting either turnout or nonvoting participation of Latino immigrants in the LINES dataset. Studies of turnout in the United States always begin by identifying education and income as key predictors of participation, and their empirical findings typically emphasize the consistency and strength of the relationships between education and turnout and income and turnout. Yet this may not be the case for Latino immigrants. In both simple bivariate relationships (table 2) and in a multivariable model conditioning on other factors (table 4), we fail to find a significant relationship between education and turnout for Latino immigrants. Failure to identify a statistically significant relationship in a multivariable model with only 264 observations could simply result from relying on a small sample size, even in our estimates based on CPS data. But even when the sample size is almost two thousand respondents (a size similar to many studies of Anglos finding the traditional relationships between education and turnout and income and turnout), we find no significant relationship between income and turnout among Latino immigrants. We note that within the ANES data, estimated coefficients for Latinos are generally comparable in magnitude to those of whites—they simply fail to achieve statistical significance because of the much smaller sample size (hundreds of observations rather than thousands).

Thus, drawing strong inferences here is extremely difficult. The lack of a consistent finding may suggest that we are simply measuring education poorly—that comparing education levels of people from countries with very different overall levels of education is not the same as measuring education for people brought up in the United States. It may also suggest that immigrants go through other routes of political activation. Evaluating these possibilities likely requires survey data—with large sample sizes—on the resources (including education and income) available to immigrants in their home countries as well as in the United States to better understand the lingering influences of immigrants' experiences in their countries of origin on voter turnout.

We also believe it is important that subsequent research consider how different sampling frames and survey research practices used to produce data sets on immigrant political attitudes and behaviors might be responsible for the many differences we observe. Understanding these differences and developing a clear understanding of best practices in terms of surveying Latinos is essential to properly studying Latino political behavior. Doing so would help sharpen our understanding of the importance of demographic, as well as nondemographic, resources to Latino immigrant political behavior.

APPENDIX

Table A1. Demographic Model of Turnout

	CPS Latino Immigrant Citizens	CPS Latino U.S.-Born Citizens
Education	0.439***	0.534***
	(0.050)	(0.032)
Income	0.070	0.136***
	(0.050)	(0.028)
Age	0.026***	0.024***
	(0.003)	(0.002)
Woman	0.075	0.200***
	(0.097)	(0.056)
Married	−0.053**	−0.008
	(0.026)	(0.014)
South	0.360	−0.202
	(0.251)	(0.161)
California	0.254**	−0.082
	(0.117)	(0.070)
Texas	−0.570***	−0.175
	(0.280)	(0.169)
Florida	0.174	0.459**
	(0.278)	(0.197)
Constant	−2.373***	−2.718***
	(0.264)	(0.165)
Observations	1,936	5,876
LR	0	0
Log likelihood	−1242	−3730

Source: Authors' calculations using U.S. Census Bureau 2012.
Note: Cell entry is the logit coefficient; standard errors in parentheses.
$*p < .1; **p < .05; ***p < .01$

REFERENCES

Abrajano, Marisa, and Costas Panagopoulos. 2011. "Does Language Matter? The Impact of Spanish Versus English-Language GOTV Efforts on Latino Turnout." *American Politics Research* 39(4): 643-63.

American National Election Studies (ANES). 2012. The ANES 2012 Time Series Study dataset. Ann Arbor: University of Michigan; Palo Alto: Stanford University. Accessed February 26, 2016. http://www.electionstudies.org/.

Barreto, Matt A. 2005. "Latino Immigrants at the Polls: Foreign-Born Voter Turnout in the 2002 Election." *Political Research Quarterly (formerly WPQ)* 58(1): 79-86.

Barreto, Matt A. and Gary M. Segura. 2014. *Latino America: How America's Most Dynamic Population Is Poised to Transform the Politics of the Nation*. New York: Public Affairs.

Barreto, Matt A., Gary M. Segura, and Nathan D. Woods. 2004. "The Mobilizing Effect of Majority-Minority Districts on Latino Turnout." *American Political Science Review* 98(1): 65-75.

Bass, Loretta E., and Lynne M. Casper. 2001. "Impacting the Political Landscape: Who Registers and Votes Among Naturalized Americans?" *Political Behavior* 23(2): 103-30.

Bueker, Catherine Simpson. 2013. "What Wakes the Sleeping Giant? The Effect of State Context on Latino Voter Turnout in the 2004 Election." *Latino Studies* 11(3): 388-410.

Cassel, Carol A. 2002. "Hispanic Turnout: Estimates from Validated Voting Data." *Political Research Quarterly* 55(2): 391-408.

García Bedolla, Lisa, and Melissa R. Michelson. 2012. *Mobilizing Inclusion: Transforming the Electorate Through Get-Out-the-Vote Campaigns*. New Haven, Conn.: Yale University Press.

Highton, Benjamin, and Arthur L. Burris. 2002. "New Perspectives on Latino Voter Turnout in the United States." *American Politics Research* 30(3): 285-306.

Jackson, Robert A. 2003. "Differential Influences on Latino Electoral Participation." *Political Behavior* 25(4): 339-66.

Jang, Seung-Jin. 2009. "Get Out on Behalf of Your Group: Electoral Participation of Latinos and Asian Americans." *Political Behavior* 31(4): 511-35.

Johnson, Martin, Robert M. Stein, and Robert Wrinkle. 2003. "Language Choice, Residential Stability, and Voting Among Latino Americans." *Social Science Quarterly* 84(2): 412-424.

Junn, Jane. 2010. "On Participation: Individuals, Dynamic Categories, and the Context of Power." In *Oxford Handbook of American Elections and Political Behavior*, edited by Jan E. Leighley. New York: Oxford University Press.

Leal, David L. 2002. "Political Participation by Latino Non-Citizens in the United States." *British Journal of Political Science* 32(2): 353-70.

Leal, David L., Stephen A. Nuño, Jongho Lee, and Rodolfo O. de la Garza. 2008. "Latinos, Immigration, and the 2006 Midterm Elections." *PS: Political Science and Politics* 41(2): 309-17.

Leighley, Jan E., and Jonathan Nagler. 2014. *Who Votes Now? Demographics, Issues, Inequality, and Turnout in the United States*. Princeton, N.J.: Princeton University Press.

Levin, Ines. 2013. "Political Inclusion of Latino Immigrants: Becoming a Citizen and Political Participation." *American Politics Research* 41(4): 535-68.

Matland, Richard E., and Gregg R. Murray. 2012. "An Experimental Test of Mobilization Effects in a Latino Community." *Political Research Quarterly* 65(1): 192-205.

McCann, James A., and Michael Jones-Correa. 2012. Latino Immigrant National Election Study, 2012. New York: Russell Sage Foundation, Carnegie Corporation of New York, Purdue University, and Cornell University.

Michelson, Melissa R. 2003. "Getting Out the Latino Vote: How Door-to-Door Canvassing Influences Voter Turnout in Rural Central California." *Political Behavior* 25(3): 247-63.

———. 2005. "Meeting the Challenge of Latino Voter Mobilization." *Annals of the American Academy of Political and Social Science* 601(1): 85-101.

———. 2006. "Mobilizing the Latino Youth Vote: Some Experimental Results." *Social Science Quarterly* 87(1): 1188-206.

Michelson, Melissa, and Lisa García Bedolla. 2014. "Mobilization by Different Means: Nativity and GOTV in the United States." *International Migration Review* 48(3): 710-27.

Mohamed, Heather Silber. 2013. "Can Protests Make Latinos 'American'? Identity, Immigration Politics, and the 2006 Marches." *American Politics Research* 41(2): 298-327.

Pantoja, Adrian D., Ricardo Ramírez, and Gary M. Segura. 2001. "Citizens by Choice, Voters by Necessity: Patterns in Political Mobilization by Naturalized Latinos." *Political Research Quarterly* 54(4): 729-50.

Parkin, Michael, and Frances Zlotnick. 2011. "English Proficiency and Latino Participation in U.S. Elections." *Politics & Policy* 39(4): 515-37.

Pearson-Merkowitz, Shanna. 2012a. "Aqui No Hay Oportunidades: Latino Segregation and the Keys to Political Participation." *Politics & Policy* 40(2): 259-95.

———. 2012b. "The Limits of the Homogeneity Model: Segregation and Civic Engagement in Latino Communities." *American Politics Research* 40(4): 701-36.

Ramakrishnan, S. Karthick, and Thomas J. Espenshade. 2001. "Immigrant Incorporation and Political Participation in the United States." *International Migration Review* 35(3): 870-909.

Ramírez, Ricardo. 2005. "Giving Voice to Latino Voters: A Field Experiment on the Effectiveness of a National Nonpartisan Mobilization Effort." *Annals of the American Academy of Political and Social Science* 601(September): 66-84.

Rosenstone, Steven J., and John Mark Hansen. 1993. *Mobilization, Participation, and Democracy in America*. New York: Pearson Education.

Shaw, Daron, Rodolfo O. de la Garza, and Jongho Lee. 2000. "Examining Latino Turnout in 1996: A Three-State, Validated Survey Approach." *American Journal of Political Science* 44(2): 338-46.

Stevens, Daniel, and Benjamin G. Bishin. 2011. "Getting Out the Vote: Minority Mobilization in a Presidential Election." *Political Behavior* 33: 113-38.

Tam Cho, Wendy K. 1999. "Naturalization, Socialization, Participation: Immigrants and (Non-)Voting." *Journal of Politics* 61(4): 1140-55.

U.S. Census Bureau. 2012. Current Population Survey dataset, November 2012. Washington: Government Printing Office.

Valdez, Zulema. 2011. "Political Participation Among Latinos in the United States: The Effect of Group Identity and Consciousness." *Social Science Quarterly* 92(2): 466-82.

Verba, Sidney, Kay Lehman Schlozman, and Henry Brady. 1995. *Voice and Equality: Civic Voluntarism in American Politics*. Cambridge, Mass.: Harvard University Press.

Wolfinger, Raymond E., and Steven J. Rosenstone. 1980. *Who Votes?* New Haven, Conn.: Yale University Press.

Wrinkle, Robert D., Joseph Stewart Jr., J. L. Polinard, Kenneth J. Meier, and John R. Arvizu. 1996. "Ethnicity and Nonelectoral Political Participation." *Hispanic Journal of Behavioral Sciences* 18(2): 142-53.

The Hispanic Immigrant Voter and the Classic American Voter: Presidential Support in the 2012 Election

MICHAEL S. LEWIS-BECK AND MARY STEGMAIER

In their classic 1960 work, Angus Campbell and his colleagues offer a model to explain political behavior. They posit a funnel of causality, whereby the causal flow moved from remote long-term forces, such as sociodemographics and party identification, to more immediate short-term forces, such as issues and candidates, finally arriving at the vote choice itself. This explanation has withstood the test of time in studies of the United States and other democracies. The question at hand in this article is how Latin American immigrants comport themselves in the national political environment of the United States. Can the political preferences of Hispanic immigrants be explained pretty much the way the political preferences of native-born Americans can be explained? In other words, does the funnel of causality apply to them? Our findings, based on analysis of 2012 American National Election Study and Latino Immigrant National Election Study survey data, indicate that it does.

Keywords: Hispanic voters, presidential approval, voting behavior, 2012 presidential election, American voters

The American Voter (TAV) established a paradigm for studying political behavior. Angus Campbell and his colleagues (1960) posited a funnel of causality to explain presidential voting behavior, whereby the causal flow moved from remote long-term forces, such as sociodemographics and party identification, to more immediate short-term forces, such as issues and candidates, finally arriving at the tip of the funnel, the vote choice itself. That paradigm has not gone unchallenged, and other approaches have competed for its place in the theoretical spotlight, for example, rational choice, political geography, historical-institutional, media and communications, campaign strategy. Even when TAV is acknowledged as the dominant approach, the extent of its reach faces challenges. For instance, if its explanation held for the originally studied presidential elections of 1952 and 1956, does it hold now? To answer that question, "Thousands of journal articles and conference papers have been published and presented on the subject of voting behavior in the decades since 1960, pieces that have reconsidered the original work of Campbell, Converse, Miller and Stokes" (Lewis-Beck et al. 2008, x). A more recent example includes a special issue of *Electoral Studies*, dedicated to revisiting TAV, its evidence and theories (Lewis-Beck 2009).

Michael S. Lewis-Beck is F. Wendell Miller Distinguished Professor of Political Science at the University of Iowa.
Mary Stegmaier is assistant professor in the Truman School of Public Affairs at the University of Missouri.

We thank Jay McCann, Michael Jones-Correa, the Russell Sage Foundation workshop participants, and the anonymous referees for their helpful comments. Direct correspondence to: Michael S. Lewis-Beck, at michael-lewis-beck@uiowa.edu, Department of Political Science, University of Iowa, Iowa City, IA 52242; and Mary Stegmaier at stegmaierm@missouri.edu, Truman School of Public Affairs, University of Missouri, Columbia, MO 65211.

Thus, the body of published work following *TAV* precepts has become vast, and some of this research has examined its empirical reach. Michael Lewis-Beck and his colleagues, revisiting *TAV* theory and applying it to the U.S. presidential elections of 2000 and 2004, draw an unambiguous conclusion: "Does the social-psychological explanation of presidential vote choice, developed in *The American Voter* and symbolized in its famous theory of the 'funnel of causality,' still hold? The essential answer drawn from our revisit must be yes" (2008, 427). Whether it applies to other advanced democracies poses a question explored early on for the British case (Butler and Stokes 1969). The funnel idea still guides much British electoral research, including refined points over the exogeneity of party identification (Clarke et al. 2004, 2009; Whiteley et al. 2013).

The Michigan model, as it is sometimes called, has found ground beyond Anglo-Saxon shores. A current cutting-edge volume, *The Nordic Voter*, by Åsa Bengtsson and his colleagues explicitly acknowledges the debt: "The general idea behind the sequencing of chapters is well known to most students of electoral behavior: the 'funnel of causality'" (2014, 10). A recent work on French presidential elections provides an acknowledgment "To Philip E. Converse," and claims, "Our approach is straightforward, drawing on the founding 'Michigan model' of political behavior . . . or at least the French variant" (Lewis-Beck, Nadeau, and Bélanger 2012, 12). They apply such a model to French voters in four election surveys from 1988 to 2007. In the first national election survey investigation of vote choice in Austria, Sylvia Kritzinger and her colleagues state in their section on theory, "we organize the work around the funnel of causality, first introduced by Campbell et al." (2013, 26–27).

None of the works cited thus far, however, examine cultures that are not clearly Western and have both lower incomes and more fragile democratic institutions. Unfortunately, systematic political behavior research based on scientific election surveys has been relatively scarce in these parts of the world. That picture has begun to change, especially in Latin America, where a considerable number of well-crafted public opinion polls have now been administered, primarily through the good offices of the Latin American Public Opinion Project at Vanderbilt University (Carlin, Singer, and Zechmeister 2015; Seligson and Zechmeister 2012; Zechmeister and Corral 2013). A question, then, is how these citizens behave at the ballot box. Does the funnel of causality argument help account for their choices? One recent study, which explicitly fits a Michigan-style model to an election survey data pool from twelve Latin American countries finds, encouragingly, that almost half the variance in national vote choice can be explained (Lewis-Beck and Ratto 2013).

That last result implies that Latin American citizens, in their democratic settings, respond to electoral cues roughly the same way as North American citizens do. Still, the suggestion does not speak to how Latin Americans behave politically when they are actually in North America, either as naturalized U.S. citizens or as immigrants as yet without citizenship. This, of course, is the burning concern of this paper. How do these immigrants from Latin America comport themselves in the U.S. national political environment? Can the political preferences of these Hispanic immigrants be explained in much the same way as the political attitudes of native-born Americans? In other words, does the funnel of causality apply to them?

Our hypothesis is that it does, because they are subject to the same forces as other democratic actors in the American system. Many immigrants came to the United States as adults, missing out on the traditional political socialization during the teenage years in the United States. But, like all people, they absorbed perspectives and attitudes in their countries of origin that likely provided guidance as they acculturated to the new political environment. Further, adjusting to life in a new country involves much change and flexibility. During such a transition, immigrants learn from their new friends, coworkers, leaders, and experiences. They are affected by the same political climate as all Americans, and therefore we anticipate that this will lead them to develop party identification, views on political issues, evaluations of the economy, and opinions about candidates.

In our analysis, we test whether the same

structural model of political preference—essentially the Michigan model—works for Hispanic immigrants and for native-born Americans, with regard to the 2012 U.S. presidential election. We find that it does. We come to this conclusion after comparative analysis of the Latino Immigrant National Election Study (LINES) and the American National Election Studies (ANES), gathered in 2012 preelection surveys conducted either by phone (LINES) or face-to-face (ANES).[1] We first explicate the dependent variable. Then, we lay out the estimation strategy, a block-recursive one, successfully employed elsewhere. Next, we consider the independent variables as sets, in order of their appearance in the funnel: sociodemographics, partisanship, issues, candidates. As we shall see, the estimated models of presidential support, LINES versus ANES, appear similar. However, that does not mean that their political choice processes are identical. On the contrary, some differences are intriguing but nevertheless seem contextually understandable.

THE DEPENDENT VARIABLE: VOTES, PREFERENCES, APPROVAL

Initially, one might suppose the preferred dependent variable would be vote intention, measured equally in both these preelection surveys, with an item something like, "If the presidential election were held tomorrow, who would you vote for?" However, upon inspection, several obstacles to such a comparison appear. First, a question of that type was not asked in the LINES survey. Instead, the closest thing to a vote question (translated into English) reads as follows (see PREVOTE_PREFPRWHO variable, LINES preelection): "Talking about the elections for president in the United States, do you have a preference for one of the presidential candidates? If 'Yes,' which candidate do you prefer?"

The obvious reason for this nonstandard formulation is that the majority of respondents in the survey are not U.S. citizens and so are not eligible to vote (as assumed by the standard formulation). Nevertheless, this preference question could perhaps be used as a vote intention proxy, assuming that an Obama (or Romney) response would reflect their vote intention (if they could vote). We did this, and uncovered the following distribution of among those who expressed a preference: Obama = 90.3 percent, Romney = 9.4 percent, Other candidate = 0.3 percent. This is a useful result, suggesting an overwhelming desire to vote for Obama (even if they could not). However, it is not very helpful beyond that, since it is a blunt instrument. Because almost everyone selects one candidate (Obama), little variance is left to explain.

Put another way, if this simple dichotomy, Obama or Romney, were used as a dependent variable in a logistic regression analysis of these data, few independent variables would be found statistically significant. We would learn very little about what caused presidential support to vary in this particular population. Thus, we need another, more finely calibrated, measure of presidential support. Also, we need a measure of support that is theoretically more universal (stretching across this immigrant population of citizens and noncitizens, and across the U.S. population of mostly native-born citizens). The ideal measure would be some continuous assessment of presidential satisfaction, or approval, which fortunately we do have. It reads (translated into English) as follows (see PRESAPP_APPPRES, LINES preelection): "Do you approve or disapprove of the way Barack Obama is handling his job as president? (Do you approve strongly or not strongly? Do you disapprove strongly or not strongly?)"

On the basic approval question, 90 percent of those surveyed provided an assessment. When constructing the approval scale, we faced the problem that respondents were not given an explicit neutral category. As Herbert Weisberg remarks in his book on survey error, "some people will not be able to translate their opinion into one of the available response alternatives, such as when they have a neutral opinion but no neutral alternative is offered" (2009, 132). Therefore, we coded responses of

---

1. In our analysis of both surveys, we weight the data. In LINES, we weight by WGTRAKE and in the ANES by WEIGHT_FTF.

don't know as the neutral category of 3, which does not seem to create theoretical or empirical difficulties.[2] On this 5-point scale, then, respondents spread themselves out well along the distribution (from 1 = strongly disapprove, to 5 = strongly approve). Fewer than half (49.2 percent) chose the 5 option, meaning that most of these respondents had less than complete satisfaction with President Obama's performance. In other words, although many were fully behind him, others were less so, and to differing degrees. The item, in sum, allows the respondents a finer calibration of their attitude, making this a patently attractive indicator of support, and one that could also be followed in the ANES preelection survey as well. Admittedly, it is not a vote variable. But, we must remember that such approval measures are routinely used in comparative electoral behavior studies to construct a "popularity function" (setting the dependent variable as some sort of approval measure) when a "vote function" (setting the dependent variable as some sort of vote measure) is not available (Nannestad and Paldam 1994; Lewis-Beck and Stegmaier 2013).

THE ESTIMATION STRATEGY

The funnel of causality theory posits a causal flow from one set of variables to another. The more remote variables influence the less remote variables, in turn, finally arriving at the tip of the funnel, where the individual political actor responds. For example, religion shapes party identification, party identification shapes gay marriage attitudes, gay marriage attitudes shape candidate feelings, and candidate feelings trigger presidential support (or its withdrawal). Movement through this causal chain proceeds from long-term forces, such as religion and party identification, to short-term forces, such as gay marriage attitudes and candidate feelings. The long-term forces tend to be enduring, stable, lasting—in a word, exogenous. The short-term forces tend to be fickle, unstable, of the moment—in a word, endogenous. The generative process of political behavior takes place over time, among many variables, and implies the operation of a multiequation system rather than a single-equation one. Precise specification, and estimation, of such a multiequation system can be daunting.

A practical solution is block-recursive modeling, first extensively employed by Warren Miller and Merrill Shanks (1996). A sequence of equations is specified, then estimated one after the other, each containing the prior causal variables. The final equation contains all the relevant causal variables and estimates their direct effects on the political behavior under study. Their indirect effects, of course, are transmitted through the coefficients of the more remote equations. Econometrically, a core assumption is that the independent variables in a prior block are exogenous to the variables in a later block. An additional assumption is that the estimation error in a prior block lacks correlation with the estimation error in a subsequent block (Kmenta 1997). Under these assumptions, estimating the series of equations with ordinary least squares (OLS) yields consistent coefficients, given the continuous measure we have of the approval variable. We estimate (OLS) a four-equation block-recursive causal system of presidential support in the 2012 election, beginning with the first block, and with the LINES data. We then go on to similar estimation for the ANES data, ultimately comparing the two sets of results.

---

2. In constructing the dependent variable, we assume that respondents who indicated don't know to the initial presidential approval question likely had a neutral opinion. Thus, we keep these sixty-one respondents in our measure as the neutral category. They are the only people who appear in this middle (3) category on our 5-point scale. Respondents who refused to answer this approval question are coded as missing, as are those who refused or did not know on the follow-up strength question.

To ensure that our results were not affected by our decision to put the don't knows in the neutral category, we ran the models on a 4-point approval variable (1= strongly disapprove, 2= not strongly disapprove, 3= not strongly approve, 4= strongly approve). This does not change the results much. For example, the complete model (model 4) in table 1, when run on this 4-point dependent variable, shows that the same variables reach statistical significance, except the gay marriage variable.

SOCIO-DEMOGRAPHICS (LINES)

An adult's socio-demographic characteristics heavily determine his or her place in the hierarchy of society. In the Hispanic community we are studying, for example, a churchgoing, college-educated man who lives with his family in a nice house and earns a respectable salary conveys a certain image of himself in the political world. We might expect such characteristics to influence the kinds of candidates he prefers. These socio-demographic variables are measured in the LINES survey, as follows, in a series of dummy variables (1,0): *Gender* (1 = female), *Church Attendance* (1 = nearly weekly or more), *Marital Status* (1 = married living with spouse), *Education* (1 = high school or more), *Class* (1 = middle or upper), *Homeowner* (1 = owner), *Income* (1 = $20K or more), *Age* (1 = forty-five or older), *Health Insurance* (1 = possess). To these standard socio-demographic variables, we add additional variables that uniquely characterize the socio-demographic status of immigrants: the dummy variable of *Citizenship* (1 = citizen), *Year of Arrival in the United States* (actual year), *Language Spoken at Home* (1= only English to 5 = only Spanish), and country of origin. Approximately 70 percent of survey respondents were born in Mexico, about 5 percent in Cuba, and 4 percent in the Dominican Republic. We create separate dummy variables for each of these countries. We also create dummies for the regions of Central America (15 percent of the respondents) and South America (4 percent). In our multivariate analysis, we include dummies for these three countries and Central America, with South America serving as the omitted category.

Before looking at these multivariate results, we ask whether these variables relate to presidential approval for Obama in a simple bivariate way. Citizenship and year of arrival achieve the standard level of statistical significance (0.05, one-tail). Their correlations (Pearson's *r*) with the 5-point approval scale (1 = strong disapproval and 5 = strong approval) are -0.058 and 0.091 respectively. These relationships mean that citizens were more likely than non-citizens to disapprove of Obama, and those who arrived in the United States more recently were more likely to approve of him than those who arrived long ago. Further, among the countries and regions of origin, dummy variables—Cuba, Central America, and South America—are statistically significant. The relationship is strongest for immigrants from Cuba, showing a correlation of -0.193. Those from Central America were more likely to approve of Obama (0.077) and those from South America less likely to do so (-0.084), though notably the strength of these relationships is much weaker than for Cuban Americans. In the bivariate correlations, Mexican origin just misses significance (a 0.055 correlation), and Dominican Republic origin is far from it.

A few other socio-demographic variables came close to conventional statistical significance. Specifically, women and homeowners were more approving of Obama's performance, correlations of 0.055, and 0.053, respectively. Also, respondents who identified as middle or upper class and those who spoke more Spanish at home held more negative assessments, both showing correlations of -0.047. Although thin, these findings merit pursuit in a multivariate context.

Our first equation, for the socio-demographic block, can be read as follows:

Approval = f (Socio-demographics)   Model 1

where the socio-demographic variables are gender, church, marriage, education, class, home, income, age, health insurance, citizenship, year of arrival, language spoken at home, and country or region of origin. In other words, the model bases itself on our sixteen available variables, which we regress (OLS) on the 5-point presidential approval scale. This estimation appears in table 1 (column 1).

Do these multivariate estimates change the picture much from the bivariate correlations? Only a little. We see that those who arrived in the United States more recently are more likely to support Obama, as are respondents who were born in Mexico, the Dominican Republic, and Central America; respondents of Cuban origin were less likely to approve of him. Citizenship and language spoken at home fail to reach statistical significance. Looking at the other variables in this model, we observe that women are more likely to support Obama, as are homeowners. The impact of homeowner-

Table 1. LINES 2012 Regression Analysis of Presidential Approval

	Model 1	Model 2	Model 3	Model 4
Sociodemographics				
Citizen	−0.105	−0.142	−0.041	−0.012
	(0.112)	(0.105)	(0.098)	(0.087)
Year arrived in United States	0.008*	0.010*	0.004	0.002
	(0.005)	(0.005)	(0.004)	(0.004)
Language at home	−0.076	−0.058	−0.066	−0.041
	(0.053)	(.050)	(0.046)	(0.041)
Female	0.164*	0.190*	0.218*	0.089
	(0.092)	(0.086)	(0.082)	(0.074)
Health insurance	0.106	0.080	0.079	0.119
	(0.095)	(0.089)	(0.082)	(0.073)
Church attendance	−0.108	−0.044	−0.057	−0.077
	(0.095)	(0.086)	(0.080)	(0.071)
Married	0.094	0.092	0.023	−0.018
	(0.093)	(0.087)	(0.082)	(0.073)
Homeowner	0.193*	0.137	0.063	0.076
	(0.099)	(0.092)	(0.086)	(0.077)
Age	0.149	0.099	0.144	0.159
	(0.108)	(0.101)	(0.095)	(0.084)
Education	0.149	0.065	−0.017	0.015
	(0.097)	(0.091)	(0.085)	(0.076)
Social class	−0.151	−0.162*	−0.110	−0.049
	(0.102)	(0.095)	(0.088)	(0.079)
Income	−0.018	−0.136	−0.223*	−0.174*
	(0.096)	(0.090)	(0.085)	(0.075)
Mexico	0.541*	0.551*	0.561*	0.438*
	(0.209)	(0.195)	(0.182)	(0.162)
Cuba	−0.595*	−0.435*	−0.266	−0.134
	(0.281)	(0.262)	(0.248)	(0.220)
Dominican Republic	0.647*	0.550*	0.586*	0.203
	(0.302)	(0.282)	(0.266)	(0.238)
Central America	0.716*	0.683*	0.724*	0.548*
	(0.229)	(0.214)	(0.199)	(0.177)
Party-ideology				
Democratic party ID		0.760*	0.593*	0.343*
		(0.085)	(0.080)	(0.074)
Liberal ideology		0.474*	0.346*	0.167*
		(0.101)	(0.095)	(0.086)
Issues				
Increase government services			0.082	0.056
			(0.079)	(0.070)
Citizenship for illegal immigrants			0.115	0.142
			(0.113)	(0.098)
Gay marriage			0.180*	0.149*
			(0.090)	(0.080)
Death penalty			0.104	0.019
			(0.080)	(0.071)
Abortion			0.015	−0.096
			(0.106)	(0.094)

Table 1. (cont.)

	Model 1	Model 2	Model 3	Model 4
Past personal finances			0.136*	0.080*
			(0.038)	(0.034)
Past national economy			0.280*	0.175*
			(0.046)	(0.042)
Future personal finances			0.004	−0.014
			(0.046)	(0.041)
Future national economy			0.161*	0.153*
			(0.044)	(0.039)
Candidate evaluations				
Obama thermometer				0.018*
				(0.001)
Romney thermometer				−0.009*
				(0.001)
Constant	−12.889	−15.748*	−6.583	−3.578
	(9.929)	(9.274)	(8.639)	(7.675)
N	723	723	705	705
R	0.280	0.449	0.574	0.688
R^2	0.078	0.202	0.329	0.473
Adjusted R^2	0.057	0.181	0.302	0.450
SEE	1.18	1.100	1.002	0.890

Source: Authors' compilation based on McCann and Jones-Correa 2012.
Note: Unstandardized regression coefficients are reported, with the standard errors in parentheses. The dependent variable, *Presidential Approval* ranges from 1 = strongly disapprove to 5 = strongly approve. Don't knows are coded in the middle category of 3. Those who refused are excluded from the analysis. Independent variables: *Year of Arrival* is the actual year reported by the respondent; *Language spoken at Home* ranges from 1= only English to 5= only Spanish. Don't knows and refusals on these questions were coded as missing. Refused and don't knows are included in the 0 category for the following dichotomous variables: all other socio-demographic variables including country of origin (coded into a set of dummy variables: Mexico, Cuba, Dominican Republic, Central America, and the excluded variable South America), party identification and ideology, and all social issue variables. The economic variables are coded as 1 = much worse to 5= much better, with don't knows included in the middle "the same" category, and refusals are excluded. The candidate feeling thermometers range from 0 to 100, with don't knows, refused, and don't recognize coded as the neutral 50. We code the variables this way to avoid drastically reducing the N. Our experiments suggest that this coding decision does not seriously influence the magnitude of the coefficients reported.
Standard errors in parentheses.
*$p < .05$ (one-tailed test)

ship suggests that "having a stake" in the economics of the community can engender more broad system support for government officials, such as the president. We return to other, short-term economic effects later.

Overall, how do socio-demographics account for differences in presidential approval? Not well. The correlation (R) between all sixteen variables and approval reaches 0.280. However, even that modest magnitude diminishes when the R-squared (0.078) and the adjusted R-squared (0.057) are examined. We must conclude that, despite applying a rather full and more or less standard battery of socio-demographic measures, they make just a small dent in our understanding of presidential support among the Hispanic immigrant community. For that understanding, we need to move farther down the funnel.

PARTISANSHIP: PARTY AND IDEOLOGY (LINES)

Given that we are working with a sample of immigrants to the United States, rather than a sample of the native born, it might be supposed that the question of party identification would be met with an overwhelming response of "don't know." Zoltan Hajnal and Taeku Lee argue that immigrants "will be motivated to remain neutral—at least in their self-identification" (2011, 277). Theoretically, they draw on both the Michigan model, which posits party identification is acquired initially through socialization (Campbell et al. 1960), as well as the rational choice approach, which emphasizes the role of information and updating (Fiorina 1981). Hajnal and Lee contend that because many immigrants spent their formative years in their country of birth, they missed out on U.S. political socialization and might not have enough information about the parties and their positions to choose which party to align with.

However, elsewhere in this issue, David Sears, Felix Danbold, and Vanessa Zavala find that many Latino immigrants have indeed acquired a party identification. Using the 2012 LINES and ANES surveys, they examine party identification among naturalized and native-born citizens, and find that Latinos are right on par with white Americans (Sears, Danbold, and Zavala, this volume, table 2). Nonincorporation is more prevalent among nonnaturalized Latinos, but they find signs of partisan crystallization in this group. Ultimately, Sears and his colleagues conclude that Hispanic immigrant incorporation into the party system has come about "following a path shaped by a combination of exogenous and endogenous forces . . . that aligns with the socialization approach put forth in *The American Voter*."

Just over half of LINES respondents identify with a party, according to responses from the standard party identification question, which reads as follows (PTYID_RPTYID): "Generally speaking, do you usually think of yourself as a Democrat, a Republican, an Independent, or what?"

The relative frequency distribution on the variable is Democrat = 43.0 percent, Republican = 8.1 percent, Independent = 31.9 percent, don't know/other party/no preference = 17.0 percent. Clearly, these respondents show knowledge of the major political parties in the country, and are able to evaluate their relationship to these parties. Of those who selected one of the two major parties, the preference slanted heavily in favor of the Democrats (84.1 percent) over the Republicans (15.9 percent).

We would expect Democratic identifiers to be much more approving of Obama, and they are, as we shall see. However, party identification does not exhaust the possible sources of partisan attachment. In particular, liberal-conservative ideology has been put forward as an additional long-term social-psychological anchor in the electorate. The extent to which Americans have a meaningful ideology remains a source of controversy. Campbell and his colleagues (1960) were actually skeptical that voters had coherent patterns of political thought that could be labeled liberal or conservative. Lewis-Beck and his colleagues echo this skepticism in their update of Campbell, reporting that "only a bare majority of our respondents (51.4 percent) consider themselves to be either liberal or conservative" (2008, 223). Further, too, is the question of what the terms *liberal* and *conservative* substantively mean, even for those who so place themselves (Lewis-Beck et al. 2008). Other work argues that these ideological orientations do have politically meaningful content (Jacoby 2002; Sears 2001). In any case, it seems worth exploring their impact in these LINES data.

In the LINES survey, an ideology self-placement item was posed, of the following form: "We hear a lot of talk these days about liberals and conservatives. How would you describe yourself? Extremely liberal, liberal, moderate or middle of the road, slightly conservative, conservative, or extremely conservative, or haven't you thought much about this?"

The distribution on this item does show a fairly large group, 24.7 percent, who simply have not thought much about it. Also, a sizable percentage, 18.9 percent, located themselves in the middle of the road. Still, a fair share were willing to call themselves liberal, 21.6 percent in all. This group is of special interest to us because President Obama has frequently been tagged with the liberal label. We reasoned that, among immigrants who explicitly saw themselves as liberal, they would be more supportive of Obama independently of whether they identified with the Democratic Party. As we shall see, that is the case.

Incorporating this second block of variables, the model now reads

Approval = f (Socio-demographics, Partisanship)   Model 2,

where partisanship includes party identification (Democrat or not) and ideological identification (Liberal or not). The estimates for this model appear in table 1 (column 2).

Clearly, these social-psychological anchors are working as expected. The coefficients of both variables are in the right direction and highly significant ($p > 0.001$). Further, party identification has special weight, as the coefficient of 0.760 shows (standardized coefficient = 0.311). Democratic identifiers, not surprisingly, are much more likely to approve of President Obama's job performance. But, beyond that, liberal identifiers (not all of whom are Democrats) also back Obama. Because these two variables—party and ideology—have the same (1, 0) metric, their relative strength can be compared in an examination of the unstandardized coefficients and are, respectively, 0.760 and 0.474. We observe that party effects are about double ideology effects, again in line with expectations.

How much does the addition of these long-term factors help the model, in terms of its explanatory power? A good deal. The multiple correlation (R) has climbed to 0.449, and the adjusted R-squared to 0.181. The model appears to be gaining traction, as the forces of electoral politics fill the funnel.

ISSUES (LINES)

We now enter into the realm of short-term forces, namely issues. Campbell and his colleagues (1960) saw that the issues of the day would influence preferences. However, they felt that that influence would be limited, because of the heavy requirements an issue must meet, to change political behavior. These criteria are three and may be summarized as follows: the voter has to see the issue, the voter must have a preference on the issue, and the voter must believe that one candidate is closer. Because these criteria are demanding, we should not expect issues to overwhelm the model. But we should imagine that some issues will make a difference.

Preferences on a number of issues were measured in the survey. First, we constructed a series of dummy (1, 0) variables on five social issues: *abortion* (1 = women should have full access), *citizenship for illegals* (1 = favor), *government services* (1 = should provide more), *death penalty* (1 = favor), *gay marriage* (1 = allow). Responses of don't know or those who refused were coded as 0 to avoid losing too many observations. The univariate distributions of these variables merit attention. For one, fewer than half (44.8 percent) felt the government should clearly provide more services, a finding that flies in the face of the stereotype that "the immigrant is looking for a handout." For another, these respondents overwhelmingly favor (at 84.1 percent) citizenship for illegal visitors, which speaks to a sense of grievance they feel over current policies. With respect to cultural issues, the findings are not surprising: only 29.1 percent favor gay marriage, only 18.0 percent favor full access for women to abortion care, and a large minority (40.8 percent) favor the death penalty. Of these issues, three reach conventional bivariate statistical significance in the expected direction, and their correlations with presidential approval are reported in parentheses: citizenship for illegals ($r = 0.079$); gay marriage ($r = 0.093$), and increasing government services ($r = 0.099$).

As well, a series of 5-point economics questions was asked (where 1 = much worse and 5 = much better): past personal finances, future personal finances, past national economy, future national economy. These economic evaluations tap the classic dimensions of time (retrospective versus prospective) and target (personal versus national) that are employed in the economic voting literature, as applied to election surveys (on the evolution of economic voting research from *TAV* to the present, see Lewis-Beck and Stegmaier 2009; for classics on economic voting in American national election surveys, see Fiorina 1981; Kiewiet 1983). Here, for example, is the wording for the past national economy item, which follows standard phrasing: "Now thinking about the economy in the country as a whole, would you say that over the past year the nation's economy has gotten better, stayed about the same, or gotten worse?"

This evaluation, a retrospective on the national economy, has been labeled sociotropic. The evaluation of past personal finances has been labeled pocketbook (see Kinder and Kiewiet 1981). The distribution on pocketbook evaluations shows more people think they became better off (38.3 percent) than worse off (31.0 percent) over the past year. The distribution on sociotropic evaluations shows the same pattern, though more lopsided: 36.5 percent saw a better national economy, but only 16.8 percent saw a worse one. Interestingly, this squares with the balance of consumer confidence in the 2012 American electorate as a whole (Lewis-Beck and Tien 2014).

Which of these issue variables sustain their effect once they are included in a multivariate model? Here is the equation to be estimated, showing the third block of variables entered:

Approval = f(Socio-demographics,
Partisanship, Issues)   Model 3

where the issues are those noted and have the same coding. The estimates appear in table 1 (column 3).

As can be seen, the only social issue to survive the controls in terms of statistical significance is gay marriage. Although its coefficient does not suggest a large effect (that is, the standardized value = 0.070, which is much less than the Democratic and Liberal standardized coefficients in this model, 0.246 and 0.122 respectively), it remains noteworthy as a lavender button issue that, when pushed, tends to distance Hispanic immigrants from Obama. But the real action rests with the economy. Three of the four economic issue variables easily attain statistical significance. Moreover, the expected pattern from the literature is reproduced, with sociotropic evaluation clearly mattering more than pocketbook (Stegmaier and Lewis-Beck 2013). Indeed, the retrospective national economic evaluations coefficient, with a standardized value of 0.225, implies that evaluations of the national economy weigh heavily in the minds of these immigrants. For them, perhaps more than any other issue, and certainly more than any issue we have in our analysis, the national economy is what counts. Given the realities of their circumstances, and their aspirations for their families, this seems unsurprising.

Overall, does consideration of the role of issues increase much our understanding of presidential support within this community? Yes. The addition of this issues battery of nine items to the explanatory mix boosts substantially our ability to account for Obama support. The multiple R now stands at 0.574. Most impressively, the adjusted R-squared has risen from 0.181 in model 2 to 0.302 in model 3.

CANDIDATES (LINES)

We now arrive at that most immediate of voter concerns, the qualities of the candidates themselves. Their traits are very much at the forefront of a presidential campaign, and the Obama-Romney contest was no exception. What is it about Obama's leadership style that increases his support? Decreases it? A considerable literature has examined this general question, beginning with Campbell and his colleagues (1960). At least three qualities seem consistently important across studies in the United States and Great Britain: competence, honesty, and empathy (Clarke et al. 2004; Kessel 2004; Kinder 1986). Two basic methods have been used to measure these leader images among electorates: one direct (specific items, such as "Is the candidate honest?") and the other indirect (general feeling thermometers, such as "rate how warm you feel toward candidate X"). The LINES survey employs the latter approach. The wording (translated into English) of the lead question (THERMPRE_THINTRO) is this: "I'd like to get your feeling toward some of our political leaders and other people who are in the news these days. I'll read the name of a person and I'd like you to rate that person using something we call the feeling thermometer. Ratings between 50 degrees and 100 degrees mean that you feel favorable."

These feeling thermometers, when applied here to Obama and Romney, are telling. First, most respondents were able to use the scale (don't knows and refusals for Obama = 3 percent, for Romney = 13.3 percent). This suggests that they are well aware of these political figures, and have opinions about them. The modal feeling toward Obama is 100, more than one in four respondents (26.7 percent) giving him this score. Obviously, he is a major object of attention in their American political universe. The median responses reveal a good deal about relative candidate evaluations: Obama median = 80, Romney median = 45. The typical Hispanic immigrant, then, likes Obama almost twice as much as Romney. One would expect this image advantage would convert to job support for Obama. We incorporate these feeling thermometers into our model, as a fourth block:

$$\text{Approval} = f \text{(Socio-demographics, Partisanship, Issues, Candidates)} \quad \text{Model 4}$$

where candidates are measured by a feeling thermometer variables for Obama (0–100) and for Romney (0–100). So as to not lose observations, respondents who did not express a thermometer score on the candidates were recoded at the neutral position of 50 on the scale. The estimates for this model appear in table 1 (column 4).

An examination of these feeling thermometer coefficients demonstrates that affect toward both candidates, positive or negative, contributes to the Obama approval score. But the respondent's feeling toward Obama counts for about twice as much as that toward Romney (from table 1, the Obama coefficient = 0.018, the Romney coefficient = -0.009). Moreover, Obama's likeability has a greater impact on his job approval than any of the other independent variables. For example, the effect of the Obama thermometer even surpasses the effect of Democratic Party identification, when we compare the standardized coefficients from model 4, 0.385 and 0.142 respectively. In other words, the most important long-term force in the causal explanation, party identification, is trumped by this even more important short-term force of incumbent candidate appeal.

What of the other direct effects captured in this final, more fully specified, model? With respect to the long-term forces, the only influences that remain are from income, immigrants who came from Mexico and Central America, party identification, and ideology. Notably, the other immigrant-specific characteristics (citizenship, year of arrival, and language spoken at home) do not improve our understanding of presidential approval in our complete Michigan model, at least in their capacity as direct effects. With respect to short-term forces, such as social issues, attitudes on gay marriage still manage to affect Obama support. Turning to economic issues, we find sharp, and multiple, effects. Both retrospective and prospective sociotropic evaluations easily achieve statistical significance, as do past pocketbook evaluations. In terms of relative magnitude, the sociotropic evaluation dominates the pocketbook, suggesting that Hispanic immigrants concern themselves, first, with the larger national picture (Kiewiet and Lewis-Beck 2011).

The fit statistics have now made it into the familiar territory of well-specified models of U.S. presidential survey data: $R = 0.688$, adjusted R-squared = 0.450. The story that they tell about the political behavior of contemporary Hispanic immigrants to the United States sheds considerable light. On the whole, the story affirms our hypothesis: their presidential support can be explained, to a considerable extent, by the classic Michigan model. Citizen status, year of arrival, and language spoken at home undoubtedly affect one's status in a community, but they do not enhance our immediate understanding of voting and presidential support among Hispanic immigrants. Next, we move on to compare the Michigan model's performance with the same model applied to the 2012 ANES national sample.

THE BLOCK-RECURSIVE MODEL: ESTIMATES FROM THE ANES

The application of the funnel of causality, via estimation of the block-recursive model with the LINES data, shows promise. The time has come to apply the same theory and estimation strategy to the parallel ANES survey (pre-2012 election, face-to-face). But first we need to examine the sample and measures of the two in order to establish similarities and differences. The dependent variable, presidential approval, is worded and calibrated the same way, though the distribution of responses clearly favors Obama less in this sample. Further, all of the independent variables available in both the LINES survey and the ANES survey are coded the same way. Finally, although race is effectively a constant in the sample of Hispanic immigrants, we do use race variables with the ANES data. In sum, the two variable sets match almost exactly. The parallel estimates (OLS), on the ANES survey appear in full, from block one to block four (see table 2). We introduce the main results from each block, beginning with socio-demographics, and compare them with the LINES findings before fully and systemically evaluating them.

In the initial block, we again relate the socio-demographic variables to presidential approval. We note right away a different pattern from the LINES data. As preface, with respect to the bivariate correlations, almost all are statistically significant, and in the expected direction. Several of these correlations exceed 0.10 in magnitude, for example, marital status, homeownership, religious attendance, social class, age, and income. Further, the correlations of race-ethnicity with Obama support stand out: $r = 0.33$ (black versus others); $r = 0.14$ (Hispanic versus others).[3] These variables, taken together in the multiple regression equation of block 1, appear in table 2 (column 1) with their respective unstandardized coefficients. Overall, they definitely yield a higher fit (an $R = 0.445$, an adjusted R-squared $= 0.193$) when compared with the LINES results. Clearly, socio-demographics matter.

What about partisanship, whose effects are estimated in table 2 (column 2)? When party and ideology are added to the model, they are again significant. Further, they again contribute substantially to an increase in model fit.

Where we see the differences are in the magnitudes of the coefficients. For LINES (table 1, column 2), the party identification coefficient is 0.760; for ANES, it is 1.403. Similarly, for LINES, the ideology coefficient is 0.474; for ANES, it is 0.810. A comparison of these unstandardized coefficients suggests that partisanship, by either measure, exercises about twice the pull on the national sample, as opposed to the immigrant sample.

In the third block, the issues variables are included, table 2 (column 3). Issues appear important for both the LINES and the ANES samples. The influence of two issues stands out: gay marriage and the economy. For both, gay marriage is the most important social issue: as judged by the unstandardized coefficients, for LINES it is 0.180 and for ANES it is 0.299. Note, further, that the issue of gay marriage has a bigger impact within the national sample than the immigrant sample.

Of all the issues under study, social or not, the past performance of the economy manages the biggest effect, in both samples. Interestingly, the coefficients of the sociotropic retrospective variable come close to each other: for LINES, 0.280, and for ANES, 0.439. For both samples, then, the national economy is highly important. Also the pocketbook variable, as measured by past personal finances, achieves statistical significance across the samples. However, interestingly, its coefficient attains nearly twice the magnitude in the Latino sample, suggesting that for hard-pressed groups, such as immigrants, personal financial well-being has more relevance.

The last set of variables to be entered is the feeling thermometers for the candidates, table 2 (column 4). For both samples, opinions about the candidates add greatly to understanding their presidential support. Moreover, of all the increments to variance explained, in moving from block to block, this makes the largest relative contribution for LINES. Candidate attributes, more than any other set of factors, distinguish their choices. This contrasts, for example, with the powerful role of partisan-

---

3. We enter the race variables in the ANES socio-demographic model since, in terms of the funnel of causality, race along with other socio-demographic characteristics, are the most exogenous variables. In the LINES socio-demographic model, race is not included because all the respondents are Hispanic.

Table 2. ANES 2012 Regression Analysis of Presidential Approval

	Model 1	Model 2	Model 3	Model 4
Sociodemographics				
Female	0.133*	0.060	0.082	0.008
	(0.070)	(0.061)	(0.197)	(0.039)
Health insurance	−0.047	−0.016	−0.054	−0.045
	(0.103)	(0.089)	(0.081)	(0.057)
Church attendance	−0.530*	−0.346*	−0.228*	−0.080*
	(0.076)	(0.066)	(0.066)	(0.046)
Married	−0.403*	−0.261*	−0.211*	−0.016
	(0.075)	(0.065)	(0.059)	(0.042)
Homeowner	−0.156*	−0.064	−0.038	−0.021
	(0.086)	(0.074)	(0.068)	(0.047)
Age	−0.054	−0.162*	0.019	0.016
	(0.074)	(0.064)	(0.061)	(0.042)
Education	0.082	0.152	0.059	0.053
	(0.115)	(0.099)	(0.091)	(0.064)
Social class	0.005	−0.110*	−0.208*	−0.060
	(0.074)	(0.064)	(0.059)	(0.041)
Income	−0.009	−0.074	−0.128*	−0.071
	(0.081)	(0.070)	(0.064)	(0.045)
Black	1.837*	1.138*	0.856*	0.125*
	(0.114)	(0.105)	(0.100)	(0.072)
Hispanic	0.987*	0.538*	0.423*	1.08
	(0.117)	(0.103)	(0.094)	(0.066)
Other nonwhite non-Hispanic	0.541*	0.428*	0.289*	−0.011
	(0.145)	(0.125)	(0.114)	(0.080)
Party-ideology				
Democratic party ID		1.403*	0.968*	0.223*
		(0.074)	(0.071)	(0.052)
Liberal ideology		0.810*	0.459*	0.118*
		(0.080)	(0.076)	(0.054)
Issues				
Increase government services			0.175*	0.065
			(0.066)	(0.046)
Citizenship for illegal immigrants			0.048	−0.059
			(0.059)	(0.041)
Gay marriage			0.299*	−0.004
			(0.064)	(0.045)
Death penalty			−0.225*	0.017
			(0.061)	(0.042)
Abortion			0.059	−0.062
			(0.063)	(0.044)
Past personal finances			0.080*	0.058*
			(0.026)	(0.018)
Past national economy			0.439*	0.129*
			(0.031)	(0.023)
Future personal finances			0.064*	−0.010
			(0.035)	(0.025)
Future national economy			0.071*	0.018
			(0.035)	(0.025)

Table 2. (cont.)

	Model 1	Model 2	Model 3	Model 4
Candidate evaluations				
Obama thermometer				0.033*
				(0.001)
Romney thermometer				-0.011*
				(0.001)
Constant	3.134*	2.545*	0.794*	1.161*
	(0.152)	(0.133)	(0.198)	(0.152)
N	2040	2040	2026	2026
R	0.445	0.636	0.715	0.874
R^2	0.198	0.404	0.512	0.764
Adjusted R^2	0.193	0.400	0.506	0.761
SEE	1.56	1.34	1.22	0.85

Source: Authors' compilation based on ANES 2012.
Note: Unstandardized regression coefficients are reported, with the standard errors in parentheses. The dependent variable, *Presidential Approval* ranges from 1 = strongly disapprove to 5 = strongly approve. Don't knows were coded in the middle category of 3. Those who refused are excluded from the analysis. Independent variables: Refused and don't knows were included in the 0 category for the following dichotomous variables: all socio-demographic variables, party identification and ideology, and all social issue variables. The economic variables are coded as 1 = much worse to 5 = much better, with don't knows included in the middle of the same category and refusals excluded. The candidate feeling thermometers range from 0 to 100, with don't knows, refused, and don't recognize coded as the neutral 50. We code the variables this way to avoid drastically reducing the N. Our experiments suggest that this coding decision does not seriously influence the magnitude of the coefficients reported.
Standard errors in parentheses
*$p < 0.05$ (one-tailed test)

ship for ANES. In sum, candidate appeal—personality if you will—helps structure immigrant preferences to a high degree, especially when understood comparatively.

COMPARING MODEL PERFORMANCE ACROSS THE TWO SAMPLES

Thus far, we have examined each survey, and each block, separately. Now we evaluate the Michigan model across samples and blocks. In table 3, a comparison is made across three criteria: contribution, structure, and strength. First, we observe that the funnel of causality provides a useful overall framework of explanation. However, at each stage, it does not always register the same value. The roles of partisanship and issues are rather similar across the two samples. That is, both sets of variables make a strong contribution to explaining presidential support. However, that does not mean that the structure and strength of the relationships within those two blocks is identical. Partisanship exercises stronger effects in the national sample than in the Hispanic immigrant sample. We expected that immigrants would acquire party identification as they assimilated into American society, but, as Sears, Danbold, and Zavala show in this volume, this is true for naturalized immigrants; among the non-naturalized, however, fewer self-identify with a party, though many show signs of nascent party identification. Because of this, and because immigrants have not spent their entire lives in the U.S. political system, the long-term anchor of partisanship has a weaker influence on vote choice. Finally, although both samples are responsive to issues, the set is not the same; the immigrants come close to being single-issue voters, in that it is mainly the economy (in its multiple dimensions) that

Table 3. Comparison Across the Michigan Model: LINES and ANES, 2012

	LINES		ANES
Socio-demographics			
Contribution+	0.057	<	0.193
Structure^	year arrived, female, homeowner, origin	≠	female, church, married, home, race-ethnicity
Strength#		≠	
Partisanship			
Contribution	0.124	<	0.207
Structure	party ID, ideology	=	party ID, ideology
Strength		<	
Issues			
Contribution	0.121	>	0.106
Structure	gay, past pocket, past and future economy	≠	government, gay, death, all economy
Strength		≠	
Candidates			
Contribution	0.148	<	0.255
Structure	Obama thermometer, Romney thermometer	=	Obama thermometer, Romney thermometer
Strength		<	

Source: Authors' calculations based on tables 1 and 2.
Note: Contribution+ refers to the increment to the adjusted R-squared, once the variables are added to the block; *Structure^* refers to the variables added to the block that have statistically significant regression slopes (in the expected direction); *Strength#* refers to the effects (slopes) of the variables added to the block that have statistically significant coefficients (in the expected direction).

moves them. In contrast, the national sample respondents have multiple concerns beyond the economy.

Now consider the role of candidate appeal, which contributes more than any other block regardless of sample. This result suggests the vital role of candidate characteristics, such as leadership, honesty, and—more generally—personality traits. These things matter a great deal for both Hispanic immigrants and the national sample. Further, the structure of the response appears the same: liking Obama generates the expected presidential approval in both groups, as does disliking Romney. In other words, both these attitudes have an independent effect. Moreover, that effect operates asymmetrically, in that feeling toward Obama has at least double the impact of feeling toward Romney.

It is with respect to the first block, socio-demographics, that we observe—ostensibly—the biggest difference across samples. In the immigrant survey, it appears to add very little to the explanation, even with the inclusion of immigrant-specific traits and country of origin. In the national survey, by way of contrast, it provides variance, structure, and strength. However, looks can be deceptive. Most of this socio-demographic power comes from the necessary addition of the race-ethnicity variables to the ANES data (in table 2, column 1). These variables are not added into the LINES analyses in an obvious sense, because that sample is racially and ethnically essentially homogenous, that is, it composes in itself a Hispanic demographic. Statistically, that means that it *is* added, but it is added as a constant, into the intercept. Demographics, then, make an important contribution to the explanation of presidential support here; but to better capture that effect structurally one needs data over time rather than cross-sectionally. This same difficulty is occurring elsewhere as analysts try to capture the effects of this restricted variance problem with regard to the observation of economic crisis (see, for example, Lewis-Beck and Fraile 2014).

Overall, how well does the funnel of causality explanation account for Obama support? One answer comes from assessment of goodness-of-fit at the last stage, with model 4. At first glance, it looks as if the national sample receives better explanation than the immigrant sample: that is, the adjusted R-squareds, respectively, are 0.761 and 0.450. However, as we know, a comparison of the R-squared (adjusted or not) can be perilous across samples, particularly if we have variation differences in the X or Y variables (Lewis-Beck and Skalaban 1990). In such a situation, which clearly is the case here, a more secure measure of comparative model fit comes from the standard error of estimate, or SEE (Lewis-Beck and Kruger 2007). As the bottom of tables 1 and 2 (column 4) show, the SEE is 0.89 and 0.85, respectively. In other words, by this measure, the models yield about the same fit. Put another way, if we wish to predict presidential support, we are able to do about equally well for either the immigrant sample or the national sample. In sum, the funnel of causality argument, taken to its last stage, receives about the same level of empirical confirmation, on either dataset.

CONCLUSION

We began with the notion that the funnel of causality explanation for political behavior, as created by Campbell and his colleagues (1960) and developed by their adherents, could be successfully applied to yet another democratic setting. In particular, we pursued the idea that it could explain the political preferences of Hispanic immigrants in the context of the 2012 U.S. presidential election. According to our findings, the Michigan model shows itself capable of rendering a more than satisfactory account of Obama support in that contest, for both Hispanic immigrants and American nationals generally.

Our finding that the Michigan model holds for immigrants suggests that people are able to assimilate to new political environments. They have common experiences with other Americans, form attachments to parties, develop opinions on political issues, evaluate the economy, and assess the candidates. These factors, following the funnel of causality, predictably affect how immigrants judge the president's performance in much the same way they affect how Americans, in general, judge the president.

REFERENCES

American National Election Studies (ANES). 2010. *Time Series Cumulative Data File dataset*. Ann Arbor: University of Michigan; Palo Alto: Stanford University. Accessed February 29, 2016. http://www.electionstudies.org/.

Bengtsson, Åsa, Kasper M. Hansen, Ólafur Þ. Harðarson, Hanne M. Narud, and Henrik Oscarsson. 2014. *The Nordic Voter: Myths of Exceptionalism*. Colchester: ECPR Press.

Butler, David, and Donald E. Strokes. 1969. *Political Change in Britain*. New York: St. Martin's Press.

Campbell, Angus, Philip E. Converse, Warren E. Miller, and Donald E. Stokes. 1960. *The American Voter*. New York: John Wiley & Sons.

Carlin, Ryan E., Matthew M. Singer, and Elizabeth J. Zechmeister, eds. 2015. *The Latin American Voter: Pursuing Representation and Accountability in Challenging Contexts*. Ann Arbor: University of Michigan Press.

Clarke, D. Harold, David Sanders, Marianne C. Stewart, and Paul F. Whiteley. 2004. *Political Choice in Britain*. Oxford: Oxford University Press.

———. 2009. *Performance Politics and the British Voter*. Cambridge: Cambridge University Press.

Fiorina, P. Morris. 1981. *Retrospective Voting in American National Elections*. New Haven, Conn.: Yale University Press.

Hajnal, Zoltan L., and Taeku Lee. 2011. *Why Americans Don't Join the Party: Race, Immigration, and the Failure (of Political Parties) to Engage the Electorate*. Princeton, N.J.: Princeton University Press.

Jacoby, William G. 2002. "Liberal-Conservative Thinking in the American Electorate." In *Research in Micropolitics: Political Decision Making, Participation, and Deliberation*, edited by Michael X. Delli Carpini, Leonie Huddy, and Robert Y. Shapiro. Greenwich, Conn.: JAI Press.

Kessel, John H. 2004. "Views of the Voters." In *Models of Voting in Presidential Elections, edited by Herbert F. Weisberg and Clyde Wilcox. Stanford, Calif.: Stanford University Press.

Kiewiet, D. Roderick. 1983. *Macroeconomics and Micropolitics: The Electoral Effects of Economic Issues.* Chicago: University of Chicago Press.

Kiewiet, D. Roderick, and Michael S. Lewis-Beck. 2011. "No 'Man' Is an Island: Self-Interest, the Public Interest, and Sociotropic Voting." *Critical Review* 23(3): 303–19.

Kinder, R. Donald. 1986. "Presidential Character Revisited." In *Political Cognition*, edited by Richard R. Lau and David O. Sears. Hillside, N.J.: Lawrence Erlbaum.

Kinder, R. Donald, and D. Roderick Kiewiet. 1981. "Sociotropic Politics: The American Case." *British Journal of Political Science* 11(2): 129–61.

Kmenta, Jan. 1997. *Elements of Econometrics*, 2nd ed. Ann Arbor: University of Michigan Press.

Kritzinger, Sylvia, Eva Zeglovits, Michael S. Lewis-Beck, and Richard Nadeau. 2013. *The Austrian Voter*. Vienna: Vienna University Press.

Lewis-Beck, Michael S., ed. 2009. "Special Issue on The American Voter Revisited." *Electoral Studies* 28(4): 521–641.

Lewis-Beck, Michael S., and Marta Fraile. 2014. "Economic Vote Instability: Endogeneity or Restricted Variance? Spanish Panel Evidence from 2008 and 2011." *European Journal of Political Research* 53(1): 160–79.

Lewis-Beck, Michael S., William G. Jacoby, Helmut Norpoth, and Herbert F. Weisberg. 2008. *The American Voter Revisited*. Ann Arbor: University of Michigan Press.

Lewis-Beck, Michael S., and James Krueger. 2007. "Goodness-of-Fit: R-squared, SEE, and 'Best Practice'." *Political Methodologist* 15(1): 2–4.

Lewis-Beck, Michael S., Richard Nadeau, and Éric Bélanger. 2012. *French Presidential Elections*. Basingstoke: Palgrave Macmillan.

Lewis-Beck, Michael S., and Maria Celeste Ratto. 2013. "Economic Voting in Latin America: A General Model." *Electoral Studies* 32(3): 489–93.

Lewis-Beck, Michael S., and Andrew Skalaban. 1990. "The R-Squared: Some Straight Talk." *Political Analysis* 2(1): 153–71.

Lewis-Beck, Michael S., and Mary Stegmaier. 2009. "American Voter to Economic Voter: Evolution of an Idea." *Electoral Studies* 28(4): 625–31.

———. 2013. "The VP-Function Revisited: A Survey of the Literature on Vote and Popularity Functions after over 40 Years." *Public Choice* 157(3–4): 367–85.

Lewis-Beck, Michael S., and Charles Tien. 2014. "Proxy Models and Nowcasting: US Presidential Elections in the Future." *Presidential Studies Quarterly* 44: 506–21.

McCann, James A., and Michael Jones-Correa. 2012. Latino Immigrant National Election Study, 2012. New York: Russell Sage Foundation, Carnegie Corporation of New York, Purdue University, and Cornell University.

Miller, Warren E., and J. Merrill Shanks. 1996. *The New American Voter*. Cambridge, Mass.: Harvard University Press.

Nannestad, Peter, and Martin Paldam. 1994. "The VP-Function: A Survey of the Literature on Vote and Popularity Functions After 25 Years." *Public Choice* 79(3–4): 213–45.

Sears, David O. 2001. "The Role of Affect in Symbolic Politics." In *Citizens and Politics: Perspectives from Political Psychology*, edited by James H. Kuklinski. Cambridge: Cambridge University Press.

Seligson, Mitchell, and Elizabeth Zechmeister. 2012. "Public Opinion Research in Latin America." In *Routledge Handbook on Latin American Politics*, edited by Peter Kingstone, and Deborah J. Yashar. New York: Routledge.

Stegmaier, Mary, and Michael S. Lewis-Beck. 2013. "Economic Voting." In *Oxford Bibliographies in Political Science*, edited by R. Valelly. New York: Oxford University Press.

Weisberg, Herbert F. 2009. *The Total Survey Error Approach: A Guide to the New Science of Survey Research*. Chicago: University of Chicago Press.

Whiteley, Paul F., Harold D. Clarke, David Sanders, and Marianne C. Stewart. 2013. *Affluence, Austerity and Electoral Change in Britain*. Cambridge: Cambridge University Press.

Zechmeister, Elizabeth, and Margarita Corral. 2013. "Individual and Contextual Constraints on Ideological Labels in Latin America." *Comparative Political Studies* 46(6): 675–701.

Incorporation of Latino Immigrants into the American Party System

DAVID O. SEARS, FELIX DANBOLD, AND
VANESSA M. ZAVALA

Are Latinos, especially immigrants, less partisan than other American ethnic groups? In the 2012 Latino Immigrant National Election Study and American National Election Studies datasets, a greater proportion of Latinos self-categorize as partisans on the standard measure of party identification than previously theorized. Only non-naturalized Latino immigrants showed unusual nonincorporation into the party system. Both continuing subjective engagement in the politics of their country of origin and nonpolitical assimilation in the United States were associated with greater partisan self-categorization, even controlling for relevant demographics. However, self-categorization may underestimate incorporation into the party system by overlooking latent partisan preferences. Indeed, Latino immigrants show quite crystallized attitudes toward the parties and their candidates, even those who did not self-categorize as Democrats or Republicans. Only non-naturalized immigrants show notably low levels of partisan crystallization. Most seemingly unincorporated Latino immigrants may simply be in the early stages of developing partisan identities rather than deliberately standing outside the party system.

Keywords: Latino party identification, Latino immigrants, partisan self-categorization, partisan crystallization, latent preferences, assimilation

In 2012, Barack Obama received between 71 and 75 percent of the Latino vote, according to the Pew Research Center's Hispanic Trends Project (2012) and Latino Decisions (2012). That was an increase from 67 percent in 2008, and an even larger increase for the Democratic ticket from the 53 percent that John Kerry arguably received in 2004 (Preston 2008). News stories following the Obama victories emphasized not only the size of his margin among Latinos but that they are the fastest-growing ethnic subgroup in the country. The subtext of these reports was that such demographic changes were inevitably moving the nation in the direction of the Democrats. That has led some to conclude that the Latino vote is a "sleeping giant" now beginning to stir.

Given that about one in three of the Latino population are foreign born, about half the U.S. total (Krogstad and Lopez 2014), the outcomes of these elections also raised anew questions about the incorporation of new immigrant groups into the American party system. In this paper, we seek to examine the degree of incorporation of Latino immigrants into the party system; which party, if any, Latino immi-

David O. Sears is distinguished professor of psychology and political science at the University of California, Los Angeles. **Felix Danbold** is a doctoral candidate at the University of California, Los Angeles. **Vanessa M. Zavala** is a doctoral student at the University of California, Los Angeles.

Direct correspondence to: David O. Sears at sears@ssgs.ucla.edu, Psychology Department, University of California, Los Angeles, CA 90095; Felix Danbold at fdanbold@gmail.com, 1285 Franz Hall, Box 951563, University of California, Los Angeles, CA 90095; and Vanessa M. Zavala at vanessamzavala@gmail.com, 1285 Franz Hall, Box 951563, University of California, Los Angeles, CA 90095.

grants are joining in the United States; and begin to explore the determinants of their adoption of a partisan identity.

LATINOS AND THE PARTY SYSTEM

Beyond statistics from the voting booth, questions about Latino immigrants' ultimate partisan loyalties remain somewhat unresolved. Many have predicted that Latinos' predominantly working-class status would lead them to economic liberalism and the Democratic Party, as has been true of many immigrant groups in the past. Carole Uhlaner and Chris Garcia (2005) find that Mexican American immigrants who have spent higher proportions of their lives in the United States, and older U.S.-born Mexican Americans, were more likely to be Democrats. They argue that longer tenure in the United States promotes Democratic partisanship, though the class explanation for that preference is less clear in their analyses, because the link between the direction of partisan preferences and socioeconomic status (SES) varies across various indicators of class. Shaun Bowler, Stephen Nicholson, and Gary Segura (2006) suggest that the political hostility displayed by Republicans toward minorities in recent years has driven Latinos even more toward the Democrats. On the other hand, it has long been argued that many Latinos are "natural Republicans," both because of their widespread social conservatism and their upward-mobility aspirations (Alvarez and García Bedolla 2003; DeSipio 1996). The ire of many Latino immigrant groups at the increased rates of deportation of undocumented immigrants under the Obama administration may also have loosened support for the Democratic Party among Latinos (Serrano 2014).

An important third possibility is that many Latinos, especially immigrants, remain largely free of partisan commitments. As Donald Green, Bradley Palmquist, and Eric Schickler say, "recent immigrants constitute one of the largest groups of unaligned citizens in the United States, but parties have been slow in recruiting them" (2002, 227–28). Janelle Wong also argues that a wide variety of other civic institutions could, but often do not, facilitate incorporation of immigrants into the political system (2006). Among the consequences may be that many adopt an apolitical "none of the above" stance toward the parties rather than a strong partisan attachment.

However, Zoltan Hajnal and Taeku Lee have made perhaps the most systematic case for the claim that many Latinos are "choosing to remain on the sidelines" of the party system (2011, 87–88). They argue that the existing literature "misses what is perhaps most distinctive about the party identification of immigrant-based groups, namely, the relative absence of any relationship to parties." They cite surveys of Latino and Asian Americans that show a "distinct lack of enthusiasm for the major parties," as reflected in the classic self-categorization measures of party identification featured in *The American Voter* (Campbell et al. 1960). The authors argue that "a clear majority" (55 percent of the 2006 Latino National Survey) are nonpartisans, not affiliated with either of the two major parties. The single largest group (38 percent) are what they call nonidentifiers, whose responses to the initial party identification question are coded as not sure, don't know, refused, something else, no preference, or do not think in those terms; another 17 percent call themselves Independent rather than Democrat or Republican (Hajnal and Lee 2011, 4–5, 88, 148; see also Wong et al. 2011). Their Independent category appears to include those who self-categorized as leaning toward one party or the other, a category of Independents who have been shown in the past to behave more like weak partisans than pure Independents, who are self-declared Independents declining to indicate any partisan "leaning" (Lewis-Beck et al. 2007; Keith et al. 1992).

The contrast between these three views has obvious political importance in terms of current partisan debates over a "pathway to citizenship" for immigrants who have not obtained citizenship. If in fact many noncitizen Latino immigrants are predisposed toward being Democrats, one could readily understand Republican anxieties about flooding the electorate with millions of new Democratic voters. On the other hand, Democrats might have every reason to emphasize noncitizen Latinos' current explicit nonpartisanship, perhaps strategically arguing that Republicans should have nothing to worry about were the electorate to be expanded to incorporate many new apolitical, nonpartisan Latinos.

THEORIES OF PARTISANSHIP

How might extant theories of partisanship help explain the likelihood and direction of incorporation among Latinos into the party system? One conception has its ancestry in Anthony Downs's early (1957) version of rational choice theories. In this view, voters are sufficiently informed about politics, adequately understand their own interests, and engage in enough instrumental reasoning linking the two to produce sensible ideologies and policy preferences, and ultimately rational proximity voting. A later variant, following V. O. Key's (1966) admonition that voters are not fools, viewed voters as adjusting their partisanship according to their perceptions of party performance. Party identification therefore becomes a "running tally" adjusted as the voter adapts it to his or her perceptions of party competence (Fiorina 1981). If Latinos feel that both parties are indifferent to their interests, they may have little incentive to favor either one.

Others argue that many Latinos will never even be firmly committed to the United States, much less to one or the other political party. Because the great majority of Latino immigrants come from adjacent or nearby nations (nearly two-thirds are from Mexico) characterized by porous borders and frequent reverse migration, some scholars predict that many Latino immigrants will opt to remain Spanish-fluent, moving freely back and forth between the two nations, and perhaps preferring to vote in the elections of their original nations rather than in the United States (Huntington 2004). Critical race theorists like Rogers Smith (1997, 2011) take a surprisingly similar view, noting the obstacles facing immigrants in the many inegalitarian exceptions to the openness of American society to newcomers, especially people of color. Racial hierarchy theorists formalize such views, depicting most Latinos as stuck in a subordinate position in a largely stable and inflexible hierarchy of racial groups (for example, Bonilla-Silva 2006; Masuoka and Junn 2013; Sidanius and Pratto 1999).

Hajnal and Lee (2011) explain the high rates of nonpartisanship they observed among Latinos in similarly rational terms. Immigrants' lack of information or information uncertainty means they are likely to distance themselves from the parties as an "affirmation of rational skepticism" about institutions they know little about and mistrust (82). Latinos also are "ideologically ambivalent" about both of the two main parties, given that neither consistently represents immigrants' interests. The rational choice approach would therefore seem compatible with an expectation that high rates of nonpartisanship are emerging in a group that receives few convincing overtures from either party.

The best-known major alternative to a rational choice approach is *The American Voter* view that preadult socialization, especially from parents, is the crucial ingredient in developing Americans' party identifications (Campbell et al. 1960; also see Lewis-Beck et al. 2008). It depicted a psychological process in which affective attachments toward the explicit symbols of the parties were acquired without much information. What information was available, or that became available later in adulthood, was often used in the service of post hoc rationalization of prior partisanship, a point later developed in more detail by Milton Lodge and Charles Taber (2014).

That canonical theory about the origins of partisan attachments might point to some specific obstacles to the acquisition of strong partisanship among immigrants. Almost all immigrants had parents who had spent their own formative years, or their adult lives, or both, in another nation's political system. Those parents probably had little information and few strong attitudes toward the American political parties. As a result, immigrants would therefore be unlikely to inherit strong preferences about the American parties from their parents. Even naturalized first-generation immigrants, lacking that crucial parental influence in their own preadult lives, might be slow to acquire an American party identification. U.S.-born Latinos in the second generation may receive more preadult socialization, but mostly again from immigrant parents who had little of that experience themselves. The second generation might also receive weak partisan socialization from other possible agents, such as peers and schools, given that low-income immigrants to America are often quite residentially segregated (Iceland and Scopilliti 2008). So even the second generation might also tend to be only indifferent partisans.

However, subsequent research has developed some elaborations and modifications of this classical account that may be more favorable to developing strong partisan identities in adulthood after immigration. Although contemporary writers range from subtle revisions of that original theory (Lewis-Beck et al. 2008) to more fundamental ones (Hajnal and Lee 2011), supporters and critics have reached consensus on a few points. Most relevant, acquisition of partisanship is now recognized as promoted by a broader set of experiences than just exposure to one's parents, and as evolving over a longer period of the life course than just the preadult years. Indeed, in the United States' steady-state party system, party identification generally continues to strengthen with age through the life course, not just plateauing as offspring leave adolescence (for reviews, see Lewis-Beck et al. 2008; Sears and Brown 2013). Even adults can be converted if the parties change positions on key issues, such as when white southerners moved to the Republican Party starting in the 1960s after the Democrats began to support civil rights more forthrightly (Carmines and Stimson 1989; Green, Palmquist, and Schickler 2002; Osborne, Sears, and Valentino 2011).

This revisionist socialization theory might suggest that, rather than rationally deciding not to enter a party system with unappealing options, the numerous nonpartisans in the heavily immigrant Latino population may merely be in the early stages of adopting a partisan identity. A straight-line assimilation process (Gordon 1964) argues that each successive generation after immigration acculturates to American society more, in language, residential integration, intermarriage, institutional engagement, subjective attachment to the nation, and weakened ethnic ties (Alba and Nee 2003; Citrin and Sears 2014). By that logic, Latino immigrants should become steadily more incorporated into the party system over time. In fact, some of Hajnal and Lee's (2011) empirical findings about Latino nonpartisanship seem to show just that, partisan identification increasing as a function of both years in the United States and higher socioeconomic status. They describe the development of Latino partisanship as also being guided in part by processes of straight-line assimilation, following a sequential process of, first, choosing to identify with a party, and then determining which party to identify with.

This proposed process of integration may have been overlooked in part due to the almost universal reliance on the conventional Michigan self-categorization measure of party identification ("Generally speaking, do you usually think of yourself as a Democrat, a Republican, an Independent, or what?"). Recent developments in psychology suggest that this conventional measure may underestimate the presence of real partisan preferences acquired earlier. Dual-process theories suggest a distinction between explicit and implicit measures of attitudes. The former involve conscious self-categorization, as in the Michigan measure. The latter reflect more automatic affective associations that the individual may or may not be fully aware of. A prominent advocate of such a distinction is Daniel Kahneman (2003), who contrasts conscious deliberate choices (System 2) with more affective, automatic, and less conscious associations (System 1). Social psychologists find that implicit attitudes are pervasive and detectable even when the individual is not consciously aware of them or is responding to subliminal stimuli. However, the case for widespread implicit attitudes does not hinge on their being wholly unconscious (Banaji and Greenwald 2013).

Are most Latinos outside the party system by choice, "rational skepticism" keeping them "on the sidelines?" Or are many simply in the early stages of incorporation because of weak prior socialization, given their recent immigration or that of their families, that early stage present primarily in terms of latent preferences, and so often not detected by the conventional self-categorization measure? We find widespread partisan affective preferences that frequently coexist with self-categorization as nonpartisan. We develop measures of attitude crystallization that we believe reflect reliable latent partisan preferences that often emerge prior to self-categorization as a partisan, during earlier stages of incorporation into the party system.

RESEARCH GOALS

Our aim in this paper, then, is to produce an up-to-date assessment of how incorporated Latinos are in the American party system, particularly Latino immigrants. Our hypothesis is that Latino immigrants may be developing partisan preferences more commonly, as well as earlier in the assimilation process, than is often appreciated. We address some determinants of partisan incorporation that seem to be more consistent with the socialization than the rational choice approach to partisanship. Finally, we suggest that the incorporation of Latinos into the American party system has been underestimated because its psychology has been specified too narrowly. We suggest that reliance on the relatively demanding criterion of conscious partisan self-categorization needs to be supplemented by recognition of the more pervasive implicit partisan preferences that we call latent preferences.

We have four goals. First, using more current data than available in previous research, we reassess Latinos' level of incorporation into the party system. We find far lower levels of nonpartisanship among Latinos as a whole than in previous work. We also find that high levels of nonpartisanship are limited primarily to Latinos who are non-naturalized immigrants, who perhaps not incidentally are prevented from voting. We also find that Latinos are as fully incorporated into the party system as whites of comparably low levels of income and education. We conclude from these analyses that Latino nonpartisanship is less a conscious decision to remain aloof from distrusted political parties than a result of their being at an early stage in the long process of integration into American society.

Second, to explain differences in self-categorization into partisan identities beyond these factors, we examine the influence of Latino immigrants' continuing political engagement with their country of origin on their incorporation into the American party system. Immigrants are unlikely to arrive as political blank slates. Political engagement in countries of origin may carry over into political lives in America, analogous to the influence of early political socialization on the more general U.S. population. But what kind of impact might it have? Most obviously, it might impede immigrants' abilities to switch gears to the U.S. system, though previous research has not uncovered such a negative impact (Wong 2006; Wong et al. 2011). Alternatively, prior political interests and experiences may be transferable to life in America, actually facilitating incorporation into the American party system. For example, Bruce Cain, Roderick Kiewiet, and Carole Uhlaner (1991) find that refugees from formerly communist nations wound up predominantly as Republicans, attracted to that party as more vigorously anticommunist than the Democrats. Earlier studies of immigrant partisanship have typically relied on reports of post-immigration experiences with American politics. Instead, we broaden our search to include data about Latino immigrants' involvement in the politics of their nation of origin.

Third, the partisan incorporation of new immigrants may be a piece of a broader process of assimilation into their new nation. Immigrants' efforts to become more subjectively and culturally invested in America even in ostensibly nonpolitical domains may contribute to their political incorporation as well. For example, once in the United States, English fluency might facilitate exposure to the mainstream media and news about elections. Indeed, Wong (2000) finds that English-language skills were linked to the acquisition of partisanship among Latino and Asian immigrants. Similarly, Karthick Ramakrishnan (2005) finds that being married or employed or having a stable residence also predicted stronger party identification. Alternatively, it could be that the adoption of a partisan identity can occur independently of nonpolitical acculturation. The benefits of being able to communicate fluently in English across contexts or being able to drive are more immediate than, and may not necessarily predict, the more abstract benefits of political incorporation and engagement. To test this, we examine ostensibly nonpolitical acculturation experiences in American society, such as intentions to stay in

America and possessing English fluency, as potential facilitators of immigrants' political incorporation.

Fourth, because the partisanship of Latinos is the central focus of this paper, the traditional self-categorization measure of party identification drawn from *The American Voter* is crucial for our initial analyses. However, we also argue that it may understate Latino incorporation into the party system. In recent years, social psychologists have distinguished such conscious, explicit attitudes from implicit attitudes that reflect automatic, often nonconscious, affective associations. Furthermore, researchers have shown that strong implicit attitudes can be held even in the absence of strong explicit attitudes (for example, Banaji and Greenwald 2013). Even with minimal political information and some ambivalence toward the Democratic Party, most Latinos, even putative nonpartisans, may nonetheless have clear latent preferences for it over the Republican Party.

To test for such latent preferences, we assess the crystallization of partisanship using the associations between relevant affectively loaded political concepts. We operationalize crystallization, borrowing from Philip Converse's (1964) classic three-part conceptualization of belief systems, in terms of the stability of party and candidate evaluations over time, consistency of party and candidate evaluations with presidential preferences, and power of party evaluations over evaluations of the parties' presidential nominees (for precedents, see Sears, Haley, and Henry 2008; Sears and Valentino 1997). We hypothesize that strong and highly crystallized latent preferences for one party over the other may exist even among those who are defined as nonpartisans according to their conscious self-categorizations, and even among many immigrants who are not citizens.

METHODS

We rely primarily on the Latino Immigrant National Election Study (LINES) conducted in 2012. As explained elsewhere in this issue (McCann and Jones-Correa), a national sample of naturalized and non-naturalized Latino immigrants from Spanish-speaking countries in Latin America was recruited to participate in telephone interviews during the two months before the November 2012 presidential election or two months after (n = 418 pre-only, n = 435 both pre- and post, and n = 451 post-only; overall sample size was 1,304).

A second source of data comes from black (n = 511), white (n = 918), and Latino (n = 472) adult U.S. citizens interviewed in the preelection and postelection surveys conducted by the 2012 American National Election Study (ANES). We analyzed data only from respondents in the Time Series face-to-face (FTF) subsample because of non-negligible differences between it and the online subsample (WEB) in the question structure of the party identification items that are at the heart of our analyses.

Measures

Party Identification

Partisanship was assessed similarly across the ANES and LINES datasets with the standard Michigan party identification items. In the preelection survey, participants were asked, "Generally speaking, do you usually think of yourself as a Democrat, a Republican, an independent, or what?" If they responded with either Republican or Democrat, they were then asked, "Would you call yourself a strong [Democrat/Republican] or a not very strong [Democrat/Republican]?" However, if they had responded with Independent, other party, no preference, don't know, or refused to answer the former question, they were then asked, "Do you think of yourself as closer to the Republican Party or to the Democratic Party?" From these two items, we computed two partisanship indices.

The first included eight categories of partisanship: Strong Democrat, not very strong Democrat, leaning Democrat, pure Independent, leaning Republican, not very strong Republican, strong Republican, and nonidentifiers. Leaning Democrats and leaning Republicans had identified as Independents to the first question and "closer" to one party or the other to the second. Pure Independents were coded as those who identified as Independents to the first question, then volunteered neither to the second. Nonidentifiers included all who refused to answer the first question or responded to it as Other, don't know, or no preference. Nonidentifiers also included those who responded to the first question as Independent and then refused to answer or answered don't know to the second question. (The online questions were somewhat different, providing more opportunities to identify as pure Independents and fewer to identify as nonidentifiers).

The second index pooled categories from the first index, reducing it to four categories: Democrat (strong Democrat and not very strong Democrat), Republican (strong Republican and not very strong Republican), Independent (pure Independents, leaning Democrat, leaning Republican), and nonidentifiers.

Naturalization

In the LINES 2012, respondents were asked, "Are you a naturalized citizen in the United States?" (yes or no). The ANES 2012 included only U.S. citizens. Respondents who had not been born in the United States indicated their immigration status in terms of the year they became naturalized U.S. citizens.

Continuing Political Engagement in Country of Origin

Continuing engagement of Latino immigrants in the politics of their country of origin was measured in the LINES 2012 only, based on four indicators: "How often did you vote in presidential elections in [country of origin]?"; "Have you voted in an election in [country of origin] while being in the United States?"; "Talking now about [your country of origin], in general how much interest do you have in politics in that country?"; "How much attention would you say you pay to politics in [country of origin, or if COO unknown: the country where you were born]?" These four items were keyed such that higher scores indicated higher levels of political involvement in the country of origin. They all loaded on a single factor and so were combined to form a *continuing political engagement index*. That index has modest reliability ($\alpha = 0.54$), despite being made up of quite different constructs rather than being alternate indicators of a common latent variable.

It was rescaled to 0 to 1, and mean scores were trichotomized, to compare the least continuingly engaged third of the Latino immigrants with the most engaged third.

Nonpolitical Assimilation

An index of assimilation into the U.S. mainstream outside of politics was based on six indicators in the LINES 2012. Respondents were asked, "Are you a naturalized citizen in the United States?"; "How often do you send money to friends or family in [country of origin]?"(reverse keyed); "Do you have plans to return to [country of origin] to live there permanently?" (reverse keyed); "Do you have a non-expired driver's license?"; "What language do you primarily speak at home with your family? Is it only English, mostly English, only Spanish, mostly Spanish, or both languages equally?"; and "For information about politics would you say you get the most information from Spanish-language television, radio, and newspapers, or from English-language TV, radio, and newspapers?" (reverse keyed). These six items were keyed such that higher numbers indicated higher assimilation into the United States and were scaled into our *assimilation* index ($\alpha = 0.53$). Mean scores were then trichotomized, as with the previous scale.

Demographic Controls

Regression analyses were run on the LINES data predicting partisanship from continuing political engagement and assimilation. They included the following demographic controls: age of respondent on arrival to the United States, years in the United States, highest level of education, and gender. Age of arrival to the United States ranged from less than one year to seventy-four ($M = 49$, $SD = 15$; median age of arrival = 24; median years in the United States = 22). Highest level of education was coded into five categories: less than high school graduate (62 percent), high school diploma or GED (20 percent), some post–high school education (12 percent), bachelor's degree (4 percent), and graduate degree (2 percent; $M = 1.66$, $SD = 1.00$). Gender was coded dichotomously: 0 = male (44 percent), 1 = female (56 percent).

Crystallization of Partisanship

Crystallization of partisanship was evaluated in terms of three types of correlations, following Converse (1964), and Sears and Valentino (1997) and Sears, Haley, and Henry (2008): stability of party and candidate evaluations over time; consistency of presidential preferences with evaluations of the parties and individual candidates; and power of party evaluations over evaluations of the parties' presidential nominees. Significant positive correlations between two items were defined as indicative of significant crystallization. One caution is that some of the correlations are based on relatively small sample sizes due to the lower number of Latino participants who were nonidentifiers, or who self-identified as pure Independents or as Republicans, or because most respondents participated in only one wave (pre- or postelection only).

Most of the correlations were based on feeling thermometers in the LINES 2012 dataset that asked respondents how they felt about the Democratic Party, the Republican Party, and presidential candidates Barack Obama and Mitt Romney, using 0 (cold) to 100 (warm) scales. Like-dislike ratings of the parties on 0 to 10 scales appeared on the postelection interview only. In all cases the pro-Democratic or pro-Obama responses were keyed high, and pro-Republican or pro-Romney responses keyed low.

We computed two *stability* coefficients, correlations between pre- and postelection evaluations of the political parties and of the presidential candidates. In each case we used the difference scores, between the Democrats and Republicans, and between the Obama and Romney items. In the tables, we refer to these as *Party Pre * Party Post* and *Candidate Pre * Candidate Post*, respectively.

We computed two *consistency* coefficients (*Candidate Pre * President Preference; Party Pre * President Preference*) reflecting correlations between presidential preference and candidate thermometers and party thermometers, using questions from the preelection survey. The presidential candidate preference scale (*President Preference*) was based on three items. The first asked respondents, "Talking about the elections for president in the United States, do you have a preference for one of the presidential candidates?" If respondents answered yes to that item, they were then asked, "Which candidate do you prefer? Barack Obama, Mitt Romney [randomize order], or another candidate?" and "Would you say that your preference for this candidate is strong or not so strong?" Among those who stated they did have a presidential candidate preference, their answers were recoded into a single item (1 = Strong preference for Romney to 4 = Strong preference for Obama).

Finally, we computed two *power* coefficients, reflecting the correlations between the preelection thermometer items of each party and of their respective candidates (*Republican Party Pre * Romney Pre; Democratic Party Pre * Obama Pre*).

RESULTS

Our first question was whether, in 2012, an exceptionally large percentage of Latinos were still unincorporated in the American party system. Specifically, when asked for their party identification, were Latinos substantially more likely to self-categorize as nonidentifiers or Independents than whites or blacks were?

Following Hajnal and Lee (2011), we start with the most expansive definition of nonincorporation, made up of all nonidentifiers and Independents (both leaning and pure Independents). As seen in the penultimate row of table 1, 46 percent of the Latino immigrants in the LINES and 40 percent of the Latino citizens in the ANES were classified as nonincorporated using this approach. Both these percentages were substantially lower than the earlier estimate of a majority (55 percent) of Latinos categorized as nonincorporated in the 2006 Latino National Survey (Hajnal and Lee 2011, 159). Moreover, both of these 2012 estimates of Latino nonincorporation are a little below the figure for whites (48 percent in the 2012 ANES). This is an early warning signal that Latinos may not be as nonincorporated as originally thought, and perhaps not as unique, either.

However, we have reservations about such an expansive method of estimating the extent of Latino nonpartisanship. It treats leaning In-

Table 1. Partisan Self-Categorization by Ethnicity

	Latino		White	Black
	LINES 2012	ANES 2012	ANES 2012	ANES 2012
Democrat	45	49	26	74
Lean Democrat[a]	13	15	14	16
Pure Independent[a,b]	8	7	6	2
Lean Republican[a]	4	5	16	2
Republican	9	11	27	2
Nonidentifier[a,b]	21	13	12	4
Total percent	100%	100%	101%	100%
Total N	847	471	915	509
Total nonincorporated including leaning Independents[a]	46	40	48	24
Total nonincorporated excluding leaning Independents[b]	29	20	18	6

Source: Authors' calculations based on ANES 2012 (FTF only), McCann and Jones-Correa 2012.
Note: The categories included in each of the total nonincorporated rows are indicated by superscripts.

dependents as nonpartisans despite the substantial evidence in previous research cited earlier that they are generally about as partisan as so-called weak partisans. The final row summarizing nonincorporation in table 1 takes the more conservative, and customary, approach of excluding these leaners in calculations of the nonincorporated, leaving only the pure Independents and nonidentifiers. By this index, 29 percent of Latinos in the LINES and 20 percent of Latinos in the ANES were classified as nonincorporated. The Latinos in the ANES, all citizens, did not show significantly higher rates of nonincorporation than whites did (18 percent). This again suggests that Latino nonincorporation may be neither as widespread nor as unique to Latinos as previously thought.

In the remainder of the paper, we exclude leaning Independents from our estimates of the nonincorporated, given prior evidence that their partisanship rivals that of those who self-categorize as Democrats or Republicans, though "not very strong." The general findings of the following analyses replicate with either treatment, however.

NATURALIZATION AND IMMIGRATION STATUS

The Latinos in the LINES show a relatively high percentage of nonincorporated, though far from a majority. The high number, however, may be due primarily to the many non-naturalized immigrants in that sample. Therefore, we break down Latinos in both surveys by naturalization and immigration status. Table 2 shows that nonincorporation among Latinos was by far the highest and highly divergent from whites only among non-naturalized immigrants. Among Latinos, noncitizen immigrants were about twice as likely to be nonidentifiers (28 percent) as either naturalized immigrants (12 and 15 percent) or U.S.-born citizens (12 percent). To estimate total nonincorporation, we pooled nonidentifiers only with pure Independents. Again the non-naturalized immigrants are the outliers. In the LINES, 36 percent were either nonidentifiers or pure Independents, whereas all samples of Latino citizens showed far less nonincorporation (naturalized immigrants, 19 percent in the LINES and 24 percent in the ANES; and U.S.-born, 19 percent in the ANES). These rates of incorporation among Latino citizens were very similar to those of whites in the ANES (18 percent). It seems clear, then, that the higher rates of nonincorporation seen in table 1 among Latino immigrants in the LINES were driven by non-naturalized immigrants, not Latino citizens.

To be sure, blacks in the ANES are substan-

Table 2. Partisan Self-Categorization by Naturalization

	Non-naturalized Latino	Naturalized Latino		U.S.-Born Latino	All White	All Black
	LINES 2012	LINES 2012	ANES 2012	ANES 2012	ANES 2012	ANES 2012
Democrat	38	55	50	48	26	74
Lean Democrat	16	10	14	15	14	16
Pure Independent[a]	8	7	9	7	6	2
Lean Republican	4	4	4	6	16	2
Republican	6	12	9	12	28	2
Nonidentifier[a]	28	12	15	12	12	4
Total percent	100%	100%	101%	100%	102%	100%
Total N	509	338	141	324	915	509
Total nonincorporated[a]	36	19	24	19	18	6

Source: Authors' calculations based on ANES 2012 (FTF only), McCann and Jones-Correa 2012.
Note: Total nonincorporated is composed of the superscripted categories (pure Independent and nonidentifier).

tially less likely to be nonincorporated (6 percent) than Latinos or whites were (20 and 18 percent, respectively), using the narrower definition excluding leaners. That whites differ from blacks at about the same rate as do Latinos emphasizes that Latinos, especially Latino citizens, are not exceptionally weakly incorporated into the party system. The distinctively strong partisanship of blacks is a phenomenon that goes beyond the scope of this paper.

Class or Ethnicity?

We followed up these analyses by looking for additional subsets of the Latino population that might show especially weak incorporation. Hajnal and Lee (2011) show that it occurred significantly more often among Latinos with less income and education. Using the ANES dataset, we attempted to replicate this finding, as well as to elaborate on it in two ways. First, we used more moderate partitions of income and education levels than Hajnal and Lee, who contrasted only the extremes of each category. Second, we ran parallel analyses among whites to see whether Latinos' generally lower SES, as opposed to their ethnicity, might produce unusually high levels of nonincorporation relative to whites,.

Table 3 shows the partisan self-categorizations of those in the ANES whose annual family incomes fell above or below $20,000. Indeed, low-income Latinos (24 percent) were more likely to be nonincorporated (that is, nonidentifier or pure Independent) than high-income Latinos were (15 percent). However, whites showed a similar but somewhat smaller difference (19 percent versus 15 percent). So low-income Latinos were not much more likely to be nonincorporated than low-income whites were. The more notable difference was that low-income Latinos showed a far stronger preference for the Democrats (47 percent) than did similarly disadvantaged whites (27 percent), and were far less likely to be Republican (9 versus 23 percent). Low-income Latinos differ from whites not so much because they are not incorporated into the party system, but because they are much more likely to be Democrats.

Another indicator of socioeconomic disadvantage is educational level. We compared less-educated Latinos with comparable white respondents from the ANES survey; specifically, those who failed to reach the level of a high school graduate or equivalent. Table 4 shows that less education, like lower income, was associated with lower levels of partisan identification among Latinos: 25 percent of the less educated were nonincorporated, against 16

Table 3. Partisan Self-Categorization by Income

	< 20k		≥ 20k	
	Latino	White	Latino	White
Democrat	47	27	49	26
Pure Independent[a]	8	8	7	5
Republican	9	23	12	29
Nonidentifier[a]	16	11	8	10
Total percent	101%	100%	100%	101%
Total N	174	252	298	666
Total nonincorporated[a]	24	19	15	15

Source: Authors' calculations based on ANES 2012 (FTF only).
Note: Leaners classified as Democrats or Republicans. Total nonincorporated is composed of the superscripted categories (pure Independent and nonidentifier).

Table 4. Partisan Self-Categorization by Educational Level

	< HS Graduate		≥ HS Graduate	
	Latino	White	Latino	White
Democrat	51	27	48	26
Pure Independent[a]	8	14	7	5
Republican	6	17	12	29
Nonidentifier[a]	17	14	9	9
Total percent	101%	100%	100%	100%
Total N	108	105	264	813
Total nonincorporated[a]	25	28	16	14

Source: Authors' calculations based on ANES 2012 (FTF only).
Note: Leaners classified as Democrats or Republicans. Total nonincorporated is composed of the superscripted categories (pure Independent and nonidentifier).

percent of the better educated. Perhaps more interesting is that Latinos and whites again did not differ very much, once education is controlled. Less-educated Latinos were not much more likely to be nonidentifiers than comparable whites (17 versus 14 percent) and were actually less likely than less-educated whites to be self-declared pure Independents (8 versus 14 percent). However, less-educated Latinos, like lower income Latinos, were far more likely to self-categorize as Democrats than comparable whites were (51 versus 27 percent) and less likely to be Republicans (6 versus 17 percent). Using controls on either income or education, then, less-advantaged Latinos did not differ much from comparable whites in their level of incorporation into the party system. Indeed, the most noteworthy difference is that Latinos are far more likely to be Democrats than whites are.

Continuing Political Engagement in Country of Origin

So far, our analyses showed that although present, nonincorporation among Latinos appears to be less common than earlier estimates suggested. Rather, it appears to be primarily characteristic of Latino immigrants lacking citizenship. As a result, we aimed next to identify factors related to immigration that might be predictive of a lack of partisan identification. We begin by examining whether immigrants' continuing political engagement in their countries of origin affects their incorporation into

Table 5. Partisan Self-Categorization Among Latino Immigrants by Continuing Political Engagement in Country of Origin

	Least Cont. Engagement	Middle Third	Most Cont. Engagement	Most-Least % Difference
Democrat	49	58	67	18
Pure Independent[a]	10	7	6	-4
Republican	13	14	12	-1
Nonidentifier[a]	28	21	15	-13
Total percent	100%	100%	100%	
Total N	275	285	286	
Total nonincorporated[a]	38	28	21	-17

Source: Authors' calculations based on McCann and Jones-Correa 2012.
Note: Leaners classified as Democrats or Republicans. Total nonincorporated is composed of the superscripted categories (pure Independent and nonidentifier).
Continuing engagement was divided into three groups as equally sized as possible.

the American party system. It could signal a lack of interest in becoming a full member of their new nation, or suck more time away from the politics of the United States, and thus be a drag on the acquisition of American-style partisanship. Alternatively, it could be associated with accelerated political engagement in the United States, much as parental political engagement prepares offspring for later political involvement.

Table 5 shows that Latinos' continuing political engagement in their country of origin was actually quite strongly positively associated with partisan self-categorization in the United States, supporting the acceleration rather than the drag hypothesis. The most engaged individuals were about half as likely to be nonidentifiers (15 versus 28 percent) as the least engaged. Combining them with the pure Independents in our total estimate of nonincorporation, those low in continuing political engagement were nearly twice as likely to place themselves outside the party system than the most engaged were (38 versus 21 percent). The most engaged third of Latino immigrants were also about a third more likely to self-identify as Democrats than their least engaged counterparts were. The vast majority of those with continuing political involvement in their nation of origin were incorporated into the American party system, and showed a strong proclivity for the Democratic Party in particular.

Nonpolitical Assimilation

Our third goal was to see whether nonpolitical forms of assimilation had similarly positive associations with partisan incorporation. Common sense would suggest that greater acculturation to the English language and watching English-language news would be associated with greater subjective involvement in the American party system. However, this is not guaranteed. The more immersed Latino immigrants become in a society with a long history of discrimination against peoples of color, the more disillusioned they might become, including alienation from a party system that may seem ineffective in promoting their group's interests in key areas such as immigration.

In table 6, we find support for the hypothesis that partisan incorporation accompanies assimilation even on dimensions that do not directly relate to politics. Those Latino immigrants who were classified as the least assimilated were twice as likely to be nonidentifiers as the most assimilated were (32 percent versus 14 percent). Combining nonidentifiers with pure Independents shows a decline from 41 percent among the least assimilated, a level that does seem to reflect widespread nonincorporation into the party system, to just 21 percent among the most assimilated, that does not seem to reflect unusual nonincorporation. The most assimilated showed higher identification with the Democrats (by 12 percent), and

Table 6. Partisan Self-Categorization Among Latino Immigrants by Nonpolitical Assimilation.

	Least Assimilated	Middle Third	Most Assimilated	Most-Least % Difference
Democrat	50	61	62	12
Pure Independent[a]	9	8	7	-2
Republican	9	12	16	7
Nonidentifier[a]	32	20	14	-18
Total percent	100%	101%	99%	
Total N	254	280	313	
Total nonincorporated[a]	41	28	21	-20

Source: Authors' calculations based on McCann and Jones-Correa 2012.
Note: Leaners classified as Democrats or Republicans. Total nonincorporated is comprised of the superscripted categories (pure Independent and nonidentifier). The nonpolitical assimilation scale was divided to create as equally sized groups as possible.

here also with the Republicans (by 7 percent), than the least assimilated did.

We should also address the question of whether continuing political engagement in one's nation of origin had a zero-sum relationship with even nonpolitical assimilation activities in America. Continuing to vote in elections in the country of origin might seem to run counter to engaging in nonpolitical activities that integrate oneself into America. This was not the case, however; the two factors were not significantly correlated with one another ($r = -0.03$, ns). Immigrants' levels of political engagement with their countries of origin seem to be relatively independent of their assimilatory efforts in their new country, contrary to Samuel Huntington's (2004) concerns. Although nonpolitical assimilation and continuing political engagement are both positively associated with incorporation into the party system, not all Latino immigrants are engaging in both sets of behaviors simultaneously.

We next tested the robustness of our findings thus far by using these predictors in regressions alongside theoretically and statistically related controls. Not surprisingly, both continuing engagement and nonpolitical assimilation among Latino immigrants were associated with demographic factors that are also usually correlated with acculturation. It was therefore important to show that any effects of these two primary predictors were not due to their serving as proxies for more relevant demographic factors. For example, both more youthful immigration and longer tenure in the United States might influence continuing engagement and assimilative behaviors by themselves, without the more specific content of those latter variables. Indeed, those older at arrival showed somewhat more continuing political engagement in their nation of origin ($r = 0.18$, $p < 0.01$), presumably having had more opportunities for pre-immigration socialization and experience in politics in the home country. More years in the United States since immigration was more strongly associated with nonpolitical assimilation ($r = 0.45$, $p < 0.01$), given more time to acculturate into their new society (the correlations of age of arrival with assimilation and of years in the United States with engagement were not significant).

Using a series of regressions, then, we tested whether the associations of engagement and assimilation with Latinos' partisanship held up with the inclusion of controls on age of arrival, years in the United States, gender, and education. Our first outcome measure was incorporation into the party system (nonidentifiers and pure Independents = 0, leaning Independents and partisans = 1). Table 7 presents two binary logistic regression models using continuing political engagement and nonpolitical assimilation as primary predictors. Model 1 shows that when entered simultane-

Table 7. Binary Logistic Regression: Partisan Identification Among Latino Immigrants

	Model 1			Model 2		
	B	SE		B	SE	
Constant	−0.08	0.22	Constant	−0.68	0.42	
Continued engagement	1.27**	0.35	Continued engagement	1.04**	0.37	
Assimilation	1.43**	0.36	Assimilation	0.88*	0.43	
			Age of arrival	0.02†	0.01	
			Years in United States	0.02*	0.01	
			Gender	−0.38*	0.18	
			Education	−0.68	0.42	

Source: Authors' calculations based on McCann and Jones-Correa 2012.
Note: 0 = nonidentifier or pure Independent, 1 = any other identification. All coefficients are unstandardized.
Two-tailed: †$p < .10$; *$p < .05$; **$p < .01$

Table 8. Linear Regression: Strength of Party Identification Among Latino Immigrants

	Model 1			Model 2		
	B	SE		B	SE	
Constant	2.50**	0.11	Constant	2.09**	0.19	
Continued engagement	0.43**	0.16	Continued engagement	0.41*	0.17	
Assimilation	0.57**	0.17	Assimilation	0.41*	0.17	
			Age of arrival	0.01**	0.00	
			Years in United States	0.01**	0.00	
			Gender	0.02	0.08	
			Education	−0.01	0.02	

Source: Authors' calculations based on McCann and Jones-Correa 2012.
Note: 1 = pure Independent, 2 = lean D/R, 3 = not very strong D/R, 4 = strong D/R. All coefficients are unstandardized.
Two-tailed significance, †$p < .10$; *$p < .05$; **$p < .01$

ously, both predictors were still positively and significantly associated with being an identifier. Model 2 shows that these effects persisted with controls, although those longer in the United States were more likely to be incorporated above and beyond the effects of engagement and assimilation. Men were also more likely to be identifiers than were women, consistent with the usual findings about political involvement.

Our second outcome variable was strength of party identification (pure Independents = 1, leaning Independents = 2, not very strong partisans = 3, and strong partisans = 4; nonidentifiers excluded). Table 8 presents two models with the same sets of predictors as in table 7, but using linear regression given a continuous outcome variable. Again, both continuing engagement and assimilation were significantly associated with stronger partisanship among Latino immigrants, even with controls. Here, being older at arrival and having spent more years in the United States were also both related to stronger partisanship above and beyond the effects of engagement and assimilation.

Table 9. Crystallization of Partisan Preferences Among Latino Immigrants by Partisan Self-Categorization

	Democrat	Republican	Nonincorporated	Full Sample
Stability				
Candidate Pre * Candidate Post	0.53**	0.87**	0.65**	0.69**
Party Pre * Party Post	0.42**	0.65**	0.33'	0.61**
Consistency				
Candidate Pre * President Preference	0.44**	0.81**	0.56**	0.68**
Party Pre * President Preference	0.31**	0.65**	0.21'	0.56**
Power				
Republican Party Pre * Romney Pre	0.70**	0.71**	0.55**	0.70**
Democratic Party Pre * Obama Pre	0.60**	0.65**	0.39**	0.61**
Sample range	169–466	21–98	36–163	136–725
Overall crystallization means	0.51	0.74	0.46	0.64

Source: Authors' calculations based on McCann and Jones-Correa 2012.
Note: Leaners classified as Democrats or Republicans. Nonincorporated classified as pure Independents and nonidentifiers.
Two-tailed significance, '$p < .10$; *$p < .05$; **$p < .01$

Strongly Crystallized Partisan Preferences

Our analyses thus far have shown that high levels of nonincorporation previously thought to characterize Latinos as a whole are primarily limited to those who are noncitizens, economically and educationally disadvantaged, low in political engagement with their country of origin, and in the early stages of acculturation. Our final set of analyses expands on the notion that nonincorporated Latino immigrants may simply be in the early stages of partisan incorporation. If so, we might find evidence of partisan preferences even among Latinos who do not yet categorize themselves as being within the party system.

To do this, we changed the criterion for partisan incorporation from self-categorization on the traditional measure of party identification, an explicit attitude, to the crystallization of latent partisan preferences, presumably implicit attitudes. Here we depart from the traditional model of partisanship. That would suggest that Latinos' self-categorization as nonidentifiers or pure Independents reflects a lack of interest in the parties or active rejection of them. They therefore would also be unlikely to possess crystallized partisan preferences, in the form of stable and coherent latent associations between relevant partisan preferences. If, however, a dual-process model of party identification is a good fit, we might see crystallized partisan preferences, reflected in systematic and consistent latent preferences, even among those who seem not to be incorporated into the party system by the standard of self-categorization.

Table 9 shows the strength of these latent preferences within each class of self-categorizers among Latino immigrants in the LINES. Because of small samples, here we combine the two nonpartisan groups, pure Independents and nonidentifiers. Very high and almost uniformly statistically significant correlations emerge even among the nonincorporated on all three types of crystallization. For example, the stability of differential candidate thermometer ratings from pre- to postelection was $r = 0.65$ among the nonincorporated and the correlation between preelection thermometer ratings of the Democratic Party and of Obama was $r = 0.33$. Overall, the mean (r to z transformed) crystallization coefficient of the nonincorporated ($r = 0.46$) was quite substantial by the standards Converse originally set for

Table 10. Crystallization of Partisan Preferences Among Latino Citizens by Partisan Self-Categorization

	Democrat	Republican	Nonincorporated	Full Sample
Stability				
Candidate Pre * Candidate Post	0.60**	0.87**	0.72**	0.79**
Party Pre * Party Post	0.43**	0.57**	0.56**	0.67**
Consistency				
Candidate Pre * President Preference	0.57**	0.80**	0.74**	0.81**
Party Pre * President Preference	0.32**	0.47**	0.29'	0.63**
Power				
Republican Party Pre * Romney Pre	0.64**	0.63**	0.55**	0.69**
Democratic Party Pre * Obama Pre	0.46**	0.61**	0.56**	0.65**
Sample range	230–298	61–73	44–87	338–459
Overall crystallization means	0.51	0.69	0.59	0.71

Source: Authors' calculations based on ANES 2012 (FTF only).
Note: Leaners classified as Democrats or Republicans. Nonincorporated classified as pure Independents and nonidentifiers.
Two-tailed significance, '$p < .10$; *$p < .05$; **$p < 0.01$

crystallized belief systems (1964; also see Converse and Markus 1979; Kinder 2006). This was true whether looking at mean crystallization coefficients for pure Independents ($r = 0.36$) and nonidentifiers ($r = 0.48$) individually or combined. On average, they were almost as great as the average crystallization of Democrats ($r = 0.51$), though lower than that of the few Republicans ($r = 0.74$). All coefficients were significant except one that was only marginally significant.

We turned to the ANES sample to replicate these results. As shown in table 10, the average crystallization of the overall sample of Latino citizens was even higher ($r = 0.71$) than it had been in the LINES sample of immigrants ($r = 0.64$; see table 9). Looking again at the nonincorporated, the mean level of crystallization ($r = 0.59$) was roughly comparable to that of either Democrats ($r = 0.51$) or Republicans ($r = 0.69$). Again, this was true for the nonincorporated in the aggregate, or for pure Independents ($r = 0.55$) or nonidentifiers ($r = 0.59$) separately. This reinforces the finding that genuine partisan preferences can be observed even among Latinos who would normally be treated as standing outside the party system, once we turn our attention from explicit self-categorizations to latent preferences.

Finally, we returned to our previous analyses of the effects of Latinos' immigration status on partisan incorporation, this time using the criterion of crystallization rather than explicit self-categorization. As we saw earlier in table 2, a lack of partisan incorporation appeared to be limited primarily to noncitizen immigrants; partisan identification was relatively high among both naturalized and U.S.-born citizens. Our argument is that latent preferences are acquired earlier than are self-conscious partisan self-categorizations. That would lead us to expect that even non-naturalized immigrants would show strong and statistically significant levels of political crystallization, though lower than their naturalized counterparts.

Indeed, table 11 shows strong latent partisan preferences, even among the non-naturalized Latino immigrants in the LINES survey. For the non-naturalized, coefficients were consistently significant, and high in absolute terms, across all three types of crystallization, ranging from $r = 0.36$ to $r = 0.60$, and averaging $r = 0.52$. To be sure, naturalized immigrants showed higher levels of crystallization than did the non-naturalized, ranging from $r = 0.68$ to $r = 0.79$, and averaging $r = 0.74$, and the difference was significant in all but one case. However, in the ANES, naturalized immigrants' partisanship was just as crystallized as that of U.S.-born Latinos, averaging $r = 0.69$ and 0.73, respectively. All but one of the differences between the naturalized and U.S. born for the six indicators of crystallization were trivial in size. This mirrors the conclusion that high levels of partisan nonincorporation among Latinos are characteristic neither of naturalized citizens nor the U.S. born. Only the noncitizen first-generation immigrants show somewhat weaker latent partisan preferences. But even among these noncitizens, statistically significant levels of crystallization were pervasive.

Looking across tables 9, 10, and 11, across all groups, crystallization coefficients are generally higher for candidate-related correlations than those focused on parties. This implies that incorporation into the party system may go through presidential candidates first, later generalizing to the parties. Noncitizen Latinos quickly appreciated that Barack Obama, not Mitt Romney, was their man. Generalizing that to a preference for the Democratic over the Republican Party may take more experience.

DISCUSSION

The phenomenon we address in this paper is the question of Latino incorporation into the American party system, or lack of it. The role of Latinos in electoral politics, especially new immigrants, is a piece of the larger conversation about their integration into American society. One large question we raise is about the accuracy of the image of Latinos as a sleeping giant, making relatively slow movement through the stages of naturalization, voter registration, and voting turnout, and so not as incorporated into the American party system as other ethnic groups. A second large question concerns the explanations for such a putative lack of incorporation into the party system. The traditional story about immigrants to America is one of straight-line assimilation (Gordon 1964). That takes time, however. The development of a partisan attachment within immigrant families, as with some other political predispositions, may be more likely to occur across generations than within them (Citrin and Sears 2014). A contrasting interpretation of Latinos' supposedly slow partisan incorporation is that they are maintaining their subjective distance from the political parties. They are said to be reluctant to identify with either party or even to self-categorize as an Independent, viewing the party system with some suspicion, perhaps viewing both parties and their candidates as seeming not to have Latinos' interests at heart (Hajnal and Lee 2011).

We first reappraise the extent to which Latinos truly are less incorporated into the party system than are other ethnic groups. We find little evidence that Latinos in general are, in fact, opting out of the American party system at unusually high levels. We use data collected in 2012, which is more recent than published so far, based on interviews with a sample of Latino immigrants as well as with the most comparable subsample of U.S. citizens in the standard ANES. Following Hajnal and Lee (2011), we initially defined nonpartisanship in terms of either nonidentification (failing to self-categorize as a Democrat, Republican, or Independent) or self-categorization as Independent. The proportion of Latinos so defined as nonpartisans fell well below the estimate derived earlier by Hajnal and Lee (2011) from the 2006 Latino National Survey. And Latinos did not especially stand out as failing to incorporate into the party system by this definition, actually falling short of the nonpartisan proportion of whites in the ANES.

However, we believe that definition of nonpartisanship is far too inclusive. The great majority of Latinos who self-classified as Independents leaned toward one party or the other. Considering such leaning Independents as not incorporated into the party system flies in the face of much evidence that they in fact behave much like weak partisans. Consequently, in the remainder of the paper we limit the nonincorporated classification to nonidentifiers and Independents with no partisan leaning. By that standard, only non-naturalized Latino immigrants showed unusually high levels of nonpartisanship (36 percent). The more numerous

Table 11. Crystallization of Partisanship by Immigration Status

	LINES 2012		ANES 2012			LINES	ANES
	Non-naturalized	Naturalized	Naturalized	U.S.-Born		Naturalized–Non-naturalized Difference	U.S.-Born–Naturalized Difference
Stability							
Candidate Pre * Candidate Post	0.56**	0.75**	0.72**	0.82**		0.19**	0.10*
Party Pre * Party Post	0.52**	0.68**	0.69**	0.67**		0.14†	-0.02
Consistency							
Candidate Pre * President Preference	0.52**	0.78**	0.78**	0.82**		0.26**	0.04
Party Pre * President Preference	0.36**	0.70**	0.64**	0.63**		0.34**	-0.01
Power							
Republican Party Pre * Romney Pre	0.53**	0.70**	0.65**	0.70**		0.17**	0.05
Democratic Party Pre * Obama Pre	0.60**	0.79**	0.65**	0.65**		0.19**	0.00
Sample range	120–429	106–312	86–120	252–339			
Overall crystallization means	0.52	0.74	0.69	0.73			

Source: Authors' calculations based on ANES 2012 (FTF only), McCann and Jones-Correa 2012.
Two-tailed significance, †$p < .10$; *$p < .05$; **$p < .01$

Latinos who were citizens, either naturalized or U.S.-born, yielded far lower levels of nonpartisanship (averaging around 21 percent), and were quite similar to whites (18 percent).

Any greater level of nonpartisanship among Latinos than whites seems to be due to the many Latinos who are recent immigrants, then. Beyond that, even those of generally low levels of income and education were about as incorporated as comparable whites. Nonpartisanship was virtually identical for Latinos and whites at similarly low levels of education and income. In short, Latinos do not show unusually high levels of nonpartisanship except among non-naturalized immigrants, whose lives present obvious obstacles to an active partisan identity (such as lack of citizenship and no opportunity to vote, and only limited access to high-wage jobs and education). In contrast, Latino citizens show high levels of partisan self-categorization, overwhelmingly as Democrats.

Our second major finding is that, surprisingly perhaps, immigrants who maintained a continuing engagement in the politics of their country of origin also showed the greatest incorporation into the American party system. Presumably this is due to socialized political identities, political interests, and general political proclivities. This finding is contrary to Huntington's (2004) expectation that many Mexican Americans will remain politically committed to Mexican society and resist integration into American society. Similarly, the findings of Waldinger and Duquette-Rury in this issue underscore the non-zero-sum nature of political investment in Latino immigrants' countries of origin and in the United States.

Our third major finding is that political incorporation accompanies other, nonpolitical forms of assimilation. Immigrants who watch more English-language television and intend to stay in America show higher levels of partisan identification than those who are less assimilated in those terms. Continuing engagement and assimilation also predicted partisan self-categorization and strength of partisanship over and above relevant controls. This too implies that Latino immigrants are joining, rather than avoiding, the party system. Information uncertainty and reservations about the Democratic Party may play a role in Latinos' political thinking, but Latinos are more engaged than sometimes characterized. The reliability coefficients for both the continuing engagement and nonpolitical assimilation scales were lower than often seen in studies of public opinion, perhaps adding credibility to the effects we nevertheless found to be significant.

Our fourth major finding goes beyond earlier studies of incorporation into the party system, all of which have used the criterion of self-categorization on the traditional Michigan party identification measure. Contemporary social psychology has suggested that latent affective preferences may often be more extensive than revealed by conscious and explicit choices. Accordingly, we tested for the crystallization of underlying partisan preferences, operationalized in terms of their stability, consistency, and power. The examination of political crystallization allowed us to look inside the minds of Latino immigrants.

We find pervasive and clear partisan preferences, even among those classified as outside the party system in terms of their conscious self-categorization. Not surprisingly, partisan identifiers showed robust levels of crystallization. But even the nonidentifiers and pure Independents, who had not explicitly categorized themselves into a partisan identity, had quite stable and consistent latent partisan preferences. Relatively lower levels of crystallization of latent preferences only seemed to emerge among non-naturalized immigrants, again highlighting this group as the one subset of the Latino population showing an appreciable lack of incorporation into the American party system. However, even they showed highly significant absolute levels of crystallization. This implies that even the least incorporated group of Latinos holds clear partisan preferences. Even if they cannot vote, noncitizens know which side they favor.

Our indicators of crystallization consisted of associations between partisan attitudes. Those attitude objects are quite similar, of course. However, as Converse (1964) showed originally, and as many others have shown since, public opinion frequently shows only modest levels of constraint. To repeatedly get correlations over $r = 0.50$ between even identical attitudes measured several weeks apart is impressive, especially in a sample of immigrants with a median educational level below high school graduate, many not fluent in English. The same is true for consistency between affects toward the parties and toward their presidential candidates. Such persistently high correlations would be unlikely unless the respondents had quite consistent partisan preferences. Later research will be required to test how far the crystallization of these latent partisan preferences reaches into the more complex territory of issues and ideologies that do not share the same manifest partisan symbolism as the most vividly partisan attitude objects used here.

This research should help inform our knowledge about the political incorporation of immigrant groups more generally. Latinos are showing patterns of incorporation more in line with the history of the European immigrants of a century ago, who also took several decades to integrate into the party system (see, for example, Andersen 1979; DeSipio 2001; Erie 1988; Sterne 2001). In the contemporary era, given the absence of well-oiled party machines making clear and consistent overtures to incoming immigrants, the idea that Latinos have been hesitant to join the party system makes a great deal of sense. It is probable that a lack of clear political information, scant ideological appeals from both parties, and an ambiguous role in the narrative of American racial tensions have all contributed to making some Latinos ambivalent about or avoidant of the party system. However, we show that many Latinos are forging psychologically robust connections with the party system even in the face of such obstacles. One potential facilitator of such connections is that Spanish-language media may help politicize Latino immigrants (see Garcia-Rios and Barreto, this issue). The active efforts of the Spanish-language news media to increase political awareness and engagement in the Latino immigrant community were largely nonpartisan in 2012. However this exposure to the American political system required Latino immigrants to contend with the party system and may have helped generate the underlying partisan preferences we find here.

Overall, however, the idea that Latino immigrants will gradually join the party system, following a path shaped by a combination of exogenous and endogenous forces, is one that aligns with the socialization approach put forth in *The American Voter* (Campbell et al. 1960). That Lewis-Beck and Stegmaier (this issue) find more converging evidence for the applicability of this classic text to the LINES dataset further bolsters our confidence in the idea that rather than being politically detached outliers, Latino immigrants are merely in the early stages of familiar paths to partisanship.

On the ground, the message is simple: most Latino immigrants quickly develop latent partisan preferences, and when they do they overwhelmingly prefer the Democratic Party. That partisanship increases with naturalization, engagement, and assimilation. We would then expect the continued steady incorporation of Latinos into the party system, specifically into the Democratic Party, as increasing proportions are either U.S. born or become naturalized. This mirrors the findings of Huddy, Mason, and Horwitz in this issue that growing partisanship among Latino immigrants is likely to favor Democrats quite heavily. In addition, the positive association of Democratic preferences with both ethnic group identification and awareness of discrimination may reflect processes that work independently and simultaneously with those we have identified. The associations between partisan incorporation and nonpolitical assimilation may seem to run against the grain of these other effects. However, our findings, and the work of bicultural identity researchers (Benet-Martínez and Haritatos 2005), suggest that Latino immigrants are able to acculturate in America without sacrificing awareness of and investment in their unique ethnic identity.

Increasing Latino incorporation into the party system still further will require overcoming the principal barrier we find to it, lack of naturalization. Furthermore, lack of citizenship is also related to other obstacles we identified, including access to education and income. Thus facilitating naturalization would probably have the largest effects on bringing more into the party system. So, surprisingly enough, would facilitating continued engagement in the politics of countries of origin (such as through enhanced access to international media) as well as facilitating nonpolitical assimilation (such as increased opportunities to learn English and access English-language media).

These strategies would appear to be primarily advantageous to the Democratic Party. Given current restraints on immigration, the Latino electorate in America is poised to become dominated by the heavily Democratic naturalized first-generation and second-generation Latinos we observed in our analyses. Obviously this is not true for all. Some, especially older Cuban Americans, prefer Republicans, but those are in the minority. Future research could usefully examine heterogeneity within the Latino population. Where immigrants come from and where they settle in America is known to influence their partisanship through differences in cultural attitudes toward assimilation and receptivity of the local community. In addition, although examined only briefly here, future research could also usefully examine second- and third-generation Latinos, for whom factors like continuing political engagement may be less relevant, and whose assimilation efforts may plateau early in life.

Our findings indicate that Latino immigrants are considerably more subjectively involved in the party system than sometimes characterized. The partisan nonidentification previously thought to characterize the Latino population as a whole seems to occur primarily under a confluence of several specific obstacles: lack of citizenship, little education and low income, weak continuing political engagement in immigrants' nations of origin, and lower nonpolitical assimilation into the United States. Even among those without citizenship, we found evidence of significant crystallization and the positive effects of both continuing political engagement and assimilation on partisanship. When those obstacles are overcome, a relatively smooth pattern of political incorporation seems to occur among Latino immigrants, with evidence of this process detectable even among non-naturalized immigrants. Instead of avoiding the party system, Latinos clearly seem to be steadily joining it as many leave the moment of immigration further and further behind.

REFERENCES

Alba, Richard, and Victor Nee. 2003. *Remaking the American Mainstream: Assimilation and Contemporary Immigration*. Cambridge, Mass.: Harvard University Press.

Alvarez, R. Michael, and Lisa García Bedolla. 2003. "The Foundations of Latino Voter Partisanship: Evidence from the 2000 Election." *Journal of Politics* 65(1): 31–49.

American National Election Studies (ANES). 2012. The ANES 2012 Time Series Study dataset. Ann Arbor: University of Michigan; Palo Alto: Stanford University. Accessed February 26, 2016. http://www.electionstudies.org/.

Andersen, Kristi. 1979. *The Creation of a Democratic Majority, 1928–1936*. Chicago: University of Chicago Press.

Banaji, Mahzarin R., and Anthony G. Greenwald. 2013. *Blindspot: Hidden Biases of Good People*. New York: Delacorte Press.

Benet-Martínez, Veronica, and Jana Haritatos. 2005. "Bicultural Identity Integration (BII): Components and Psychosocial Antecedents." *Journal of Personality* 73(4): 1015–50.

Bonilla-Silva, Eduardo. 2006. *Racism Without Racists: Color-Blind Racism and the Persistence of Racial Inequality in the United States*. Lanham, Md.: Rowman & Littlefield.

Bowler, Shaun, Stephen P. Nicholson, and Gary M. Segura. 2006. "Earthquakes and Aftershocks: Race, Direct Democracy, and Partisan Change." *American Journal of Political Science* 50(1): 146–59.

Cain, Bruce E., D. Roderick Kiewiet, and Carole J. Uhlaner. 1991. "The Acquisition of Partisanship by Latinos and Asian Americans." *American Journal of Political Science* 35(2): 390–422.

Campbell, Angus, Philip E. Converse, Warren E. Miller, and Donald E. Stokes. 1960. *The American Voter*. New York: John Wiley & Sons.

Carmines, Edward G., and James A. Stimson. 1989. *Issue Evolution: Race and the Transformation of American Politics*. Princeton, N.J.: Princeton University Press.

Citrin, Jack, and David O. Sears. 2014. *American Identity and the Politics of Multiculturalism*. Cambridge: Cambridge University Press.

Converse, Philip E. 1964. "The Nature of Belief Systems in Mass Publics." In *Ideology and Its Discontents*, edited by David E. Apter. New York: Free Press.

Converse, Philip E., and Gregory B. Markus. 1979. "Plus ca change...: The New CPS Election Study Panel." *American Political Science Review* 73(1): 32–49.

DeSipio, Louis. 1996. "Making Citizens or Good Citizens? Naturalization as a Predictor of Organizational and Electoral Behavior Among Latino Immigrants." *Hispanic Journal of Behavioral Sciences* 18(2): 194–213.

———. 2001. "Building America, One Person at a Time: Naturalization and Political Behavior of the Naturalized in Contemporary American Politics." In *E Pluribus Unum? Contemporary and Historical Perspectives on Immigrant Political Incorporation*, edited by Gary Gerstle and John Mollenkopf. New York: Russell Sage Foundation.

Downs, Anthony. 1957. *An Economic Theory of Democracy*. New York: Harper Collins.

Erie, Steven P. 1988. *Rainbow's End: Irish-Americans and the Dilemmas of Urban Machine Politics, 1840–1985*. Berkeley: University of California Press.

Fiorina, Morris P. 1981. *Retrospective Voting in American National Elections*. New Haven, Conn.: Yale University Press.

Gordon, Milton Myron. 1964. *Assimilation in American Life: The Role of Race, Religion, and National Origins*. New York: Oxford University Press.

Green, Donald P., Bradley Palmquist, and Eric Schickler. 2002. *Partisan Hearts and Minds: Political Parties and the Social Identities of Voters*. New Haven, Conn.: Yale University Press.

Hajnal, Zoltan L., and Taeku Lee. 2011. *Why Americans Don't Join the Party: Race, Immigration, and the Failure (of Political Parties) to Engage the Electorate*. Princeton, N.J.: Princeton University Press.

Huntington, Samuel P. 2004. *Who Are We?: The Challenges to America's National Identity*. New York: Simon and Schuster.

Iceland, John, and Melissa Scopilliti. 2008. "Immigrant Residential Segregation in US Metropolitan Areas, 1990–2000." *Demography* 45(1): 79–94.

Kahneman, Daniel. 2003. "A Perspective on Judgment and Choice: Mapping Bounded Rationality." *American Psychologist* 58(9): 697–720.

Keith, Bruce E., David B. Magleby, Candice J. Nelson, Elizabeth Orr, Mark C. Westlye, and Raymond E. Wolfinger. 1992. *The Myth of the Independent Voter*. Berkeley: University of California Press.

Key, V.O., Jr. 1966. *The Responsible Electorate: Rationality in Presidential Voting*. New York: Vintage.

Kinder, Donald R. 2006. "Belief Systems Today." *Critical Review* 18(1–3): 197–216.

Krogstad, Jens Manuel, and Mark Hugo Lopez. 2014. "Hispanic Nativity Shift: U.S. Births Drive Population Growth as Immigration Stalls." Washington, D.C.: Pew Research Center's Hispanic Trends Project.

Latino Decisions. 2012. "Obama Wins 75% of Latino Vote." *Latino Decisions*, November 7, 2012. Accessed January 31, 2016. http://www.latinodecisions.com/blog/2012/11/07/obama-wins-75-of-latino-vote-marks-historic-latino-influence-in-presidential-election/.

Lewis-Beck, Michael S., William G. Jacoby, Helmut Norpoth, and Herbert E. Weisberg. 2008. *The American Voter Revisited*. Ann Arbor: University of Michigan Press.

Lodge, Milton, and Charles S. Taber. 2014. *The Rationalizing Voter*. New York: Cambridge University Press.

Masuoka, Natalie, and Jane Junn. 2013. *The Politics of Belonging: Race, Public Opinion, and Immigration*. Chicago: University of Chicago Press.

McCann, James A., and Michael Jones-Correa. 2012. *Latino Immigrant National Election Study, 2012*. New York: Russell Sage Foundation, Carnegie Corporation of New York, Purdue University, and Cornell University.

Osborne, Danny, David O. Sears, and Nicholas A. Valentino. 2011. "The End of the Solidly Democratic South: The Impressionable-Years Hypothesis." *Political Psychology* 32(1): 81–108.

Pew Research Center. 2012. "Latino Voters in the 2012 Election." November 7, 2012. Washington, D.C.: Pew Research Center's Hispanic Trends Project. Accessed February 29, 2016. http://www.pewhispanic.org/files/2012/11/2012_Latino_vote_exit_poll_analysis_final_11-09.pdf.

Preston, Julia. 2008. "In Big Shift, Latino Vote Was Heavily for Obama." *New York Times*, November 6, 2008, p. 7.

Ramakrishnan, S. Karthick. 2005. *Democracy in Immigrant America: Changing Demographics and Political Participation*. Stanford, Calif.: Stanford University Press.

Sears, David O., and Christia Brown. 2013. "Childhood and Adult Political Development." In *The Oxford Handbook of Political Psychology*, edited by Leonie Huddy, David O. Sears, and Jack S. Levy. New York: Oxford University Press.

Sears, David O., Hillary Haley, and P. J. Henry. 2008. "Cultural Diversity and Sociopolitical Attitudes at College Entry." In Jim Sidanius, Shana Levin, Colette Van Laar, and David O. Sears, *The Diversity Challenge: Social Identity and Intergroup Relations on the College Campus*. New York: Russell Sage Foundation.

Sears, David O., and Nicholas A. Valentino. 1997. "Politics Matters: Political Events as Catalysts for Preadult Socialization." *American Political Science Review* 91(1): 45-65.

Serrano, Alfonso. 2014. "Obama faces immigration protests in 40 U.S. cities." *Al Jazeera America*, April 4, 2014. Accessed January 31, 2016. http://america.aljazeera.com/articles/2014/4/4/immigration-advocatespressureobamaondeportations.html.

Sidanius, James, and Felicia Pratto. 1999. *Social Dominance: An Intergroup Theory of Social Hierarchy and Oppression*. New York: Cambridge University Press.

Smith, Rogers M. 1997. *Civic Ideals: Conflicting Visions of Citizenship in US History*. New Haven, Conn.: Yale University Press.

———. 2011. "Living in a Promiseland: Mexican Immigrants and American Obligations." *Perspectives on Politics*: 9(3): 545-57.

Sterne, Evelyn Savidge. 2001. "Beyond the Boss: Immigration and American Political Culture from 1880 to 1940." In *E Pluribus Unum? Contemporary and Historical Perspectives on Immigrant Political Incorporation*, edited by Gary Gerstle and John Mollenkopf. New York: Russell Sage Foundation.

Uhlaner, Carole J., and F. Chris Garcia. 2005. "Learning Which Party Fits: Experience, Ethnic Identity, and the Demographic Foundations of Latino Party Identification." In *Diversity in Democracy: Minority Representation in the United States*, edited by Gary M. Segura and Shaun Bowler. Charlottesville: University of Virginia Press.

Wong, Janelle, S. 2000. "The Effects of Age and Political Exposure on the Development of Party Identification Among Asian American and Latino Immigrants in the United States." *Political Behavior* 22(4): 341-71.

———. 2006. *Democracy's Promise: Immigrants and American Civic Institutions*. Ann Arbor: University of Michigan Press.

Wong, Janelle, S. Karthick Ramakrishnan, Taeku Lee, and Jane Junn. 2011. *Asian American Political Participation: Emerging Constituents and Their Political Identities*. New York: Russell Sage Foundation.

Political Identity Convergence: On Being Latino, Becoming a Democrat, and Getting Active

LEONIE HUDDY, LILLIANA MASON, AND S. NECHAMA HORWITZ

The majority of Latinos in the United States identify with the Democratic Party, a tendency with broad political implications as Latinos become an increasingly large segment of the population. Little research, however, has delved into the origins of this preference. In this research, we contrast two explanations for Latinos' Democratic proclivities: an instrumental explanation grounded in ideological policy preferences and an expressive identity account based on the defense of Latino identity and status. In analysis of data from two large national datasets, the 2012 Latino Immigrant National Election Study and American National Election Study focused on Latino immigrants and citizens respectively, we find strong support for the expressive identity explanation. Hispanic and partisan identities have converged among Latinos in the United States to create a large number of Latino Democrats regardless of citizenship status. Those who identify strongly as Latinos and see pervasive discrimination against Latinos are the strongest Democrats, a process that further intensified over the course of the 2012 election. A strong partisan preference increased political campaign activity, though this activity level was modest overall. Relatively few Latinos had worked on a campaign or given money to a candidate; somewhat larger numbers had tried to convince others about a candidate or worn a button or displayed a sticker. Finally, some support was evident for an instrumental account. Latino support for government-provided health insurance in 2012 consistently increased support for the Democratic Party.

Keywords: Latino identity, partisanship, political participation, social identity

Latinos are a growing segment of the U.S. electorate, and their political proclivities matter. The 2012 presidential election underscored Latinos' increasing political clout, an election year in which they were part of a nontraditional coalition of young people, women, Asians, and blacks that provided a decisive victory to Democrat Barack Obama over his Republican opponent Mitt Romney. The election outcome, coupled with the likely growth of the Latino voter population from 11 percent of the eligible electorate in 2012 to 16 percent in 2030, sparked considerable debate on the future of party politics in the United States (Taylor et al. 2012). Latinos have historically identified with the Democratic Party, roughly 57 percent over the

Leonie Huddy is professor of political science at Stony Brook University. **Lilliana Mason** is assistant professor of government and politics at the University of Maryland, College Park. **S. Nechama Horwitz** is a doctoral student in political science at Stony Brook University.

We extend our thanks to Jay McCann, Michael Correa-Jones, David Sears, and members of the RSF LINES working group for helpful comments on an earlier version of this project. Direct correspondence to: Leonie Huddy at leonie.huddy@sunysb.edu, Department of Political Science, Stony Brook University, Stony Brook, NY 11794; Lilliana Mason at lmason@umd.edu, 3140 Tydings Hall, University of Maryland, College Park, MD 20742; and S. Nechama Horwitz at snhorwitz@gmail.com, Department of Political Science, Stony Brook University, Social and Behavioral Sciences Building, 7th Floor, Stony Brook, NY 11794.

Figure 1. Latino Party Identification over Time

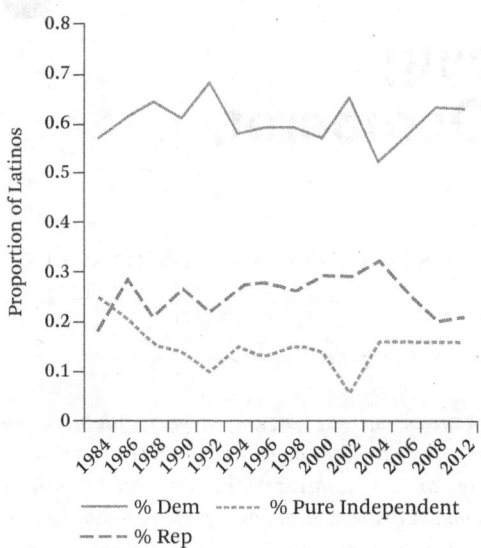

Source: Authors' compilation based on ANES 2008, 2012.
Note: Partisans include Independent leaners. In 1996 and 2002, percentages should be interpreted with extreme caution, as the sample size is thirty-two and seventeen, respectively. In all other years, sample size ranges from sixty-nine (1992) to 140 (1990), with Latino oversamples increasing sample sizes in 2008 (470) and 2012 (1005).

last fifteen years, more than double the number who identify as Republicans (25 percent in the 2000 Latino Voter Study conducted by Knight-Ridder, see Alvarez and García Bedolla 2003). Shaun Bowler and Gary Segura (2011) note that although Latino support for Democrats has fluctuated to some extent over time it remains generally stable. Strong Democratic identification also translates into support for Democratic candidates, some 71 percent of Latinos voting for Obama in 2012 and 67 percent in 2008, according to network exit polls (*New York Times* 2012, 2008).

Evidence of Latinos' general Democratic proclivities is pervasive. Figure 1 demonstrates that in every year since 1984, Latinos have been far more likely to identify with the Democratic than the Republican Party. Far less research has been conducted, however, on why Latinos are more likely to be Democrats than Republicans. Country of origin and past political history each play a role. Data collected over the past fifteen years—the 1989–1990 Latino National Political Survey (LNPS) and the 2000 Latino Voter Survey (LVS)—indicate that roughly 67 percent of Mexicans and between 64 and 69 percent of Puerto Ricans are Democrats, and that between 66 and 69 percent of Cubans are Republican (Alvarez and García Bedolla 2003; Uhlaner and Garcia 1998). Some evidence indicates that more recent Cuban migrants are less Republican than those who came to the United States in the immediate aftermath of the Cuban revolution in 1959 (Garcia 2011). Overall, country of origin influences Latino partisanship. Nonetheless, attributing trends in partisanship to country of origin is a static way to understand current and future trends in Latino political proclivities. We look to factors inherent within contemporary American politics as an alternative and more dynamic account of Latino partisan preferences.

Instrumental Partisanship

Political party policy stances and political ideology are an ongoing and dynamic aspect of American political life. From an instrumental perspective, partisanship is a running tally of party performance, ideological beliefs, and proximity to the party in terms of preferred policies (Fiorina 1981; Franklin and Jackson 1983). Michael Alvarez and Lisa García Bedolla (2003) view Latino partisanship as instrumental in an account that also explains why partisanship differs among Latinos of different national backgrounds. From this perspective, partisanship rests on a preference for a political party's policy stances on social or economic issues. Alvarez and García Bedolla demonstrate, with data from the 2000 LVS, that issues and ideology provide a strong foundation for partisanship among Latinos. Holding a liberal stance on a mix of issues such as abortion, affirmative action, school vouchers, health care, gun control, and tax cuts distinguishes Democrats from Independents and Republicans. Carole Uhlaner and Chris Garcia (1998) argue along similar lines that Cubans who left Cuba after the Mariel boatlift incident (during a period of Cuban economic downturn) are more likely to ground partisanship in economic considerations.

Interestingly, immigration attitudes do not

explain Latino partisan preferences in Alvarez and García Bedolla's (2003) data. This is at odds with numerous suggestions that Latinos' position on immigration explains their support for Democratic candidates (Garcia 2011). For example, Shaun Bowler, Stephen Nicholson, and Gary Segura (2006) argue that anti-Latino and anti-immigrant propositions sponsored by the Californian Republican Party in the 1990s reversed Latino flight from the state Democratic Party. Sophia Wallace (2012) also argues that immigration reforms feature heavily in Latino support for Obama despite some disappointment in his immigration policy. From Wallace's perspective, Latino support for Obama arises because his administration has taken small measures designed to improve the daily life of Latino immigrants.

From an instrumental perspective, then, Latinos' preference for the Democratic Party stems from their generally liberal position on a range of social and economic issues. This support for the Democrats does not appear to be a direct defense of self-interest because less well-educated Latinos are only somewhat more likely to be Democrats than their better-educated counterparts are; no connection can be made between low income and increased Democratic identification (Alvarez and García Bedolla 2003). In other words, Latino support of liberal economic policies and expanded government welfare programs is not concentrated among those in lower-income households or those who are less well educated, suggesting that support for such policies, and the Democratic Party that promotes them, is not a matter of simple self-interest. This is a somewhat puzzling finding given that the instrumental model would predict a link between low income, support for social welfare policies, and the Democratic Party.

But another possible explanation for Latino partisanship has not been well tested as yet. We refer to this as an expressive approach in which partisanship is viewed as a social identity (Huddy, Mason, and Aaroe 2015). This account of partisanship is inherently dynamic, partisans showing increased or decreased enthusiasm for their party in direct proportion to the strength of their partisan identity and potential partisan status threats and gains. The strongest partisans respond most emotionally to partisan threats and reassurances, and therefore work hardest for the party. One way in which expressive partisan identities form is in the merger of partisan identities with broad demographic identities based on race, ethnicity, gender, and class. This can occur when one political party better represents and respects group members than another. Lilliana Mason (forthcoming) has demonstrated the merger of evangelical and Republican identities, black, secular, and Democratic identities, and the particular political potency of partisan identities formed through identity convergence.

Expressive Partisanship and Convergent Identities

Social identity theory provides a strong foundation for the study of expressive partisanship among Latinos. First, the approach can account for the conditions under which Latinos develop a cohesive political outlook, revolving around Latino or Hispanic identity. Second, it can account for the political engagement of Latino Democrats once Latino and Democratic identities merge. The general approach to the study of social identities that Henri Tajfel (1981) developed is agnostic to the nature of the group under study. From a social identity theory perspective, once group members identify as Latinos or Democrats they are motivated to protect and advance their group's status as a way to maintain their positive distinctiveness (Huddy 2001). In developing the theory, Tajfel and John Turner (1979) placed key emphasis on the need among group members "to differentiate their own groups positively from others to achieve a positive social identity" (Turner et al. 1987, 42). In that sense, Latinos who identify strongly with fellow ethnics are motivated to protect the social status of Latinos from Anglo prejudice and disrespect. Likewise, Democrats are motivated to defend their party against partisan threats and electoral loss. The more strongly individuals identify with their group, the more strongly they defend the group's status (Huddy 2013).

Political cohesion is especially likely when multiple identities, one of which contains strong political content, converge. Sonia Roccas and Marilynn Brewer (2002) develop the concept of identity complexity to capture this. They measure the extent to which different social groups were perceived to share characteristics and members, and discover that individuals who are members of highly overlapping groups (those in which members have similar characteristics or include many of the same people) are more reactive to group-based threats than members of groups that are not seen as overlapping. Thus a Latino Democrat will react more to threats against Latinos than a Latino Republican would because Latino and Democratic identities overlap. Political identities have exhibited this type of fusion in the United States in recent years as political partisans become sorted more fully along the lines of political ideology (Levendusky 2009). Mason (2015) examines this process and finds that convergent partisan and ideological identities lead to greater political activism and increased emotional reactivity to group threats. Factors such as group threat can promote identity convergence. For example, in Northern Ireland threat reduced social identity complexity, leading to increased overlap between an identity as Catholic and Irish, and Protestant and British (Schmid et al. 2008).

It is possible to follow the roots of identity convergence all the way back to seminal voting studies that introduced the idea of cross-pressured voters (Lazarsfeld, Berelson, and Gaudet 1944; Campbell et al. 1960). Early electoral studies indicated that partisans who identified with groups associated with the opposing party were less likely to vote. Seymour Lipset went so far as to call these cross-pressured voters "politically impotent," suggesting that "the more pressures brought to bear on individuals or groups which operate in opposing directions, the more likely are prospective voters to withdraw from the situation by 'losing interest' and not making a choice" (1960, 211). Further research found that these voters would be less strongly partisan (Powell 1976) and that such "cross-cutting cleavages" would mitigate social conflict (Lipset 1960; Nordlinger 1972). More recent work has begun to suggest that, in fact, cross-pressures do reduce the strength of partisan affiliation and levels of political activism (Brader, Tucker, and Therriault 2013; Mason 2015; Mutz 2002).

As Democratic and Latino identities move into alignment, Democrats are likely to become increasingly sensitive to ethnic threats, and Latinos to become increasingly sensitive to partisan threats. The more aligned the two identities, the more important it is to a group member that the in-group prevails and maintains status because declining status of one group means declining status of the other. If your party loses an election, your ethnic group loses some of its positive distinctiveness. In that case, according to Tajfel, a group member has two options: to leave the group or to work to make it better. As partisan identity grows stronger, and more identities line up behind it, leaving the party becomes less possible and action becomes necessary. As political identities come into alignment, the effects of identity on political action should thus increase.

African Americans provide a powerful example of identity convergence, involving party and race. They exhibit an impressive degree of racial identity and loyalty, are staunch Democrats, and are far more likely than whites to vote for black Democratic candidates (Reese and Brown 1995; Philpot and Walton 2007; Sigelman and Welch 1984). The electoral effect of group loyalties is most pronounced among African Americans who identify with both the Democratic Party and their racial group (Tate 1994; Dawson 1994). In exit polls conducted during the 2008 Democratic presidential primaries (pitting Barack Obama against Hillary Clinton), respondents in thirty-one states were asked whether race was the single most important factor, one of several important factors, or not important in their vote choice. This is admittedly a crude way to get at the influence of racial loyalties because not everyone is aware of or willing to admit that their vote was affected by such considerations. Nonetheless, roughly 30 percent of black men and women said that race was important to their vote, and they voted overwhelmingly for Obama. Moreover, in a 2008 Democratic primary poll conducted in Pennsylvania by *Time* magazine, blacks strongly supported Obama based on their concern about racial discrimination in

American society (Huddy and Carey 2009). The fusion between black and Democratic identity is palpable.

Political Action and the Defense of Group Status

One of the real strengths of an expressive approach to partisanship is its ability to explain the link between partisanship and political activity, and the conditions most likely to foster partisan political action (Huddy, Mason, and Aaroe 2015). Researchers have documented the past influence of partisanship on electoral engagement and voter turnout (Abramson and Aldrich 1982; Campbell et al. 1960; Rosenstone and Hansen 1993). But they have paid far less attention to the origins of partisan-driven political engagement. The link between partisanship and political engagement is critical to the study of Latino political behavior and civic incorporation. It may seem odd at a time of growing partisan incivility in the United States to promote partisanship as a path to civic engagement but that is indeed the reality (Iyengar, Sood, and Lelkes 2012). Electoral engagement increases as one becomes a more staunch partisan (Huddy, Mason, and Aaroe 2015). And, as noted, the link between identity strength and political action is even larger when several identities converge, as we believe is the case for Latino and Democratic identities. The link between partisanship and engagement is a compelling reason to examine closely the origins of Latino partisanship.

Research investigating political emotion helps shed light on why strongly convergent identities generate political action. Anger and enthusiasm are highly relevant political emotions known to increase political engagement (Groenendyk and Banks 2013; Marcus, Neuman, and Mackuen 2000; Smith, Cronin. and Kessler 2008; van Zomeren, Spears, and Leach 2008; Valentino et al. 2011). Both emotions are felt more intensely by strong group identifiers and are especially likely to arise during a political campaign. A threatened electoral loss and related loss of power and status generates the action-oriented emotion of anger, whereas reassurance of electoral success and status gains arouse the action-oriented emotion of enthusiasm. And both electoral success and threat are pervasive in competitive elections. Thus we would expect Latino Democrats with highly convergent identities to be the strongest and most politically active partisans. They will take greatest umbrage at a status threat directed at either Latinos or Democrats, and should be more politically active as a consequence. Symbolic grievances concerning perceived ethnic discrimination or other forms of potential ethnic status threat may be especially prone to identity-based intensification, in which the strongest identifiers are angrier and take the greatest offense in response to a specific campaign situation or event.

Republican politicians have pushed Latinos increasingly toward the Democratic Party in recent years. For example, over the last decade, Republicans have taken a series of actions and positions that have alienated and offended many Latinos. These moves are not so much economic as symbolic, involving anti-immigrant legislation, negative rhetoric and portrayals of Latinos, offensive political campaign ads, and an unwillingness to consider immigration reform legislation. The House passage of HR 4437, the Border Protection, Antiterrorism, and Illegal Immigration Control Act of 2005, which included harsher penalties for illegal immigrants, sparked the 2006 immigration reform protests. Most recently, Republicans have advocated repeal of President Obama's Deferred Action for Childhood Arrivals (DACA) program and voted to deport unaccompanied minors who have been arriving at the border from Central America. According to social identity theory, these are exactly the kinds of threats likely to push Latinos toward the Democratic Party or further enrage Democratic Latinos to take political action.

In this study, we examine the connections of Latino identity, partisanship, and political engagement among two groups of Latinos: citizens included in the main and oversample component of the 2012 American National Election Study (ANES) Time Series and Web component, and immigrants included in the 2012 Latino Immigrant National Election Study (LINES) survey. The inclusion of immigrants is central to this project. The majority of the Latinos in the LINES survey are not citizens, but they are politically important and vastly understudied. In one sense, we might expect noncitizen immigrants to be more likely than citizens to hold merged partisan and ethnic identities because a Latino identity provides a simple cue to the political system. All one needs to know is that Democrats are more supportive than Republicans of Latino concerns. In that sense, Latino identity is a convenient decisional heuristic. But identity politics may be equally effective among citizens who pay close attention to American politics.

HYPOTHESES

In summary, we examine several hypotheses in this research. First, we assess both the degree to which Latino-Hispanic and Democratic partisan identities have converged among American Latinos and the degree to which Democratic identity is further strengthened among Latinos who believe anti-Latino discrimination is pervasive in American society. Second, we assess the degree to which a strong Democratic identity increased political action in the 2012 presidential campaign (because it involves the convergence of an ethnic and political identity) and contrast that with the effects of a strong (nonconvergent) Republican identity, which we expect to be weaker. Third, we examine the degree to which the 2012 campaign increased the link between Latino identity, Democratic partisanship, and political engagement. The election was characterized by presidential candidate Mitt Romney's anti-immigrant rhetoric in the Republican primaries, something that could have aroused Latino anger and heightened engagement. Latinos may have also felt increased enthusiasm for Democrats after the election because their support was viewed as instrumental to Obama's victory, leading to further identity convergence.

We assume throughout that Latino identity is a social identity built on cultural, familial, and geographic factors. We test the notion that Latino identity is convergent with a Democratic identity and in that sense also has political aspects. But we see it as being grounded in a broader array of factors. In that sense, it is distinct from ideology and related stances on economic and social issues, allowing us to contrast its effects on partisanship with such instrumental political factors.

RESEARCH STUDIES

The Latino Immigrant National Election Study is based on data from a sample of adult immigrants from Spanish-speaking countries in Latin America. A sample of 855 Latinos was interviewed by telephone in the preelection survey. Interviewing began on October 4, 2012, and was completed on November 5, 2012. Of those 855 adults, 435 were reinterviewed in the postelection survey for a reinterview rate of 51 percent. An additional new sample of 451 Latino respondents was also interviewed in the postelection survey. The postelection telephone interviews occurred between November 12 and December 20, 2012. This resulted in a total of 886 Latino respondents interviewed in the postelection survey.

Respondent contact information was obtained from the marketing research firm Geoscape; both landlines and cellular numbers were randomly selected for national coverage. Sampling was not conditional on naturalization status. The overall response rate (AAPOR RR4) was 0.320. Professional bilingual interviewers conducted the surveys, most of which were conducted in Spanish. To a large extent, questions were developed to mirror questions asked in the 2012 ANES to facilitate comparison between Latino citizens and noncitizen immigrants.

All LINES data reported in this manuscript were weighted. Weights were created by raking the data to conform to marginal distributions of education, age, and gender of Latino immigrants based on data from the American Community Survey (ACS). The raking calculates weights based on an iterative proportional fitting procedure.

American National Election Studies Time Series and Panel: Latino Sample

Hispanic respondents from the ANES are drawn from both the nationally representative sample and the Hispanic oversample. Data were collected both face-to-face (FTF) and over the Internet (Web). Preelection interviews were collected beginning two months before the

2012 elections and postelection interviews until two months after the elections. Overall, 472 (141 foreign-born) Hispanic respondents were gathered through FTF methods and 533 (232 foreign-born) through the Web for a total of 1,005. Further, 438 of the FTF sample and 482 of the Web sample completed the postelection survey for respective reinterview rates of 93 percent and 90 percent and a postelection sample of 920.

Web interviews were conducted through GfK Knowledge Networks, which is based on a randomly selected sample drawn from both an address-based sampling frame and a random-digit dialing (RDD) frame of nationally representative telephone numbers. FTF sampling was conducted by Abt SRBI under the oversight of ANES. The forty-eight states were first stratified and then random residential addresses were selected based on information contained in the Delivery Sequence File maintained by the U.S. Postal Service. The Hispanic oversample was collected from tracts in which 20 percent of the population was Hispanic. The overall response rate for the FTF sampling was 38 percent and for the Web sampling 2 percent.

All ANES data are weighted using the overall population weights created by ANES. Weights for the FTF population were created using: age, a cross-classification of age and sex, race-ethnicity, a cross-classification of race-ethnicity and sex, educational attainment, a cross-classification of race-ethnicity and educational attainment, marital status, income, census region, home ownership, and nation of birth. Internet weights were developed using: cross-classification of race-ethnicity and educational attainment, a cross-classification of age and sex, metropolitan status, household Internet access, income, marital status, and home ownership.

SAMPLE CHARACTERISTICS

Demographic differences are dramatic between the foreign and native-born U.S. Latino populations and are mirrored in the LINES and ANES samples as seen in table 1. Based on estimates of the entire Latino population from the ACS, native-born Latinos are slightly younger than foreign-born (an average age of thirty-seven to forty-four). Native-born Latinos are also far better educated and more likely to speak English than their foreign-born counterparts. More than half (52 percent) of all native-born Latinos have at least some college, versus just over a quarter (27 percent) of their foreign-born counterparts. Interestingly, both groups of Latinos live in relatively low-income households. More than half of all Latinos regardless of nativity live in households earning less than $20,000 per year (ACS).

The native-born ANES sample is very similar to the ACS statistics on native-born Latinos and in that sense quite representative. In contrast, the foreign-born ANES sample stands out in part because they are citizens, a feature of the ANES design. They are also somewhat wealthier, better educated, and a little older than the entire foreign-born Latino population. Latinos in the LINES data mirror the foreign-born population more accurately when it comes to citizenship, age, and education. They are less representative when it comes to income, however. They earn far less than the foreign-born population, and fully 50 percent live in households earning $20,000 or less, versus only 24 percent among foreign-born Latinos in the ACS. The ANES foreign-born sample is somewhat more likely to speak English (although a near majority speak mostly Spanish). And the ANES foreign-born sample, especially those obtained on the Internet, had been in the United States for longer than respondents in the LINES sample. These differences should be kept in mind when drawing comparisons between the two studies.

MEASURES

Except where noted explicitly, identical measures were used in the LINES and ANES studies. Typically, these measures appeared on the same survey (pre- or postelection) in the two studies. Unless noted otherwise, all measures were rescaled to vary from 0 to 1.

Partisan Preferences
The expressive approach to partisanship and the study of political action requires a more finely differentiated measure than the traditional measure of partisanship, which captures

Table 1. Demographic Profile of LINES and ANES Latinos

	LINES	ANES Foreign Born FTF	ANES Foreign Born Web	ACS Foreign Born 2012	ANES Native Born FTF	ANES Native Born Web	ACS Native Born 2012
Citizen (percentage)	36	100	100	35	100	100	100
Age (years)	43	47	49	44	35	38	37
Gender (male percentage)	52	44	52	51	50	48	50
Income (percentages)							
< $20,000	50	32	34	24	33	25	23
$20,000 to $40,000	31	27	28	31	25	22	24
$40,000 to $60,000	12	14	15	19	15	18	18
> $60,000	8	28	23	25	26	33	35
Education (percentages)							
< = Sixth grade	25	11	14	25	0	2	2
7–12 no diploma	24	18	20	22	14	11	16
HS diploma, GED	26	21	28	26	42	35	29
Some college/AA	17	21	25	17	30	34	38
BA +	9	30	13	10	13	16	14
Language (percentages)							
Only or mostly English	2	22	19		67	67	
Both equally	29	31	31		27	25	
Only or mostly Spanish	68	47	50		6	8	
Years in United States							
< Ten	16	13	0				
Eleven to twenty	34	25	2				
Twenty-one to fifty	43	45	51				
> Fifty	6	16	46				
N	1,304	141	232	174,932	329	299	167,900

Source: Authors' compilation based on U.S. Census Bureau 2012, ANES 2012, McCann and Jones-Correa 2012.

Note: LINES data is weighted (based on education, age, and gender) to the 2012 American Community Survey foreign-born population; weights for the ANES were developed to match the entire US population. Numbers for the ANES are not dramatically different with and without weights.

minimal variation in partisan strength between strong identifiers, not so strong identifiers, and leaning independents. In past research, we have developed a direct measure of partisan identity (Huddy, Mason, and Aaroe 2015). These identity questions were not available in the current study, and we thus created a new fine-grained measure of partisan preferences in the pre- and postelection LINES and ANES studies. We regard this as a de facto measure of identity but refer to it throughout as a measure of partisan preference because it contains component measures of party preferences and identification.

In the preelection study, we developed a reliable measure of partisan preference by additively combining three measures of partisanship: self-reported partisan identification (which was not asked in the postelection survey) and Democratic and Republican feeling thermometers ($\alpha = 0.71$, LINES; $\alpha = 0.86$, ANES). Those who reported no partisanship affiliation

Table 2. A Political Profile of LINES and ANES Latinos

	LINES	ANES Foreign Born		ANES Native Born	
		FTF	Web	FTF	Web
Preelection PID Scale (0=Reps, 1=Dems)	.63	.66	.66	.65	.59
Postelection PID Scale (0=Reps, 1=Dems)	.65	.64	.63	.66	.57
Panel PID Scale (0-1) (0=Reps, 1=Dems)	.67	.65	.65	.66	.58
Party identification					
Republican	14	19	20	18	26
Independent	25	15	21	15	23
Democrats	61	67	60	66	51
Ideology (conservative-liberal)	.46	.50	.48	.54	.50
Hispanic identity (1): How important is being Hispanic to your sense of yourself?					
Extremely	26	36	26	30	17
Very	55	28	32	29	21
Moderately	11	17	24	13	29
A little/not at all	7	12	6	17	26
Hispanic Identity (2): What happens to Hispanic people in this country affects you?					
Yes, a lot	17	27	7	21	8
Yes, some	22	31	34	30	27
Yes, not much	7	3	6	7	11
No	55	38	53	43	55
Discrimination: How much discrimination is there in the United States against Hispanics?					
A great deal	16	16	25	10	11
A lot	38	41	26	39	19
A moderate amount	19	23	33	32	45
A little/none	27	21	16	19	25
Political activities in 2012: participation					
Tried to convince people to vote a certain way?	30	35	36	29	29
Attended a rally?	4	2	6	1	4
Wore a button, sticker, or sign?	11	6	17	8	12
Worked for a party/candidate?	2	1	5	1	3
Gave money?	3	3	7	3	10

Source: Authors' compilation based on ANES 2012, McCann and Jones-Correa 2012.
Note: All numbers other than scales in percentages. LINES data is weighted to the ACS 2012 foreign-born population; weights for the ANES were developed to match the entire U.S. population. Numbers for the ANES are not dramatically different with and without weights.

in response to the traditional question were coded as Independents. Second, a postelection measure of partisanship was created by combining three measures: the party to which one feels closest, liking for the Democratic Party, and liking for the Republican Party (α = 0.71 LINES, α = 0.84, ANES). Finally, a joint measure of partisanship was created from all six items for those in both waves of the panel (α = 0.82, LINES; α = 0.91, ANES).

As seen in table 2, a majority of Latinos identified as Democrats in both the LINES and ANES in terms of self-placement in the preelection survey. All subsamples of Latinos gained a mean score well above 0.5 on the party preference scale, indicating a preference for the Democratic Party both before and after the election. The native-born ANES Latino Web sample was the weakest subgroup of Democrats across the two studies, only 51 percent identifying as Democrat versus 60 percent of the foreign-born ANES Web component and 61 percent of the LINES sample.

Hispanic Identity and Perceived Discrimination

Respondents were asked in the postelection survey how important Hispanic identity is to them on a 5-point scale that ranged from extremely to not at all important. This was rescaled from 0 to 1, 1 indicating that Hispanic identity was extremely important. Respondents were also asked about linked fate with other Hispanics ("Does what happens to Hispanics in the United States have something to do with what happens in your life?"). These two questions were combined despite modest correlations ($r = 0.11$, LINES; $r = 0.17$, ANES) to create a scale of Hispanic identity.[1]

For the most part, Latinos were strongly identified as Hispanic with over 80 percent of the LINES sample, roughly 60 percent of the foreign-born ANES sample, and just under 60 percent of the native-born ANES FTF sample saying it was extremely or very important to them to be Hispanic. Native-born Latinos in the ANES Web sample were the only subgroup in which a majority did not feel this way. Only 38 percent of this group said Hispanic identity was extremely or very important to them, whereas 26 percent said it was not at all or only a little important.

Respondents were also asked in the postelection survey about how much discrimination exists against Hispanics in the United States today on a 5-point scale ranging from none to a great deal. Responses were recoded so that 1 represented a great deal of perceived discrimination. Perceived discrimination against Hispanics was pervasive. More than half of the LINES sample and roughly 40 percent of the ANES sample saw a lot or a great deal of discrimination. A small minority of Latinos in both studies said there was only a little or no discrimination.

Political Engagement

Participation

Respondents were asked in the postelection survey whether they had participated in each of five political activities during 2012: trying to convince another about politics, attending a rally, displaying a sign or button, working for a candidate or party, or donating to a candidate or party. These five items were combined to create an index of the number of political activities engaged in during the 2012 election. The scale ranged from 0 to 1 ($\alpha = 0.37$, LINES; $\alpha = 0.61$, ANES). Levels of activity are low overall, with the exception of trying to influence another's vote, something to keep in mind when considering later analyses of the determinants of activity.

Ideology and Policy Issue Stance

Ideology

Ideological self-placement was measured in both the pre- and postelection surveys. Respondents were asked to place themselves on a 7-point scale from extremely liberal to extremely conservative. Respondents who did not respond were asked to choose one of the labels. Those who responded liberal to the second question were given a score of 3 on the 7-point scale, and those who chose conservative were given a score of 5. Those who did not respond were coded as moderate and placed at the scale midpoint (4).

Immigration Policy

In the preelection survey, respondents were asked three questions concerning their support for the Dream Act, status checks by state and local officers to determine the immigration status of anyone they suspect of being illegal, and whether illegal immigrants should be criminalized, deported, legalized with penalties, or legalized without penalty. These three items were combined but do not form espe-

---

1. In subsequent analyses, this combined variable has greater predictive validity than either variable alone.

cially strong scales (α = 0.18, LINES; α = 0.50, ANES). In the postelection survey, respondents were asked whether they felt that the level of immigration should be increased, decreased, or maintained.

Health-Care Policy

Support for government health care was assessed by two questions in the preelection survey. Respondents were asked how strongly they supported or opposed the 2010 Affordable Care Act and then asked their position on a scale that ranged from 1, support for a government health insurance plan that covers everyone, to 7, support for private health insurance. This was also rescaled from 0 to 1, 1 being the most supportive of the government plan. The two questions were combined to form a measure of support for government-provided health insurance (α = 0.14, LINES, and α = 0.43, ANES).

Abortion Policy

Respondents were asked whether they supported legal abortion and under what circumstances.

Gay Rights Policy

Respondents were asked if gay couples should be allowed to adopt children, their support for gay marriage, and whether they favored or opposed laws to protect homosexuals from job discrimination. Responses were rescaled and combined to form a scale that ranged from 0 to 1, with 1 indicating greater support for gay rights (α=.64, LINES; α=.74, ANES).

Political Mobilization and Patriotism

Several other factors that could influence levels of political activity were also assessed. To ensure that mobilization efforts were controlled in models analyzing political action, respondents were asked in the postelection survey whether they had been contacted by a political party or some other political entity during the 2012 election. Respondents were also asked in the postelection survey about their feelings for the United States and the American flag. These two questions were combined to form a measure of patriotism (α = 0.16, LINES; α = 0.60, ANES).

Demographics

In addition, a series of additional questions were asked to assess immigrant status and background. Country of origin was asked of Latinos in the LINES but not the ANES study.

RESULTS

The LINES study, an entirely foreign-born sample, is a productive place to begin an examination of the elements that inform Latino partisan identity. In the first column of table 3, a Democratic Party preference is regressed onto Hispanic identity and perceived discrimination against Hispanics, key facets of an expressive account of partisanship. These analyses are confined to the postelection survey because it contained the ethnic identity and discrimination measures. The dependent variable in column 1 is a partisan preference scale that ranges from 0 (strongly pro-Republican) to 1 (strongly pro-Democratic). Among foreign-born Latinos in the LINES study (column 1), even when controlling for ideological identification, Hispanic identity and perceived discrimination against Hispanics are both strongly tied to an affiliation with the Democratic Party in the postelection survey. The coefficients for Hispanic identity and perceived discrimination are both similar in magnitude to the effect of ideology, usually one of the strongest determinants of partisan identity. In an immigrant sample, therefore, simply identifying as Hispanic or viewing Hispanics as subject to discrimination are linked to stronger support for the Democratic Party. This analysis also confirms the widespread finding that Mexican, Central American, and Dominican Latinos are more likely than Cubans (the omitted category) to gravitate toward the Democrats. These analyses provide preliminary support for the convergence of Latino and Democratic affiliations.

In additional analysis of immigrant Democrats in the LINES study (those who show at least some preference for Democrats over Republicans on the preference scale), Hispanic identity and perceived discrimination further intensify a preference for the party. In this analysis (column 2, table 3), substantial missing data on ideology lead us to omit it from the

Table 3. Determinants of Latino Postelection Partisan Preference

	1. LINES Postelection Republican-Democrat Preference	2. LINES Democrats Democratic Preference	3. ANES 2012 Panel Republican-Democrat Preference	4. ANES 2012 Democrats Democratic Preference	5. ANES 2012 Republicans Republican Preference
Ideology (conservative-liberal)	0.14 (0.03)***	—	0.46 (0.05)***	0.30 (0.09)***	−0.50 (0.10)***
Identity politics					
Hispanic identity (post)	0.15 (0.03)***	−0.15 (0.14)	0.14 (0.04)***	−0.12 (0.20)	0.08 (0.09)
Discrimination – Hispanics (post)	0.12 (0.03)***	−0.16 (0.12)*	0.13 (0.04)***	−0.19 (0.17)	0.02 (0.10)
Hispanic ID X discrimination	—	0.48 (0.20)***	—	0.45 (0.27)*	—
Immigration status					
Citizen	−0.01 (0.02)	0.05 (0.04)*			
Undocumented on arrival	−0.02 (0.02)	0.01 (0.03)			
Years in United States of foreign born	0.00 (0.00)*	0.00 (0.00)	−0.00 (0.01)	0.01 (0.02)	−0.02 (0.02)
Foreign born			0.02 (0.05)	−0.07 (0.07)	0.10 (0.10)
Country or region of origin					
Mexico	0.13 (0.04)***	−0.15 (0.06)***			
Central America	0.20 (0.04)***	−0.04 (0.06)			
South American	0.05 (0.05)	−0.25 (0.07)***			
Dominican	0.17 (0.06)***	−0.03 (0.07)			
(Cuba omitted category)					
Demographics					
Gender (male)	−0.02 (0.02)*	−0.02 (0.03)	−0.03 (0.02)*	0.02 (0.03)	0.08 (0.04)**
Age (decades)	−0.00 (0.01)	0.01 (0.01)	0.00 (0.01)	0.02 (0.01)	0.04 (0.02)***
Education	0.04 (0.03)	0.10 (0.06)**	−0.08 (0.06)*	0.03 (0.09)	−0.13 (0.11)
Family income	−0.02 (0.01)**	0.01 (0.01)	−0.07 (0.04)*	0.09 (0.07)*	0.19 (0.08)***
Constant	0.33 (0.07)***	0.50 (0.13)***	0.35 (0.07)***	0.25 (0.16)***	0.24 (0.09)***
N	649	548	875	589	182

Source: Authors' compilation based on ANES 2012, McCann and Jones-Correa 2012.

Note: Entries are unstandardized regression coefficients with standard errors in parentheses. Analyses were conducted with multiple imputations (twenty times) for income in both data sets and age in LINES. Standard errors are adjusted to account for error in these imputations using the STATA multiple imputation routine. All variables are coded 0 or 1 except age, which is in decades, and years in United States, which is in years.

One-tailed: *p ≤ .1; **p ≤ .05; ***p ≤ .01

Figure 2. Effect of Perceived Discrimination on Democratic Party Support

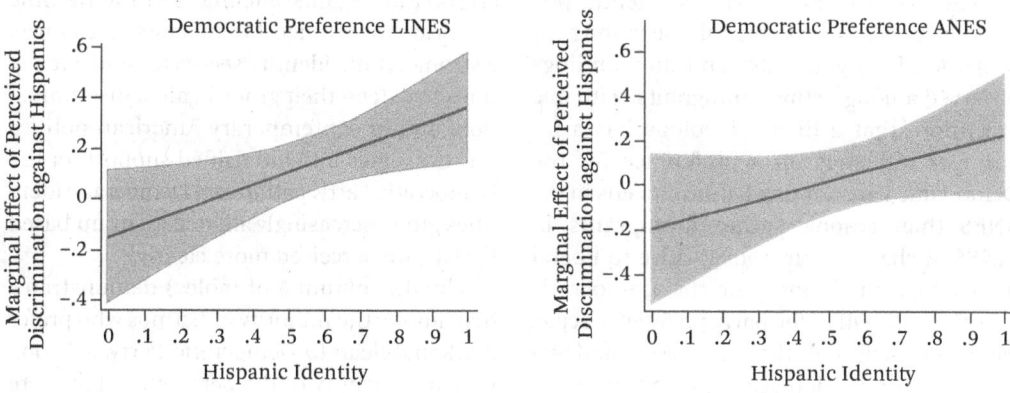

Source: Authors' compilation based on ANES 2012, McCann and Jones-Correa 2012.
Note: Marginal effects calculated using the OLS model found in column 2 of table 3 (LINES) and column 4 of table 3 (ANES). All variables set at their means, except for dichotomous variables, which are set at their modes. The LINES modal values generate marginal effects for Mexican, female, non-naturalized citizens who arrived with documentation. The ANES modal values generate marginal effects for native-born women.

analysis in order to increase sample size.[2] In this model, Latinos who strongly identify as Hispanic and perceive ethnic discrimination strongly prefer the Democratic Party to the Republican. The interaction between Hispanic identity and perceived discrimination against Hispanics is large and significant, showing that a Latino with a strong Hispanic identity who perceives ethnic discrimination is nearly 48 percent more likely to prefer the Democratic Party to the Republican than a weakly identified Latino who does not perceive discrimination.

Figure 2 depicts the marginal effects of perceived discrimination against Hispanics on Democratic Party identity strength at different levels of Hispanic identity. At low levels of identity, perceived discrimination dampens Democratic identity, but as Hispanic identity strength increases, perceived discrimination increases a preference for the Democratic Party. This is the expected pattern of findings if status politics and identity threat are driving strongly identified Latinos toward the Democratic Party. Thus, among Latino immigrants, identity politics plays a powerful role in driving support for the party. Both Hispanic identity and perceived Hispanic discrimination increase a preference for Democrats over Republicans (despite no interaction between identity and discrimination in the sample as a whole). Also, a preference for the Democratic Party is especially strong among Democrats who identify strongly with and perceive discrimination against Hispanics. Evidence in these analyses indicates that Hispanic and Democratic Party identities have converged as hypothesized. The interaction between Hispanic identity and discrimination also helps rule out the notion that Democratic identification increases Hispanic identity, the reverse causal order to that hypothesized. It is difficult to see why a Democratic identification would only intensify Hispanic identity among those who perceive ethnic discrimination.

The influence of Latino identity and perceived Latino discrimination on Democratic partisan preference in the LINES study may arise because noncitizen immigrants (the bulk of the LINES sample) do not know enough about American politics or the stance adopted by the parties on specific issues to base their partisanship on instrumental concerns. In column 3 of table 3, we turn to the 2012 ANES

---

2. The omission of ideology does not change the substantive results of the model in additional analyses not shown here.

sample of Latino citizens (immigrant and non-immigrant), to determine whether identity politics plays an equally powerful role among citizens. Model 3 generally replicates findings observed among Latino immigrants, with one exception, that a liberal ideology has a far stronger influence on a preference for the Democratic Party among Latino citizens in the ANES than among Latino immigrants in LINES. A change from conservative to liberal increases a preference for the Democratic Party by fully half of the party preference scale, whereas the effect of Hispanic identity and perceived discrimination against Hispanics is essentially the same as that observed in the LINES sample. Even controlling for the large effect of ideology in the ANES study, a Latino with a strong sense of Hispanic identity is significantly more likely than someone with a weak identity to prefer the Democratic Party. Similarly, perceived discrimination against Hispanics significantly pushes Latinos closer to the Democratic Party. Interestingly, the magnitude of these effects is not that different among immigrants in the LINES and foreign- and native-born citizens in the ANES. Even after accounting for a potentially strong instrumental component of partisan affiliation among Latino citizens via ideology, status and identity influence partisan affiliations. Once again, no interaction is evident between Hispanic identity and perceived discrimination when looking at the ANES sample as a whole.

Identity politics—based on an interaction between Hispanic identity and perceived discrimination—does, however, intensify a preference for the Democratic Party among Latino Democrats in the ANES. Model 4 in table 3 is confined to Latinos in the ANES who express a preference for the Democratic Party over the Republican Party. In this model, even after controlling for ideology, someone who strongly identifies as Latino and perceives widespread ethnic discrimination is 45 percent more positive about the Democratic Party than a comparable Latino who perceives no discrimination and has weak Hispanic identity. This model replicates the same finding among Democratic supporters in the LINES study. Figure 2 depicts this relationship graphically. Again, in line with the expectations of social identity theory, strongly identified Latinos who perceive discrimination against members of their ethnic group are the strongest Democrats. In essence, a strong ethnic identity seems to motivate Latinos to defend their group against discrimination, and in contemporary American politics this translates into intensified support for the Democratic Party. Latino and Democratic identities grow increasingly aligned as group-based threats are perceived more clearly.

Finally, column 5 of table 3 demonstrates that among the minority of Latinos who prefer the Republican to Democratic Party, a strong Hispanic identity or the perception that there is widespread discrimination against Hispanics does nothing to intensify the strength of Republican support. In the (admittedly small) subsample of Latinos who call themselves Republicans, the strength of their attachment to that party lies in their ideological leanings and to a smaller extent in demographic characteristics. Latinos who are wealthier, older, and male are more strongly Republican than Democratic. Conservatism has an even greater effect on a preference for the Republican Party among Latino citizens in the ANES. For conservative Latino citizens, Hispanic identity has nothing to do with their support of the Republican Party.

Identity politics appears to have played a substantial role in the development of Democratic partisanship among Latinos, at least after the 2012 election. The election may have intensified the role of identity-based partisanship because it involved Republican anti-Latino rhetoric and potentially boosted Latino pride in effecting a Democratic victory. To assess this possibility, we draw more fully on both the pre- and postelection survey waves to examine the potential intensification of Latino and Democratic identity convergence. Examination of the LINES panel also allows us to contrast the role of issues and identity politics in driving partisan preferences because most issue questions were included in the preelection survey whereas identity questions were in the postsurvey.

Thankfully, both the LINES and the ANES data include an assessment of partisanship before and after the election, which allows us to simplify our model and analyze the role of ethnic identity and policy issues in affecting changes in party preference intensity over the course of the election. To analyze potential change, we confine analyses to the panel respondents interviewed at both time points. This results in a substantial reduction in the LINES but not ANES sample sizes. In table 4, the direction and strength of party preference is assessed after the election, whereas controlling for party preference is measured before the election. In all five models of table 4, preelection party preference is by far the strongest predictor of postelection party preference, as expected. However, both Latino identity and issue stances also influenced partisanship.

In model 1 of table 4, the full Republican-to-Democratic scale of partisanship is predicted after the election, using the full scale measured before the election. In the LINES data, Hispanic identity is aligned increasingly with Latino preference for the Democratic Party over the course of the election after controlling for their party preference before the election. The analysis in this model also makes clear that party preferences are not based solely on identity politics. Support for government-provided health insurance and gay rights both intensified support for the Democratic Party among Latino immigrants in the LINES study.

Latino identity also intensified Democratic preferences among those who initially preferred Democrats over Republicans in the preelection survey. Support for government health insurance, legalized abortion, and gay rights also intensified a preference for the Democrats. As seen in model 2 of table 4, however, the strongest factor that accounted for the intensity of Democratic support after the election was intensity prior to the election.

In fact, the results from model 1 are also replicated in model 3, in the ANES sample of Latino citizens. Party support after the election is linked most strongly to the choice of party preelection, but Hispanic identity also plays a role. As Hispanic identification increased in the ANES sample of Latinos, Latino postelection support for the Democratic Party also increased. In addition, support for health care and gay rights intensified support for Democrats as it did in the LINES sample. The main difference between the LINES and ANES samples is that ideology matters more in the ANES sample. Among Latinos in the ANES, ideology is a significant predictor of partisan direction postelection, even when controlling for preelection partisanship, indicating that liberals became more supportive of Democrats and conservatives more supportive of Republicans over the course of the election.

Even when only looking at Democrats from the ANES sample in model 4 of table 4, and controlling for preelection Democratic identification, a stronger identification with Hispanics leads to a stronger affiliation with Democrats over the course of the election in the ANES sample. Health-care and abortion attitudes also increased Democratic support over the course of the election among ANES Latino Democrats.

Finally, among the few Republican identifiers in the ANES sample of Latinos, preelection Republican support and conservative ideology had the most significant influence on the strength of Republican identification after the election. More conservative Latinos preferred the Republican Party more strongly. As seen in table 3, Hispanic identification did not intensify Republican identification during the 2012 election. However, instrumental concerns about health care and gay rights had a significant effect on Latino Republicans, conservative positions on those issues increasing the intensity of support for the Republican Party.

In sum, evidence is ample that Latinos, regardless of citizenship status, are moving toward the Democratic Party in part because of ethnic identity politics, merging Hispanic and Democratic identities. A strong Hispanic identity differentiates Democrats from Republicans and when combined with an awareness of Latino discrimination creates especially strong Latino support for the Democratic Party. Identity-based status politics is thus alive and well. But identity politics is not the only basis for party preferences among Latinos. Instrumental support for government-provided health insurance and the Affordable Care Act increased support for the Democratic Party over the course of the 2012 election in both the LINES and ANES studies. And, on average, more Latinos supported than opposed these policies, providing a boost to the Democrats.

Table 4. Determinants of Latino Postelection Partisan Preference

	1. LINES Panel Republican-Democrat	2. LINES, Panel Democrats Democratic Preference	3. ANES Panel Republican-Democrat	4. ANES 2012 Panel Democrats Democratic Preference	5. ANES 2012 Panel Republicans Republican Preference
Republican-Democrat preference (pre)	0.56 (0.05)***	—	0.61 (0.04)***	—	—
Democrat-Republican preference (pre)	—	0.28 (0.03)***	—	0.27 (0.05)***	0.34 (0.06)***
Ideology (conservative-liberal)	0.03 (0.03)	-0.00 (0.03)	0.08 (0.04)**	0.07 (0.05)	-0.12 (0.07)*
Identity politics					
Hispanic identity (post)	0.07 (0.03)**	0.04 (0.03)*	0.06 (0.02)**	0.07 (0.03)**	-0.07 (0.05)
Discrimination – Hispanics (post)	0.03 (0.03)	0.04 (0.03)	0.01 (0.03)	0.03 (0.03)	0.06 (0.07)
Policy issues					
Pro-immigration (pre)	0.03 (0.06)	0.00 (0.06)	0.02 (0.03)	-0.00 (0.04)	0.00 (0.06)
Pro-government health insurance (pre)	0.08 (0.04)**	0.08 (0.03)***	0.15 (0.04)***	0.11 (0.05)**	-0.21 (0.06)***
Pro-abortion (pre)	0.00 (0.00)	0.004 (0.001)***	0.02 (0.015)	0.04 (0.03)*	0.03 (0.03)
Pro-gay rights (pre)	0.045 (0.025)*	0.04 (0.03)*	0.04 (0.02)*	0.04 (0.03)	-0.07 (0.04)*
Constant	0.12 (0.07)*	0.45 (0.07)***	0.01 (0.02)	0.36 (0.05)***	-0.66 (0.05)
R^2	0.473	0.294	0.697	0.326	0.577
N	403	293	903	608	216

Source: Authors' compilation based on ANES 2012, McCann and Jones-Correa 2012.

Note: Entries are unstandardized regression coefficients with standard errors in parentheses. Data are weighted. Democrats in the LINES survey include all respondents who indicated a preference for the Democrats in the postelection survey on the Republican-Democrat preference scale. Republicans and Democrats in the ANES are identified based on their response to the standard partisanship question in the preelection survey. Leaners are included as partisans. All variables are coded 0 or 1.

One-tailed: *$p < .1$; **$p < .05$; ***$p < .01$

Attitudes toward government-provided healthcare assistance also intensified support for the Republican Party among those opposed to it. Gay rights influenced party support over the course of the 2012 election, but Latinos are quite divided in this area, and thus it provides no net benefit to either party. Finally, despite popular conceptions to the contrary, Latino views on immigration had no effect on party preferences. Presumably, if immigration does influence Latino partisanship, it does so through Latino identity and perceived Republican negativity toward Latinos.

CAMPAIGN ACTIVITY IN 2012

We had expected the concordance of partisan and ethnic identity to be especially powerful politically, leading to greater political activity among Latino Democrats than Latino Republicans. To test this theory, we first looked at Latinos in the LINES study, regressing activity in the 2012 campaign (the most common activities of which were talking to others and wearing a sticker or button or displaying a sign) on party preferences folded to indicate strength and then unfolded to indicate strength and partisan direction. Consistent with an expressive view of partisanship (Huddy, Mason, and Aaroe 2015), folded partisanship was a powerful predictor of campaign activity. Our hypothesis of additional activity among Democrats was not supported, however. In model 1 of table 5, no added effect of the Republican to Democrat (direction) scale after controlling for partisan strength was evident.

The hypothesis that merged Hispanic and Democratic identities would more powerfully influence political campaign action than a strong Republican identity had merit, as shown in additional analyses. A preference for the Democratic Party interacted with Hispanic identity to increase political campaign activity in 2012, as seen in model 2 in table 5. When presented visually in figure 3, it becomes clear that Hispanic identity dampened political activity among Latinos who preferred the Republican Party rather than further boosted political activity among Democrats. A similar finding emerges when analyses are confined to the LINES Panel (see model 3, table 5). In sum, Hispanic identity plays a double role in driving Latino political activity. It strengthens Democratic identity and thus elevates action, and it reduces political activity among Republicans, presumably because it generates paralyzing conflict between one's party and ethnic identity. This conclusion is confirmed by simple bivariate correlation coefficients. On balance, the correlation between Latino identity and 2012 campaign activity is modestly positive for Latinos in the LINES study who preferred the Democratic Party ($r = 0.09$) and sizeable and negative among those who preferred Republicans ($r = -0.22$).

Finally, we turn to Latinos in the ANES to further assess the influence of partisan preferences and identity politics on political activity in the 2012 campaign. Once again, as expected, folded partisanship increased political activity. Thus both strong Democrats and Republicans were more likely to take action during the campaign, as shown in model 1 of table 6. No evidence, however, indicated that strong Democrats took greater action than strong Republicans in the ANES data. Interestingly, in this same model, Latinos who identified strongly as Hispanic and perceived widespread ethnic discrimination were also more likely to have been active within the campaign.

The activating effect of ethnic identity and perceived discrimination were somewhat larger among Democrats than Republicans, as seen in models 2 and 3 of table 6. Interestingly, when analyses were confined to Latinos who regarded themselves as Democrats in the pre-election survey (based on the standard partisanship question) the interaction between identity and discrimination was significant. This is generally consistent with findings observed in the LINES study of immigrants. At odds with the LINES study, however, the interaction is positive and sizeable among Republicans, though it did not reach significance because of its smaller sample size (model 3, table 6). When the interaction is plotted for Democrats in figure 4, it is clear that perceived discrimination against Latinos has little effect on activity among Latinos who lack a strong Hispanic identity but an increasingly positive effect among Democrats with a stronger Hispanic identity. Oddly, the same trend is apparent among Republicans, suggesting that they

Table 5. Determinants of Latinos' 2012 Campaign Activity, LINES

	1. LINES, Postelection Sample	2. LINES, Postelection Sample	3. LINES, Panel
Ideology (conservative-liberal)	—	—	0.49 (0.26)*
Folded party preference scale (post)	1.15 (0.22)***	1.06 (0.22)***	0.73 (0.30)**
Republican-Democrat preference (post)	-0.17 (0.32)	-0.89 (0.53)*	-1.42 (0.78)*
Identity politics			
Hispanic identity (post)	-0.05 (0.21)	-1.22 (0.64)*	-1.62 (0.97)*
Republican-Democrat preference X Hispanic ID	—	1.63 (0.92)*	2.32 (10.32)*
Discrimination – Hispanics (post)	0.13 (0.17)	0.11 (0.17)	0.02 (0.23)
Political interest			
Mobilized (post)	0.36 (0.11)***	0.36 (0.11)***	0.40 (0.14)***
Immigration status			
Patriotism (post)	0.85 (0.34)**	0.83 (0.34)**	1.19 (0.46)**
Citizen	-0.06 (0.15)	-0.07 (0.15)	-0.21 (0.22)
Undocumented on arrival	0.28 (0.13)	0.27 (0.13)**	0.02 (0.20)
Years in United States of foreign born	0.01 (0.005)*	0.01 (0.005)*	0.01 (0.01)
Foreign born			—
Demographics			
Gender (male)	-0.14 (0.10)	-0.13 (0.10)	-0.27 (0.14)*
Age (decades)	-0.01 (0.04)	-0.01 (0.04)	-0.01 (0.07)
Education	0.74 (0.21)***	0.71 (0.21)***	0.76 (0.31)**
Family income	0.05 (0.04)	0.05 (0.04)	0.01 (0.06)
Cut 1	1.95 (0.46)	1.38 (0.54)	0.72 (0.79)
Cut 2	3.18 (0.47)	2.62 (0.55)	2.02 (0.80)
Cut 3	3.89 (0.46)	3.34 (0.55)	2.70 (0.78)
Cut 4	4.37 (0.48)	3.82 (0.57)	3.15 (0.82)
Cut 5	5.04 (0.53)	4.48 (0.58)	—
N	782	782	382

Source: Authors' compilation based on McCann and Jones-Correa 2012.
Note: Entries are unstandardized ordered probit coefficients with standard errors in parentheses. Data are weighted. Income and age are imputed (twenty times). Ideology is not included in models 1 and 2 due to missing data in the postelection survey but is included in the panel. All variables are coded 0 or 1 except age, which is coded in decades. Values were truncated in the panel and no one scored in the top category.
One tailed: *$p < .1$; **$p < .05$; ***$p < .01$

were motivated to work for the Republican Party based on the same identity factors. Admittedly, the ANES sample includes relatively few Republican Latinos, but they largely supported Romney. We are forced to conclude that they were motivated to work on his behalf driven by issues of concern to Latinos, though further research is needed to fully understand this finding.

Finally, among Latinos who were classified as pure Independents in the preelection wave of the ANES (based again on the standard partisanship question), Hispanic identity and a sense of perceived ethnic discrimination both

Figure 3. Effect of Hispanic Identity on 2012 Campaign Activity

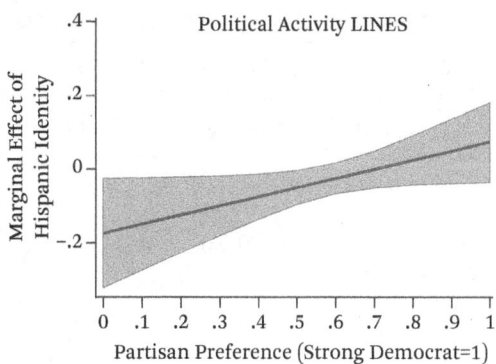

Source: Authors' compilation based on McCann and Jones-Correa 2012.
Note: Marginal effects calculated using the OLS model found in column 2 of table 5. All variables set at their means, except for dichotomous variables that are set at their mode (female, non-naturalized, arrived with documentation).

weakly intensified political activity. Even among individuals with no clear partisanship, politically independent Latino citizens were propelled to take action. Roughly a third of Independents voted in the 2012 election and did so overwhelmingly for Obama, suggesting that heightened political activity among political Independents also favored the Democratic Party.

We also examined the data to see whether living in a swing state with increased levels of political ads and enhanced mobilization efforts increased political activity among Latinos, or among strongly identified Latinos, but it did not. The one exception was that strongly identified Latinos who preferred the Republican Party were less politically active in a swing state, suggesting demobilization. This is consistent with our initial hypothesis that Republicans who identified as Latino would be less active politically. This is apparently true in swing states with heightened levels of statewide political mobilization.

AFRICAN AMERICANS

The current analyses raise questions about whether a similar dynamic can be observed among African Americans. The 2012 candidacy of Barack Obama, an African American, and the strong ties between African Americans and the Democratic Party should also arouse identity politics among blacks. From that perspective, Democratic partisanship should be linked to a black identity and perceived racial discrimination among African Americans.

When partisan preferences among blacks in the 2012 ANES were subject to the same analyses as those shown in columns 3 through 5 of table 3, we observed parallel findings. Black identity (assessed as the importance of being black) and perceived discrimination against blacks are associated with a postelection preference for the Democratic Party and a stronger partisan identity among black Democrats. Likewise, black identity and perceived racial discrimination are associated with a greater preference for the Democratic Party in the ANES panel after controlling for preelection party preference and several issues (immigration, government health insurance, abortion, and gay rights). Moreover, the link between ethnic-racial identity and support for the Democratic Party is comparable among blacks and Latinos. This lends added support to an identity convergence model of American partisanship among racial and ethnic minorities. Racial identity and perceived racial discrimination have no additional effect on political activity among blacks, however. As for Latinos, strong partisanship elevates levels of political activity among all blacks, and identity thus has an indirect influence on political activity via partisan preferences. Black identity and political activity are not directly linked in 2012, however. This difference between blacks and Latinos may arise because racial identity has been a part of Democratic politics for quite some time, whereas it has emerged more recently among Latinos.

CONCLUSION

Overall, we find ample evidence that Hispanic and partisan identities have converged among Latinos in the United States to create a large number of Latino Democrats. This conclusion holds for immigrants in the LINES study and foreign- and U.S.-born American citizens in the ANES. In that sense, our conclusions are similar to those drawn by Sears, Danbold, and Za-

Table 6. Determinants of Latinos' 2012 Campaign Activity, ANES

	1. Panel	2. Panel, Democrats	3. Panel, Republicans	4. Panel, Independents
Ideology (conservative-liberal)	−0.23 (0.27)	0.01 (0.33)	−1.22 (0.72)**	0.58 (0.70)
Folded party preference (post)	0.72 (0.21)***	—	—	—
Republican-Democratic preference (post)	−1.03 (0.73)*	1.15 (0.47)***	−0.74 (0.62)	1.10 (1.05)
Identity politics				
Hispanic identity (post)	−1.05 (0.76)*	−1.17 (0.69)**	−1.02 (0.93)	2.14 (1.37)*
Party preference X Hispanic ID (post)	0.38 (0.84)	—	—	—
Discrimination – Hispanics (post)	−0.58 (0.75)	−0.51 (0.65)	−0.34 (0.99)	1.51 (1.04)*
Party preference X Hispanic discrimination	0.48 (0.98)	—	—	—
Hispanic identity X Hispanic discrimination	1.57 (0.92)**	2.08 (0.99)***	1.61 (1.88)	−0.58 (1.74)
Political interest				
Mobilized (post)	0.63 (0.12)***	0.64 (0.15)***	0.59 (0.22)***	0.63 (0.34)**
Immigration status				
Patriotism (post)	−0.38 (0.34)	−0.18 (0.36)	0.01 (0.62)	−0.87 (0.80)
Years in United States of foreign born	0.01 (0.01)***	0.02 (0.01)***	−0.00 (0.01)	0.02 (0.02)
Foreign born	−0.44 (0.25)**	−0.75 (0.31)***	0.64 (0.52)	−0.50 (0.69)
Demographics				
Gender (male)	−0.11 (0.11)	0.05 (0.13)	0.14 (0.22)	−0.67 (0.33)***
Age (decades)	0.03 (0.04)	0.07 (0.05)*	0.08 (0.07)	−0.21 (0.13)*
Education	0.12 (0.35)	0.35 (0.38)	−1.68 (0.64)***	0.94 (0.99)
Family income	0.01 (0.24)	−0.22 (0.29)	0.59 (0.48)	1.20 (0.69)**
Cut 1	−0.33 (0.67)	1.47 (0.69)	−0.90 (0.66)	1.66 (1.19)
Cut 2	0.90 (0.68)	2.66 (0.69)	0.70 (0.69)	2.97 (1.28)
Cut 3	1.43 (0.66)	3.21 (0.71)	1.24 (0.60)	3.76 (1.24)
Cut 4	1.82 (0.67)	3.54 (0.72)	2.08 (0.78)	4.10 (1.2)
Cut 5	1.95 (0.67)	3.59 (0.73)	2.59 (0.75)	—
N	874	554	183	137

Source: Authors' compilation based on ANES 2012.
Note: Note: Entries are unstandardized ordered probit coefficients with standard errors in parentheses conducted. Data are weighted. Income is imputed (twenty times). Republicans and Democrats are identified based on their response to the standard partisanship question in the preelection survey. Leaners are included as partisans. All variables are coded 0 or 1 except age, which is coded in decades. Data are weighted.
One tailed: *$p < .1$; **$p < .05$; ***$p < .01$

Figure 4. Effect of Perceived Discrimination on 2012 Campaign Activity

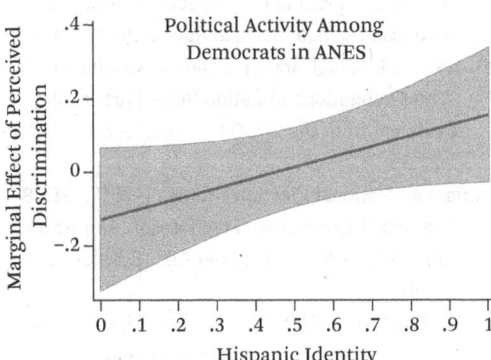

Source: Authors' compilation based on McCann and Jones-Correa 2012.
Note: Marginal effects calculated using OLS model using same variables found in column 2 of table 6. All variables set at their means, except dichotomous variables set at their modes (native-born women).

vala in this volume. Moreover, the same identity factors strengthen a preference for the Democratic Party once someone develops a pro-Democratic orientation. This strengthening of Democratic identity is most pronounced among those who see pervasive anti-Latino discrimination in the United States and identify strongly with their ethnic group. We were able to document this process of Democratic preference intensification in action in the few months between the 2012 pre- and postelection ANES surveys. Even taking prior party preferences into consideration, a strong Hispanic identity pushed Latinos even closer to the Democratic Party during the course of the election. All in all, Latinos exhibit clear evidence of identity politics at work as their Hispanic and Democratic identities become increasingly fused.

An increasing alignment between Hispanic and Democratic identities holds powerful implications for Latinos' political engagement now and into the future. We found that a strong partisan preference increased political campaign activity, consistent with an expressive view of partisanship in which a strong partisan identity increases emotional reactivity to campaign events, in turn driving political engagement (Huddy, Mason, and Aaroe 2015). As identity politics moves Latinos even more firmly into the Democratic camp, they are also more likely to get involved in political campaigns. Sergio Garcia-Rios and Matt Barreto document a similar trend elsewhere in this issue, finding that those who felt linked fate with other Latinos (an element in our Latino identity scale) and consumed Spanish language television were more active in the 2012 campaign. Admittedly, Latino action in 2012 was fairly modest. Few Latinos had worked on a campaign or given money to a candidate. Somewhat larger numbers had tried to convince others about a candidate or worn a button or displayed a sticker. But this leaves much room for future Latino political activity.

We found less evidence, however, that Democrats were more politically active than Republicans. We had hypothesized that this would occur because Latino and Democratic identities had converged. There was some evidence along these lines: Latinos in the LINES study who identified strongly as Hispanic and preferred the Democratic Party were even more politically active than others. Democratic Latinos in the ANES who identified as Hispanic and perceived discrimination were more active within the campaign. But so were Republicans in the ANES (albeit to a lesser degree), suggesting something of a contrary movement to reclaim Latino concerns for their party. In the end, identity politics does drive greater Latino activity on behalf of Democrats simply because it has pushed many more Latinos toward the Democratic Party and helped intensify their attachment.

Finally, we began with a discussion of two very different approaches to partisanship: instrumental and expressive perspectives. In the end, both account to some degree for stronger Democratic proclivities among Latinos. We have demonstrated stronger Democratic support among Latinos with a strong Hispanic identity. This preference is even stronger among those who also perceive widespread anti-Latino bias. But we should also return to evidence that majority Latino support for government-provided health insurance in 2012 also played a consistent role in increasing support for Democrats and weakening it for Republicans among Republican identifiers. Support for pro-immigrant policies did not intensify a preference for the Democratic Party above initial preelection partisan preferences. But the issues of both immigration and government health insurance were tightly connected to identity politics, raising questions about how easy it is to disentangle the two approaches among Latinos. The ANES is the best study in which to look at this because of the large sample retained within the panel (which included preelection questions on issues and postelection questions on Hispanic identity). In these data, support for pro-immigration and government health insurance was significantly correlated with Hispanic identity ($r = 0.25$ and $r = 0.21$ respectively) and perceived ethnic discrimination ($r = 0.21$ in both instances). This link persists even after removing the common effects of partisan preferences, suggesting that both issues have become entwined with identity politics.

In conclusion, perceived Republican animosity toward Latinos is pushing them ever closer to the Democratic Party. As some observers have noted, this is odd because many Latinos are religious and socially conservative, which might incline them in the other direction. But instead, recent discussions of immigration and government health insurance policies have become entwined with Latino identity politics, placing Latinos closer to Democrats than to Republicans. There is no sign that Republicans will relent any time soon and repair their image among Latinos. Unless things change, Latinos will move increasingly into the Democratic camp and work on behalf of Democratic politicians. A policy that legalizes current illegal immigrants will have an especially profound effect on American politics (as Democrats hope and Republicans fear) creating an even larger Democratic Latino community. Without a change in Republican course, Democrats will benefit from continued and intensifying Latino loyalty over the coming years. Identity politics is alive and well in contemporary American society.

REFERENCES

Abramson, Paul R., and John H. Aldrich. 1982. "The Decline of Electoral Participation in America." *American Political Science Review* 76(3): 502-21.

Alvarez, R. Michael, and Lisa García Bedolla. 2003. "The Foundations of Latino Voter Partisanship: Evidence from the 2000 Election." *Journal of Politics* 65(1): 31-49.

American National Election Studies (ANES). 2008. The ANES Cumulative File dataset. Ann Arbor: University of Michigan; Palo Alto: Stanford University.

———. 2012. The ANES 2012 Time Series Study dataset. Ann Arbor: University of Michigan; Palo Alto: Stanford University. Accessed February 26, 2016. http://www.electionstudies.org/.

Bowler, Shaun, Stephen P. Nicholson, and Gary M. Segura. 2006. "Earthquakes and Aftershocks: Race, Direct Democracy, and Partisan Change." *American Journal of Political Science* 50(1): 146-59.

Bowler, Shaun, and Gary Segura. 2011. *The Future Is Ours: Minority Politics, Political Behavior, and the Multiracial Era of American Politics*. Thousand Oaks, Calif.: CQ Press.

Brader, Ted, Joshua A. Tucker, and Andrew Therriault. 2014. "Cross Pressure Scores: An Individual-Level Measure of Cumulative Partisan Pressures Arising from Social Group Memberships." *Political Behavior* 36(1): 23-51.

Campbell, Angus, Philip E. Converse, Warren E. Miller, and Donald E. Stokes. 1960. *The American Voter*. New York: John Wiley & Sons.

Dawson, Michael C. 1994. *Behind the Mule: Race and Class in African-American Politics*. Princeton, N.J.: Princeton University Press.

Fiorina, Morris P. 1981. *Retrospective Voting in American National Elections: A Micro-Analysis*. New Haven, Conn.: Yale University Press.

Franklin, Charles H., and John E. Jackson. 1983. "The Dynamics of Party Identification." *American Political Science Review* 77(4): 957-73.

Garcia, John A. 2011. *Latino Politics in America: Community, Culture, and Interests*. Lanham, Md.: Rowman & Littlefield.

Groenendyk, Eric W., and Antoine J. Banks. 2013. "Emotional Rescue: How Affect Helps Partisans Overcome Collective Action Problems." *Political Psychology* 35(3): 359-78.

Huddy, Leonie. 2001. "From Social to Political Identity: A Critical Examination of Social Identity Theory." *Political Psychology* 22(1): 127–56.

———. 2013. "From Group Identity to Political Commitment and Cohesion." In *Oxford Handbook of Political Psychology*, edited by Leonie Huddy, David O. Sears, and Robert Jervis. New York: Oxford University Press.

Huddy, Leonie, and Tony E. Carey Jr. 2009. "Group Politics Redux: Race and Gender in the 2008 Democratic Presidential Primaries." *Politics and Gender* 5(1): 81–96.

Huddy, Leonie, Lilliana Mason, and Lene Aaroe. 2015. "Expressive Partisanship: Campaign Involvement, Political Emotion, and Partisan Identity." *American Political Science Review* 109(1): 1–17.

Iyengar, Shanto, Gaurav Sood, and Yphtach Lelkes. 2012. "Affect, Not Ideology A Social Identity Perspective on Polarization." *Public Opinion Quarterly* 76(3): 405–31.

Lazarsfeld, Paul, Bernard Berelson, and Hazel Gaudet. 1944. *The People's Choice*. New York: Columbia University Press.

Levendusky, Matthew. 2009. *The Partisan Sort: How Liberals Became Democrats and Conservatives Became Republicans*. Chicago: University of Chicago Press.

Lipset, Seymour Martin. 1960. *Political Man: The Social Bases of Politics*. Garden City, N.J.: Doubleday.

Marcus, George E., W. Russell Neuman, and Michael Mackuen. 2000. *Affective Intelligence and Political Judgment*. Chicago: University of Chicago Press.

Mason, Lilliana. 2015. "I Disrespectfully Agree: The Differential Effects of Partisan Sorting on Social and Issue Polarization." *American Journal of Political Science* 59(1): 128–45. doi: 10.1111/ajps.12089.

———. Forthcoming. "A Cross-Cutting Calm: How Social Sorting Drives Affective Polarization." *Public Opinion Quarterly*.

McCann, James A., and Michael Jones-Correa. 2012. Latino Immigrant National Election Study, 2012. New York: Russell Sage Foundation, Carnegie Corporation of New York, Purdue University, and Cornell University.

Mutz, Diana C. 2002. "The Consequences of Cross-Cutting Networks for Political Participation." *American Journal of Political Science* 46(4): 838–55.

New York Times. 2008. "Election Results 2008." Accessed October 14, 2014. http://elections.nytimes.com/2008/results/president/exit-polls.html.

———. 2012. "President Exit Polls." Accessed October 14, 2014. http://elections.nytimes.com/2012/results/president/exit-polls.

Nordlinger, Eric. 1972. *Conflict Regulation in Divided Societies*. Cambridge, Mass.: Harvard University Center for International Affairs.

Philpot, Tasha S., and Hanes Walton. 2007. "One of Our Own: Black Female Candidates and the Voters Who Support Them." *American Journal of Political Science* 51(1): 49–62.

Powell, G. Bingham. 1976. "Political Cleavage Structure, Cross-Pressure Process, and Partisanship: An Empirical Test of the Theory." *American Journal of Political Science* 20(1): 1–23.

Reese, Laura A., and Rupert E. Brown. 1995. "The Effects of Religious Messages on Racial Identity and System Blame Among African Americans." *Journal of Politics* 57(1): 24–43.

Roccas, Sonia, and Marilynn B. Brewer. 2002. "Social Identity Complexity." *Personality and Social Psychology Review* 6(2): 88–106.

Rosenstone, Steven, and John Hansen. 1993. *Mobilization, Participation, and Democracy in America*. New York: MacMillan.

Schmid, Karin, Nicole Tausch, Miles Hewstone, Joanne Hughes, and Ed Cairns. 2008. "The Effects of Living in Segregated vs. Mixed Areas in Northern Ireland: A Simultaneous Analysis of Contact and Threat Effects in the Context of Micro-Level Neighbourhoods." *International Journal of Conflict and Violence* 2(1): 56–71.

Sigelman, Lee, and Susan Welch. 1984. "Race, Gender, and Opinion Toward Black and Female Presidential Candidates." *Public Opinion Quarterly* 48(2)(Summer 1984): 467–75.

Smith, Heather J., Tracey Cronin, and Thomas Kessler. 2008. "Anger, Fear, or Sadness: Faculty Members' Emotional Reactions to Collective Pay Disadvantage." *Political Psychology* 29(2): 221–46.

Tajfel, Henri. 1981. *Human Groups and Social Categories: Studies in Social Psychology*. Cambridge: Cambridge University Press.

Tajfel, Henri, and John Turner. 1979. "An Integrative Theory of Intergroup Conflict." In *The Social Psychology of Intergroup Relations*, edited by William

G. Austin and Stephen Worchel. Monterey, Calif.: Brooks/Cole.

Tate, Katherine. 1994. *From Protest to Politics: The New Black Voters in American Elections*. Cambridge, Mass.: Harvard University Press.

Taylor, Paul, Ana Gonzalez-Barrera, Jeffrey S. Passel, and Mark Hugo Lopez. 2013. "An Awakened Giant: The Hispanic Electorate Is Likely to Double by 2030." Washington, D.C.: Pew Hispanic Center. Accessed February 1, 2016. http://www.pewhispanic.org/2012/11/14/an-awakened-giant-the-hispanic-electorate-is-likely-to-double-by-2030/.

Turner, John, Michael Hogg, Penelope Oakes, Stephen Reicher, and Margaret Wetherell. 1987. *Rediscovering the Social Group: A Self-Categorization Theory*. Oxford: Blackwell.

Uhlaner, Carole J., and F. Chris Garcia. 1998. "Foundations of Latino Party Identification: Learning, Ethnicity and Demographic Factors among Mexicans, Puerto Ricans, Cubans and Anglos in the United States." Irvine: University of California, Center for the Study of Democracy. Accessed February 1, 2016. http://escholarship.org/uc/item/3qq4v57p.

U.S. Census Bureau. 2012. Current Population Survey dataset, November 2012. Washington: Government Printing Office.

Valentino, Nicholas A., Ted Brader, Eric W. Groenendyk, Krysha Gregorowicz, and Vincent L. Hutchings. 2011. "Election Night's Alright for Fighting: The Role of Emotions in Political Participation." *The Journal of Politics* 73(1): 156–70.

van Zomeren, Martijn, Russell Spears, and Colin Wayne Leach. 2008. "Exploring Psychological Mechanisms of Collective Action: Does Relevance of Group Identity Influence How People Cope with Collective Disadvantage?" *British Journal of Social Psychology* 47(2): 353–72.

Wallace, Sophia J. 2012. "It's Complicated: Latinos, President Obama, and the 2012 Election." *Social Science Quarterly* 93(5): 1360–83.

PART IV
Study Appendix

Key Design Features of the 2012 Latino Immigrant National Election Study

JAMES A. McCANN AND MICHAEL JONES-CORREA

The Latino Immigrant National Election Study (LINES), conducted in two installments during the fall of 2012, is a nationally representative telephone survey of foreign-born adult residents of the United States who emigrated from one of the Spanish-speaking countries of Latin America. The Russell Sage Foundation, the Carnegie Corporation of New York, Purdue University, and Cornell University provided support for the study. Much of the instrumentation for LINES was adapted from the questionnaire of the 2012 American National Election Study (ANES), so that the political attitudes and behaviors of Latino immigrants can be systematically compared with other groups within the United States. Unlike the ANES, sampling for LINES was not conditional on civic status or voting eligibility.

How politically engaged are Latino immigrants vis-à-vis Latinos who were born and raised in the United States? Vis-à-vis African Americans or Anglos (whites)? Are immigrants without voting rights less inclined to take part in civic life? Are immigrants who remain involved in politics in their country of birth less likely to follow public affairs in the United States? Or does engagement in one national context complement involvement in the other? Such questions, among others, may be examined as never before through the 2012 LINES. The articles in this issue of *RSF* amply demonstrate the diverse scholarly literatures to which this survey contributes.

The first installment of the study was fielded at the height of the campaign season, between October 10 and November 5, 2012. In total, 853 immigrants took part in the preelection survey. Contact information for respondents was obtained from the marketing research firm Geoscape. Individuals identified on Geoscape's Hispanicity index as likely to have emigrated from Latin America were contacted at random and invited to take part in the investigation once it was confirmed that they fit the study profile. Both landline and cellular numbers were selected (AAPOR RR 4 = 0.31; Cooperation Rate = 0.93). Professional bilingual interviewers affiliated with the polling firm Latino Decisions conducted the surveys; nearly all (95 percent) were in Spanish.

Following the elections on November 6, 2012, we contacted as many immigrants as possible again for another round of interviewing. The fielding period for this installment lasted until December 20, 2012. Up to fifteen attempts were made to reach each respondent. A total of 435 participants from the preelection study took part in this second round, for a recontact rate of 51 percent. This rate is less than what is typically obtained in household panel surveys such as the ANES, but it is somewhat better than that in recent election-year telephone panel surveys of the Mexican-born population (see McCann, Cornelius, and Leal 2009; McCann and Nishikawa Chávez, forthcoming). As noted in the LINES codebook, panel attrition biases were relatively minor. Immigrants who were politically attentive were slightly more likely to take part in the second survey wave, as were those who primarily spoke Spanish at home. Age, level of formal education, family income, gender, naturalization status, the number of years spent in the United States, and frequency of church attendance were not significantly correlated with panel attrition.

While this second survey round was being administered, an additional 451 Latino immigrants were randomly selected and interviewed, so that the postelection N is comparable in size to that from the preelection wave. The full N for LINES is thus 1,304. Interviewing Services of America surveyed these fresh 451 postelection respondents, who were recruited for the study using procedures that were identical to those employed in the preelection round.

The distributions of socio-demographic variables in LINES were compared with those of Latino immigrants over eighteen in the 2011 American Community Survey (ACS). In most respects, the LINES sample conformed to the ACS, though significant discrepancies were found for education, age, and gender. A weighting variable was consequently calculated through iterative proportional fitting (that is, "raking"). When the LINES data are weighted, the distributions for educational group, age group, and gender match the ACS. Users wishing to pool LINES with the 2012 ANES may calculate additional weights as needed.

Table A1 provides a breakdown of selected social and demographic variables for LINES respondents. These variables have long been associated with orientations toward politics and participation: formal education, family income, gender, age, marital status, country of birth, years living in the United States, and civic status. For each of these items, variation is considerable. Researchers wishing to examine how socioeconomic resources, exposure to American society, or civic status, among other factors, shape democratic engagement among immigrants have much analytical leverage. At the same time, comparative benchmarks from the 2012 ANES indicate how foreign-born Latinos differ from the public at large. Most notably, Latino immigrants tend to be younger, less educated, and less affluent.

Nearly all of the telephone contact records for LINES respondents also included current street addresses. To protect anonymity, these addresses cannot be publicly archived. Users wishing to incorporate contextual geographical variables into multilevel analyses may contact the PIs for five-digit Federal Information Processing Standard (FIPS) codes, which identify the counties of residence for respondents. In the current version of the study, a number of politically relevant county and census tract-level variables have been incorporated, including age distributions, home values, education levels, percent receiving public assistance, and size of the noncitizen population. A full listing of these variables and the data sources is given in table A2. The 2012 LINES is archived for general use; citation instructions are given in the study codebook. Questions concerning the design and use of LINES data can be directed to the PIs.

Table A1. Socio-Demographic Profile of Participants

	LINES	ANES
Education		
Less than high school	49	10
High school graduate	26	30
Some college	16	30
College degree	9	29
Family income (2011)		
Less than $20 K	40	15
$20 K to $40 K	25	19
$40 K to $60 K	9	13
$60 K to $80 K	3	12
$80 K to $150 K	2	19
More than $150 K	1	7
No answer	20	17
Gender		
Male	52	48
Female	48	52
Age		
Eighteen to thirty-four	34	29
Thirty-five to forty-four	26	18
Forty-five to fifty-five	19	17
Fifty-five and older	20	36
Marital Status		
Married	59	53
Divorced/separated/widowed	17	26
Never married	24	21
Country of birth		N/A
Mexico	68	
Central American country	9	
Cuba	5	
Dominican Republic	5	
Other	13	
Time in United States		N/A
Less than ten years	14	
Ten to nineteen years	36	
Twenty to twenty-nine years	29	
Thirty or more	21	
Civic status		N/A
Naturalized U.S. citizen	36	
Noncitizen, legal permanent resident (LPR)	13	
NonCitizen, non-LPR, valid photo ID from U.S. government	29	
NonCitizen, non-LPR, no valid photo ID from U.S. government	22	

Source: Authors' compilation based on ANES 2012 and McCann and Jones-Correa 2012.
Note: Numbers in percentages. Weighted N = 1,306 (LINES) and 2,054 (ANES).

Table A2. Contextual Variables Currently Incorporated in the 2012 LINES

Variable Name	Variable Description	Data Source
otpop	Total population	2010 Census Summary File 1 Demographic Profile (DP1)
Tothouse	Total housing units	2010 Census Summary File 1 Demographic Profile (DP1)
Over18	Percent over the age of eighteen	2010 Census Summary File 1 Demographic Profile (DP1)
Over65	Percent over the age of sixty-five	2010 Census Summary File 1 Demographic Profile (DP1)
Owner	Percent owner occupied housing	2010 Census Summary File 1 Demographic Profile (DP1)
Med_homeval	Median home value	2006–2010 ACS Five-Year Estimates, Selected Housing Characteristics in the United States (DP04)
Hiq_homeval	Home value upper quartile	2006–2010 ACS Five-Year Estimates, Selected Population Tables (B25078)
Lowq_homeval	Home value lower quartile	2006–2010 ACS Five-Year Estimates, Selected Population Tables (B25076)
Hsgrad	Percent with a high school diploma or equivalent	2006–2010 ACS Five-Year Estimates, Selected Social Characteristics in the United States (DP02)
Collgrad	Percent with a college degree	2006–2010 ACS Five-Year Estimates, Selected Social Characteristics in the United States (DP02)
HSgrad_plus	Percent with at least a high school degree or equivalent	2006–2010 ACS Five-Year Estimates, Selected Social Characteristics in the United States (DP02)
collgrad_plus	Percent with at least a bachelor's degree	2006–2010 ACS Five-Year Estimates, Selected Social Characteristics in the United States (DP02)
foreign	Percent foreign born	2006–2010 ACS Five-Year Estimates, Selected Social Characteristics in the United States (DP02)
25k	Percent making less than $25k annually	2006–2010 ACS Five-Year Estimates, Selected Economic Characteristics in the United States (DP03)
50k	Percent making $25k to $50k annually	2006–2010 ACS Five-Year Estimates, Selected Economic Characteristics in the United States (DP03)
75k	Percent making $50k to $75k annually	2006–2010 ACS Five-Year Estimates, Selected Economic Characteristics in the United States (DP03)
100k	Percent making $75k to $100k annually	2006–2010 ACS Five-Year Estimates, Selected Economic Characteristics in the United States (DP03)
150k	Percent making $100k to $150k annually	2006–2010 ACS Five-Year Estimates, Selected Economic Characteristics in the United States (DP03)

Table A2. (cont.)

Variable Name	Variable Description	Data Source
150k_pl	Percent making $150k or more annually	2006–2010 ACS Five-Year Estimates, Selected Economic Characteristics in the United States (DP03)
noncitz	Percent noncitizens	2006–2010 ACS Five-Year Estimates, Selected Social Characteristics in the United States (DP02)
esl	Percent ESL speakers	2006–2010 ACS Five-Year Estimates, Selected Social Characteristics in the United States (DP02)
esl_ltvw	Percent ESL speakers who speak less than very well (less than very well/total population)	2006-2010 ACS Five-Year Estimates, Selected Social Characteristics in the United States (DP02)
esl_vw	Percent ESL speakers who speak very well (very well/total population)	2006-2010 ACS Five-Year Estimates, Selected Social Characteristics in the United States (DP02)
medinc	Median income	2006-2010 ACS Five-Year Estimates, Selected Economic Characteristics in the United States (DP03)
pubast	Percent receiving public assistance	2006-2010 ACS Five-Year Estimates, Public Assistance Income or Food Stamps/SNAP in the Past 12 Months for households (B19058)
sqkm	Square kilometers	2010 Census TIGER/Line Shapefiles
sqmi	Square miles	2010 Census TIGER/Line Shapefiles
latino	Percent Hispanic/Latino, nonwhite	2010 Census Summary File 1 Demographic Profile (DP1)
black	Percent African American	2010 Census Summary File 1 Demographic Profile (DP1)
native	Percent Native American	2010 Census Summary File 1 Demographic Profile (DP1)
asian	Percent Asian	2010 Census Summary File 1 Demographic Profile (DP1)
white	Percent white, non-Hispanic	2010 Census Summary File 1 Demographic Profile (DP1)
api	Percent Asian-Pacific Islander	2010 Census Summary File 1 Demographic Profile (DP1)
othrace	Percent some other racial-ethnic group	2010 Census Summary File 1 Demographic Profile (DP1)

Source: Authors' compilation based on McCann and Jones-Correa 2012.
Note: Contextual variables collected by the firm Latino Decisions.

REFERENCES

McCann, James A., Wayne Cornelius, and David L. Leal. 2009. "Absentee Voting and Transnational Civic Engagement Among Mexican Expatriates." In *Mexico's Choice: The 2006 Presidential Campaign in Comparative Perspective*, edited by Jorge Dominguez, Chappell Lawson, and Alejandro Moreno. Baltimore, Md.: Johns Hopkins University Press.

McCann, James A. and Michael Jones-Correa. 2012. Latino Immigrant National Election Study, 2012. New York: Russell Sage Foundation, Carnegie Corporation of New York, Purdue University, and Cornell University.

McCann, James A., and Katsuo Nishikawa Chávez. Forthcoming. "Partisanship by Invitation: Immigrants Respond to Political Campaigns." *Journal of Politics*.